D1566036

Military Theory and Practice in the Age of Xenophon

MILITARY THEORY
AND PRACTICE
IN THE
AGE OF XENOPHON

J. K. ANDERSON

University of California Press
Berkeley and Los Angeles 1970

University of California Press
Berkeley and Los Angeles, California
University of California Press, Ltd.
London, England

Copyright © 1970, by
The Regents of the University of California

Standard Book Number: 520–01564–9
Library of Congress Catalog Card Number: 74–104010

Printed in the United States of America

To H. R. W. Smith

ACKNOWLEDGMENTS

This book was written during a year of sabbatical leave from the University of California at Berkeley. The generosity of the John Simon Guggenheim Memorial Foundation enabled me to spend the time in Europe, and my special thanks are due to its president, Dr. Gordon N. Ray, to Professor Sterling Dow, and to Dr. Henry Allan Moe for their help and encouragement. Mr. D. E. L. Haynes and Mr. D. E. Strong showed me the kindness that is characteristic of the Department of Greek and Roman Antiquities at the British Museum, especially in making the blocks of the Nereid Monument available for me to study at a time when they were dismantled and not yet on public display. The late Professor Sir Frank Adcock, Miss Joyce Reynolds, Professors R. M. Cook, A. H. M. Jones and G. S. Kirk, and Mr. R. V. Nicholls were most hospitable and helpful in all sorts of ways during my stay at Cambridge. Miss Sylvia Benton was, as always, a fount of useful advice and curious information. Mr. John Boardman, Dr. W. G. Forrest, and Mr. D. M. Lewis showed me much kindness, and I am particularly grateful to Dr. Forrest for reading and improving the Appendix, although I know he does not fully agree with its conclusions. In Athens, Mrs. Jane Rabnett, Professor and Mrs. A. W. Lawrence, and Mr. A. H. S. Megaw were among those who spared no pains to smooth over what appeared to be serious difficulties. For a most instructive visit to the Metropolitan Museum of Art, and for a constant flow of information, criticism, and encouragement, I am indebted to Mrs. V. S. Littauer. In particular, if there is any merit in my remarks on chariots, the credit is hers.

The late Mr. John Huston by his generosity, enthusiasm and wide-ranging knowledge, constantly encouraged and advanced my work.

My colleagues at this University, especially Professors G. Azarpay, D. A. Amyx, J. Fontenrose, A. E. Gordon, C. H. Greenewalt, E. S. Gruen and L. A. Mackay have given valuable help, including improvements to the first draft of the typescript. Mrs. Louise Berge helped me in my search through *Corpus Vasorum Antiquorum* for illustrations of different forms of armour, and she and other members of my seminar classes, especially Mrs. Marian Sagan and Mrs. Yvonne Schwarz, have repeatedly suggested fresh ideas. My wife typed and retyped successive drafts from an almost illegible manuscript. My thanks are also due to Mrs. M. Weir and Mrs. M. Riddle of the University of California Press, and to Mrs. A. Morgan, who drew the figures.

The extent to which I have benefited from Professor W. K. Pritchett's earlier studies of Greek topography will be apparent from the footnotes. His *Studies in Ancient Greek Topography: Part II (Battlefields)* (Berkeley, University of California Press, 1969) did not reach me until my own book was in the printer's hands, though he very kindly presented me with a copy. His account of "The Battle near the Nemea River in 394 B.C.," placing the battlefield not on the Nemea itself but on the banks of the Rachiani, which crosses the coastal plain further to the east, supersedes all earlier topographical discussions.

My greatest gratitude is due to Professor D. L. Page, who spared time from his many important duties to read each chapter as it was produced in its original form and to criticise it in detail, immeasurably improving both form and content.

My predecessor in the Chair of Classical Archaeology at Berkeley, Professor H. R. W. Smith, has for ten years been unfailing in his kindness and in the generosity with which he has placed his great learning at the service of my pupils and myself. I offer this book to him as a small return.

CONTENTS

I

INTRODUCTION

"The Greeks," said Mardonius, the evil counsellor of King Xerxes of Persia, "are accustomed to wage war in the most irrational manner through senselessness and stupidity. For whenever they declare war on each other, they seek out the fairest and most level ground and go down to battle on it. In consequence, even the victors come off with great loss. I say nothing of the vanquished, for they are annihilated. But since they all speak the same language, they ought to exchange heralds and envoys and so make up their differences by any means rather than by fighting. And if it were absolutely necessary to make war on each other, they should try to discover the most impregnable positions on either side and make trial of them." [1]

Three centuries after the Persian wars, Polybius contrasted the open and honourable warfare of the ancients with the deceitfulness of his own age. In former times there were no secret weapons, stratagems, or missiles, and armies met openly on pre-arranged battlefields. But in his day, people actually said that the open conduct of any military operation was bad generalship. Among the Romans, admittedly, some trace of the ancient virtue survived, but the rest of the world was altogether degenerate. [2]

It is true that a ban on missiles seems to have been arranged at least once in early Greek warfare, [3] though we cannot be sure of the precise date or circumstances, and that challenges to fight on particular fields were not unknown. [4] But the preference for hand-to-hand fighting was due less to a feeling that missiles were

unfair and unmanly than to a belief in their comparative in-
effectiveness.[5] Pitched battles on the level ground were less irrational than Mardonius supposed. For the terrain on which the
Greeks fought consists of pockets of flat land, seldom more than
a few miles in extent, separated by steep, eroded, rocky, scrub-
covered mountains, useless except to the goatherd and the char-
coal burner. Profitable agriculture was and is practically confined to the plains and the lower foot-hills round them. Each
city-state had its own patch of plain (where there were no good
plains, the people still lived in villages), and most lived hand to
mouth. The loss of a single harvest might be endured, but the
loss of two in succession meant ruin to the smaller agricultural
towns. Commerce and manufacture, which need not necessarily
be interrupted by an enemy invasion, helped to support the
economy of the larger cities, but in the fifth century B.C., only
Athens among the cities of the Greek mainland had accumulated
a sufficient reserve of capital to enable her to support a protracted
war in which her farm lands were abandoned to the enemy.[6]

A Greek state, therefore, making war upon its neighbour, could
hope to reduce the enemy to submission by gaining possession
of his agricultural land for a few weeks, "when the corn was in
the ear." His total destruction was only sought in exceptional
circumstances. Greek cities did not normally seek to annex territory farther from their walls than would permit its possessors
to take part personally in political life. The total overthrow of
another state would permanently alter the balance of power in
Greece, perhaps not to the conqueror's advantage. Lysander recognised the value of Athens as a counterpoise to Thebes; and
Epaminondas saw that the threat of Sparta would make the
Peloponnesians look for Theban help.[7] There was also a repug-
nance against the destruction of an irreplaceable part of the
Greek world. Polydorus, after the defeat of Argos, said that he
came to recover territory, not to conquer a city. When Agesipolis
heard that Philip had taken only a few days to destroy Olynthus,

he replied that it would be many times as long before Philip built another such city.[8]

The destruction of the year's harvest could be achieved simply by marching the army through the fields, trampling the growing crop or beating it down with sticks.[9] More lasting injury could be inflicted by the destruction of farm buildings and tools, and the capture or escape of livestock and slaves. Most serious of all was the destruction of vines and fruit trees, whose growth represented the labour, not of a single season, but of generations. But to devastate a wide area quickly, the army must be dispersed, and small parties with their weapons laid aside for spades or axes were vulnerable to counter-attack. Such work could not, therefore, be undertaken on a large scale until the enemy had been beaten from the field, or had voluntarily abandoned it. For the invader to "go down to battle" on "the fairest and most level ground" was, therefore, the obvious strategy. Why the defending side should accept the challenge of open battle on the plain, instead of holding the difficult passes that led to it, is a harder question to answer.[10]

The fact that the first object of victory was to gain possession of the battlefield helps to explain the curious conventions that ruled the conduct of victors and vanquished in the classical era. To abandon the bodies of dead friends and kinsmen to carrion birds and beasts was a disgrace and a violation of divine law; accordingly, much of the fighting in the *Iliad* takes place around the bodies of slain heroes, which must be dragged out of the fighting and carried back by their friends to receive their due funeral rites. But in classical warfare, when a man fell, the ranks closed up and pressed on; the dead were left until after the battle. So there developed the custom of formally sending a herald after a lost battle to ask permission from the victors to take up the dead from the battlefield. If the losers did not do so, they did not admit that the enemy were masters of the field, and so did not formally acknowledge defeat. A skirmish in

which the Athenian cavalry lost a few dead, but recovered the
bodies the same day without a truce, hardly counted as a victory
for the enemy.[11] On the other hand, when the pious Nicias, after
re-embarking his men from a successful raid on enemy territory,
found that two dead bodies had not been taken up and sent a
herald to recover them under truce, his action turned a clear victory into a formal defeat.[12]

Religion compelled the victor to allow the recovery of the dead
bodies, but their arms were regularly dedicated to the gods, in
their temples in the victor's city or at the great sanctuaries like
Delphi and Olympia. Probably in the late sixth century B.C., the
custom arose of also making a dedication on the battlefield itself
—a trophy, erected at the point where the enemy had been turned
to flight. This consisted of a tree trunk, to which were affixed
captured arms, often a helmet, a shield, and cuirass arranged as
though on a man. (Plates I, II) These weapons were dedicated
to the gods of war. To overthrow them was therefore an impious
act, though Thucydides records one instance of a trophy being
pulled down because its builders "were not really masters of the
ground at the time when they erected it." In a later age, the
people of Rhodes erected a building to hide a hostile trophy which
their religious scruples would not allow them to destroy.[13]

It has been well observed that "the principal idea behind the
ordinary trophy is the sign of defeat, not the monument of victory," and that permanent war memorials were therefore not
normally erected on the battlefield. The stone columns erected by
the Athenians at Marathon and Salamis were as exceptional
as the victories that they commemorated. The Theban victory over
the Spartans at Leuctra was, according to tradition, the first
victory of Greeks over Greeks to be commemorated by a permanent trophy, and its erection is said to have brought odium on
its victors.[14]

The erection of a trophy did not by any means imply a decisive victory. The Athenian expedition to Sicily in 415–413 B.C.
ended in total disaster, but the Athenians remembered that their

army had set up seven trophies over the Syracusans, while the gods held the balance even between them. Even a beaten army or fleet might claim victory in one part of the action, and set up a trophy accordingly.[15]

The failure of ancient Greek states to defend the strong positions on their frontiers is to be explained by economic and political reasons, as well as by purely tactical ones, such as those that governed the conduct of the Thebans and Athenians in the campaigns of 378 and 377 B.C. The want of accumulated capital in most Greek states has already been mentioned, and for maintenance of a standing army, a full treasure-chest is the first essential. But without a standing army of full-time soldiers, strong positions (whether artificially fortified or not) could not be permanently garrisoned. Without a properly organized commissariat, the garrisons could not be supplied. And mountain warfare required special equipment and training and was therefore not for amateurs from the cities or the plains.

The richer citizens in Greek states professed their readiness to serve with person and fortune; and their conduct proved their sincerity. But though every man was ready to lay out his money to equip himself to the best of his ability, he was not ready to pay taxes to support a standing army. Indeed he would have thought it disgraceful to pay someone else to relieve him of one of the most perilous and difficult of his obligations. And to disgrace was added danger. The ancient Greeks, like the Englishmen of the seventeenth century, regarded a standing army as an instrument of tyranny. For the property-owning citizens to sit back in idleness, letting their bodies grow soft and their fathers' weapons blacken in the chimney smoke, while foreigners or—perhaps worse still—their poorer fellow-citizens were armed and trained at their expense, was to invite the overthrow of constitutional government.

In the fifth century B.C. then, we do not find states using professional troops, lightly armed for mountain warfare, to guard their frontiers. Some, notably Athens, maintained outlying forts

of considerable strength,[16] but these forts were without professional garrisons and could not delay a full-scale invasion. The
ordinary Greek army consisted of part-time soldiers, citizens of
sufficient substance to arm themselves, but unwilling to leave their
homes and unable to desert their regular occupations for more
than a short period each year. Their campaigns were conducted
in the season before harvest, when the farmers were free and the
enemy's crops most vulnerable.

Among these amateur soldiers, the Spartans stood out as a
nation of professionals. As early as the Persian wars, and no
doubt earlier, their army, "Lacedaemonian" rather than "Spartan,"
contained elements drawn from different levels of society and
from other towns than Sparta itself. But the heart of both the
army and state was the small group of Spartiate "peers," a ruling
class whose lives were dedicated to holding by force what their
ancestors had forcibly won. Their households, and the military
messes in which the adult men normally ate, were maintained
from the produce of estates worked by the helots, supposedly
descendants of the original occupiers of the land, who had been
conquered by the first Dorian invaders. Their labour freed the
Spartans from the necessity of making a living, but their numbers
and their oppressed condition, "like asses worn by heavy burdens," compelled their rulers to remain constantly under arms.
Being constantly engaged in drill and the study of tactics, the
Spartans showed more originality and enterprise in these fields
than is sometimes allowed to them. But their strategic concepts
never developed beyond the old assumption that ravaging the
enemy's farm land would force him to submit in the end.

"Do you not know," asks Socrates in the *Memorabilia*, "that
men cut the corn that others have sown, and chop down the
trees that they have planted, and blockade in every way those
who, though weaker than themselves, are unwilling to serve
them, until they bring them to choose slavery rather than war
with their betters?"[17] The Spartans behaved as though this
was all there was to know about strategy; Agesilaus conducted

his campaigns in Asia as though the Great King could be made to conform to Spartan demands by the devastation of an out-lying province. Before the end of the war, they, and their admirer Xenophon, had certainly come to realize that by destroying the estates of their former friend Pharnabazus they were achieving nothing, injuring their own reputation for fair dealing, and turning friends who might have supported their position in mainland Greece into bitter and powerful enemies. But they never devised any better plan of operation.

Because the object of the usual Greek campaign was to occupy temporarily, or to defend, the level agricultural land, the troops were equipped to fight on this land, in large masses drawn up in close order, engaging hand-to-hand with spear and shield. Because the invading army did not intend to stay, it did not need to keep its lines of communication clear behind it. The helplessness of Greek heavy infantry when attacked by light-armed troops in broken ground has been often remarked, but if the heavy infantry were not trying to drive the enemy off the hills and occupy them themselves, but merely to pass from one plain to another, they could often fight their way through with their strength substantially intact. Behind them, their enemies were left in the hills, uninjured but unable to do anything more to save their farms and open villages. The march of the Ten Thousand described in Xenophon's *Anabasis* is the most cele-brated instance of the success of Greek spearmen in passing through mountains strongly defended by light-armed troops, but examples are not wanting from the Spartan wars of the early fourth century. It is true that these wars also provide some examples of the successful defence of mountain barriers by light-armed professional soldiers. But on the whole, attempts to defend the passes failed more often than they succeeded, even when suitable troops were available, as they had not been in the fifth century B.C. Had the Greek armies had to keep their lines of communication open behind them, the story would have been different; but they came bringing enough provisions for a

short stay, supplemented them where they could by living off
the country they had invaded, and were not dependent on long
unarmed convoys repeatedly threading the passes behind them.[18]
For the same reason, the enemy's frontier forts, if any, could
be left untaken and unmasked. Their garrisons were not strong
enough to deal with anything larger than raiding parties; they
had no artillery except bows and slings and therefore did not
really command the ground they overlooked. An army might
pass them uninjured both on its outward and on its homeward
march.[19]

The neglect of the arts of fortification and siege warfare by
the Spartans has been often remarked and perhaps exaggerated.
The siege of Plataea was begun with as much enterprise, and
seen through with as much determination, as any comparable
operation undertaken by Athens. In the war in Asia at the beginning of the fourth century, Spartan generals often successfully
directed the capture of small fortresses, though certainly they
were not risking Spartan lives in the storming parties. And the
capture of Mantinea in 386 B.C. was as ingenious as any brilliancy
of the Hellenistic age. But Sparta contributed nothing to the
fourth-century development of siege-engines and of fortifications
to counter them, and the Spartans boasted that they had no need
of either, until Epaminondas taught them better. Lacedaemon
was difficult of access, the "citadel of the Peloponnese," a rich
but mountain-girt valley. In the middle stood a cluster of unwalled
irregular villages, the capital. No Spartan woman had seen the
smoke of an enemy's camp fires, nor had her ancestresses as far
as tradition could be carried. The Argive who boasted that many
Spartans lay buried in his land was answered that not one
Argive lay in the land of Sparta. Sparta needed no fortifications
except the bodies of her sons.[20] And Spartan offensive strategy,
which generally aimed at the submission of the enemy, not his
total subjection, was based on the assumption that that submission
could be obtained by mastery of the open field. To assault fortifications cost men; to blockade them, money. But a destructive

march through the enemy's farm lands might be both profitable and enjoyable. For this method of warfare, the hoplite army was the perfect instrument. The Spartan mistake lay in supposing that this strategy was as applicable to Periclean Athens or to the Persian Empire as to the country towns of the Peloponnese.

The purpose of this book is to investigate Spartan military techniques, the art of drilling hoplites and handling them on the battlefield, and the way in which their own skills were finally turned against the Spartans. The Spartan military art is more easily studied in the period of decline than in the heroic age of Thermopylae, or even during the great Peloponnesian War. This unfortunate fact is partly explained by the nature of our sources. Herodotus and Thucydides wrote for readers familiar with the general principles of warfare, and did not profess to instruct in tactics, having in any case more important matters to describe. Neither had served on campaigns with the Spartan army. Thucydides was interested in Spartan military organization, and passed on to his readers information which the ordinary Athenian can hardly have known; but he himself admits that the truth was hard to come by,[21] and his account presents difficulties.

Our chief contemporary authority for the history of the fourth century B.C., Xenophon, is in almost all respects far inferior to his predecessors. Like Herodotus, he had travelled widely, but though he often gives a lively picture of whatever presented itself directly to his notice—the hunting of wild ass and ostrich, date-palm wine and barley beer, the dolphin blubber which the Black Sea tribes used instead of olive oil—he did not look round to see what was not thrust directly under his nose. It is true that he did not travel, as Herodotus did, for the purpose of historical inquiry, and for most of his march through Asia he was preoccupied with military responsibilities. Even more superficial than his account of the actual state of the Persian Empire were his enquiries into its past history. Passing the ruined Assyrian fortresses, he was told that these were strongholds of the Medes, whom Zeus struck with lightning when they were besieged by the Persians. Obviously he could not have investigated the matter further at the time, but he never tried to do so, and passes on to his reader as historical fact the empty tale of an ignorant guide, given no doubt through an interpreter and in answer to a casual question.[22]

In his *Hellenica*, Xenophon's superficiality is again apparent. Many incidents are vividly, indeed stirringly, narrated, and this is especially true of those at which we may suppose that Xenophon himself was present, though he does not mention his own participation.[23] At other times we may imagine narrators of like character and interests to Xenophon himself, probably personal friends, telling the historian of their own experiences. The various actions around Phlius in 368 B.C., especially the brilliant affairs of horse,[24] or the death of Stasippus, leader of the Spartan party at Tegea in Arcadia—a man of whom Xenophon writes as of a personal acquaintance[25]—may be supposed to have been described to him by eyewitnesses. For most of his active life, he was in close touch with the leaders of Sparta and of the Spartan allies, and so in an excellent position to hear one side of the story. With the other side he hardly troubled himself. He is often and justly charged with prejudice in favour of Sparta, but he does not seem to tell lies deliberately. He reports what he saw and heard, but he does not trouble to find out the other point of view. Nor does he succeed in combining the separate incidents that he describes into a complete historical pattern. He leaves out too much. His omissions have been explained as due to a desire to suppress what was painful to his Spartan friends. But his neglect of the earthquake of Helice, the battle of Tegyra, or the foundation of Megalopolis might perhaps have been due less to a conscious desire to suppress painful facts than to a failure to seek out informants when they did not present themselves. He cannot deny that Messenia was liberated from the Spartans or that Megalopolis was founded in their despite, and does not seek to do so. But he was not there himself and none of his friends told him what had happened. So he leaves these events out of his narrative and we hear nothing of the new cities until they suddenly appear unexplained in his story. The historian of the Persian or Peloponnesian Wars must follow Herodotus or Thucydides, adding where he can detail derived from other sources. But one cannot reconstruct an intelligible history of the early fourth century B.C. from Xenophon alone. That his book should have been preserved complete when so many of his contemporaries are known only through quotation by later writers is due no doubt partly to his gift for storytelling. But it is perhaps also due to the amount of technical information that he imparts, which we do not always appreciate because it is of no practical use to us today. Thucydides had been an Athenian general, which means that he was experienced in great affairs of state, as well as in military matters, but not necessarily that he had had a more thorough training in the technique of warfare than his fellow-citizens. Xenophon had been a brigadier of mercenaries, and for many years probably a senior staff officer in the Spartan service. He could not answer, or even ask, the wider questions that we regard as the concern of history, but the minute details of active service he could claim to understand better than almost any other Athenian. His book on horsemanship was written, he tells us, in order to pass on to his younger friends the fruits of his superior experience, and it was perhaps in the same spirit that he set out the details of quite minor military operations. Thucydides tells us that the Spartan King Agis, after leading his army in order of battle to within a stone's throw of a strongly-posted enemy, suddenly withdrew it in haste without actually engaging.[26] He does not tell us how the operation was carried out. Xenophon gives us every detail of how King Agesilaus withdrew his army from a dangerous position,[27] no doubt so that the reader will know what to do if ever he is in like difficulty.

Where strict history fails him as a vehicle for instruction he makes use of historical fiction. The *Cyropaedia*, written near the end of Xenophon's life after the defeat of Sparta, interests the modern reader because it is the fullest statement of Xenophon's ideas on education, or because it is the forerunner of the European novel. If we are interested in the battle pieces, it is for the deeds of heroes and the romantic fate of kings. The raising, training, and manoeuvering of the rank-and-file infantry seem tedious obstacles to the flow of the story. Yet perhaps Xenophon would have regarded these as the truly useful parts of the book, the pill in the jam. The issue of historical events is not always according to the textbook theories. At the battle of Leuctra, Spartan tactics failed, but Xenophon no doubt continued to believe that their system was theoretically sounder than that of their Theban enemies. His account of the battle is mostly explanations of why things did in fact go wrong. But in a novel, he could start with the bare fact that Cyrus the Great of Persia did defeat Croesus of Lydia, and make that victory the result of textbook manoeuvres carried through to a happy conclusion by troops trained in the ideal system of tactics. This system is the subject of the present work

II

HOPLITE ARMOUR
AND WEAPONS

Between the seventh century B.C. and the fourth, the essential principles of land warfare in southern Greece remained the same. "Fight, standing fast by each other, and do not begin shameful flight or fear," said Tyrtaeus.[1] "Whoever is willing to stand fast in his rank and resist the enemy and not run away" was Laches's definition of a brave man when questioned by Socrates two and a half centuries later.[2] To both Tyrtaeus and Laches, the good soldier was one who stood fast by his comrades. The cohesion of the whole mass of men counted for more than individual heroics. The Homeric kings, who went out before their people to challenge their equals in single combat, had no place in the phalanx; pre-eminent strength, beauty, and swiftness of foot were no longer the first qualities demanded of a leader.

But though the essential concept of the heavy infantryman and his method of fighting remained unchanged during this long period, the monuments reveal important variations in his equipment over the centuries, reflecting changes in the details, though not the broad principles, of warfare. The items are best examined separately. This chapter is mainly concerned with presenting in detail the evidence, archaeological and literary, for the conclusions presented in its Summary (pp. 40–42), to which the reader who is not particularly interested in the finer points of these topics is advised to turn directly.

THE SHIELD

This essential item of equipment was in the fourth century B.C. very much what it had been in the seventh. The round shield (*aspis*) was the only heavy infantry shield used in classical Greece. The so-called "Boeotian" shield (Plate 2A) represented on coins and works of art, has been shown by Miss H. L. Lorimer to be a "romantic archaism," introduced by vase-painters into heroic scenes in recollection of the "Dipylon" shield that had really been used in the eighth century B.C. The Boeotians stamped it on their coinage, but the vase-painters gave it to Thessalian Achilles and Salaminian Ajax, and it was the helmet, not the shield, that distinguished Boeotian hoplites in real life.[3] The "Boeotian" shield survives in Attic vase-painting into the early red-figure period, but disappears about the time of the Persian Wars. Perhaps the Persians, when they sacked Athens in 480 B.C., destroyed actual examples of the "Dipylon" shield, that had been preserved in temples to inspire, and mislead, the artists of the Archaic period.[4]

In the Hellenistic period, the *thyreos* (Latin *scutum*), a long oval shield with a central boss or a rib down the middle, was often used instead of the round *aspis* (Latin *clipeus*) by Greek armies, as well as by the Romans and Celts. Some scholars have held that the Achaeans of the northern Peloponnese had used the *thyreos*, or something like it, since remote antiquity, and that this type should therefore be counted as a direct descendant of one type or other of prehistoric long shield surviving into the classical period.[5] The theory rests upon the fact (no doubt correctly stated by Plutarch and Pausanias) that Philopoemen, upon being elected general of the Achaean League in 208–207 B.C., made his soldiers give up the *thyreos* for the *aspis*. But the "Achaean" army of the time was largely Arcadian, like Philopoemen himself, or Sicyonian, like his predecessor Aratus. Aratus had constantly been defeated in pitched battles, though often recovering his losses in skirmishes and surprises, and Plutarch explains that Philopoemen wanted to do away with light-infantry tactics and replace them by a firm and steadfast order of battle. The Achaean League had been using shields like those of the Roman legions, and light spears, but without adopting the Roman manipular formation. They were still drawn up in the continuous phalanx, but a phalanx that was undefended by a hedge of long spears or an unbroken wall of large shields.[6] The Achaeans, as well as their Arcadian and Sicyonian neighbors and the Argives, who also joined the Hellenistic League, all used the round *aspis* in the classical period. This Xenophon expressly states of the Achaeans among the Ten Thousand, and it may be inferred from references to Achaeans fighting side by side with other Peloponnesians, either in Greece as allies of Sparta, or abroad as mercenaries.[7] The *thyreos* never appears in classical Greek art, but often in that of the Hellenistic period.

The round *aspis* was then the only shield used by the classical Greek hoplite. It was designed for the tactics of the phalanx and introduced together with them. Demaratus of Sparta is said to have replied to one who asked him why the Spartans disgraced those who threw away their shields but not those who lost helmets or breastplates, "Because they wear those for their own sakes, but carry shields for the sake of the whole line." [8]

The shield was generally over thirty inches in diameter, and slightly convex, with a broad flat rim of bronze round the edge. Its distinctive feature was the manner in which it was carried (Plate 2B).[9] The bearer's left arm was thrust up to the elbow through a metal arm-band in the centre of the shield, and his left hand grasped a handgrip just inside the rim.

In the fifth century, to judge from the vase-paintings, this handgrip was often made from a short length of heavy plaited cord, sometimes fastened at either end to metal pegs, which are decorated with tassels. Similar pegs are set some distance within the rim, sometimes two above and two below the armband, sometimes more. A single cord, fastened so as to leave plenty of slack, runs from one end of the handgrip round these pegs and back to the other end of the handgrip. On black-figured vases, both Corinthian and Attic, and on some red-figured vases, the pegs alone, with their conspicuous tassels, are to be seen. In some cases, the cord may have been added in paint which has disappeared. I believe that the purpose of the cord is to enable the shield to be slung over the back, either for ease of carrying on the march, or, less often, for protection in retreat (Plate 3). The shield would be turned through ninety degrees, and one arm passed through each of the slack loops that were normally at the top and bottom. (The cord is also explained as spare material from which a new handle could be made if the first should break. But the hoplite could not simply pull a new length round into the required position: he would have, at the very least, to stop and secure the new handle to its pegs).[10]

In action, the left arm, with the shield on it, was thrown up in front of the body, with the elbow bent and the forearm horizontal. In consequence, nearly half the bearer's shield projected to the left of his own body, and, when the phalanx was drawn up in close order, protected his left-hand neighbour rather than himself. A man could not bring his own shield round to guard his own right side, and the right-hand file of the phalanx was therefore vulnerable; that of the column of march still more so.

The shield was made of perishable material, almost certainly wood. Its fittings, including the rim and armband, were of bronze. In the Archaic period, a blazon, such as a dolphin or griffin cut out of sheet bronze, was often attached to the front of the shield, or the whole front might be bronze-covered. The Spartans adopted the bronze-covered shield, according to Xenophon, because it was most quickly polished and tarnished most slowly,[11] and their ranks gleamed with bronze and scarlet.[12] The complete covering of metal gave little or no additional protection, being very thin, as may be seen from an actual Spartan shield, captured by the Athenians at Pylos in 425 B.C., which was found during the excavation of the market-place at Athens.[13] The hoplite shield seems never to have been completely proof against the well-delivered blow of a spear. Many vase-paintings show shields pierced, and Brasidas was wounded when his shield turned traitor.[14]

In some works of art (Plates 4A, 13), a rectangular apron of leather or heavy cloth is shown fastened to the lower edge of the shield by studs or rivets, and hanging down almost to the bearer's ankles. This shield-apron is sometimes borne by leaders of files or by other prominent figures, and so at one time was believed to be a distinguishing badge of officers or heralds.[15] This unlikely explanation has long been discarded in favour of the true one. The apron is an attempt to modify a shield originally designed for use by spearmen against other spearmen in order to give better protection against arrows. It appears first in a Clazomenian painting, after the middle of the sixth century B.C., when the collapse of Lydia had exposed the Greeks of Asia Minor to Persian attack.[16] The latest examples are also from Asia Minor, upon Lycian grave monuments of the fourth century B.C.[17] In Attic vase-painting, it is fairly common in the Late Archaic and Early Classic periods—that is, in the generation of the Persian invasions and of the Athenian counter-offensive in Asia—but is very rare thereafter.[18] We do not know its ancient name.[19]

The size of the hoplite shield was roughly determined by the length of the bearer's forearm. The shields from Olympia vary from about 0.80 to 1.00 m. in diameter, and that from Pylos measures 0.95 by 0.83 m. Its oval shape is unusual, but does not have any obvious military significance and does not seem to have been a distinctive feature of Spartan shields. The shields carved on the base of the trophy set up by the Thebans after their victory over the Spartans at Leuctra are round and 0.97 m. in diameter.[20]

The blazons that decorate hoplite shields in Archaic vase-paintings are splendid or terrifying, but those portrayed after the Persian wars are comparatively tame and dull (Plate 4).[21] They seem to have been chosen at the whim of the individual and, though a particular device might refer to the distinguished ancestry of its bearer, there was no College of Heralds to regulate the matter. In the sixth century B.C., the hoplite armies of many Greek states were perhaps still small enough and aristocratic enough for the identity of individuals to be a matter of interest. But in the fifth and fourth centuries, national emblems generally replaced personal ones. The Mantineans displayed the trident of their guardian god Poseidon;[22] the Thebans, the club of Heracles. But in 362 B.C., the Theban general Epaminondas caused his allies to paint the Theban club on their shields and no patriotic or sentimental objections seem to have been raised. Nor did the Athenian democrats at the Piraeus in 403 B.C. place any traditional emblems on their improvised wooden and wicker shields. In the civil war in which they were engaged, those marks would have lost their practical value as means of distinction, and they were not retained for sentimental reasons. The shields were simply whitened, and nobody seems to have thought it an objection that white shields were proper to the Argive army.[23]

Epaminondas's tomb was decorated with a shield bearing the device of a dragon, alluding to his descent from the race that sprang from the dragon's teeth, but he does not seem to have borne this blazon in his lifetime.[24] Alcibiades shocked Athens by displaying Eros grasping a thunderbolt instead of an ancestral blazon,[25] but this seems to mean that it would have been proper for him to have alluded to his ancestors in his choice of device, not that they had always borne some emblem that he gave up. In any case, the story shows that he had freedom of choice in the matter.

In the Spartan army, the initial lambda, for Lacedaemonians, marked alike the shields of the Spartiate peers, their less-privileged fellow-Spartans, and the *perioeci*—the inhabitants of the small subordinate villages, who in the fourth century B.C., fought side by side with the Spartiates, though at the time of the Persian invasion they had been brigaded separately. This prosaic letter had by the later fifth century become more dreadful than any legendary monster. At Amphipolis in 422 B.C., Cleon, the general, was not the only Athenian to be "terror-stricken when he saw the lambdas gleaming." [26]

It was doubtless in imitation of the Spartans, if not by their orders, that the Sicyonians displayed the letter sigma on their shield. But no prestige attached to it. In an action in which a party of Spartan cavalry were left unsupported by the flight of their Sicyonian allies, "Pasimachus, the captain of the horse, with a few cavalrymen, when he saw the Sicyonians being crushed, tied the horses to trees and took up the Sicyonians' shields. He went to meet the Argives with those who would follow him, but the Argives, seeing the sigmas on the shields, took them for Sicyonians and felt no fear of them. Thereupon Pasimachus is said to have exclaimed: 'By the Great Twin Brethren, Argives, these sigmas here will trick you,' and closed with them. And so, fighting with few men against many, he and some others of his company fell." [27]

No doubt other cities displayed their own initial letters on their shields, but the evidence records only the M borne by the Messenians after their liberation from Sparta.[28] Prosaic efficiency is to be expected of Spartans, and they may have introduced the practice of using letters instead of blazons. But the literary evidence goes back only to the late fifth century B.C., whereas on a few Attic vases, from about 500 B.C. onwards, are figures bearing shields with the initials of Athens.[29] Curiously, at least one of these figures represents not an Athenian but a foreign mythical hero. Perhaps the painter's fancy had been caught by a novel practice and he painted the shield in the latest fashion, without regard to the meaning of the letters. The expulsion of the tyrant Hippias in 510 B.C. and the establishment of the Athenian democracy were followed by victories over Chalcis and Boeotia,[30] which may have been the result of an expansion of the Athenian hoplite army.[31] Either the democratic character of the new force or the influence of the Spartans, who had been chiefly responsible for the liberation, might explain the appearance of the A on Athenian shields at this time; but we cannot be certain that they really did adopt this practice, and if they did, the use of personal blazons was certainly not given up entirely. It is possible that the letter does not even stand for the city of Athens, but for the goddess Athena. Some of the bearers of this device are youths apparently taking part in the hoplite race, possibly in the Panathenaic Games.[32]

Even the Spartans seem to have made some concessions to individual fancy, for Plutarch tells a story of a Spartan (nameless and dateless) whose device was a life-sized fly. When mocked for trying to escape the enemy's notice, he replied that, on the contrary, he wanted to force the enemy to notice him by closing to a distance from which they would see his emblem in its actual size.[33] Perhaps the Spartans were allowed to combine a small personal badge with the national insignia, just as crews of military aircraft do today.

BODY ARMOUR

In the art of the seventh century B.C. and most of the sixth, hoplites are generally shown in a state of "heroic nudity" or wearing the "bell cuirass" (Plate 2A).[34] This consists of bronze back- and breastplates, fashioned separately and fastened together above the shoulders. The cuirass ends above the hips in a sharply out-turned flange, which would keep the edge off the wearer's thighs when he moved and might also serve to deflect a spear thrust delivered overarm, downwards against the lower abdomen or thigh. The prominent features of the anatomy that the cuirass is intended to protect are roughly engraved upon it, and may be curiously combined with other decoration. This type of cuirass persisted until the end of the sixth century, when it was replaced by one in which the out-turned flange was generally reduced or done away with and replaced by *pteryges*, long narrow strips of metal or reinforced leather hanging from the straight lower edge and hinged to allow free movement. This improved form seems (on the evidence of vase-paintings) to have lasted only for about a generation—the generation of the Persian wars—

and to have been replaced in the second quarter of the fifth century B.C. by a type that remained essentially unchanged until the Roman Imperial period.[35] The anatomical modelling of the cuirass progressively becomes subtler and more accurate (just as it does in the sculpture of the time). But this is not always easy to judge in vase-painting, and the clearest distinguishing feature of the fully developed *muskelpanzer* of the Classic period is that its lower edge is no longer straight but shaped to fit the lower edge of the abdomen. The armholes, as well as the lower edge, are sometimes guarded by *pteryges*.[36]

But already in the middle of the sixth century B.C., a lighter corslet* of leather or linen sometimes appears in art as a substitute for the plate cuirass,[37] and in literature it can be traced back further still. Down to the end of the sixth century B.C., the plate cuirass still appears to be standard equipment, at least in Athenian and Corinthian vase-painting; but, if we are to judge from the frequency with which the corslet appears in fifth-century art, it had become the regular armour of the rank and file by the time of the Persian wars.[38] From this time on there is great variety in the body armour of hoplites depicted in works of art, with the cuirass appearing most frequently on large vases depicting mythological subjects (especially in the work of Niobid Painter and his group in the Early Classic period). Even in these vases, when there are more hoplites than one, their equipment is generally mixed, and we find on the same vase the fully developed *muskelpanzer* cuirass, the leather corslet, and heroic nudity.[39] Sometimes there seems to be no special significance in the cuirass,[40] but on other vases it seems to be reserved for a special hero, as Neoptolemus at the Sack of Troy. In the Niobid Painter's Amazonomachy in Palermo,[41] two Greeks wear cuirasses. One, the slayer of the Amazon queen on the front of the vase, is no doubt marked out for special distinction, but the other is a minor combatant, in the restricted space below one

---

* For the sake of convenience, the words "cuirass" and "corslet" are not used interchangeably. The former is restricted to the plate cuirass.

handle, with one foot on a pile of rocks, half-crouching before his larger adversary. But, whether the artist used the plate cuirass to distinguish individual figures or not, the fact that it is seldom introduced into scenes of ordinary life painted on minor vases, but is reserved for major works of art depicting mythological scenes, suggests that it had become an unusual piece of equipment, and that its wearers were men of distinguished qualities. It certainly had not become a museum piece, given as "period dress" to mythological characters. Panoplies, complete sets of armour, which presumably included the cuirass, were given by the Athenian generals as a form of military decoration.[42] Actual examples of cuirasses of the fifth and fourth centuries B.C. have survived in Thracian and Italian tombs.[43] "Period dress" was not affected by the painters of the Early Classic period, who had forgotten even the "Boeotian" shield. The particular painters in whose work the plate cuirass is most often found were completely up-to-date in their ideas of armour, as is proved by the fact that they show such novelties as the shield-apron and "Thracian" helmet. But the most common form of armour is no longer the cuirass, but the corslet.

The form of the corslet is clearly shown on many works of art (Plate 5). It was wrapped round the left side of the body and fastened on the right, being secured by large flaps brought over the shoulders from the back and fastened down on the breast with tie-strings. The lower edge was cut into a large number of narrow vertical strips, which provided a flexible covering for the lower abdomen. This arrangement no doubt suggested the use of *pteryges* for the same purpose to the makers of cuirasses. Sculptures and vase-paintings do not indicate the material from which the corslet was made. Xenophon speaks of the *spolas*,[44] which was of leather.[45] Other authors mention linen corslets, but we can only conclude that they were made to the same pattern as the leather ones; at least the monuments do not distinguish them. I imagine the linen corslet to have been of coarse stiffened material, like Shakespeare's buckram, which might have much the same appearance as leather when depicted in sculpture or vase-painting. On the other hand, Mr. Michael Goldstein points out to me that on some vase-paintings contemporary with the Persian Wars, Persian soldiers are shown wearing over oriental dress corslets which are generally similar to the Greek type, but seem slightly more bulky and are covered with crisscrossing fine lines. The lines do not resemble the usual representations of scale-armour, which was also in use among the Persians, and it may be that these corslets are supposed to be of padded or quilted linen. Herodotus notes that the Persians borrowed their corslet from the Egyptians, and the general similarity to the Greek type might be explained by the supposition that the Greek corslet was also copied from an Egyptian model, probably by the mercenaries who served the Twenty-sixth Dynasty. In Greece, leather must have been more generally available than linen; hence the development of the *spolas*.[46]

Linen corslets, according to Pausanias, who saw one dedicated in a temple but may have lacked practical experience, gave protection against the bites of wild beasts but not against the thrust of iron, and he seems to have thought that they were used only in hunting.[47] But the sabres of the Heavy Brigade at Balaclava are said to have "rebounded like cudgels" from the Russian greatcoats,[48] and stiffened linen might turn a slashing blow. The linen corslet was certainly still used in Greek warfare in the fourth century B.C.,[49] though Xenophon only mentions it as part of the equipment of Asiatics, real or fictitious.[50] Alexander the Great is said to have worn one at Arbela, but it was a Persian corslet, captured at the earlier victory of Issus.[51]

Small plates or overlapping scales of metal were often added in the fifth century, and probably earlier,[52] to the body of the corslet, for additional protection (Plate 6). Scale-armour was an oriental invention,[53] but the Greeks applied it to their own form of corslet, instead of copying the Asiatic mail shirt.

The corslet with metal reinforcement seems to be less common in Attic fifth-century vase-paintings than the unreinforced type,[54] and was perhaps rarer in actual life.

Ancient armourers rarely attempted to make plate-armour with flexible joints. When it was desired to provide protection for the limbs, separate pieces were fashioned to clip round the thighs, shins, and upper arms. Thigh- and arm-guards appear in vase-painting in the third quarter of the sixth century, when hoplite armour seems to have reached its fullest development,[55] but were no longer used as infantry armour after the end of the century. During the fifth and fourth centuries, only the greaves were in common use, and even they are often omitted in works of art, and may not always have been worn. Surviving examples are of thin sheet bronze, which must originally have been reinforced by a backing of padded cloth. Round the edge of the metal runs a line of small holes through which passed the stitches holding this backing in place. The metal is shaped to fit round the shins and calves, the muscles being indicated in relief, and the back being left open so that the greaves could be clipped round the leg from the front, and held in place by the springiness of the metal, without any additional fastening.[56] Many red-figured vases show warriors putting on their greaves in this manner, before the corslet or cuirass, presumably because it was hard to bend when wearing body armour.[57]

Under his body armour, whether cuirass or corslet, the hoplite normally wore a short tunic (*chitoniskos*), probably of linen, to protect him against chafing, and against the heat of the sun upon his armour. Attic red-figure vase-painters sometimes show hoplites wearing the *chitoniskos* with no armour over it (Plate 7).[58] It appears at first sight that this is no more than an artistic convention, like that of "heroic nudity," which also persists through the fifth century B.C.,[59] though perhaps in many cases we should speak rather of "athletic nudity," as some pictures are certainly of athletes taking part in the hoplite race, which was a feature of many of the great athletic contests. These runners have shields on their left arms, carry helmets in their right hands, and are naked except for their greaves.[60] Dancers performing the Pyrrhic dance under arms are similarly shown naked.[61] Other vases show hoplites naked except for a *chlamys* or short cloak,[62] which, down to the Early Classic period, is sometimes worn tucked round the loins.[63] A curious "three-tiered loin-cloth" has also been recognised in the Late Archaic period,[64] but is perhaps no more than a *chitoniskos* that has been allowed to slip down from the shoulder and caught by the girdle round the waist.[65] In general, it would be reasonable to suppose that the vase-painters were influenced, even in their battle scenes, by what they saw in the gymnasia, and that young men at exercise did not always take on the burden of full armour.

But there remains a body of evidence which cannot be explained in this manner. On a number of Attic vases from the Early Classic period onwards, the thin *chitoniskos* is replaced by a tunic of heavier patterned material (Plate 8),[66] such as is used to cover cushions or couches, or for the dress of barbarians, or occasionally for the shield-aprons already mentioned. It might be questioned whether these tunics were worn for the slight additional protection given by the heavy cloth, or merely for the decorative quality of their patterns. But a very few vases show an apron of patterned stuff worn, without body armour, over the ordinary *chitoniskos* and obviously designed to protect the wearer's thighs and loins (Plate 9). The wearers are ordinary hoplites taking leave of their families before going off to the wars. There is nothing either "heroic" or "athletic" about their dress, and the apron is not pleasing aesthetically. The only reasonable explanation for its appearance is that the artist really had seen hoplites equipped in this manner, and that the protective value of the thick patterned material was recognised, perhaps as a result of encounters with Asiatics. The Mossynoeci whom Xenophon encountered wore a *chitoniskos* coming to above the knee, "as thick as blanket-weave linen," apparently for protection instead of a corslet, and at least one Persian, on a vase-painting of about 460 B.C., is shown with a protective apron about his loins.[67]

I do not know any certain reference to the apron in ancient literature. The early poets mention a defensive girdle, called *zoma* or *zoster*,[68] but this was of metal, and in any case to identify it with our apron would be an anachronism. Polybius says that the Roman cavalry used in former times to wear a *perizoma*,[69] which is perhaps the fringed semicircular apron, hanging down from the front of a broad girdle, that appears on some fourth-century Italian vases.[70] The word may serve for the Greek hoplite's apron; it is also used of the workman's apron and the athlete's loin-cloth, and in this last sense has given a name to the "Perizoma Group" of Attic black-figure vases.

Instead of the *chitoniskos*, which was fastened over both shoulders, hoplites in works of art sometimes wear the *exomis*, a short tunic of coarse cloth fastened over the left shoulder only.[71] This is rare in vase-painting, and not found very early,[72] but a comparatively high proportion of hoplites in sculptured works of the late fifth and early fourth century wear this garment (Plate 10). It was traditionally associated with rough living, or the appearance of it, being worn by workmen[73] and by those who affected the Spartan fashion of dress.[74]

Hoplites without body armour are suggested by several historical passages. In 401 B.C., the younger Cyrus paraded his Greek mercenaries for the benefit of the Queen of Cilicia. Xenophon says that the Greeks all had bronze helmets, red tunics, greaves, and their shields uncovered, which on the line of march would be carried in bags to save them from tarnishing. The generals had been ordered to draw up their men in battle formation, and presumably they were also armed as for battle. When body armour (whether corslet or cuirass) is shown in paintings or sculpture, it is always worn over the tunic. It cannot therefore be supposed that the troops were really wearing armour but that Xenophon only mentions the tunics because they alone were visible.[75]

Again, after the death of Cyrus, when the Greeks were deserted by the Asiatic divisions of his army and compelled to improvise a small force of cavalry to cover their retreat, Xenophon expressly notes that corslets (*spolades*) and cuirasses (*thorakes*) were provided for the troopers. Presumably, therefore, not all these men had body armour when they served in the infantry.[76] That the cavalry wore heavier armour than the infantry is certain.

> Soteridas of Sicyon said: "It's not fair, Xenophon. There you sit on your horse, and I struggle along under the weight of my shield." When Xenophon heard this he jumped down from his horse and pushed him out of his rank and took his shield from him and made his way with it as quickly as he was able. But he had his cavalry cuirass on too, so that he was overloaded. So he ordered those in front to lead on and those behind to pass him, and followed with difficulty. But the other soldiers struck Soteridas and threw stones at him and cursed him, until they forced him to take his shield and come on.[77]

Clearly Xenophon was wearing the plate cuirass, and the foot-soldiers were relying mainly on their shields. The hoplite shield could not be managed at the same time as the reins, so Xenophon did not carry one on horseback, though (as seems to have been customary for general officers) he had a shield-bearer to assist him when he led his men on foot.[78] Some, at least, of the infantry certainly wore *spolades*, for Xenophon records the death of the Laconian Leonymus, shot in the side, through his shield and *spolas*, by a Kurdish cloth-yard arrow.[79] (Compare the equipment of the mercenaries on the Nereid Monument: Plates 13, 14.)

The Ten Thousand were not, as far as we can judge from our evidence, equipped differently from other Peloponnesians or Boeotians of the same period. And in Sicily too, at about the same period, Dionysius I of Syracuse provided body armour for his general officers, cavalry, and guards, but not for the rank-and-file infantry, when equipping an army to fight against Carthage.[80] This evidence is slight and scattered, but it does suggest that the hoplite of about 400 B.C. was not a "heavy infantryman" encased as completely as possible in plate of proof, but, though still trained to fight hand-to-hand and in close order, depended chiefly on his shield for protection.[81]

THE HELMET

In their head covering too, the soldiers of the late fifth and fourth centuries B.C. were ready to sacrifice protection to freedom and lightness. The standard type of hoplite helmet in the Archaic period was that called nowadays, and probably in antiquity too, "Corinthian" (Plates 1, 5, 8). This completely enclosed the back and sides of the head as well as the crown. No opening was left for the ears, though in all but the earliest examples a definite distinction was made between the parts intended to enclose the cranium, the back of the head and neck, and the face. The cheek pieces were fixed, and a fixed nasal protected the nose, leaving narrow slits for sight, speech, and breathing. The helmet was made of bronze, and well padded on the inside, probably with felt. Holes for sewing in the padding are often visible round the rim. A crest of horsehair, usually fitting closely to the crown but sometimes raised above it on a short stem or stilt (Plate 2A), might be attached to the helmet.[82]

This type is still found in fourth-century works of art, but it must have obstructed both sight and hearing, besides being excessively hot and uncomfortable in the Greek summer. It belongs properly to the period of the bell cuirass, when protection was evidently thought more important than mobility. In works of art, it is often shown pushed to the back of the head, leaving the face free (Plate 13A). In real life it was no doubt worn in this way, for comfort's sake, until the last moment before going into action. But the vase-painters often show their subjects barefaced, even in the heat of battle.

Less obstructive types, such as the "Chalcidian," which left the ears free, were experimented with in the sixth century, and from about 500 B.C. helmets with hinged cheek pieces, which could be lifted up except in action, were usual. The type nowadays called "Attic" commonly has a nasal, also hinged (Plates 6, 4B, 16; with no nasal, Plates 2A, 4A, 7). The rare "Thracian" helmet, which appears in Attic vase-painting soon after the Persian Wars, has no nasal, but a narrow reinforced rim projecting over the brows.[83]

But a more remarkable development is the replacement of the head-enclosing helmet by a pointed cap, covering the crown of the head only (Plates 10, 11, 12, 13A, 15, 19). This pointed cap, best known by its ancient name, *pilos*, becomes common in works of painting and sculpture at the end of the fifth century B.C., and at that time and in the fourth century is often worn by hoplites without body armour. Miss K. M. T. Chrimes has pointed out the tactical significance of the new active hoplite, clad in tunic and *pilos* instead of corslet and helmet, but the archaeological evidence presented below shows that many cities used the new equipment, not, as she suggested, Sparta alone. Nor did the Spartans take advantage of their new nimbleness to rush in upon a heavy and slow-moving enemy. On the contrary, their ordered and deliberate advance is contrasted by Thucydides with the rapid movements of their enemies.[84]

The root meaning of the word *pilos* is "felt," and the first headgear to receive this name is the rough home-made conical peasant's cap,[85] which is sometimes shown worn by the attendants of hoplites on Attic black-figured vases of the sixth century B.C. A smoother conical or bell-shaped cap appears in Attic red-figured vase-painting from the Archaic period onwards, worn by hunters, travellers, and horsemen as an alternative to the more usual *petasos*, or broad-brimmed sun-hat. A vase-painting does not tell one the material of which the cap is made, but there is no real reason for supposing that the *pilos*, when shown in peaceful contexts, is not simply a hard felt cap, useful protection against the accidents of the road or the cudgels of robbers. In war, the felt cap seems at first to have been worn not in place of the helmet, but under it, as a substitute for a fitted lining of felt,[86]

or for a headband on which the helmet might sit (Plate 8).[87]
But the light-armed attendants who accompany hoplites[88] on
campaign seem to have found the *pilos* protection enough in
their skirmishes. On the vases, they sometimes fight side by side
with their masters, a spear in the right hand, the left arm wrapped
in the *chlamys*, or short cloak, and thrown forward for defence,
but in real life they seem to have had little importance on the
battlefield.

The earliest Attic pictures of hoplites wearing the *pilos* instead
of the helmet are from the Early Classic period—perhaps just
before the middle of the fifth century—and they are at first extremely rare. Probably from this time onwards, the shape was
copied in metal, or reinforced with metal hoops like the mediaeval
spangenhelm.[89] Actual examples of bronze *piloi* have been found
at Dodona and elsewhere, whose tautly curving crowns and narrow, sharply out-turned rims come very close to many painted
and sculptured representations.[90] By 411 B.C., the word *pilos* had
come to mean simply "helmet of *pilos* shape," and no longer
necessarily suggested the material felt, for in the *Lysistrata* of
Aristophanes, a cavalry commander is made fun of for using
his bronze *pilos* as a porridge bowl.[91]

I believe that this passage shows that Thucydides too uses the
word *pilos* to mean headgear in his account of the Spartan defeat
at Sphacteria in 425 B.C., though the Spartan *pilos* was perhaps
still actually made of felt. Four hundred and twenty hoplites, cut
off on the narrow, precipitous, scrub-covered island, were assailed
by greatly superior numbers of light-armed troops. "Thereupon
matters went hard with the Lacedaemonians. For their *piloi* were
not proof against the arrows, and javelins broke off in them when
they were struck." [92]

The ancient commentary (apparently guessing) offers two different explanations, both of which can be supported by archaeological evidence. Either "the *piloi* are garments compacted of
wool, like corslets under the breast, which we put on"—this explanation might be applied to the tunic (Plate 8) or to the apron

(Plate 9) of blanket material, whose appearance in vase-painting in the Classic period, about the beginning of the Peloponnesian War or slightly earlier, has already been noted—or "But some people say that they are the coverings of the headgear." [93] Some helmets depicted on Attic red-figured vases are covered with a chequer pattern, explained by Sir John Beazley as a cloth cover intended to protect the wearer against the sun (Plate 16; compare the cloth covering of Priam's stool). But I believe that Thucydides means helmets of the *pilos* shape.[94]

That felt *piloi* were used in war appears from a tombstone of about 420–410 B.C., found at Megara, but probably of Attic workmanship, so that the nationality of the soldier portrayed on it is not certain. He stands with his right arm hanging down by his side, his *pilos* in his hand. Sir John Beazley writes: "The hand sinks into the hat and presses it out of shape. . . . I have no doubt that the material is felt and that felt piloi were used in war as in peace. The hat of Odysseus on the Dolon vase in London certainly seems to be soft." [95] The warrior wears an *exomis*, with no body armour or greaves. His sword hangs at his left side from a baldric. A heavy cloak hangs over his left shoulder, and his shield is on his left arm. He carries his spear at the slope in his left hand.

There is also some late literary evidence that suggests that the Spartans may simply have substituted the strong cap of the mountain shepherds for the metal helmet. The Laconian or Arcadian *pilos* is mentioned by Arrian (early second century after Christ) as a possible alternative to the helmet in the arming of heavy hoplites. And his contemporary, Dio Chrysostom, speaks of the irrational behaviour of humans who cut off their own hair and weave that of animals into Arcadian or Laconian *piloi* as a substitute.[96] I think it is quite possible, therefore, that the Spartans at Sphacteria had no better head protection than strong felt caps. The Athenian archers, like the Normans at Hastings, may have shot into the air, to clear the wall of overlapping shields. At this time, the *pilos* was no doubt standard equipment in the Spartan

army, and the vase-paintings suggest that individuals were experimenting with it at Athens, which may have been one reason
why the conservative Thucydides pointed out the inadequacy of
the new-fangled headgear.

Hoplites wearing *piloi*, some of which are distinguished by
the addition of a crest, are not uncommon on Attic vases of the
late fifth century, and continue into the fourth both in Attic and
South Italian vase-painting (Plates 15, 19).[97] But for the late
fifth and fourth centuries, the evidence of sculptured monuments
is more impressive than that of painted vases. Athenian grave
monuments, whose style suggests a date before the end of the
fifth century B.C., show hoplites wearing the *pilos* and without
body armour (Plate 12).[98] Most of them are Athenians, but not
all. A relief in the Metropolitan Museum of Art (Plate 10) shows
a bearded warrior wearing an *exomis*, a hoplite shield on his left
arm, but no body armour, and a sword slung at his left side from
a baldric. He bestrides a fallen adversary, whom he is about to
dispatch with the butt-end of his spear. The top of the slab has
been sawn off, so it is not known what sort of helmet he was
wearing. But his fallen opponent wears a *pilos* and a short cloak
hanging from his left shoulder. He is otherwise naked, but has
unsheathed a short stabbing-sword which he points at his victorious adversary's body. Miss G. M. A. Richter assigns the relief
to the late fifth century on stylistic grounds. Its material (Pentelic
marble) and workmanship attest its Attic origin, and it evidently
represents an Athenian warrior triumphing over an opponent,
whom we might take to be a Spartan even if his nationality were
not established by the short sword, a weapon characteristically
Spartan, as Miss Richter points out.[99] Such a sword (perhaps
not quite as short) and *pilos* also form part of the equipment of
certain hoplites depicted on gravestones from Boeotia; they have
been claimed as Spartans, but I believe that their nationality is
less certain than that of the fallen warrior in New York. They
wear red *exomides* and no body armour.[100]

Admittedly, figures on tombstones may be heroic, and a sculp-

tured block from Athens indicates the wearing of the corslet under the *exomis* by soldiers who were presumably either Spartans
or allies of Sparta (Plate 11). On the faces of this block are
trophies carved in relief, beside one of which stands a hoplite in
cuirass and Attic helmet, and beside another a winged Victory.
The trophies consist of tree stumps, from each of which a lopped
branch projects like an upraised right hand. A *pilos* crowns the
main trunk, on which the shoulder-straps and neck- and armholes of a corslet are indicated by incised lines. The trophy by
which the hoplite stands is complete, with cloak and shield.
Victory is still dressing the other trophy, and raises a fold of the
cloak in her left hand.[101]

The *pilos* also found favour with the Greek mercenaries,
mostly Arcadians, who were employed by the Persian satraps
and by the almost independent rulers of Caria and Lycia on the
southeast seaboard. Kherei, ruler of Xanthus in Lycia from about
430 to after 411 B.C., boasts that he slew seven hoplites in one day,
men of Arcadia. On the reliefs decorating his monument,[102] his
gigantic figure strides forward to deal with the last of the seven,
who is unhelmeted, with the shields of the other six in relief
above his head. On another face of the block are three more
hoplites, probably Greek, of whom two wear *piloi*, the better
preserved of which has the sharply offset rim of the bronze *pilos*
from Dodona. These figures are heroically nude (though Kherei's
victim wears a cuirass) and Kherei himself is depicted on a
gigantic scale. The details of equipment are therefore not wholly
reliable.

On the early fourth-century monument of Payava from Xanthus, heroic conventions seem less marked. The principal figure,
a horseman, is clad in complete and elaborate armour. But of the
five hoplites whom he opposes, two are naked (one bare-headed,
one wearing a rough felt cap). The other three wear the *exomis*,
with bare right shoulders, and have *piloi*, presumably of metal,
two of them with curving cheek pieces and all with crests.[103]
These men are perhaps Greeks being broken by Lycian cavalry,

but the *pilos* occurs elsewhere on the monument, worn by foot soldiers (one crested) and by a charioteer, who is accompanied by a hoplite wearing plate cuirass and Attic helmet. The crested *pilos,* on this and other monuments, has been taken as proof of Lycian nationality, being identified with the *pilos* encircled with feathers that Herodotus mentions as the distinctive head-dress of the Lycians in the army of Xerxes. But the crest does not encircle the *pilos* on the monuments, and there are similar crested *piloi* in Attic and South Italian vase-painting.

Something very like the crested *pilos* also appears in Cypriot art as early as the Archaic period. But metal caps from Cyprus, crested or otherwise, might be derived from Asiatic prototypes and form part of a tradition separate from that of mainland Greece. I only mention the Cypriot examples to show that this form of helmet was known at an early period outside Lycia. Besides, the Lycians in the army of Xerxes were archers, not hoplites,[104] though their Carian neighbours had their own tradition of hoplite fighting.[105]

The finest of the Lycian monuments, and one of the finest illustrations of hoplite warfare, is the Nereid Monument, of about 400 B.C., from Xanthus. The armour depicted upon it is in some respects different from that usual in European Greece at the same time, but these differences are not so great as to render unlikely the usual view that these soldiers are Greek mercenaries, serving Asiatic rulers and adapting themselves to local conditions. It is of course highly probable that Carians as well as Greeks were employed in Lycia, or even that the Lycians themselves had by this time changed their armament, but I do not now believe that the hoplites on the Nereid Monument are demonstrably un-Greek.

Hoplites appear on the west pediment of the Nereid Monument, and upon the first and second friezes. The first frieze is heroic, not historical, with small groups of combatants engaged in separate fights over the bodies of the slain, in the epic manner. There are hoplites on both sides. Some have corslets, others tunics only;

still others are nude. All have the hoplite shield and helmet.[106] The combatants include horsemen, several of whom are being worsted by the hoplites, and Asiatics of rank, wearing the soft tiara of Persian nobles.

Like this frieze, the west pediment has an air of theatrical unreality. It seems originally to have depicted a battle of hoplites (probably Greeks) against Asiatic cavalry, but of the latter there survives only the foreleg of a rearing horse. Six hoplites are fairly well preserved; the foremost, crushed beneath the horse's hooves, is naked and wears a *pilos*. At least two of the others (the head of one is mutilated) have *piloi*, and no body armour, though they have short cloaks and one has a tunic. Two only of the six have leather corslets, and they also wear helmets.

The most interesting part of the Nereid Monument, for our present purpose, is the second frieze (details, Plates 13, 14), which apparently shows a historical incident—the capture of a walled Lycian city by a disciplined hoplite army in the service of an Asiatic ruler. The hoplites, who are often shown in regular formation, bear the brunt of the fighting, though a few archers and stone-throwers also appear. The defenders of the city, also armed as hoplites, throw stones instead of wielding spears, even when they sally out of the gates. Most of the hoplites wear corslets, though there are a few with tunics only.[107] Helmets of various types are the usual head-dress, but there are also several *piloi* (mostly badly battered and so not very clear in the published drawings), whose shape is very close to that of the metal ones found at Dodona.[108]

These soldiers, who prefer the helmet to the *pilos*, and most of whom, even the archers, wear corslets (probably leather *spolades*), seem not to have followed the fashions reflected in the contemporary art of mainland Greece. Still more striking is the retention of the rectangular shield-apron, carried by a few hoplites, both defenders and attackers, half a century after its usual appearance in Attic vase-paintings (Plate 13A).[109] Hoplites fighting in Asia would still need to take special precautions against

Asiatic arrows, whatever their own origin. But the long tunics worn under their armour by the soldiers of the Nereid Monument do seem at first sight to be Asiatic. In Attic pictures of Greek soldiers, the tunics rarely come below the middle of the thigh. On the Nereid Monument, they come down to the knee, or even below it (Plate 14B). Such long tunics are often shown over the trousers and long-sleeved jackets of Asiatics, but I have noted only one in fifth-century Attic vase-painting worn by a hoplite as his only garment, and he is probably intended to be an Oriental.

But even the long tunic is not necessarily Asiatic. Xenophon notes that the Thracians wore under their heavy horsemen's cloaks, "*chitons* not only about their torsos but about their thighs too," to protect themselves from the cold; and other soldiers seem to have found the longer garment valuable. Professor H. R. W. Smith points out to me that it is worn by at least two hoplites (both certainly Greeks of Southern Italy) on fourth-century Apulian vases (Plate 15).[110] Perhaps, therefore, we cannot safely say more about this second frieze than that it suggests differences between Asiatic conditions and those of mainland Greece.

In the heroic scenes, fanciful variations are introduced, which may be compared with those in the remarkable sculptures of the Heroon of Gjölbaschi, the ancient Trysa, to the east of Xanthus.[111] Since their subjects are legendary, these sculptures do not necessarily represent contemporary armour, but there is certainly no deliberate antiquarianism about them. Many of them are concerned with the Trojan War, and most of the combatants on both sides are represented as hoplites. Both the *pilos* and the helmet are common, and some of the figures have corslets, others tunics only, apparently without reference to the form of their headgear.[112] The *pilos* is also worn by archers and unarmed stone-throwers,[113] by most of the hunters of the Calydonian Boar, and by Odysseus and Telemachus slaying the Suitors.[114] Some of the figures in the battle scenes wear a *pilos* with a short crest at the peak, which, on one part of the frieze representing the Sack of Troy, seems to distinguish friend from enemy.[115] But almost directly below[116] comes a group of five figures assailing a gate, all in *piloi,* the central one crested, and here the crest might be taken as a badge of rank. Generally it has no obvious significance.

OFFENSIVE WEAPONS

The offensive weapons of the hoplite were, at all periods, the spear and the sword. Of these the spear was always the more important. The Greek says, "taken by the spear" not "conquered by the sword"; the shields and the firm array of spears are the essential features of Greek equipment that Aeschylus contrasts to the archery of the Asiatics.[117] Spears shown in art vary in length, from a man's height to half as much again—perhaps generally from seven to eight feet[118]—with a heavy iron point,[119] and a solid metal butt, which might be used for finishing off fallen opponents,[120] but more usually for sticking the spears into the ground when the troops rested in bivouac.[121] Ash wood was used for the shafts of spears in the heroic age,[122] but cornel seems to have been used in the classical period and later.[123] The spear was wielded with the right hand only (the left being fully occupied with the shield) and was intended for hand-to-hand fighting, though of course it could be thrown if its bearer wanted. But in the classical period, this seems only to have been done from high ground, and generally by fugitives turning on their pursuers, never as part of the preliminaries of a set battle.[124]

The swords shown on Attic vase-paintings of the fifth and fourth centuries B.C. fall into two main groups. One is the straight cut-and-thrust, usually with a leaf-shaped blade, not shorter than the bearer's forearm, and generally rather longer. An iron sword of this type found at Dodona was 0.58 m. long, without most of its hilt, and the best preserved of several from Olympia was 0.68 m. long. Its original length is supposed to have been about 0.80 m.[125] The other kind is a slashing sword, of about the same length, with a curved single-edged blade. Xenophon calls this a *machaera* (the word is also used of other cutting implements, including small knives) and recommends its use in the cavalry.[126]

Vase-paintings often show the *machaera* being used by infantry, but in the close press of hoplite battle the straight thrusting sword may have been more useful. It was for this close press that the Spartans were equipped. The short sword of the fallen Spartan on the relief in New York (Plate 10) has already been mentioned, and the Spartan sword was the subject of several of the famous sayings recorded by Plutarch. The Athenian Demades told King Agis III that jugglers found Spartan swords easy to swallow, because of their shortness. The king replied, "Yet the Spartans reach their enemies with their swords." [127] Antalcidas replied to the question why the Spartans used short swords in war, "Because we fight close to our enemies," [128] and a Spartan mother whose son complained of his sword's shortness told him to "Add to it one step forward." [129] The short sword does not seem to have been as widely adopted as the *pilos,* but it won some favour among military adventurers. The murderers of Dion, being unable to strangle him with their bare hands, called for a sword, and Lycon the Syracusan passed them one which was "short, like the Spartan swords." It was probably not of Spartan make, being finely ornamented, and so was easily recognized when a few years later it was used to kill Callipus, the leader of the plot against Dion.[130]

As Miss Chrimes justly points out,[131] a sword-swallower's sword must have been straight—such a weapon, in fact, as is shown on the New York relief. Ancient writers also mention the *xyele,* which the lexicographers of late antiquity describe as "a small sword which some call a sickle." [132] Xenophon says that the Chalybes, whom the Ten Thousand encountered on their retreat, had at their belts knives as big as a Laconian *xyele,* with which they butchered and beheaded those who fell into their hands. And he also says that the Spartiate Dracontius, whom the Ten Thousand chose to preside over their games, had been exiled from home as a boy because he struck another boy with his *xyele* and accidentally slew him.[133] Plutarch has a story of how two Spartan boys fought with sickles (he does not use the word *xyele*) and one was mortally wounded, but would not let his friends avenge him, because he would have done as much to his opponent if he had got his blow in first.[134] I have not recognized the *xyele* on any classical representations of soldiers, and believe that it was not used by the Spartans in battle in the classical period.[135] Iron sickles were, in later times, dedicated by boys to the goddess Artemis Orthia,[136] and I believe that the *xyele* is to be identified with these ceremonial weapons.

UNIFORMS

For uniforms, in the sense of distinctive standardized military dress, there is little evidence in antiquity, and most of what there is refers to Sparta, or to armies trained on the Spartan model. The short tunic, worn under the body armour or by itself, was not confined to soldiers. Indeed in ancient Greece, where every citizen accepted military service as a matter of course, there was no need for a distinctive dress to mark out the military from the civilians. Sparta differed from the other cities, not because her citizens were soldiers, but because soldiering was their only occupation. And in Sparta, the soldier's tunic was coloured red, because this colour "has the fewest womanish associations and is the most warlike." [137] On red tunics, blood was least visible, and in their red tunics the Spartans were buried.[138] The red tunic was chosen, later ages believed, by Lycurgus, the half-mythical author of the Spartan constitution, and it can at least be traced back to the Third Messenian War, when the Spartan who came to beg Athenian help "sat by the altars white in his red coat." [139] But this uniform was not restricted to the Spartiate peers, whose bodies on the battlefield could not be distinguished from those of commoners or *perioeci*.[140] Even allied contingents and mercenaries serving with the Spartans were dressed in the red coat,[141] and other soldiers might adopt it for themselves, as the Ten Thousand did.

The Spartan army was elaborately organized into units and sub-units under officers of different ranks, but it seems clear that they bore no distinguishing badges on their dress.[142] There was,

of course, no officer class. Even the private soldiers were gentlemen, and brought their personal servants on campaigns with
them. This was also true of other Greek armies; the hoplite was
not required to perform "fatigues." There was no need for the
officer to be instantly recognizable as an officer, even off the
parade ground. On parade, or in the battles for which the parades
were the rehearsal, he led his own section, company or other unit,
whose members would know him by sight. Moreover, as will be
seen, each officer had his own position allotted to him, and his
duties consisted largely in passing on to his men orders received
from above, and in carrying them out according to a prescribed
drill. The Spartans did not envisage a situation in which a subordinate officer might suddenly have to take control of a body of
strange men and lead them by his own initiative.

In the Athenian army, the *taxiarchs,* or regimental commanders, apparently wore helmets with triple plumes and red or purple
tunics or cloaks,[143] which may have been an official badge of rank.

To distinguish between friend and foe, the classical Greeks
relied on letters or other shield badges, and uniforms in the modern sense were therefore the less necessary.

SUMMARY

Hoplite armour reached its heaviest development on the Greek
mainland in the late sixth century B.C., about a generation before
the Persian invasions of Europe. The hoplites who faced those
invasions were more lightly equipped than their fathers, having
discarded the clumsy thigh-and arm-pieces and, for the most part,
replaced the plate cuirass by the corslet of linen and leather. The
"Corinthian" helmet had also been generally replaced by the
"Attic" or similar types. These changes were not accidental. It
was necessary to create a more active type of soldier in order to
deal with a lightly-equipped enemy, whose chief weapon was the
bow. At Marathon in 490 B.C., the Athenians were "the first of
all Greeks whom we know to advance against the enemy at the
double," [144] though we need not suppose that, even in their modi-

fied armour, they ran for a full mile as Herodotus says. At Thermopylae ten years later, the Spartans showed their skill in active manoeuvre.[145] But this was a small picked force. Next year at Plataea, where the whole army of the Spartans and of their allies was engaged, the battle was not won by skillful manoeuvre but by the ability to hold fast under the Persian arrows until the barbarians, by their own miscalculations, were so crowded together that they could not escape the final charge. Once at close grips, the Persians continued to fight with a bravery that won their enemy's respect, but the heavier armament and regular formation of the Greeks prevailed.[146]

During the Peloponnesian War of 431–404 B.C., we find evidence of a new-style hoplite, without body armour, sometimes without greaves, and wearing a *pilos* instead of a helmet. The main task of hoplite armies was still to fight in close formation on level ground against other hoplites, but their equipment had obviously been lightened in an attempt to give them a chance against light infantry on broken ground. The archaeological evidence suggests that the Athenians were experimenting, not very systematically and probably as the result of personal preferences rather than official policy, with different forms of light hoplite equipment before the beginning of the Peloponnesian War, and that by the end of it, the *pilos* and *exomis* had become standard. The Spartan hoplites on Sphacteria seem to have been already equipped in the new fashion; if so, it seems probable that, as Miss Chrimes suggested, they had adopted it before the outbreak of war, perhaps as a result of lessons learned from the guerrilla fighting around Mount Ithome in the Third Messenian War. The archaeological evidence from Sparta fails us at about the beginning of the Persian Wars, up to which point the Spartans seem to have worn body armour and helmets like other Greeks. The fighting in Sphacteria showed that light-armed troops armed with missile weapons could destroy even the best hoplites upon difficult ground, however they were equipped. The latter part of the war and the early fourth century saw the development of still more

formidable light infantry, professional peltasts armed with javelins and light shields. Brilliantly led and in combination with
other arms, peltasts were able to defeat Spartan hoplites on a level
plain. The Greeks, and especially the Spartans, are blamed by
modern writers for clinging to cumbrous equipment and obsolete
tactics instead of transforming their whole armies into light infantry when the latter had demonstrated their superiority. But,
on the evidence presented in this chapter, they had in fact changed
their equipment to meet the new developments in warfare. And it
was still by pitched battles that wars were won, and hoplites, not
peltasts, won the pitched battles. It was by hoplites that the Spartan power was broken in the end.

III

COMMISSARIAT AND CAMPS

Spartan professionalism extended beyond the training of the fighting troops. Xenophon records the arrangements made for the supply of the army in the field. "First of all the ephors proclaim the year-classes that are to be called up on service, both for cavalry and for hoplites, and then for the craftsmen also. And so the Lacedaemonians are well supplied, even in the field, with all that men use in cities. Regulations prescribe the transport, by wagon or pack-animal, of all the tools required by the army in common, and so there is small chance of anything being accidentally forgotten." [1] The *Cyropaedia,* written some twenty years later than this passage, with the battle of Leuctra in between, provides an interesting commentary. For a march expected to last "not less than fifteen days" through barren country, Cyrus's soldiers were to take "not less than twenty days' provisions" for man and beast. Enough grain was essential, but they were to take only enough wine to make the transition to water-drinking gradual, instead of endangering their health by immediate total abstinence. Water would suffice for mixing barley groats and wheat cakes, cooking in general and drinking at meals: a few sips of wine after meals were to be allowed at first. The men were to reduce their bedding so as to be able to carry more provisions, but they were to take plenty of clothing, serviceable both in sickness and in health. The basic ration was barley or wheat, but sharp, pungent, salty foods, which keep well, were to be carried as appetizers. When the army again reached territory where grain was available, hand-mills (that is, the saddle-querns which were to be found in most houses) would be obtained on the spot. Medical supplies were mentioned, but not specified; they would not weigh much, but would be greatly in demand if necessity arose. Straps for harness and men's equipment, spokeshaves for trimming the shafts of javelins, and rasps for sharpening spear points were essential. "For the man who whets his spear point whets his courage along with it." Spare timbers for chariots and wagons, and the essential carpenter's tools, had to be brought. Even if skilled craftsmen were not everywhere available, most men could improvise running repairs. Each wagon was to carry a shovel and a mattock, each pack-animal an axe and a sickle. The officers of both the fighting troops and the transport service were made responsible for the equipment of their men. Pioneers, whose corps was made up of rejects from the light infantry, were to have axes, shovels, and mattocks to clear the way for the wagons. Smiths, carpenters, and leather-workers of military age accompanied the expedition. They were not required to bear arms in the ranks, but formed part of the regular establishment of the army in their own capacities, and served for hire those who needed them.

But even this completely equipped army relied to a considerable extent upon supplies voluntarily brought by merchants trading for their own profit. It is true that they were forbidden under pain of confiscation to trade before the end of the twenty days for which the soldiers were to supply themselves, but thereafter they might sell freely. Cyrus not only promised rewards and honours to those who brought the most provisions, but undertook to advance capital to those who gave security that they would accompany the expedition.

The first day's march was deliberately made short, so that anything that had been forgotten could be sent for. On the march across the plains, many tracks were prepared for the baggage train, which followed the cavalry screen, with the infantry phalanx following behind in order to hurry on any stragglers. But when the army passed through defiles it did so in three columns, the baggage in the middle with a column of infantry on each side. Any obstruction was to be removed by the accompanying soldiers, and as far as possible each regiment was to accompany its own baggage, so that the soldiers might work willingly to clear the way, and might have everything handy when the time came to halt.[2]

The superiority of the Spartan system no doubt consisted in the fact that supply and transport were provided for in the regular routine of mobilization. The Athenian citizen, when called suddenly to arms for the defence of the frontier, could not count on an organized commissariat. When the Athenians planned in advance a distant expedition, they well knew the importance of supplying it properly, and in the time of their greatness they acted according to their knowledge. For the attack upon Sicily, where during the four winter months the army could hardly hope for messages from Athens, let alone supplies, they provided thirty large merchant-ships and a hundred smaller vessels to carry provisions. By the advice of the general Nicias, each of the mills at Athens provided a quota of conscripts to grind flour for the expeditionary force, and stone-masons and carpenters, with the necessary tools, were enrolled for the work of fortification.[3] But normally each man served as his own provant-master. "Report with three days' rations"[4] was the order; the lists of those required for duty were posted in the market-place; and the man who only noticed his name at the last moment had to scurry round for what he could find in the shops, or go hungry.[5]

Barley groats were the regular staple of the soldier's diet.[6] They were helped down with cheese and onions, and later ages sentimentalized over the time when "the generals often gave the order to bring uncooked rations and led their men out to battle. And so did the trierarchs, issuing barley to the rowers, with cheese and onions for relish, when they embarked them on the triremes."[7] But the "good old days" are sometimes less enjoyable for those who have to live through them. To Aristophanes's chorus, the return of peace brought freedom from helmet, cheese, and onions.[8]

The rations were carried in a haversack, to which the smell of the onions clung.[9] The gentlemen ranker was not expected to carry this himself, being accompanied even in the field by a personal servant. The fictitious Cyrus of the *Cyropaedia* secured the loyalty and ready obedience of these camp-followers by giving them the same rations as the fighting troops and by treating their calling as no less honourable than that of his heralds and ambassadors.[10] His opinion that servants should have an understanding of military affairs seems to have been shared by less capable soldiers, for Theophrastus makes his coward skulk in his tent "and send out his servant with orders to reconnoitre the enemy's position." [11] But outside the story-books, Athenian camp-followers were generally untrustworthy slaves, ready to desert when their masters were in danger.[12] Nor was their calling in fact considered honourable. A speech of Isaeus reproaches the villainous Dicaeogenes, who, not content with cheating his nephew Cephisodotus out of a fortune, added disgrace to injury by sending the poor boy on the expedition to Corinth (that of 394 B.C.) as servant to his own brother Harmodius. Indeed, he even had the impudence to scold his victim for disgracing the family by wearing a rough cloak and slippers, "as though he had suffered some injustice by Cephisodotus wearing slippers and had not himself unjustly stripped him of his possessions and brought him to poverty." [13]

Fifth-century vase-paintings often show hoplites attended by young men, but they are usually dressed more smartly and more practically than poor Cephisodotus.[14] They often wear boots and leggings made of thongs wound round and round their legs like puttees, and their short cloaks are like those of hunters or horsemen (Plate 8). Moreover they are generally armed with javelins, and often engage in the fighting, whereas in actual practice the servants added nothing to the strength of the army in a pitched battle.[15]

Nor did Spartan practice come close to Xenophon's ideal. Far from trusting the helots who accompanied the army, the Spartans kept them away from the arms, always carried their spears where-ever they went, and posted sentries during the day looking in-wards towards the stands of arms "not for their enemies but for their friends."[16] Nor did the servants receive the same quantity of rations as the fighting men, though the quality was apparently the same. Delicacy in diet was not encouraged in Sparta, and once, when an ally provided a feast of cakes for Agesilaus's army, the king, with characteristic discourtesy, ordered the dainties to be given to the attendant helots.[17]

Equality of rations and living conditions between the rank and file hoplites and their officers (who were, after all, their social equals) was accepted. Aristophanes makes Lamachus in the *Acharnians* (he was apparently a *taxiarch* at the time the play was produced) shoulder his own haversack, containing thyme-fla-voured salt, stockfish, and the usual onions. But even though he had been hurriedly called out on a snowy winter night to repel a frontier raid, he took his servant with him and trusted him with his shield, to which the bedding was strapped.[18] The scene re-calls Timotheus's remark that his rival Chares was fitter to carry the general's bedding than to be general himself.[19]

At Sparta, the rule of equality did not apply to the kings, whose double portion at dinner is quaintly said to have been "not so that they might eat twice as much, but so that they should have the wherewithal to honour whomsoever they desired."[20] In the *Cyropaedia,* Cyrus distinguished those who pleased him in the same manner, but on the lavish scale that befitted an oriental monarch, inviting to dinner both senior and junior officers and sometimes private soldiers, even whole companies and regiments. It was only the size of the dinner that was lavish, not its quality, and the same food that was set before his guests was served to the king.[21]

Soldiers who had to provide for themselves at a moment's notice could not be expected to stay in the field very long. So Greek

armies when operating near home might start out with three days'
rations,[22] or five,[23] or seven,[24] or even as little as one.[25] Indeed,
once when the Athenians were pouring libations before a descent
upon the coast of Epidaurus, Iphicrates sarcastically remarked
that they had already expended their provisions for the campaign. Thirty days seems to have been considered a reasonable
time for an army to live off its own supplies, if there was time
for proper preparation.[26] The treaty of 420 B.C. between Athens,
Argos, Elis, and Mantinea stipulated that a city sending troops to
help another should provide them with food for thirty days from
the date of their arrival, and also on their departure. But it does
not follow that the troops were actually to carry the food with
them. Perhaps their cities were only responsible for seeing that
they had money to buy it with. For the treaty continued by reg-
ulating the money that was to be paid by the state asking for
help if it wanted to keep the troops for more than thirty days.[27]
To carry thirty days' supplies was at least not physically impossible: Dionysius I of Syracuse demanded as much of his men at
least once.[28] But he belonged to an age when mercenaries were
introducing new professional standards. In calculating the supplies and allowances of the ordinary army of citizen hoplites, the
servants had to be allowed for.[29]

The middle of the fourth century saw the development of the
magnificent Macedonian army. King Philip's soldiers were not
respectable citizens who could vote him out of office at the end
of the year, and they did not expect to be waited upon like gentlemen when they were in the field. "From the time that he first
raised an army, he allowed nobody the use of wheeled transport.
He allowed the cavalry not more than one camp-follower each,
the infantry one to each ten men, to carry the hand-mills and
ropes. When they marched out in the summer he ordered them
to carry thirty days' rations on their backs." But, if Philip took
no more in his baggage train than was necessary, he treated it
with respect: "Once he intended to encamp in an excellent place
but learned that there was no pasture for the baggage animals.

'What a life!' he said, 'if we have to live to suit even the donkeys' convenience.' " [30] And the Macedonian army did not distintegrate amid the cries of "Treachery!" at the end of the thirty days, when the men had to face bad weather and shortage of food, as had the Thracian tribesmen of Sitalces.[31] Philip may have laid the burdens that he put on his own men on his allies too, though a letter requiring them to bring forty days' food with them for an invasion of Phocis is of doubtful authenticity.[32] The training program of the Macedonians included forced marches, with arms, rations and equipment,[33] whereas young Athenians undergoing training in the frontier garrisons were waited on by their own servants, who cooked their masters' meals.[34]

The scale upon which hand-mills were provided for Philip's army, or even the fact that they were provided at all, may surprise the modern reader. But to carry unground grain reduced the bulk of the ration and the risk of spoilage. Even at home, most soldiers were used to seeing each day's supply ground out by hand on the stone quern. There was no portable machinery by which the rations of a marching army could be ground in bulk every day,[35] and soldiers were not asked to put their hands to the labour of slaves. Unground barley was issued instead of wheat to Roman soldiers who had disgraced themselves.[36] When Plataea was about to be besieged in 429 B.C., it was obviously necessary to cut down the number of mouths within the walls, but a garrison of four hundred and eighty combatants was still left with one hundred and ten women to make bread.[37] Nor was it only in antiquity that armies campaigning in Southern Europe needed hand-mills. They were issued to the Duke of Marlborough's soldiers when he proposed to cross the Alps and join Prince Eugene in Italy in 1706.[38]

The terms of the armistice between the Athenians and Spartans during the Sphacteria campaign of 425 B.C. inform us of the rations thought suitable for a Lacedaemonian hoplite and his servant in the field. The soldiers cut off in the island were provided daily with two Attic *choinikes* (more than half a gallon) of barley groats, ready-mixed, and two *kotylai* (about a pint) of wine, and also meat. Servants received half these quantities.[39] This is certainly not a starvation allowance (half a *choinix* of barley and a *kotyle* of water was all that was given to the Athenian prisoners at Syracuse)[40] and it was no doubt to prevent the besieged from laying aside part of their ration every day that the Athenians required that it should be issued ready-mixed and not as dry grain. A *choinix* of barley a day seems to have been the standard daily ration for a slave.[41]

For the peacetime allowance in the Spartan messes, we have only the evidence of late writers, for what it is worth. Athenaeus's figures are, for each month, "approximately one and a half Attic *medimni* [72 *choinikes*] of barley, some eleven or twelve *choeis* of wine [144 *kotylai,* or more than double the Sphacteria allowance every day] and in addition a fixed weight of cheese and figs." [42] Plutarch says that the cheese ration was about five *mnai* (five pounds) and the fig ration two.[43] A small money contribution to buy a "relish" was certainly not a feature of the earliest Spartan system, and it is questionable whether the whole amount was for the personal consumption of the Spartiate himself,[44] especially as boiled pork, and the notorious black broth made from it, seem to have appeared regularly at table; if the members of the mess had been hunting, there might be game.[45]

On active service, it may have been impossible to provide a regular meat ration for the rank and file, though Agesilaus at least recognized the importance of giving the troops hot meals, and once specially sent fire enclosed in earthenware pots to a regiment bivouacking in bad weather on a rough hillside.[46] The army was accompanied by a small herd of sacrificial beasts, as the gods had to be consulted through sacrifice whenever any decision had to be made, and upon the very field of battle. The kings were entitled to the hides and chines of the victims,[47] and no doubt the officers and officials who attended the ceremony sometimes came in for a share.[48] The Spartan soldier probably missed a regular supply of meat much more than did most

Athenians,[49] to whom sacrifices and the fine meat meals that
followed them were treats for special occasions. To most Greeks,
shortage of meat was an accepted part of daily life, but shortage
of grain was a great hardship. On the last stage of the march to
Cunaxa, the Greek mercenaries could only obtain wheat and
barley at impossibly high prices from the Lydian merchants who
accompanied the Asiatic divisions of the army, and the soldiers
pulled through on a meat diet.[50] Xenophon does not say where
the meat came from; probably worn-out and starving pack-
animals. The soldiers were glad to be given meat when it was
a supplement to the barley ration, not a substitute for it. At
Heraclea on the Black Sea a "hospitable entertainment" was
offered them, consisting of three thousand *medimni* of barley, two
thousand jars of wine, twenty oxen and a hundred sheep. One
malcontent stated emphatically that this would not feed the
army for three days,[51] but as they were now reduced to about
8500 combatants, besides women and children,[52] the barley (144,-
000 *choinikes*) ought to have lasted them for more than a week
even on the generous scale of two *choinikes* a day. Presumably
therefore the shortage of meat was the cause of complaint; but
at Sinope the "entertainment" had included no meat, only three
thousand *medimni* of barley and fifteen hundred jars of wine.[53]

A peaceful city might well be moved to "hospitality" by the
sudden appearance of a large armed force on its borders, but a
prudent general, planning to extend his campaign over a period
longer than that for which supplies could be carried, would
consider the problem of supply in advance. If he was going to
invade hostile territory, there was the hope of plunder: "abun-
dance of supply in wartime from the enemy's territory brings not
only provisions but glory in the eyes of the world." [54] But in
practice "living off the country" was an uncertain business, and
of course impossible in allied territory, if the general was to retain his allies' goodwill and his reputation as a man of honour.[55]
To attract to the camp a swarm of merchants was therefore considered desirable. The arrangements made in the *Cyropaedia*

have already been noted. A great number of merchant ships accompanied the Athenian expedition to Sicily voluntarily for the sake of trade, in addition to the pressed supply-ships, which was just as well because none of the South Italian cities would "provide a market" until the fleet reached Rhegium.[56] The Spartan fleet blockading Mytilene in 406 B.C. was accompanied by merchant ships, and they were sufficiently under control of the commander, Eteonicus, to join in the swift and silent evacuation that followed the defeat of Arginusae.[57]

No doubt all generals would have preferred to keep their markets under strict discipline. At the siege of Samos in 366 B.C., Timotheus forbade the sale of grain by smaller measures than the *medimnus* and of wine and oil except by the *metretes* (144 *kotylai*), and prohibited all mills except those attached to each company. This meant that supplies were bought in bulk by the regimental and company commanders for distribution to the troops; chance travellers, being unable to buy their needs on the spot, brought their own provisions with them, and sold the surplus when they left.[58] But unless the prospective market was attractive, merchants would not come at all, and so it seems to have been usual to allow them and the individual soldiers to bargain freely. The fictitious Cyrus of the *Cyropaedia* proposed to allow a free market in his own army once the soldiers' own supplies were exhausted; and the real Cyrus the Younger allowed the Lydian merchants to sell grain at famine prices without using his reserve of four hundred wagon-loads of flour and wine to ease the situation.[59]

When a market was provided by a friendly city instead of by travelling merchants, regulations were likely to be made by magistrates for the benefit of the sellers rather than by the general to protect the soldiers, as when the Ten Thousand reached Cerasus on the Black Sea. Here the officials narrowly escaped stoning at the hands of the soldiers, who thought themselves cheated, and the generals were unable to intervene.[60]

But the most serious consequence of the system of individual purchase was that the men could not be kept together and constantly ready for action. An important cause of the defeat of the Athenian squadron at Eretria in 411 B.C. and the disaster at Aegospotami six years later was that the crews of the galleys had to buy their food at some distance from the ships.[61] Of course, poor rowers would not have personal servants to make their purchases for them, and a fleet must therefore have suffered more than a hoplite army from this trouble. Even willing allies (which the Eretrians were not) could not be expected to provide an adequate and convenient market for a large body of men without notice in advance, and a prudent commander would warn friends along his proposed line of march to have food ready.[62] A trick practised successfully by Agesilaus against both the Persians and the Thebans was to draw the enemy's attention to one possible line of march by sending notice to the allied towns along it, and then to strike in a different quarter.[63]

It was unusual to establish a fixed magazine and base of supplies, as Dercylidas did at Atarneus after its capture in 398 B.C. Nothing like the elaborate chain of bases that supported the Persian invasion of Greece in 480 B.C. could ever have been organized by any Greek state. Cyaxares in the *Cyropaedia* sent wagons of corn forward on the route that he intended to march, but obviously this could seldom be done without risk of capture.[64]

It is notable that, when an army had to depend on travelling merchants rather than markets in allied towns, the merchants seem normally to have accompanied the march, not followed after, and the general did not have to keep his lines of communication clear for their passage. Exceptions to this rule are provided by the campaigns of Plataea in 479 B.C. and Tanagra in 457. At Plataea, the Persian cavalry successfully raided a train of five hundred animals bringing supplies from the Peloponnese.[65] The battle of Tanagra was brought on by a treacherous attack upon an escorted convoy that was bringing supplies for sale to the Athenian army in the field.[66] In both campaigns, the armies seem to have waited a considerable time in the presence of the enemy before fighting a general engagement. Perhaps this delay was unexpected, and this is why supplies had to be brought from the rear.

Soldiers who had to buy their own food had of course to be given money for the purpose, whether they were mercenary professionals or not. Several issues of coinage by Greek cities, beside the splendid coins struck by the Persian satraps of Asia Minor, can be directly connected with the payment of fleets and armies.[67] In Xenophon's time, the pay of mercenary soldiers was comparable with that of other skilled craftsmen, with double and quadruple rates for captains and generals. A verbal distinction was drawn between pay and maintenance allowance, but to a modern reader the line between the two is not always clear. Even the "soldier of fortune" seems to have looked on his pay as a sort of retainer. Anaxibius's failure to pay the Ten Thousand angered them because it left them without money to support themselves on their march to the Chersonese, and the suggestion that they should help themselves to provisions from the Thracian villages provoked a mutiny.[68]

"Living off the country" theoretically combined glory with economy, but it is of course far easier for a party of soldiers to destroy the enemy's harvest than to gather it for themselves. Profitable raids did not necessarily free the general from dealing with the merchants: they only made his dealings less one-sided. Teleutias, taking over an unpaid, beaten, demoralized force at Aegina in 386 B.C., began by stating frankly that he had brought no money with him, but promised his men to find them plenty of provisions, and added that he would rather go two days without food than that they should go one. In the meantime, his quarters would be open to all petitioners, and they could see that he himself was sharing their reduced rations. His own city of Sparta had gained wealth and honour through the willingness of her citizens to undergo danger and hardship. And now, rather than fawn on some Greek or barbarian paymaster, they should supply themselves, and gain renown on doing so. In wartime, to supply oneself fully from the enemy brought honour in the eyes of the world as well as provisions.

These sentiments were given practical effect by the surprise of the Piraeus and the capture of merchant shipping and civilian prisoners. Some of the prizes were laden with grain, but Teleutias did not make a general distribution of plunder directly to his men. Instead, he held a sale after his return to Aegina, and gave his men a month's advance pay from the proceeds. Thereafter he sailed round and took what he could, and so kept his ships fully manned and his soldiers quickly and cheerfully obedient.[69]

A less capable and less honest commander than Teleutias was the Spartan Mnasippus, who destroyed his army by trying to let it live at the enemy's expense. In 374–373 B.C., the Spartans and their allies sent an expedition to Corcyra. A Lacedaemonian contingent was included, but fifteen hundred mercenaries formed the largest part of the land forces, and should have been well supplied with pay, since the allies had for the most part compounded with money payments rather than send their own men to serve overseas.[70] The open country, naturally rich and flourishing with farms and vineyards after a generation of peace, fell at once into the hands of the invaders. Slaves and cattle were seized; no wine that lacked a bouquet would satisfy the soldiers' luxurious taste. After overrunning the fields, Mnasippus settled down to finish the business by blockading the city by land and sea. An Athenian relief force was slow in arriving, and food ran short in the city. Slaves who had deserted were left to die outside the walls. The besiegers drove them back with whips and their masters would not re-admit them. Mnasippus, seeing that the Corcyraeans were in extremities, began to cheat his mercenaries as though he had no more need of their services, dismissing some without pay and keeping the rest two months in arrears. In consequence discipline was relaxed, guard duties were neglected, and the soldiers scattered through the countryside (perhaps because they had to forage for their food instead of buying it in camp, though Xenophon does not say so). The defenders seized the opportunity for a sortie; Mnasippus got his own men under arms and called upon the officers of the mercenaries to follow. When they replied that, unless they gave them supplies, they could not keep their troops disciplined, he struck them, "one with his stick and another with his spear-butt," and got them into battle order, "dispirited and hating their general. Which is the worst possible condition for men to fight in." His defeat and death followed, and the Corcyraeans would have forced the stockade and taken the camp if they had not mistaken the crowd of merchants, servants, and slaves for a reinforcement. As it was, Hypermenes, Mnasippus's secretary, who took over the command, was able to evacuate the captured slaves and livestock in the merchant ships that accompanied the expedition and to hold the camp for a time with the surviving soldiers and the marines from the fleet. But the Corcyraeans now had the upper hand, and the besiegers, demoralized still further by rumours of the Athenian relief force, eventually embarked on their warships and escaped, in great disorder and abandoning quantities of corn and wine in their camp.[71]

It is remarkable that even with as rich a land as Corcyra to support his army, Mnasippus did not manage without the usual crowd of merchants and camp-followers. In the midst of plenty, his captains complained that they could not give their men provisions. Of course, they were not starving, as Teleutias's men had been, but, quite apart from their resentment and unwillingness to serve at all when they were being cheated, they could not perform their military duties efficiently if they had to go and look for their own food instead of buying it in the camp. Mnasippus does not seem even to have organized the collection of the booty into a common stock, as Teleutias had done.

The story of the Athenian relief expedition is instructive. The original commander, Timotheus, had failed to man his fleet of sixty ships in Athens, and had taken them for a combined recruiting and training cruise in the Aegean. The Athenians thought he was wasting time and replaced him by Iphicrates, who forced his captains to make up their crews at once and added to his fleet all the ships round the coast of Athens, even the two sacred galleys. He trained his crews on the actual voyage to Corcyra, sailing fully prepared for a sea battle, and bringing his fleet to a high state of efficiency without delaying his voyage by constant exercise in different formations. The news of Mnasippus's death reached him while he was still rounding the Peloponnese and the main enemy fleet fled before his arrival, though he was in time to capture a squadron sent by Dionysius of Syracuse. But thereafter he had to provide for his men by hiring out most of the sailors to work the farms of the Corcyraeans, who had lost so much of their labour force during the siege, and by taking his peltasts and the hoplites from the ships on a plundering expedition to Acarnania.[72] But Iphicrates did manage to reassemble his force for a descent on Cephallenia and Spartan territory.

The survivors of the Spartan defeat at Arginusae in 406 B.C. had supported themselves through the summer by gleaning seasonal fruit and working as hired labourers,[73] but a victorious fleet should not have been brought so low. The diversion of an expeditionary force from its true purpose to plundering raids for want of proper supplies was to become a feature of the wars between Athens and Philip of Macedon. And even Demosthenes, critical as he was of the conduct of the war against Philip, was inconsistent in his attitude towards plunder as a source of supply. He recalled with approval that a generation before his time, Chabrias and his mercenaries had brought more than a hundred and ten talents into the city.[74] Timoleon, the liberator of Sicily, was admired for maintaining a force of mercenaries by sending them to plunder Carthaginian territory until he was ready to use them in his campaign against the tyrants; he was perhaps taking a hint from the younger Cyrus. Xenophon evidently approved when Dercylidas, to spare his allies the burden of supporting his army through the winter, made a truce with Pharnabazus and went off to plunder the neutral Bithynians.[75]

The vulnerability of small foraging parties to cavalry attack made them a precarious source of supply. The cavalry of ancient Greece, mounted without stirrups upon small horses, were ineffective against large masses of infantry drawn up in regular formation. But Xenophon seems to have considered that, on ridable ground, cavalry could deal even with peltasts if it was properly handled, though it was the business of peltasts to skirmish in open order;[76] detached parties of hoplites and unarmed camp-followers were of course easy victims. The Athenians in 455 B.C. and the Boeotians in 368 B.C. failed in invasions of Thessaly because the Thessalian cavalry did not allow the invading infantry to scatter and forage.[77] In 395 B.C., the satraps of Asia Minor were heavily defeated when they attacked the scattered followers of the Spartan army, and the horse and foot counter-attacked in good order.[78] But in 392 B.C., Thibron failed to keep his troops in hand to support his camp-followers and was defeated and killed when he ran out at the Persian cavalry without even stopping to issue proper orders to his men.[79]

To sum up, the surest supplies of a Greek army were those it brought with it. These, with whatever could be added from the enemy's territory, had sufficed for the old style of campaign, exemplified by the Spartan invasions of Attica at the beginning of the Peloponnesian War, which are expressly said to have lasted as long as the invaders' supplies,[80] except for that of 430 B.C., supposedly cut short by fear of the plague,[81] and that of 425 B.C. This last continued only fifteen days, because it had been made when the corn was still green, so that the invaders lacked food. But in fact the Spartans had been thoroughly alarmed by the Athenian landing at Pylos and were glad of an excuse to march home.[82]

For sieges, overseas campaigns, and protracted operations involving professional troops, a different system of supply was needed. Greek armies never had a regular commissariat to supply them and were forced to rely upon the private enterprise of merchants, but at least it was recognized that it might be better to choose a successful businessman as general rather than a drill-master.[83] Xenophon spares no sympathy for Coeratidas of Thebes, whose attempt to take command of the survivors of the Ten Thousand ended when he could make no better provision for them "twenty men carrying barley meal, and another twenty with wine, and three with olive oil, and one man with the very biggest bundle of garlic that he could carry, and another with onions." [84]

As for provisions, so for weapons the Greek army usually relied on the production of private manufacturers trading with the individual soldiers rather than on the output of state arsenals.[85] It was the soldier's own responsibility to fit himself out properly, though of course he would be inspected by the magistrates. Employers of mercenaries, like Dionysius I and Timoleon, sometimes purchased arms in bulk.[86] Before his march to Europe in 394 B.C., Agesilaus rewarded the mercenary officers whose contingents were best armed, implying that they were responsible for the state of the men's equipment. But the arms of the Ten Thousand were their personal property, or at least they sold them as such.[87]

A Greek camp of the fourth century B.C., crowded with sutlers and personal servants and generally unfortified, was of course very different from a Roman camp of two centuries later. But it must in fairness be acknowledged that the Romans themselves admitted that they had learned from the camp of Pyrrhus of Epirus, captured at Beneventum in 275 B.C.,[88] and the Hellenistic generals upon whose plans the Romans improved were themselves improving upon the work of the professional soldiers of Xenophon's time. Alexander's successors were no doubt also influenced by the very ancient Asiatic tradition of castrametation. No visitor to the Assyrian Room at the British Museum[89] will accept Frontinus's statement that Pyrrhus was the first to enclose his whole army within the same rampart. The square camp of the Persians at Plataea[90] continued the Assyrian tradition, which was known to Xenophon, though he had plausible arguments against it.

Scholars, accustomed to tracing the outlines of Roman fortified camps even below the street plan of modern cities, wonder at the

Spartans for leaving their camps open, in spite of all their boasted
professionalism, and praise Iphicrates, who used to entrench himself even in friendly territory, remarking that "I didn't think
. . ." was no proper remark for a general.[91]

But the Spartans trusted to their lookouts against surprise. Their
camp was not normally a fixed base for holding down conquered
territory; it was merely a temporary halting place for the army,
whose movements were intended to bring the enemy to battle in
the open field. When it was necessary to conduct a siege or to
leave a detachment to hold a strategic point, the Spartans fortified
themselves.

The discipline of the Spartan camp in the period before the
battle of Leuctra is described in the *Constitution of the Lacedaemonians*.[92] The camp was circular, "because the corners of a
rectangle are useless"—an obscure remark which has been well
explained as meaning that the corners were considered inde-
fensible salients.[93] But the circular form was adapted to existing
features of the landscape—mountains, rivers, or walls, and at the
battle of Leuctra there happened to be a ditch in front of the
Spartan camp.[94] The habit of fitting the camp into the irregular
features of the landscape persisted into the Hellenistic age and
was criticized by Polybius, who preferred the Roman system of
always following the same plan, so that every man could always
find his own place without confusion.[95]

In the Spartan camp, sentries were posted by day over the piled
arms, looking inwards to watch their friends, not outwards
against the enemy, to warn of whose approach cavalry outposts
were placed on commanding view-points. At night, when the
cavalry would be at a disadvantage, the outpost duty was taken
over by the Sciritae, light infantry from the mountainous northern frontier of Lacedaemon.[96] But, for all their precautions against
surprise, the Spartans kept their spears with them wherever they
went, "for the same reason that they keep the slaves away from
the arms." Even in the field the Spartans were never free from
the danger of a helot rising, though they were probably not as

heavily outnumbered by their servants in the camp as they were at home.[97] Constant readiness for action was also the object of regulations forbidding the soldiers to take exercise beyond the lines of their own regiments, or to go further for necessary purposes from their arms and their comrades than was necessary to avoid giving offence. This seems to have been the only sanitary regulation. At Cerasus, the Ten Thousand purified their camp, on the advice of Xenophon and the prophets, but, like the purification of the Greek camp in the first book of the *Iliad,* this was a religious measure necessitated by impious disregard of the law of nations.[98] Field sanitation had advanced no further than the recognition that marshes and the like made unhealthy camping grounds. The father of bacteriological warfare is Clearchus of Heraclea, who, wishing to secure his position as tyrant by destroying the citizens, encamped them in the heat of the dog-days in a marsh full of stagnant water.[99]

The fouling of the ground may have been one reason why the Spartans constantly moved their camps, but Xenophon says that it was in order to injure their enemies and help their friends —that is, so that, on hostile ground, the army's devastations might be spread as widely as possible, and in friendly territory the burden might be passed on quickly from one district to another. Polyaenus relates that Agesilaus, during the invasion of Boeotia, moved his camp two or three times a day, so that his allies, who were reluctant to ravage the ground in the usual way, might keep on cutting down trees to make huts for themselves, and so destroy the orchards without really wanting to.[100] There is usually no hardship in sleeping out of doors in a Greek summer, and improvised huts and bivouacs seem to have been more usual than tents. Even in the depth of winter, Lamachus took no tent with him to the frontier, only bedding.[101] The Athenians captured at Chaeronea and released by Philip without ransom asked for their cloaks and bedding back, provoking the comment that they were behaving as though they had lost a game of knucklebones.[102] But either they had no tents or they did not claim them as personal property. When the Athenians landed in Sicily in 415 B.C., they first built a camp at Catana, and then went into winter quarters at Naxos, which they fortified. The Syracusans marched out and laid waste the territory of Catana "and burned the *skenái* of the Athenians and their camp." [103] *Skenái* (here and often elsewhere) are more probably huts and shelters of timber and brushwood than tents, which would surely have been struck and stored, if they were not wanted, rather than left standing empty all the winter.

In the *Cyropaedia,* Xenophon makes Cyrus house each complete military unit in a single *skené*. This is no doubt based on the Spartan system (maintained in the peacetime *syssitia* as well as in war) though the Spartan unit was of course smaller than the "Persian" *taxis* of a hundred men. The Ten Thousand also formed groups which shared bivouacs and baggage animals, and these no doubt also corresponded to the tactical units, though we are not expressly told so. That they camped "by *taxeis*" does not necessarily mean that each *taxis* occupied a single shelter.[104]

Iphicrates preferred one-man bivouacs. When he outnumbered the enemy, he used to make his numbers appear less by allotting a single bivouac to each pair of men, who took turns to sleep in it. When the enemy outnumbered him, each man built two bivouacs.[105] Apparently these were shelters, constructed out of whatever material came to hand, rather than tents.

Improvised materials seem also to have been used when fixed camps had to be fortified. A stockade, made like Agesilaus's huts by cutting down the nearest trees, was the usual defence, possibly reinforcing a ditch or bank. When the Thebans and their allies invaded Laconia in 369 B.C., "the Thebans, wherever they encamped, immediately threw down before their positions as many of the trees that they cut down as they were able, and so defended themselves." Here again, the cutting down of olives and other fruit trees was part of the procedure of ravaging the country. Xenophon evidently approves of the Theban conduct, which he contrasts with that of the Arcadians, who took no such precautions and left their posts to go plundering.[106] The Greek hoplite, whether citizen or mercenary, did not carry a pointed stake for the palisade, like the Roman legionary. Polybius criticizes the Greeks of his own day for preferring to build their stockades out of branching, bushy material; the line could be quickly completed, but quickly breached if a storming party dragged only a few pieces aside. The Romans, using stakes with two or three side-branches at most, had to work harder and use more stakes to begin with, but produced a stronger work.[107] The same criticism would probably have applied to most of the Greek stockades of the fifth and fourth centuries. The stockade that Pelopidas fired so that the smoke might cover his retreat sounds as though it was made of brushwood, not bare stakes.[108]

But in the classical age, Greek marching camps generally had no fortifications at all. In Paphlagonia, the barbarians harassed the outskirts of Xenophon's camp by night, but no entrenchments were made against them.[109] Nor did the Ten Thousand entrench the villages in which they sheltered from the attacks of Tissaphernes, probably because they relied upon an active defence with constant sorties.[110] In the Thracian villages, Xenophon warned Seuthes that the position was dangerous, but the Greeks did not try to convert the stockaded sheep-folds with which each house was surrounded into an organized system of defence. When the night attack came, it was by vigorous sorties from their separate billets, co-ordinated by a trumpet call from the general's headquarters, that they saved themselves.[111]

Unfortified camps could therefore be justified by strong arguments. Fixed bases and siege-works required fortification, but an army in the field could best protect itself by closing with the enemy, and its own entrenchments might prove an obstacle. In the *Cyropaedia,* Xenophon remarks on the entrenchments that Asiatic armies regularly dug round their camps, and their dependence on cavalry made it necessary. "For they know that a cavalry army is easily thrown into confusion at night, and hard to handle, especially a barbarian one. For their horses are hobbled at their mangers, and if they are attacked, it is hard work to loose the horses in the dark and bridle them and saddle them and arm themselves, and to mount and ride through the camp is altogether impossible. For all these reasons, men, and especially barbarian kings, entrench themselves, and they believe that the fact that they are in a strong position enables them to fight when they want to." [112] It has been justly pointed out that these remarks have been drawn from Xenophon's own experience.[113] But the sequel, in which their own fortifications were a chief cause of the downfall of Cyrus's Assyrian enemies, also illustrates a lesson learned, though not at first hand, in the foreign wars. For the Assyrian camp was fully visible to the Medes and Persians, who themselves took advantage of hills and villages to screen their movements from the enemy. The Assyrians chose their own day to advance, but, defiling through their gates in full sight of the enemy, "handed themselves over for the Persians to count out the exact number they wanted to fight with." [114] When Cyrus attacked, a large part of the enemy army was still within the camp, and those who were outside were thrown back into their own ditches amid slaughter and confusion.[115]

Agesilaus in Egypt once used the enemy's own fortifications to "count out the exact number he wanted to fight with" in a somewhat similar way. The story, told by Plutarch,[116] is omitted by Xenophon, but Xenophon passes very quickly over the Egyptian affair.[117] Agesilaus and the Egyptian pretender whom he was backing at the time were besieged by a rival, whose army was numerically superior. The enemy began to construct lines of circumvallation, and Agesilaus's ally begged him to try to break out before the ring was closed. But Agesilaus waited and waited, though coming daily under deeper suspicion of treachery, until the gap in the lines was narrow enough to suit his own numbers. He then attacked and routed the Egyptians, most of whose men were hindered by their own works from coming to the rescue.

Xenophon himself records an incident of the Asiatic campaigns in which the fortifications of a camp helped the attackers, not the defenders. The Spartan general Dercylidas, to spare his allies the burden of supporting his army, had allowed himself to be diverted from the war against the Persians into a plundering expedition in Bithynia. Here he was joined by a Thracian contingent of two hundred cavalry and three hundred peltasts, who made a stockade about two miles from the Greek camp. Here they collected their prisoners and plunder, for which they required a guard of two hundred Greek hoplites while they continued their raids. The Bithynians learned of this arrangement and made a dawn attack. The stockade, being about a man's height, did not protect the defenders from the stones and javelins that were rained down on them, but penned them in, so that they were unable to act until they broke the defences down themselves. Then they charged out, but the enemy gave way wherever they did so, "and easily escaped, being peltasts against hoplites, and threw javelins at them from all sides, and struck down many of them at each sortie. And at last they were all shot down as though they had been penned in a sheep-fold." [118] And the Hellenistic age provides one actual example—a victory of the elder Scipio—of the defeat of an army because its entrenchments delayed its deployment.[119]

But the danger of being surprised in an unfortified camp seems to have been far greater, even allowing for the difficulties facing ancient generals when they attempted night operations without maps, compasses, or any of the modern aids to moving across country in the dark. The Athenian general Demosthenes surprised the Ambraciots in their beds, after the sentries had been deceived by the Dorian accents of his Messenian allies.[120] Even troops trained in the Spartan system could be surprised. The expulsion of the Thirty Tyrants from Athens began with the surprise of the troops they had sent to blockade Thrasybulus in Phyle—"the Laconian guards, except for a few of them, and two tribes of [Athenian] cavalry." This force was encamped in the scrub about a mile and a half from Phyle, and Thrasybulus, with seven hundred men, was able to approach under cover of night to within some six or seven hundred yards. Here his men grounded their arms and remained quiet. "But as the day was breaking, and the men were rising and dispersing for necessary purposes from their weapons, and the grooms were making a noise as they groomed their horses, at this moment Thrasybulus's men picked up their arms and fell upon them at a run." The enemy fled, apparently without striking a blow, and a hundred and twenty of their Laconian hoplites were killed. But all the cavalry escaped except three, who were surprised in their beds,[121] so presumably the horses were at least bridled.

These Laconians were of course second-class troops, perhaps freed helots. But Agesilaus himself, during his first invasion of Acarnania in 393 B.C., was dislodged in broad daylight by the Acarnanian peltasts and slingers from a camp that he had imprudently pitched close to a mountain, and was forced to move his army on to level ground, though it was actually preparing the evening meal at the time. Sentries were of course posted before the men slept, but there seems to have been no attempt to fortify either camp.[122] Even if the omission arose from tactical theory and not mere neglect, this was one part of the Spartan military system that did not commend itself to future ages.[123]

IV

THE GENERAL
AND HIS OFFICERS

The Greek general had no specially trained staff to help him. He had only simple means of signalling, no maps, or at best primitive ones that can hardly have been carried with the army in the field,[1] and no better way of telling the time than by the movement of sun and stars. He therefore usually kept his forces united and did not try to coordinate the movements of different units moving separately towards a common end. Simple combinations, such as sending a detachment to turn the enemy's position, were successfully attempted. But when Agis III in 418 B.C. tried to trap the Argives between three columns marching separately by night, the result was that the Spartans were separated from most of their allies when the actual encounter with the enemy took place, and the Argives, no less than the Spartans, felt that they had lost an opportunity when the armies parted without a battle.[2] It was hard to ensure that widely-dispersed forces would act even on the same day, as was shown by the failure of the Athenian plan for the conquest of Boeotia in 424 B.C., and of the Spartan plan in 395.[3]

The simple supply system did not require constant written returns—not even exact daily strength returns.[4] At the Spartan headquarters, the chief paper-work seems to have been the correspondence with the home government, conducted by a single officer, and sometimes at least with true Laconic brevity.[5] The encipherment of dispatches by writing them on a strip of paper wound round a rod of known diameter, the famous *skytale*, could be done without specialist help. It was perhaps less effective in concealing the content of messages that fell into the enemy's hands than in proving the authenticity of those that were safely delivered, for once the principle was known, a captured message could be fitted to an appropriate rod by trial and error. But a forged message would be instantly detected by the recipient if it had not been written on a rod of the right size. It has been suggested that the *skytale* was originally a simple token— a broken staff of which the commander took one half and the government kept the other until the time came to send a message, when it was given to the messenger so that the exact fitting of the two parts could establish his identity when he reached his destination. But such an arrangement could be used only once. Xenophon uses the word *skytale* for a warrant for the arrest of suspects, and for instructions sent by the Spartan government to subordinate allies; in such cases it was probably more important to establish the authority of the document than to keep its contents secret. The emissary seems to have displayed the rod itself as a token of his authority, like a wand of office or an old-fashioned constable's staff.[6]

When Spartan expeditionary forces were sent abroad under some other commander than the king, the commander, who bore the title *nauarch*—or admiral if the force included a naval armament—was accompanied by a second in command, who was in charge of dispatches and took over if the original commander was killed or disabled.[7] But a king was accompanied in the field by thirty Spartiates,[8] if his army did not include any of the regular citizen regiments, and his secretary seems to have been a person of minor importance among them. Idaeus, whose golden horse-trappings Agesilaus presented to the son of Pharnabazus,[9] did not later attain high command, as far as we know. When king Agesipolis died at Olynthus in 380 B.C., the Spartans sent out a successor from home.[10]

"Those about the public tent" is the phrase used by Xenophon for advisers and officers particularly attached to the king. These did not include the officers in charge of the military chest, or the contractors who sold the plunder, or the *hellanodikai*—judges concerned with the settling of disputes rather than with the enforcement of discipline, and with the allies rather than with the Spartans themselves, as appears from their title, which is the same as that of the umpires of the Olympic games. Xenophon only mentions the existence of these persons to emphasize that the king was relieved of administrative duties and left free to act "as a priest in what concerns the gods and as a general in what concerns men." Of course in practice he supervised the administrative officers too. Agesilaus took advantage of his dealings with the contractors to put opportunities for money-making in the way of his friends.[11]

"About the public tent" were "such of the peers as share the royal tent, the prophets, the doctors, the officers of the army and any volunteers who are present."[12] The "peers who share the royal tent" included the *polemarchs,* who in Xenophon's time were the regimental commanders, three Spartiates appointed to wait upon them and upon the king,[13] and the two Pythii, who were sent to Delphi when the king wished to consult the oracle.[14]

For ascertaining the purposes of the gods from day to day there were the prophets, without whose skilled technical advice no Greek commander took the field, whatever he may have felt privately about old-fashioned religious observances.[15] Unfavourable omens seem sometimes to have been used as an excuse for not doing something,[16] or for holding back soldiers until their general's plans became ripe. In the campaign of 397 B.C., Dercylidas lay for four days outside the town of Cebron, inactive "much against his will," because the sacrifices continued unfavourable. Immediate action, before Pharnabazus came to relieve the town, seemed imperative to the professional officers in the army, one of whom tried on his own initiative to cut the water supply, and was repulsed with loss. But at this point a mutiny of the Greek mercenaries in the garrison forced the governor to fling open the gates—at the very moment that Dercylidas, having received favourable sacrifices at last, was leading his men to the assault.[17] We may draw our own conclusions about his "inaction."

Agesilaus, who was ready to hide the news of disaster by sacrificing as though to celebrate a victory,[18] is said by late writers to have imposed upon his men by imprinting VICTORY upon the sacrificial liver, and by reporting the answers of the gods as suited him best. Iphicrates, when the prophets refused him the answer that he wanted, used to change his position and sacrifice again and again.[19] But Xenophon seems to have found relief in letting the gods decide at critical moments,[20] and is at pains to point out how omens that at first seemed to mislead were triumphantly fulfilled in the end.[21] He reports in all sincerity that his penniless condition after the return of the Ten Thousand was found by Euclides the seer to result from neglect of the rites of Zeus Meilichios, and that when he sacrificed according to the prophet's advice, his wants were relieved that very same day.[22]

The specialist advice of the doctors Xenophon valued less highly. Practicing their art upon the sick, they were like patchers of torn cloaks. The general's business was to see that his army did not fall sick to begin with, by choosing healthy camping grounds, and by providing the men with a spare diet and constant activity.[23] The advice of trained doctors might not always be available. The eight "doctors" appointed by the Ten Thousand to deal with their numerous wounded during the retreat through Mesopotamia[24] were presumably only orderlies, who did what they could in the way of bandaging.

The principal officers of the army were kept close to the king, not only for consultation but to be immediately ready to receive his personal orders. Once the plan of action had been fixed and the army committed to it, the commander-in-chief had little opportunity to change his dispositions to meet the unexpected, and the subordinate officers had usually no discretion to act independently if things went wrong. This was one inheritance from

the early days of hoplite warfare, when, as has been justly pointed
out, the first shock of battle decided the issue, and so the general
put in every man to the first charge. After he had drawn up
his men and encouraged them to the best of his ability, there
was nothing more he could do except take his place in the ranks
and set the best example he could.[25] In the fourth century, experiments with manœuvre on the battlefield and the use of
reserves had begun, but the commander-in-chief, be he king or
general, was still expected to join the hoplite phalanx in person,
and so was denied a general view of the development of the
battle and the opportunity to make new plans if his first mis-
carried.

It was therefore important that the subordinate officers should
go into action with a clear understanding of what was required
of them. Thucydides describes the chain of command in the
Spartan army in his account of the battle of Mantinea in 418 B.C.
"When the king is in command, everything is governed by him,
and he personally issues verbal orders to the *polemarchs,* they to
the company commanders (*lochagoi*), they to the commanders
of fifty, they again to the commanders of *enomotiai,* and they to
the *enomotia*. And the orders, if they require anything [that is,
presumably, supplementary orders] go through the same channels
and quickly reach their destination. For almost the whole of the
Lacedaemonian army, with a few exceptions, are officers commanding subordinate officers, and the executive responsibility is
shared by many." [26]

This apparently straightforward account conceals difficulties.
It was one thing for the king to give his orders directly to the
senior officers when they were all "round the public tent" together, quite another to issue supplementary orders after he had
taken his place in the ranks and they had dispersed to their
separate commands. In this very battle of Mantinea, King Agis
changed his mind after his army had been drawn up, and sent
supplementary orders for a last-minute change of dispositions.
How were these orders issued? Thucydides uses a word which,

taken literally, would imply passing the orders from man to man down the ranks.[27] But there were several allied contingents between the king and the Lacedaemonian companies on the right wing. The "Sciritae and Brasideans" on the left were originally in direct contact with the main body, but after they had been ordered to extend to the left, a gap opened between them and the rest of the army. The order for their recall cannot therefore have been passed down the ranks, but must have been sent by messenger, which in any case was a better way of doing it. Passing the watchword down the line and back again, after the army had been drawn up in battle order, was an impressive ceremony,[28] but long messages became confused when passed on in this way. The textbook writers recommend that orders, passwords, and countersigns should be given out through the officers, to avoid the delay caused by passing them down the line, and the confused noise of everybody asking everybody else at once, which leads to addition or omission.[29]

Mounted dispatch-riders are sometimes mentioned,[30] and Agis may have had some waiting in readiness behind the line. But there is no suggestion in Thucydides that he did, or in other writers that such an arrangement was usual. At the battle of Cunaxa, Xenophon rode out in front of the line to learn if Cyrus had any fixed instructions. But Xenophon's position with the army, "neither general nor captain nor soldier," was exceptional, and there is no reason to suppose that he was acting as "galloper" to his friend Proxenus. Agesilaus had a mounted escort on his march back from Asia, but when at the head of the citizen army, he and the other kings marched and fought on foot.[31] However Agis's orders were conveyed, they reached their destination without the authority of the king's person to back them, and were in fact disobeyed by two of the officers concerned.

Xenophon was familiar with the system of issuing orders through the officers even before he entered the Spartan service. At the storming of the stronghold of the Drilae in the hills behind Trebizond, he halted the hoplites on the edge of the ravine that surrounded the place and made a personal reconnaissance, together with the company commanders. When, encouraged by their advice and that of the prophets, he resolved on an assault, he issued his orders directly, leaving each commander responsible for drawing up his own company as he thought it would fight best. To the peltasts and the crowd of light-armed followers who had already been driven back from the place, he gave orders to be ready to cover the final assault with a general discharge of missiles when the trumpet sounded. These orders were not just passed on from man to man, because "he sent the appropriate men to see to them." [32] Who these "appropriate men" were we are not told. The phrase is one that recurs in the *Anabasis,* but it is clear that it does not always refer to the same people, and that there is no specially trained body of staff officers concealed behind it.[33]

In the *Cyropaedia,* Cyrus gives orders for an attack to his officers and those of his allies, and sends them to their posts with orders to pass on the same instructions to their own "captains of ten" on the march. "For the captains of ten formed the front rank, so that they could hear. And he gave orders for each of them to pass on the word to his own ten." [34]

To make every front rank man an officer in command of the file of men that followed him was a part of the Spartan system. "In the Laconian order of battle the front-rank men are officers, and each file is a self-contained unit." [35] The file commanders took their orders directly from the commander of their *enomotia,* a sub-unit of rather over thirty men. "The orders for leading up the files beside each other are given verbally by the commander of the *enomotia* as though by a herald, and the depth of the line of battle is increased or diminished." [36] That is to say, the commander, according to the orders he himself received, would order his own *enomotia* to form up in a few files, so making a deep formation, or more files, so covering a wider front with a shallower formation.

In the *Cyropaedia,* Xenophon describes the civil organization

of the Persian Empire after the overthrow of its enemies as corresponding to that of the army, in which commanders of ten are
responsible for their tens, company commanders for the commanders of ten, commanders of a thousand for the company
commanders, and they in their turn are under the orders of
commanders of ten thousand, "and so everybody is under authority, even if there are very many ten thousands of men, and
when the general wishes to employ the army in anything, it is
sufficient to give orders to the commanders of ten thousand." [37]
Xenophon is here projecting upon a colossal scale the military
organization with which he was himself familiar, rather than
describing the actual Persian system, similar though that no
doubt was, at least on paper. It is notable that it is not just orders
that pass through these channels; booty and rewards are divided
among tens of thousands and subdivided among smaller units
until the most junior officers, "commanders of six," give them
out to the private soldiers of their squads. [38]

Unfortunately Xenophon's description of the actual Spartan
organization is in some respects less clear than that of the imaginary Persians, and, though the general sense can be recovered,
is further obscured by corruptions in the text. [39] There were six
morai, or regiments, of horse, and six of foot. Each hoplite *mora*
had one *polemarch,* four *lochagoi* or company commanders,
eight "commanders of fifty" (though in fact their commands were
no more "fifties" than the Roman "centuries" were hundreds), [40]
and sixteen commanders of *enomotiai.* From these *morai* they
were drawn up by word of command, with the *enomotiai* sometimes in single file, [41] sometimes in threes, sometimes in sixes.
This agrees with the information to be obtained from the *Hellenica* about the battle of Leuctra and the immediately preceding
period, and the differences between this account and that of
Thucydides, who does not mention the *morai* and describes the
Spartan army at Mantinea as being drawn up in seven *lochoi,*
may be explained as due either to changes in the Spartan organization, or to the inadequacy of the information available to

Thucydides, or to both. It is also clear that each officer passed on his orders to a small group of men only, and that the rank and file received their orders from their own commanders of *enomotiai*, with whom they were personally familiar.

The importance of knowing subordinate officers by name is very properly stressed in the *Cyropaedia*. Cyrus paid special attention to this point, because

> it seemed to him to be most remarkable that, when workmen all know the names of the tools of their particular crafts, and doctors know the names of all the instruments and medicines that they use, a general could be so negligent as not to know the names of his subordinate officers, whom he has to use as his tools whenever he wants to capture anything or defend it, or to issue encouragement or warning. And when he wanted to signal someone out for distinction, it seemed to him proper to address him by name. For it seemed to him that men who think that their officer recognizes them are keener to be seen doing something honourable and more desirous of avoiding disgrace. Another negligent practice seemed to him to be to issue orders when required in the way in which some masters give orders to their slaves—"Go for water, somebody! Somebody cut wood!" For he thought that when men are given orders like that, they all look at each other and nobody goes to do what has been ordered, and they are all to blame, and nobody is either ashamed or afraid in the same way, because there are many of them to share the blame. So of course he addressed by name everybody to whom he gave an order.[42]

These excellent principles applied in the Spartan army all the way down the chain of command, until, at the lowest level, "it is so easy to learn this system of tactics that nobody who can recognize men could go wrong. For it is given to some to lead and appointed others to follow." [43]

The *Cyropaedia* gives a picture of an army going into battle which is certainly taken from what Xenophon had seen during his own service. The Persian and Assyrian armies were encamped confronting each other, and it was clear that a battle was imminent. Cyrus sacrificed, with a garland on his head, and attended by his peers, also garlanded. He announced that the prophets confirmed the imminence of battle and foretold a bloodless victory. After further exhortations, the peers were instructed to take their morning meal with garlands on their heads, to pour libations, and to take their places in the ranks still garlanded. Cyrus then addressed the sturdy veterans who had been chosen to serve as rear-rank men of the files, and dismissed them with similar orders.

Meanwhile the Assyrians were issuing out of their camp and being drawn up by the king in person. His fine speeches to his men were reported to the Persians by deserters, and Cyrus was advised to call his men together and address them. He replied that a single fine speech could no more turn cowards into brave men than it could turn men who had never practised the arts of war into archers or javelin-men or horsemen. Only those soldiers could truly be relied on who had learned long ago, from the laws of their state and the teaching of its rulers, that honour and freedom belonged to the brave and disgrace to the cowards. Without the example shown them by the "peers," he could not count on even the Persians to stand firm.

The advance against the enemy is described as follows:

> When he began to lead, he led fast from the beginning, and they followed, in good order because they understood and had practised marching in formation, boldly because of their emulation, their hard physical condition, and the fact that the front-rank men were all officers, and cheerfully because of their ordered state of mind. For they knew and had learnt long ago that it was safest and easiest to come to grips, especially since the enemy were archers and javelin-men and horsemen. While they were still beyond range of the enemy, Cyrus passed down the ranks

the watchword, "Zeus, ally and leader." And when the watch-word came back again along the ranks, Cyrus himself raised the customary paean, and his men all piously joined in the cry with loud voices. For surely at such moments those who fear the gods are less afraid of men. At the sound of the paean, the peers advanced together, with cheerful faces, and glancing at one an-other. They called by name upon their neighbours in the ranks, and their second-rank men, and repeating "Come on, friends! Come on, brave men!" encouraged one another to follow. And those behind, when they heard them, replied by encouraging the leaders to lead on boldly. And Cyrus's army was full of eager-ness, ambition, strength, confidence, encouragement, steadiness, and good discipline, which last I think was most terrifying to the enemy.

Xenophon makes the Assyrians of this imaginary battle, like the Persians whom he had actually fought at Cunaxa, discharge their missiles long before the enemy came into range.

And when the Persians advanced past the spent missiles, Cyrus called out, "Gentlemen, now increase the pace! Show what you are made of! Pass the word along!" They passed on the order, and in their eagerness and fury and haste some began to break into a double together, and the whole line of battle followed at the double. And Cyrus himself gave up all thought of march-ing and led at the double, and at the same time called out "Who will follow? Who is a brave man? Who will be the first to strike down his man?" And when his soldiers heard this they all called out the same, and through the whole army like a password the word ran "Who will follow? Who is a brave man?" and in this frame of mind the Persians were carried on togther.[44]

This is very different from the traditional picture of the Spartan army going into action

> In perfect measure to the Dorian mode
> Of flutes and soft recorders.

Xenophon had himself seen hoplites charge at the double, not just against Asiatics but against other hoplites, at the battle of Coronea, the one major pitched battle of Greeks against Greeks in which he himself must have taken part, though he does not mention his own presence. But it was the Thebans who charged first, and the mercenaries, not the Spartans, in Agesilaus's army who began the countercharge, apparently without orders from the king.[45] The Spartans themselves may have continued to advance steadily at the marching pace, for all that we are told, as they had done at Mantinea in 418 B.C.

None the less, it is clear that not all the details given in the *Cyropaedia* are taken from the conduct of mercenaries, and the preliminaries to the battle are not taken from what Xenophon had seen at Cunaxa, for at Cunaxa the Greeks had to deploy into line hurriedly, to meet the surprise advance of Artaxerxes, and there was no time for sacrifices and garlands, or even to see that the men went into action properly fed. The preliminaries to action, as well as the part played by the "peers," are modelled on the custom of the Spartan service. The reliance on previous good training, rather than last-minute speeches, and the substitution of the exchange of encouragement for a formal address by the general most strikingly recall Spartan practice. At Mantinea in 418 B.C., Thucydides tells us, the Argives and their allies were suitably addressed in set speeches. But the Spartans exchanged private words of encouragement among themselves, and reminded one another of their past training, "knowing that salvation lies in deeds practised over a long period rather than in words finely spoken in exhortation for a few moments." [46] The exchange of words of encouragement is also mentioned in the *Constitution of the Lacedaemonians,* though in an obscure and misplaced digression. Xenophon breaks away from the subject that he is properly discussing, the military functions of the kings and their assistants, the officers "about the public tent," to list

some other extremely useful contrivances of Lycurgus for armed conflict. For when, in full sight of the enemy, the she-goat is sacrificed, it is the custom for all the flute-players present to play and for none of the Lacedaemonians to be without a garland. And the order has been given beforehand for shields to be polished. And the young man can join in the battle anointed with oil [47] and have a cheerful face[48] and good repute. And they pass words of encouragement to the commander of the *enomotia*. For, except from each *enomotarch,* the voice does not carry to the whole of each *enomotia*.[49] The *polemarch* must see to it that this is well done.

That is to say, the senior officers were responsible for seeing that the words of encouragement reached the junior officers. They did not attempt to make their voices carry to every man in every *enomotia* under their command. Heralds, with specially trained voices, were used when the army was in bivouac to summon the senior officers or make announcements at moments of emergency,[50] but they did not play the part of sergeant-majors in drilling large units, and only exceptionally were their voices used to transmit orders on the field of battle.[51]

The system of issuing orders through the officers of units and sub-units ensured that every man knew what to do, but it was also necessary to tell him when to do it, or rather to coordinate the movements of the different units, which had received their orders separately, so that the whole army acted together. For this purpose it was usual to treat the verbal order as cautionary, and to act upon an executive signal, usually given by trumpet. Instances of this practice, both on the parade ground and on the field of battle, have already been noted. It was at the sound of the trumpet that the Greeks threw forward their shields and advanced during the review in honour of the Queen of Cilicia, and lowered their spears and charged in the battle against Pharnabazus in Bithynia.[52] The trumpet might also be used to control the movements of a fleet at night (in the daytime visual signals seem to have been more usual at sea, probably because signals between ships often had to be made over wide distances), but again the verbal orders were issued first and the trumpet merely gave the signal to execute them.[53]

It is, however, clear that a very limited number of specific trumpet-calls for particular movements—perhaps only the "Charge!" and "Retire!"—were used in Greek armies. This is made evident by stories of generals who deceived the enemy by ordering their men to act in the opposite way to the usual significance of the call. After the repulse of repeated Syracusan assaults upon the walls of Motya, Dionysius ordered his men to renew the attack when the trumpet gave the signal to retire. The tired defenders, who had thought that the fighting was over for the day, were caught off their guard.[54] The opposite trick was played by Xenophon upon the Carduchi at the crossing of the Centrites by the Ten Thousand. After the main body and the baggage were safely over the river, the enemy pressed upon the hoplites of the rearguard, but were afraid to close with them, being equipped with missile weapons for skirmishing in the mountains, not for close combat. Xenophon therefore ordered his men to charge as soon as an enemy slingstone rang on a shield. When the enemy turned, the trumpeter would sound the war note, and upon this signal the Greeks were to turn to the right-about and run back to the river and cross as fast as they could. The success of the plan depended upon the enemy's having learned during the course of the previous few days to recognize the Greek war note as a signal for attack; and the event proved that they had, for when the trumpet sounded, they ran faster than ever, and the Greeks were able to run back to the river and cross with the loss of only a few men wounded by arrows.[55]

But, though the general could signal "Advance!" or "Retire!" by the trumpet, there was no elaborate code of calls by which he could give orders in detail. It was therefore absolutely necessary that the preliminary orders should be precisely given out and thoroughly understood before the trumpet sounded. The confusion in the Athenian ranks at Amphipolis may have been largely due to Cleon's giving the trumpet signal at the same time as the verbal order for retreat, so that most of the army knew only that their commander wanted them to move, but had no idea how he wanted the movement to be carried out.[56]

The Greeks said "In war the trumpets sound reveille, in peace the cocks," [57] but this does not necessarily imply a special call for the purpose.

For the signal to rest in the evening, or to strike camp and move off in the morning, the less warlike horn took the place of the trumpet, an arrangement foreshadowing the elaborate system of signals on different instruments used by the Roman Imperial armies.[58]

That in the Spartan armies the flute-players should have been "about the public tent" while the trumpeter was not is perhaps surprising. The value of having the trumpeter close to the general in camp appears from Xenophon's own experience, when the Thracians attacked his quarters by night, "and Silanus of Macistus, who was about eighteen years old, sounded upon the trumpet. And immediately the men in the other billets leaped out with drawn swords." [59] Perhaps trumpeters were usually too young to be counted among the officers. Among flute-players, we know by name Thersander, the tent-companion of Thibron in his last campaign in Asia, and apparently not himself a Spartan, since Xenophon says that he set out to rival his general in "feats of valour" as one who affected the Spartan way of life. They were killed together when they were surprised by the Persian cavalry.[60]

The functions of the flute-players are best described in Thucydides's famous account of the battle of Mantinea. The Argives and their allies came on rapidly and tumultuously, but "the Spartans slowly, and to the time of many flute-players, who are appointed by law, not for religious reasons, but so that they may advance marching smoothly and in time, and that their formation may not be broken, as is likely to happen to great armies in the advance." [61]

In talking of "religious reasons," Thucydides is probably referring only to the customary presence of flute-players at sacrifices, or on other ceremonial occasions, such as the raising of a trophy.[62] But a story was later told that when the descendants of Heracles first came to Sparta, they were surprised by the enemy as they were conducting the sacrifice customary upon crossing a frontier. They ordered the flute-players to lead on, and the hoplites followed, "stepping to the tune and measure and keeping their formation unbroken." After this, the Spartans resolved "always to have the flute as general in their battles. The flute leads the Laconians when they go to war, and the flute sounds the charge to them in battle." At Leuctra, the Spartans were not led by flutes, and were beaten by the Thebans, to whom flute-playing was a native accomplishment, so fulfilling an oracle.[63] There is no reason to suppose that any of this is true. But it illustrates the impression created upon the Greeks by the ordered Spartan advance, and perhaps also a belief that their defeat at Leuctra was due to their falling short of their usual high standards, as well as to the skill and valour of their enemies.

Plutarch also speaks of the tune to which the Spartans advanced, "Castor's tune," and of sacrifices to the Muses before battle. But he seems to have appreciated the moral and inspirational effect of the music rather than its purely mechanical value in giving the time to the marching men, for he tells of other nations using trumpets for the same purpose, "even down to our own time," and of the use of flutes at a wrestling match at Argos.[64] It is a curious fact that the "drum's discordant sound," to modern ears the essence of martial music, was by the ancients associated with the orgies of Dionysus, though certainly in his wars the god "gave the signal with cymbals and drums instead of the trumpet." [65]

It is surprising that the classical Greeks, unlike the Romans, did not use standards, and so the list of Spartan officers does not include a standard-bearer.[66] Commanders sometimes used a prearranged visual signal, such as a helmet raised on a spear,[67] or the display of a white or red flag,[68] to control the movement of their troops or to coordinate the operations of the separate bodies.

Xenophon saw in Asia the Persian standard, a winged disc raised on a staff.[69] And though he does not seem to have thought much of it at the time, he later recognized its value as a rallying point and indication of the commander's presence, and as a guide on which the line could dress in the advance.[70] He made the commanders in the *Cyropaedia* all have standards on their tents so that they could be quickly found.[71] The later tacticians give each battalion of the Macedonian phalanx its own standard, but they may be transferring Roman practice to their textbook armies, as we hear very little about these standards in actual accounts of battles.[72]

To sum up, the Spartan army was excellently organized to ensure that the commander's plan of action should be thoroughly understood and carried out in an orderly manner. But he had little opportunity to form a fresh plan in the middle of a battle which developed unexpectedly, or to pass on new orders to his subordinates.

V

WEAPON TRAINING

Greek military theory, as represented by the ancient writers on tactics, and no doubt Greek practice too, attached great importance to drilling men to manoeuvre in formation, but very little to teaching the individual to handle his weapons. Xenophon's own opinion, and probably that of his Spartan friends, seems to have been that missile weapons required each its special skill, but that at close quarters it was impossible to miss, and that men who had been trained to close with the enemy would not need to be shown what to do once they reached him. This belief is put into words in the *Cyropaedia,* in which Cyrus's first care is to equip the Persians—until that time ineffective skirmishers—with weapons and armour suitable for hand-to-hand combat. He does not, of course, give them those of Greek hoplites; that would be too great a strain on his readers' credulity. Cuirass for the body, buckler in the left hand, and sabre or scimitar in the right[1] are an oriental fancy-dress. But troops equipped in this way manoeuvre and fight like Spartans, not like the historical Persians, who did not renounce the bow and whose nobles fought on horseback, not in the ranks of the heavy infantry. Xenophon emphasizes that there is no special art in the handling of the new weapons. His Cyrus, encouraging the Persian commoners to adopt them, says that in time past they have been inferior to the nobility, but now they have their chance to arm themselves in the same way, undergo the same dangers, and, if they show themselves worthy, win the same rewards. In the past, gentle and simple alike have been archers and javelin-men, and the common people have been inferior to the nobles for want of leisure to practise. But in the new equipment, the nobles will have no advantage, for "the cuirass round the breast will fit each man individually; in his left hand will be a buckler, which we are all accustomed to carry; and in the right a cutlass or scimitar, with which, it needs no saying, we must strike those who confront us, with no danger of missing our stroke." [2] The experiment is taken up enthusiastically, and the commoner Pheraulas says that with common rations, common quarters and common discicipline, all are now on the same footing. Their new way of fighting is natural to man, just as the ways of fighting natural to other animals are those that they use of themselves, both in attack and defence, without need of instruction.

> And I myself from my earliest childhood knew how to throw up a guard before the things that I thought were going to hit me. If I had nothing else, I would hold my hands before me and hinder the man who hit me as far as possible. I did this not because I was taught to do it; indeed I was even hit just for throwing my hands before me. As for knives, from the time I was a baby I grabbed them whenever I saw them, and I never learned from anybody how to hold them either, except from nature, as I say. Anyway, this was another thing that I did without teaching and though it was forbidden, just as there were other things that both my mother and my father stopped me doing but I was compelled to do by nature. I promise you, I cut with my knife everything that I could without being noticed. It not only came by nature, like walking and running, but seemed to me to be pleasant as well as natural. Well then, since we are left with a sort of fighting that calls for courage rather than skill, why should not we, as well as the peers here, fight with enthusiasm? [3]

The assumption that if you gave a man a shield in his left hand and a weapon in his right he would instinctively guard himself with the one and hit with the other, without being taught how to do it, was not universally held, and from the late fifth century B.C. onwards, we hear of experts in *hoplomachia,* that is, fencing with hoplite weapons. Their art, which later received official recognition at Athens and became a regular part of the training programme of the *ephebes,*[4] was at first regarded with suspicion, partly for the very reason that the Spartans despised it. In Plato's *Laches,* the discussion of courage begins with reflections on a demonstration of *hoplomachia* by a professional instructor before an Athenian audience. The general Nicias pronounces the art to be of value primarily as an exercise, and only secondly in actual warfare. "This knowledge will also bring some advantage in an actual battle, when you must fight in formation with many others. But it will be of most benefit when the ranks are broken and you must now fight man to man, either in pursuit, to attack someone who is trying to beat you off, or in retreat, when you yourself must beat off someone who is attacking you." The expert "would come to no harm from one opponent, and perhaps not from several, but in all circumstances it would give him an advantage." From weapon training the student may proceed to drill and tactics, and so to the whole art of generalship. His courage will be heightened, and—a small point, says Nicias, but worth mentioning—smartness will be encouraged at the time when it is most necessary to impress the enemy.

But Laches replies that, if this art were of any use, it would not have been overlooked by the Lacedaemonians, whose whole lives are dedicated to searching out and practising whatever studies or pursuits will give them a military advantage. But the professors of *hoplomachia,* instead of making straight for Sparta in the certainty of honour and reward, think of Lacedaemon as an inviolable sanctuary, and do not venture to tread it even with the tips of their toes, and would rather display themselves to anyone else, especially to those who freely confess that they have many superiors in the art of war.[5]

Yet it is clear that Greek hoplites were drilled in a few standard movements with spear and shield. This was of course necessary to avoid confusion in the ranks, and we may well suppose that this drill included a few blows and parries. The repetition of certain poses in works of art raises the interesting possibility that the artists, or their models, had been regularly taught the movements represented.[6] But perhaps Pheraulas would have said that some at least of these movements were taught by nature, not by the fencing masters. And some of the repetition is certainly due to the copying by one artist of another. In trying to reconstruct the ancient arms-drill, it seems safer, therefore, to use works of art mainly to provide illustrations of the ancient texts, while admitting that there must have been several movements for which no literary evidence has survived. We have no ancient account of a Greek sword-exercise like that recommended by Vegetius for the training of Roman legionaries.[7]

Even if it were not necessary to assume that hoplites, in handling their weapons, were trained to move simultaneously at the word of command or trumpet call, it could be shown from several historical incidents that they did so. The younger Cyrus, in his first review of the Greek mercenaries, drove past their ranks, then halted his chariot before the middle of the line and sent Pigres the interpreter to the generals, with orders for the whole phalanx to throw forward their shields and advance. The generals gave the preliminary word of command to the soldiers, and they acted upon the sound of the trumpet.[8] Again, in action against Pharnabazus during the march through Bithynia,

the command was given to carry the spears upon the right shoulder until the trumpet sounded, and then to level them to the attack and follow at the marching pace, and for nobody to pursue at a run. . . . But the hoplite phalanx, marching quickly, encountered the enemy, and as the trumpet sounded the men raised the paean, and after that they cheered and at the same moment levelled their spears. Then the enemy held out no longer, but ran.[9]

The "slope" position, with the spear on the right shoulder, point uppermost, held by the right hand at the point of balance, is frequently illustrated (Plate 4A).[10] A single movement, without shifting the hold, would bring the spear down to an "attack" position, held level at the full extent of the right arm, with the point forward, ready for an underhand thrust (Plate 2B). The underhand blow, usually delivered waist high at a run, is common in classical art,[11] and I believe that it was to this position that Xenophon's men brought down their spears. In Archaic art, the thrust is generally delivered overarm, with the right arm bent at the elbow and the spear pointing forwards and slightly downwards, its shaft resting on, or carried just above, the right shoulder, behind the point of balance (Plate 4B). To bring the spear into this position from the "slope," a change of grip is needed, and more than one movement. If the reader will experiment with a broomstick or other suitable staff, he may find it easiest to bring his "spear" down from the "slope" to the "underhand position," shift the grip, and bring the spear up to the "overhand"—three movements in all. Merely reversing the grip leaves the spear head pointing backwards. Of course we do not know exactly how the ancients carried out these movements. The overhand thrust seems to be proper for hoplites drawn up in close order, aiming over their own line of overlapping shields at the enemy's throat, or trying to pierce his shield by downward blow with the weight of the body behind it (Plate 2A). When the underhand thrust does appear in early art, it is usually delivered by retreating or even wounded men, who turn and try to surprise their pursuers with a thrust below the cuirass.[12] It seems possible that lighter armour and more active open tactics brought this thrust into increasing favour, though the overarm blow was, of course, used at all periods.

The spear seems sometimes to have been carried upright on the march, instead of sloped on the shoulder. Lysander, marching through Boeotia at a time of doubtful truce, sent to ask whether he should march with spears upright or levelled [13] (that is, ready for peace or war). The upright position would look smarter than the slope, if it was well maintained, but would of course be more tiring over a long distance. At the halt, when the spear-butt could be rested on the ground, the upright position seems to have been used for "stand at ease," when troops were drawn up to await further orders. To save the left arm, the heavy shield was lowered to the ground and leaned against the knees, where it could be picked up at a moment's notice (Plates 6, 7). If the troops were not being held in instant readiness, both spear and shield would be put right on the ground, and no doubt the helmet would be laid aside whenever possible.[14]

Good soldiers did not just put their weapons down, but were drilled to act smartly together. A remarkable tribute to good drill was paid by Agesilaus when he invaded Boeotia in 378 B.C. with eighteen thousand foot and fifteen hundred horse. The Thebans were joined by five thousand infantry and two hundred cavalry from Athens, and the combined Boeotian and Athenian army was drawn up on a ridge. After some preliminary skirmishing, Agesilaus ordered a general advance upon the allied position, but

> Chabrias the Athenian, being in command of the mercenaries, ordered his soldiers to receive the enemy with contempt, standing fast in their ranks, and, leaning their shields upon their knees, to remain with spears upright. Agesilaus marvelled at the good discipline of the enemy and at their disdain,

and changed his mind about forcing a pitched battle, being unwilling to attack such good soldiers in their strong position and unable to draw them down into the plain.[15] Chabrias's action, since it was instantly copied by the Theban Sacred Band, was clearly a standard drill movement for hoplites, and the point of the references to his "contempt" for the enemy is that he ordered his men to "Stand at ease" while waiting for the enemy to advance, instead of fatiguing them by keeping them standing with shields and spears levelled. He knew, and Agesilaus realized, that when the right moment came they could pick up their shields as smartly as they had put them down.

Since Agesilaus comes off second best in this story, Xenophon leaves it out of the *Hellenica*. But he mentions the "stand at ease" position in the *Anabasis,* in his account of the quarrel between Clearchus and Menon. Menon's men, resenting Clearchus's strict discipline, attempted to stone him, but he escaped to his own camp, called his soldiers to arms, and ordered the hoplites to remain in position, with their shields placed against their knees, while he himself rode off with the Thracian auxiliaries to demand justice.[16]

A tribute to the drill of the Ten Thousand was paid by Cleander, *harmost* of Byzantium, who longed to command them when he saw their orderly obedience.[17] It cannot have been their general good behaviour that impressed him, as he himself had just narrowly escaped death in a riot. But the omens were unfavourable and he declined the command.

Bad drill at once impressed professionals as the mark of bad soldiers. Brasidas was encouraged to attack by the confusion of wavering heads and spears in the Athenian ranks in 422 B.C., and the Athenians were discouraged by their own disorder as well as by his daring.[18] Had Cleon's men moved as smartly as Chabrias's, there might have been no battle of Amphipolis.

Iphicrates once refused to draw out his army for battle, though he outnumbered the enemy and the prophets told him that the omens were good. For, though his soldiers were many, they did not even know how to throw their shields forward together or to raise the paean. And when they were ordered to "Slope spears!" the clash of arms could not be heard above the chattering of teeth.[19]

That there was a regular drill for other movements with the shield and spear—for example, for slinging the shield on the back during a retreat[20]—is possible, but I have found no certain evidence for it. In practice, the hoplite could not fling his shield over his back the moment he turned, as the peltast could,[21] as he had to disengage his left arm from the central buckle. In works of art, hoplites appear rarely with their shields slung on the march, possibly from the slack cord that runs round the inside of the shield in some pictures. The arm band and handgrip could not be used for slinging.

I know of no reference to purely ceremonial drill movements, such as formal salutes with sword and spear. The need for salutes may not have been felt in the absence of an officer class.

The arms drill of the later Macedonian phalanx was apparently also simple. The manuals give words of command for

> Stand to your arms!
> Fall out the shield-bearers!
> Silence and attention to the word of command!
> Pick up shield! Up!
> Take distance!
> Up spears!

and then proceed to the ordering of the ranks and to parade-ground manoeuvres.[22]

Alexander the Great himself owed one of his early victories to the good drill of the phalanx that he had inherited from Philip. The Taulantians were drawn up in an inaccessible position, which he proposed to storm with his men in column one hundred and twenty deep. He wished to confuse the enemy as to the exact point where the blow would be struck, and so, after calling his men to attention, "first he ordered the hoplites to raise their spears upright, then, on the word of command, to extend them for the charge, and now to extend the array of spears to the right, and again to the left." When he finally struck, the enemy were not only bewildered but overawed by the keenness and good discipline of the Macedonians.[23]

To sum up, ancient hoplites were certainly drilled to handle their arms in unison, but the movements taught were few and simple (though no doubt not quite as few as those for which literary evidence has survived). War-dances and mimic battles may have been used to teach the basic movements of attack and defence. Spartan boys, from the age of five up, are said to have learned the Pyrrhic war-dance, using stalks of fennel instead of spears.[24] The grown men may also have fought sham battles with fennel stalks; at least, a story in the *Cyropaedia* reads like an adaptation of something that Xenophon had seen and tried for himself. Cyrus honoured with a dinner invitation a commander and his men whom he had seen divided into two parties for a mock battle. Both parties were armoured alike with breastplate and buckler, but one was armed with thick stalks of fennel and the other told to pick up and throw clods. Upon the signal being given, the second party threw their clods,

> and some hit breastplates and bucklers, but some did hit a thigh or a shin. But when they closed, the men with the stalks hit the thighs of one opponent, the hands of another, the shins of a third, and some who were stooping were hit on the neck and back. At last the stalk-carriers routed their opponents and chased them, hitting out with much laughter and joking.

The parties then changed places and repeated the exercise. Cyrus was delighted, "because they were being at once exercised and encouraged, and at the same time the victors were the party that imitated the Persian armament." At dinner he noticed some with bandaged shins or hands, and asked what had happened. Being told that they had been hit by clods, he asked if it had been at close quarters or at a distance, and was told "At a distance; but at close quarters the stalk-carriers had the most wonderful sport." Whereupon those who had been hit with the stalks called out that being hit at close quarters did not strike them as sport at all, and they showed the marks of their beatings, on their hands and necks, and some even on their faces.[25]

One can imagine Agesilaus, before the Corinthian War, encouraging his men by such rough play to despise the peltasts as nursery bogies.[26] But it is no use being superior to the enemy at close quarters if they never let one close. Spartan tactics against light-armed troops will be discussed in due course.

War-dances, whether they were regarded as a serious part of training or merely as mimicry, were not found only in Sparta. When the Ten Thousand entertained the Paphlagonians, two Thracians performed a sham combat to the sound of the flute. This was followed by the Thessalian Karpaia, in which

> one man puts his weapons on one side and sows and ploughs, often turning round as though in fear, and a robber approaches. And when the first man sees him coming, he snatches up his weapons, and goes to meet him, and fights for the plough-oxen. They act this in time to the music of the flute. Finally the robber binds the husbandman and leads off the oxen, or sometimes the husbandman binds the robber, and yokes him beside his oxen and drives him with his hands bound behind his back.

Next a Mysian danced, clashing *peltae* in time to the flute, and then "certain Mantineans and other Arcadians stood up in their finest armour, and sang to the accompaniment of the war tune on the flute, and raised the paean and danced as they do in their processions to the gods." Finally a dancing-girl with a light shield danced the Pyrrhic dance amid great applause, and when the Paphlagonians asked if the Greeks actually had women fighting by their side, they were told that it was the girls who had driven the King of Persia from the camp.[27]

VI

TACTICAL TRAINING

"Without good order the hoplite arm is worthless," said Aristotle, and added (his purpose being to show that military and political developments proceed hand-in-hand) that the ancients who lived in the time of the heroic kingdoms lacked the experience and tactical skill necessary for hoplite warfare.[1] Demetrius of Phalerum observed, in a figure borrowed from Xenophon, that, as the strength of a building depends upon the laying of each individual brick and the observation of the bond between each course, so in an army, exactitude in drawing up each individual man and each company makes the whole force strong.[2] "Tactics," to a Greek of the classical period, meant the art of marshalling men in formation, although, as the formation to be chosen would depend upon the "tactical situation" in the modern sense, "tactics" involved more than parade-ground drill; or rather, parade-ground drill by itself was not enough to make a good tactician.

The study of "tactics," in the narrow sense, under professionals who might also offer instruction in subjects which appear to the modern scholar to be quite unrelated, was in Xenophon's time a new feature of the higher education of ambitious young men of the upper classes. But though these professors represented an innovation, and in old-fashioned eyes an undesirable one, the art that they taught must have existed, and no doubt developed, for nearly three centuries. From the moment that the Greeks began to fight "with bronze shields and in the phalanx,"[3] they must have been regularly drawn up in rank and file and not just crowded together "like a mob pouring out of a theatre." [4] The special place of athletics in Greek civilization, and the setting aside by Greek cities of extensive exercise grounds for the training of their youth, have been connected with the introduction of hoplite warfare.[5] If at Sparta the gymnasium was less important than in other Greek states, it was because the whole city was a training-ground.

The professors to whom the whole art of "generalship" consisted in "tactics" are criticized by Xenophon in the *Memorabilia*. Socrates encourages one of his young friends to take a course in "generalship" from Dionysodorus, but when he comes back teases him with questions. "Tell me, so that if one of us commands a regiment or company under you we may have a better understanding of the art of war, where did he begin to teach you generalship?" The young man replies, "The beginning and end of his teaching were the same. For tactics is what he taught me, and nothing else." Socrates acknowledges the importance of tactics. "For an army regularly marshalled is a very different thing from one not drawn up, just as stones and bricks and wood and tiles thrown down in a disorderly heap are of no use, but when they are properly arranged, with the materials that neither rot nor dissolve, that is, the stones and the tiles, at the bottom and top, and the bricks [sun-dried mud-brick] and wood in between, as in a building, then they become a very valuable possession, a house." The young man acknowledges that Socrates's analogy fits what he has been taught. "For in war one must post the best men in the front and rear ranks, and the worst in the middle, so that they may be led by those in front and pushed on by those in the rear"—a principle as old as Homer and constantly recurring in Xenophon and the later writers on tactics, down to the disappearance of the pikeman at the end of the seventeenth century.

First therefore there must be especial choice made of the leaders of each file or first front ranks of the Battallion, of the most expert, ablest and best-armed men: because that as from them the rest are to receive directions of their after-motions, so in them the greatest hope of the day doth consist.

Next unto the first it must be provided, that the bringers up or last rank, called *Tergiductores,* be little inferior, well experienced, wise and valiant, that they may both know when to reprehend their former Ranks, and urge them forward, if they see them declining or yielding upon false occasions; as also upon any sudden alarm given in the rere to turn faces about and make themselves a front for the best resistance.[6]

Of course, Socrates points out that Dionysodorus's teaching is of no use unless he also teaches how to tell good men from bad.[7]

Even a practical soldier, with campaigns and wounds to his credit, might be fit only to command a regiment under a general with administrative experience gained in the world of business, if his own knowledge extended only to "tactics." [8] But professional "tacticians" were certainly valuable men—like Diomilus the Andrian exile, who was chosen to lead the Syracusan picked troops in 415 B.C., but was killed before he could give proof of his quality, or Phalinus the Greek, who served under Tissaphernes.[9] In 255 B.C., when Sparta had been in eclipse for a century, Carthage was saved and a Roman consular army destroyed by a Lacedaemonian drillmaster.[10]

The importance of "tactics" to Xenophon himself is clear from the care with which he records the formations adopted in particular actions, especially in the *Anabasis.* His historical writings, however, gave him no scope for an account of the training of recruits, beginning with squad and company drill and going on to the manoeuvring of larger formations and eventually of whole armies. This is found in the *Cyropaedia.*

It has been maintained that the tactics of the *Cyropaedia,* although agreeing closely in general principle with those of the Spartans, reflect a specifically Athenian system.[11] Certainly such details as the names of the units and of their officers are not taken directly from Sparta. But we have no independent evidence for these details in the actual Athenian army of the time, of which we can say with certainty only that it was organized in ten *taxeis,* or tribal regiments, subdivided into *lochoi.* Lamachus, who is teased for his "crests and companies" by Aristophanes, "rebuked one of the *lochagoi* for some fault, and when the man said that he would never do it again replied that there were no second chances in war." [12] To this not very adequate evidence for the subdivision of the Athenian *taxeis* into *lochoi* in the first half of the Peloponnesian War, we can add the testimony of Xenophon in the second.[13]

The name *taxis* was applied not only to the tribal regiments at their full strength, a thousand men or more when the whole Athenian army went on campaign, but to the much smaller contingents that took part in distant expeditions.[14] When therefore we find in the *Cyropaedia taxeis* of a hundred men divided into four *lochoi,* the names used may be those that would have been applied to the sub-units of an Athenian expeditionary force of a thousand men, drawn from all the tribes. On the other hand, Xenophon also uses these names when speaking of mercenaries in the Spartan service in Asia, or at the siege of Corcyra—not necessarily because he falls naturally into Atticisms.

It does not seem that either *lochos* or *taxis* conveyed in itself a definite indication of number, but where both words are used, the *lochos* is always a subdivision of the *taxis.* In the *Anabasis,* *taxis* is used of formations of about two hundred men, that is two *lochoi* temporarily united for a specific purpose.[15]

Beyond this the evidence does not take us. There is no proof that any smaller subdivisions existed at Athens, and, since the system by which every front-rank man was an officer is noted as a special feature of Spartan tactics, it probably was not in force in Athens, at least in Xenophon's youth. On the other hand, our evidence is quite unsystematic. A chance reference in the *Hel-*

lenica shows that "fives" formed part of the military organization of Phlius, which was presumably based on that of Sparta.[16] A similar casual allusion might have done as much for Athens.

The tactics of the *Anabasis* are sometimes regarded as Athenian, but Xenophon (who was not even the chief general of the Ten Thousand until well after they had reached the Black Sea) could not possibly have introduced a new system of drill in the very heat of action.

To move men from place to place in an orderly column, to deploy them into line on the field of battle, to vary the depth of the line and the front that it covered, and to change direction without falling into confusion, were the objects of tactics. Under the Spartan system the essential movements were efficiently carried out, and Spartan drill therefore provided a model not only to contemporary Greece but to the larger and more elaborately organized armies of the Hellenistic period. But because the armies of the early fourth century B.C. were smaller and less complicated than those of Alexander's successors, their drill was less complicated too. It had of course already acquired a precise technical vocabulary, but one which was narrower than that employed by the later writers on tactics. Between Xenophon's time and Arrian's, words changed their significance[17] or became precise where before they had been general. I believe therefore that we should look for Xenophon's meaning in Xenophon himself, and not insist that because later writers give precise meanings to certain words he cannot still be using them in a more general way.

Recruit-drill began with the men being pushed into single file and taught to follow the file leader. Xenophon gives a picture of an awkward squad, which is clearly drawn from life. A *taxiarch* is describing his efforts to pass on to his *taxis* the lessons that he has learned from Cyrus. He begins with a single *lochos* of twenty-four men.

> I stood the commander (*lochagos*) in front, and placed behind him a young man, and the others as I thought right. Then I

stood in front of them facing the *lochos,* and at what seemed to me the proper moment I gave the order to advance. And— would you believe it?—that young man came past the *lochagos* and marched before him. When I saw him I said, "You there! What are you doing?" and he said, "I'm advancing, like you told us." And I said, "I gave the order for everyone to advance, not just you." When he heard this, he turned round to the rest of the *lochos* and said, "Don't you hear him bawling us out? He means us all to advance." And every man jack passed the *lochagos* and came up to me. And when the *lochagos* tried to make them go back, they got angry and said, "Which of them are we to obey? One of them tells us to advance and another forbids us!" But I kept my temper and made them go back and begin all over again, and said that nobody in the rear was to move until the man in front of him led, and that they were all only to see to one thing, namely following the man in front. At this moment somebody who was going home to Persia came to me and told me to give him the letter that I had written for home. The *lochagos* knew where the letter was, so I told him to run and bring it. Well, he ran and that young man followed him, sabre, breastplate, and all, and when all the rest of the *lochos* saw him they ran too. Then they came bringing the letter.[18]

This passage has an additional interest in that it shows how very far the officers were from forming a separate class, as in a modern European army. On the one hand, the company commander is sent on an orderly's errand; on the other, the men talk back to their officers without being punished for it.

The *lochos* must next be taught to form in several files side by side, and to combine with the other *lochoi* of its *taxis* (Figs. I–II). Again, the *Cyropaedia* indicates how this was done.

Once he saw another *taxiarch* leading his men from the river to the morning meal in single file, and when he thought proper, ordering the second *lochos* to come up beside the first, and the third and the fourth, into line; and when the *lochagoi* were in

line, he gave the order to lead each *lochos* in twos. On this, the
leaders of ten led up by the side into line. And when he judged
it proper, he gave the order for each *lochos* to form fours. And
thereupon the leaders of five in their turn led up by the side to
form fours.[19]

The files were regularly brought up on the left, "the shield hand,"
so that the commander, who was at the head when his unit was
in single file, was at the head of the right-hand file after it had
deployed. Xenophon does not think it necessary to mention this
explicitly, and we must also take it for granted that the men who
are to form the right-hand file halt while the left-hand file comes
up. In this passage, the *taxis* is clearly supposed to consist of four
lochoi, each of which consists of two tens, each of which is subdivided into two fives. Later on these become, without explanation, "twelves" and "sixes," probably because Xenophon decided
that each *taxis* should consist of a hundred men—four *lochoi,*
each of a *lochagos* and twenty-four men—and forgot to revise
what he had written already. The men when formed in line of
battle are, of course, drawn up in rank and file, but the line is
formed not by drawing up one rank behind the other but by
drawing up one file beside the other. The number of files can
be varied, to give a front of four, eight, or sixteen men, and a
depth of twenty, ten, or five (Fig. I). Whatever the number of the
files, each forms a distinct unit, and the file leader is also the
officer in command of the men at his back.

   This system would actually be less flexible than Xenophon
wishes it to appear, at least when it was applied to a large number of *taxeis*. We are not told what interval was allowed between
the files in the first place, but it would not be unreasonable to
allow between the four *lochoi* on an exercise of this sort the six-
foot intervals of the Macedonian phalanx in open order. Arrian
gives the drill for doubling the number of men in the ranks of
the Macedonian phalanx, by bringing up the rear half of each
file through the intervals. This could be done without extending

the front, and corresponds to Xenophon's forming each *lochos* in twos. But Arrian continues with drill for doubling the length of the front, by bringing the men from the rear to the left and right wings through the intervals between the ranks, for which there is no corresponding manoeuvre in Xenophon.[20]

An original interval of six feet between the *lochoi* of the *Cyropaedia* would allow the "leaders of ten" to bring up their "tens" (hitherto forming the rear half of each *lochos*) in the intervals between the files. But thereafter, unless the original intervals were improbably large, the *taxis* would have to extend its front, taking ground probably to the left, in order to make room for the "leaders of five" to bring their "fives" up from the rear. This might be done without much difficulty when the *taxis* was on its own in a large open space, but when it formed part of a long line it could not extend its own front without crowding upon its neighbours.

No Spartan drill for forming open or close order, like that given in the textbooks for the Macedonian phalanx, is described in our sources. But the Ten Thousand at Cunaxa, both hoplites and peltasts, were able to open intervals for the harmless passage of the Persian chariots and cavalry; and at Coronea, Agesilaus's men were forced to open ranks to let the Thebans pass.[21] Xenophon gives no details of how this was done. The files of the phalanx going into action were probably close enough together for the shields of each rank to form a continuous line, with each man protected by his right-hand neighbour's shield as well as by his own, in the manner described by Thucydides.[22] This would allow just under three feet of front for each file—room enough to countermarch the files in an orderly manner when it was desired to face the phalanx to the rear, but not enough still to leave room for the countermarch after the rear halves of the files had been brought up into the intervals. When, therefore, we are told that "instructions for the *paragogai* [leading up the files] are given out by word of mouth by the *enomotarch,* as though by a herald, and the phalanxes become thinner and deeper," we may suppose that this means that the Spartan commander could choose to deploy his army in either a deep or a shallow line, not that he could easily change its depth after it had been deployed.

From the line, the column could easily be re-formed in its original order. The right-hand file led off forward, and the others followed, each in its turn. This is how the *taxiarch* in the *Cyropaedia* brought his men in through the door of their bivouac. But it was also necessary sometimes to retire from the position upon which the line had been formed, and another *taxiarch* told Cyrus how he drilled his men for this. He brought them into their meals in the same manner as the first one, and after the meal was over,

> the rear-rank man of the last *lochos* leads out his *lochos,* with the men who in action are posted in front at the rear. And then the second [i.e., the rear-rank men of the second-last *lochos*] leads out the men of the next *lochos* after them, and the third and the fourth in the same way, so that when they have to lead away from the enemy, they may know how to come off. And, on parade on the exercise ground, when we lead to the east, I lead, and the first *lochos* is first, and the second in its proper place, and the third and the fourth, and the tens and fives of the *lochoi*, until I give the word of command. But when we go towards the west, the rear-rank man and the last *lochos* lead off first. But they still obey me though I am at the rear, to accustom them to be equally obedient whether they are leading or following.

This double form of exercise is duly rewarded with a double dinner invitation—"not both dinners on the same day, please," says the *taxiarch* "unless you give us double stomachs too!" [23]

This system is straightforward and clear when applied to small units, and theoretically it still seems sound when Xenophon jumps to the handling of three myriad men in mass formation. But of course all his experience had been with smaller numbers.

"If thirty thousand men were drawn up in close order in Hyde Park," the Duke of Wellington once said, "there are not three men in Europe who could get them out again," and perhaps Cyrus could not really have shown the way. However, Xenophon has no doubts. When Cyrus was reviewing his men, he was summoned by his uncle Cyaxares to attend at the reception of some Indian ambassadors. Instead of putting on the robe of state provided for him, Cyrus

> ordered the *taxiarch* who was posted first to halt facing the front, leading his *taxis* in single file, having Cyrus himself on his right hand, and told him to pass on the same order to the second *taxiarch,* and so through the whole army. And they in obedience passed the order on quickly, and quickly did what had been ordered; and in a short time, they were formed on a front of three hundred men (for that was the number of the *taxiarchs*)[24] and a depth of one hundred. And when they had formed up, he ordered them to follow his own lead, and immediately led off at the double.

The final formation is clear enough, and also the manner in which it was formed, by leading each *taxis* up in single file on the left of the one in front of it, and halting when the *taxiarch* came level with the other *taxiarchs*. But did they start with one *taxis* following behind another, thirty thousand men in single file twenty miles long? Obviously Xenophon has not really imagined the consequences of multiplying fifty-fold the numbers to which he was accustomed. Cyrus now led towards the palace of Cyaxares.

> But when he perceived that the road leading to the palace was too narrow for the whole force to pass through in line, he gave the order for the first thousand to follow him immediately, the second thousand to follow in the rear of the first, and so through the whole army. He himself led on without pausing, and the

other thousands followed each other in the rear of the preceding one. And he sent two aides [there is no suggestion that these were trained staff officers] to the entry into the road, so that if anybody was in doubt, they could direct the proper action. But when they arrived at the gates of Cyaxares, he ordered the first *taxiarch* to form his *taxis* twelve deep, and the leaders of twelve [who correspond to the "leaders of ten" in the passages already quoted] to halt in line round the palace, and told him to pass the same orders on to the second *taxiarch,* and so through the whole army.

Once again one feels that Xenophon had not really visualized the scale of the problem, or the time that it would take for the orders to be passed to three hundred *taxiarchs.* But in the story-book everything comes out all right (as it no doubt did when a Spartan *mora* of six hundred men practised this drill), and Cyaxares confesses that thirty thousand men marshalled in good order set his nephew off more finely than any court dress.[25]

The *Cyropaedia* also describes the execution on the battlefield of complicated manoeuvres which would in practice have needed to be rehearsed beforehand, but it has no more pictures of parade-ground drill. Something more can be learned from the sketch of Spartan tactics in the *Constitution of the Lacedaemonians,*[26] which is not related to any particular battle and so may be considered here, though it refers to active service rather than to peace-time training.

After describing the organization of the Spartan hoplites in six *morai,* each consisting of four *lochoi,* eight *pentekostyes,* and sixteen *enomotiai,*[27] Xenophon says:

From these *morai* they are drawn up at the word of command with the *enomotiai* sometimes in single file, sometimes in threes, and sometimes in sixes.[28] [At Leuctra, the *enomotiai* were formed in threes, giving a depth of not more than twelve in a line. Cf. Fig. III].[29] The common opinion, that the Laconian hoplite drill is most complicated, is a complete misunderstanding of the facts. For in the Laconian drill the front-rank men are officers and each file is a self-contained unit. It is so easy to learn this drill that nobody who can recognize men could make a mistake. For it is given to some to lead, and ordered to others to follow. And the orders to lead up the files are given verbally by the *enomotarch,* as though by a herald, and the depth of the phalanx is increased or diminished. There is not the slightest difficulty in learning any of this. But to fight in the same way with chance companions, and if they have been thrown into confusion, is no longer easy to learn, except for those who are educated under the Lycurgan laws.

It was perhaps of this passage that Plutarch was thinking when he boasted of the achievement of Pelopidas in throwing the Spartans into confusion at Leuctra.[30]

Xenophon continues:

And the Lacedaemonians also make very easy the movements which seem to the professors of tactics to be extremely difficult. For when they are marching in column, one *enomotia* of course follows at the tail of another. If in such circumstances, an enemy phalanx appears from the opposite direction, the word is given to the *enomotarch* to form front on the shield hand, and so through the whole army, until the phalanx is formed facing the enemy [Fig. IV].

This is of course the same manoeuvre for deploying from column into line of battle as that described in the *Cyropaedia* (Fig. II). The leading *enomotia* halts facing the front. The second comes up on the left, the third on the left of the second, and so on. The original orders would no doubt also specify whether each *enomotia* was to be formed in one, three, or six files. So the phalanx was formed by drawing up one file beside another, not one rank behind another, though in the phalanx the men were of course ordered by rank and file.[31] "Phalanx" in Xenophon is constantly used of an army deployed in line of battle,[32] and the situation envisaged here is comparable to that at Mantinea in 418 B.C., when the Spartan army, marching northwards, encountered the enemy deployed for battle some miles south of the position in which they were expected.[33]

Xenophon next describes how the Spartans met an enemy who appeared behind the phalanx, as at Coronea in 394 B.C., when the Thebans defeated the left wing of Agesilaus's army while Agesilaus himself, with his Spartan regiments and veteran mercenaries from Asia, chased their allies off the battlefield. After this first phase of the battle, the Spartan phalanx was facing its original front, but the only organized enemy was now behind it.[34] Merely to order the phalanx to "About turn!" would have left the rear-rank men in front, and the file leaders at the rear of the files that they were supposed to command. Accordingly: "If when they are in this formation [i.e., deployed in phalanx] the enemy appear from the rear, each file countermarches,[35] in order that the strongest men may always be facing the enemy." The later tacticians[36] distinguish the "Laconian countermarch" from the "Macedonian" and "Cretan." In the "Laconian" drill, the rear-rank man turned about and stood fast while the file leader led the rest of the file in order up to their new position. This had the advantage over the "Macedonian" system (in which the file leader turned about and stood fast, while the other members of the file took up their positions behind him) that during the manoeuvre the phalanx appeared to the enemy to be advancing upon him, not retiring.

After the countermarch, the phalanx was not, of course, in the original order, as the right flank had now become the left. Normally the Spartans accepted this situation, and made the best they could of it. "As for the fact that the commander is on the left flank, they consider this no disadvantage, but on occasion actually advantageous. For if anyone were to attempt an encircling movement, they would not envelop the unshielded but the protected side." This passage is variously interpreted. Either the commander's own safety was increased when he was on the left wing, because an encircling attack directed against him personally would now be delivered against his shielded side, not against his bare right;[37] or the meaning is that any outflanking attempt would be made against the left (as at Mantinea in 418 B.C. or the Nemea in 394), not against the right, and that therefore it was sometimes desirable to have the commander on the left, not for his own better protection, but because this was the point of danger to the army as a whole.[38] I believe that this is the correct interpretation.

However, tradition, if nothing else, laid it down that the commander's usual post was on the right wing, and accordingly the Spartans had a drill for exchanging the flanks of the reversed phalanx and bringing the commander back to the "spear hand." "If for any reason it seems expedient for the commander to have the right wing, they turn the *agema* into column and countermarch the phalanx, until the leader is on the right and the 'tail' is on the left." That is, the army is turned into column, and the left-hand man of each rank leads his own rank in countermarching until the two ends have changed places, when the army is turned back into line again. Not surprisingly, no instance of this manoeuvre being carried out in the face of the enemy is recorded. This is parade-ground drill, and even on the parade ground, better suited for small units than for the whole army deployed in line, with several hundred men in each rank.

Although the general meaning is clear, the word *agema* remains obscure. It appears to mean the leading unit of the army, but the ancient evidence does not allow us to define it more precisely.[39]

Xenophon next[40] considers the action to be taken when the enemy appears on the right or left of the column of march. I believe that these enemies are supposed to be light-armed troops; they are not spoken of as "a phalanx." A column commanded by the Spartan Anaxibius was destroyed when it was ambushed by Iphicrates and his peltasts in hilly country,[41] and detachments of hoplites were sometimes successfully concealed in positions from which they could emerge to attack the enemy's flank or rear.[42] But a whole army ranged in order of battle, on ground suitable for hoplites, could not very well be hidden, and we are not to imagine that any Spartan commander would be so fool-hardy as to march his men in column across the front of the enemy phalanx. We need not suppose, therefore, that the Spartans must have themselves deployed into phalanx to the left or right to meet an attack upon the flank of their column. The *Constitution of the Lacedaemonians* does not say that they did so; and if what it does say makes sense, we need not assume either that its author takes the final stage in the deployment for granted, or that he was an ignorant fellow who did not understand what he was writing about.[43]

Xenophon says: "Again, if a formation [*taxis*] of enemies appears from the right, when they are marching in column, the only action they take is to turn each *lochos* like a trireme head-on to the enemy, and so again the rear *lochos* is on the spear hand." "*Lochos*" is of course here used in its technical sense of a formation of four *enomotiai*, or about a hundred and forty men, and the *mora* on the line of march would consist of a single column, with four *lochoi* following one behind the other. To meet the attack, the *lochoi* simultaneously wheeled to the right, so that now instead of a single column there were four parallel columns, moving at right angles to the original line of march, at intervals corresponding to their own length (Fig. V).

This formation, *orthioi lochoi,* or "*lochoi* in column," is repeatedly mentioned in Xenophon's other writings, and was particularly suitable for hoplites operating against skirmishers on rough ground. Its advantages are most clearly set out in the *Anabasis,* in the account of the fight with the Colchians. The enemy were drawn up upon a high but accessible hill, and the Greeks began by deploying into phalanx to attack them. But upon further consideration, the generals, by Xenophon's advice, substituted *lochoi* in column for the phalanx.

For the phalanx will be broken immediately. For we will find the mountain hard to climb in one place and easy in another. And this will at once cause despondency when, after being drawn up in phalanx, the soldiers see the line broken. Again, if we advance in a deep line, the enemy line will be longer than ours, and they will use the extra men as they please. But, if we are in shallow formation, it would be in no way surprising if our phalanx were to be broken through by a concentrated discharge of missiles and the massed onslaught of many men. If this happens at any one point, the whole phalanx will suffer. I think we should form the *lochoi* in column, at sufficient intervals to take enough ground for the flanking *lochoi* to be outside the enemy's wings. In this way we shall outflank the enemy's phalanx, and, moving in column, the best of us will advance in the van, and each *lochos* will advance where the way is good. Moreover it will not be easy for the enemy to penetrate into the intervals, with a *lochos* on each side of them, and it will not be easy to break through a *lochos* advancing in column. And if any of the *lochoi* is being overwhelmed, its neighbours will come to the rescue. If one of the *lochoi* is able at any point to gain the heights, none of the enemy will stand fast any longer.[44]

Xenophon's plan was approved and answered to expectations. But it is to be noted that though the enemy are here spoken of as a phalanx (being deployed in a continuous line), "*lochoi* in column" were not used in pitched battles against a hoplite phalanx drawn up on level ground. Though this formation possessed some of the advantages of the later Roman *quincunx,* it was not really an anticipation of it.[45]

"*Lochoi* in column" were of course used by the Spartans to meet an attack on the left of the column of march. But the drill recorded in the *Constitution of the Lacedaemonians* includes an interesting variation. "If the enemy approach on the left, they do not allow this either, but run out on them, or turn the *lochoi* to meet them. And in this case the rear *lochos* is stationed on the left."

The simultaneous wheeling of the *lochoi* into parallel columns is of course the counterpart of the manoeuvre carried out when the enemy appeared on the right. The "running out" confirms that the hypothetical enemy are not hoplites in line of battle. For the Spartans regularly met the attacks of light-armed skirmishers by ordering the younger men (who must have been evenly distributed throughout the army)[46] to break out from the ranks and give chase. Why the *Constitution of the Lacedaemonians* only mentions "running out" against an attack from the left is not clear to me; and in fact the Spartans did pursue light-armed infantry who attacked from the right.[47] But the practice (as distinct from the theory) of hoplite tactics in minor actions requires a separate discussion.

VII

HOPLITES AND
OTHER ARMS

Hoplites were developed in order to fight pitched battles on level
ground. But most of Greece is not level, and pitched battles were
rare. Xenophon himself fought in two only, and one of them
was against Asiatics, not against other hoplites. He saw innu-
merable skirmishes, in many of which hoplites, hampered by their
big shields and lack of missile weapons, proved ineffective against
light-armed troops, and in some of which they were disastrously
defeated. Yet he remained to the end convinced that the flower of
the infantry should be equipped for close combat, not for skirmishing. It was not that pitched battles were necessarily decisive. The
Spartan victories at the Nemea and Coronea did not end the
Corinthian War, and the last words of the *Hellenica* comment
on the failure of the second battle of Mantinea to fulfill the
general expectation that it would settle the affairs of Greece one
way or the other.[1] At Cunaxa, the Greeks, in their own estima-
tion, won the battle; but there was no doubt who had won the
war. Leuctra, where the Spartan power was broken in an afternoon, was outstanding among the battles of Xenophon's lifetime; but even Leuctra did not end a war, though its course was
decisively changed. Modern scholars have sometimes held that the
hoplite was obsolete in the fourth century, and blamed Xenophon
and his Spartan contemporaries for not recognizing the fact. But,
though Xenophon may have underestimated the power of the

new professional light-armed infantry, it does not follow that the Greeks would have done well to rely on that power alone.

The missile weapons available to classical Greek armies were the bow, the sling, and the javelin. The catapult, which appeared in Sicily as a siege engine during the wars of Dionysius I against Carthage, was hardly known in Greece except as a curiosity until the time of Philip of Macedon, and was seldom used as field artillery even by Alexander and his successors.[2] Bow, sling, and javelin had of course been known to the Greeks for centuries, but in the early fourth century, the javelin, which has the shortest range and seems the most feeble of the three, suddenly acquired a special importance. The reason was the development of the professional peltast.

The peltast was named for his shield, a light buckler, of which the ancient descriptions are all drawn from Aristotle's lost *Constitution of the Thessalians*.[3] According to Aristotle, it was rimless, and covered with goat or sheepskin, instead of bronze or oxhide. The quotations from him do not specify shape or size, though some modern scholars deduce from his language that he was referring to a round target.[4] If so, this must be a variant, for the *pelta* in art is crescent-shaped, perhaps two feet long between the horns, and carried usually with both horns pointing upwards (Plate 18). It is managed either by a handgrip placed centrally, or by a handgrip and armband. The armband is not, however, in the middle, like that of a hoplite shield, and so the *pelta* would not project far to the bearer's left. It was for his own protection only, not for that of his neighbour, for he did not fight in rank and file, but as an individual. Sometimes at least the *pelta* was also provided with a sling, so that it could be thrown over the back when the bearer turned to fly, and Xenophon tells how some of the Thracians who made a night attack upon the village where he was quartered were hung up by their shields when they jumped over the fences surrounding the houses in order to escape.[5] Xenophon also mentions bronze *peltae,* but probably (like hoplite shields) they were only faced with a thin covering of bronze. By flashing their *peltae* in the sunlight, a small party half concealed on a scrub-covered hillside was able to give the impression that there was a large force in ambush.[6] The frame of the *pelta* was probably of close-woven wicker, and it may sometimes have been left uncovered, to judge from a few of the artistic representations.[7]

The popularity of the *pelta* with Greek artists from the Late Archaic period onwards arises not from its actual use in contemporary warfare, but from its association with the legendary Amazons, which became so strong in later ages that Roman soldiers who found some *peltae* lying on a stricken field were disappointed that there were no women's bodies among the slain.[8] But, though the *pelta* was used north of the Black Sea by the Scythian horsemen,[9] it was certainly in Thrace that the infantry peltast originated.[10]

Thracian peltasts in their original dress—a heavy patterned cloak fastened round the neck, covering both shoulders and coming down nearly to the feet, high boots, and fox-skin cap with earflaps against the cold[11] (Plates 17, 18)—are not common in Attic vase-painting, but they start early. Two examples date from the third quarter of the sixth century B.C. when Athens was acquiring new interests in the Thracian Chersonese, the modern Gallipoli Peninsula.[12] At least one Archaic Amazon wears Thracian dress instead of the Scythian habit of her sisters,[13] and there is a picture of a Thracian peltast of about the time of the Persian Wars in the David M. Robinson collection.[14] These peltasts are all javelin-men (as are most of the other Thracians illustrated in vase-painting, even when they do not actually carry the *pelta*) and carry two light, short throwing-spears. There are other pictures of Thracians, especially in illustrations of the legend of Orpheus[15] (Plate 17), and young Athenians of fashion are sometimes shown wearing Thracian cloaks and boots. But they do not carry the *pelta*.

During a period of several centuries, the Thracians were formidable enough to keep the Greeks from penetrating beyond the coasts of their country, but too savage and disunited to rank among the great powers. Peltasts were only one among several types of light infantry. But after the beginning of the Peloponnesian War, their importance was increased. Nothing came of the wild hopes that the Athenians built upon the great host of Sitalces, but mercenary peltasts, most of them Thracians, proved useful to both sides in the fighting to the north of the Aegean.[16] The relief expedition to Syracuse under Demosthenes, who had learned in Aetolia what light infantry could do to hoplites on rough ground, and made good use of the lesson at Sphacteria, was to have been accompanied by thirteen hundred Thracians.[17] They arrived at Athens too late to sail for Sicily, and achieved nothing on their way home except the sack of the defenceless country town of Mycalessus. But from this begins the extensive use of peltasts outside their own native land, and the arming of Greek light infantry as peltasts soon follows.

In the early summer of 408 B.C., the Athenian Thrasyllus armed as peltasts five thousand sailors from the crews of the fleet of fifty ships with which he was operating in the eastern Aegean.[18] This large-scale attempt to equip the poorer citizens as an effective infantry may have been preceded by experiments at the time of the attack on Melos in 416 B.C. and the Syracusan expedition.[19] The new peltasts proved effective in the first coastal raids, but Thrasyllus was later heavily defeated at Ephesus, partly because he unwisely divided his forces, and partly, perhaps, because the marshy ground upon which the cavalry, peltasts, marines, and other sailors were landed was not suitable for skirmishing tactics. But at least he had tried to make some of the poorer citizens into something better than an unarmed mob.[20]

Athens had long possessed a small but effective corps of archers. But I suppose that it is much easier for the unpractised to learn to throw a javelin than to shoot effectively with the bow, and that this is why peltasts' equipment was given to Thrasyllus's men. They represent, in fact, an attempt to make better use of unskilled manpower (for they were unskilled by land, whatever they may have been afloat), not the creation of a new professional arm.

Professional peltasts, some Thracian, some Greek, the latter mainly from the mountians of Epirus, accompanied the Ten Thousand and did good service at Cunaxa and on the retreat.[21] But it was the very much smaller body of archers and slingers who were of most value in beating off the Persian attacks upon the rearguard, once the Cretan archers had acquired Asiatic bows and the Rhodian slingers had been given lead bolts with which to out-range the Persian stones. The fighting against Tissaphernes and Mithradates[22] showed that hoplites and peltasts by themselves could do nothing but endure the attack of cavalry, archers, and slingers. But if the hoplites were supported by even a very few horsemen and a small force equipped with long-range weapons, the advantage was on their side.

On the first day after the crossing of the Zapatas, Mithradates with two hundred cavalry and four hundred light and active slingers and archers greatly distressed the Greek rearguard, who

> suffered badly and did nothing in return. For the Cretan archers shot shorter than the Persians, and moreover, being without armour, were enclosed within the hoplites, and the javelin-men did not throw their javelins far enough to reach the slingers. Accordingly it seemed to Xenophon that they should give chase, and the hoplites and peltasts who were with him in the rearguard did so. But in their pursuit they overtook none of the enemy. For the Greeks had no cavalry, nor could their infantry overtake the enemy infantry, who had a long start, in a short distance. For it was not possible to pursue far from the rest of the army.

That night, two hundred Rhodians were persuaded to volunteer as slingers, and a squadron of cavalry was improvised out of fifty men mounted on captured animals from the baggage train and Xenophon's own horses and those of the dead Clearchus. This scratch force was sufficient to change the whole situation, even against a far greater number of enemies. Tissaphernes had reinforced Mithradates, who, when the advance was resumed after a day's pause, attacked confidently with a thousand cavalry and four thousand slingers and archers. But the Greeks laid a trap for him. They had a ravine to cross, and might have been in serious difficulties had he attacked them during the crossing. But by starting early in the morning they got safely over before he appeared. Xenophon observes that, for fear of being caught unarmed and with unsaddled horses by a night attack, the Persians always camped at a distance of "not less than sixty stades"—six or seven miles—from the Greeks.[23] Evidently Mithradates, knowing that he could always find his slow-moving enemy, had not even troubled to keep them under close observation. Mithradates allowed the Greeks to get a mile or so on their way before crossing himself, evidently judging from his earlier experience that this would leave his cavalry and light infantry room to escape the short and clumsy charges of the Greeks. But meanwhile, the Greek generals

> gave orders to those of the peltasts who were to pursue, and to those of the hoplites, and told the cavalry to give chase with the confidence of being followed up by a sufficient force. When Mithradates overtook them and they were already in range of slings and arrows, the trumpet-signal was given to the Greeks, and immediately those who had been ordered charged together, and the cavalry galloped. And the enemy did not receive them, but fled to the ravine. In this pursuit, many of the barbarian infantry were killed, and of the cavalry some eighteen were taken alive in the ravine.

These two actions against Mithradates illustrate the proper use of auxiliary troops in combination with hoplites against superior enemy cavalry and light infantry. It was no good the hoplites' merely suffering under the enemy's fire and hoping that their own supporting troops would make him keep his distance with their long-range weapons. It is true that, when Tissaphernes again attempted to harass the Greek retreat, the Rhodian slingers, whose leaden bolts out-ranged all the Persian missiles, kept him off, and the hoplites did not have to charge.[24] But he and his men were by that time shaken by the earlier defeat, and showed no wish to press their attacks. In normal circumstances, even if the hoplites' auxiliaries out-ranged the enemy (as Demosthenes's archers had out-ranged the Aetolian javelin-throwers in 426 B.C.),[25] they were bound to run out of ammunition, whereas the attacking enemy had more opportunity of retrieving spent missiles, even if he was not kept supplied from outside the battle-field.[26] The hoplite must charge out on his tormentors. Being burdened by his great shield (even if the rest of his equipment had been lightened in the manner suggested in Chapter II), he had little chance of catching the enemy by himself. If he carried pursuit too far from the body of his friends, the enemy would easily turn and overwhelm him from all sides, and short rushes, which did not bring him to grips, only tired him to no purpose.

But to avoid the hoplites' pursuit, clumsy though it was, the enemy had to turn and run away. And now the hoplites' auxiliaries, if they were themselves prepared to pursue fearlessly, had their chance, however small their numbers and inferior their quality. Even a few cavalry could overtake and cut down fleeing light infantry, if the enemy was given no opportunity to rally. If his flight was checked by a natural obstacle, so much the more chance of doing damage.

At Sardis in 395 B.C., Agesilaus was able to repeat the success of the Ten Thousand against a far larger force of Persian cavalry, this time unsupported, or unencumbered, by infantry. Xenophon's account of this battle differs entirely from that in the *Hellenica Oxyrhynchia,* according to which Agesilaus, being pressed by the Persian cavalry, concealed fourteen hundred hoplites in a wood, and after drawing the enemy past the ambush, trapped them between it and his main body. This story is told in convincing detail, but we do not know its source, whereas it is certain that Xenophon, if he was not present at the battle, had the chance to discuss it shortly afterwards with the Spartan leaders, including Agesilaus himself. As a professional soldier and a devotee of Agesilaus, he must have been interested in the details of the greatest victory of the king's Asiatic campaign. I cannot believe that he would have heard only a few scraps of genuine information, and risked the displeasure of Agesilaus by making up a wholly fictitious narrative. I therefore follow his account,[27] according to which Tissaphernes, the Persian commander, was deceived as to Agesilaus's intentions, and was preparing to meet an invasion of Caria, while Agesilaus marched north into Lydia.[28] The Greek army thus marched and plundered unopposed for three clear days before the Persian army overtook them on the fourth, apparently fairly late in the day.

During the retreat of the Ten Thousand, Mithradates had despised his enemy for their want of cavalry, and been surprised by the squadron that they had organized overnight. Something of the same sort seems to have happened at Sardis. In the campaign of 396 B.C., Agesilaus had been compelled to fall back to the coast after his cavalry had been beaten in a skirmish by those of Pharnabazus. But during the winter he had reorganized it, inviting his rich allies to supply professionals "to die for them" instead of serving in person, and approving the conduct of Agamemnon, who, when a lesser king offered his chariot team instead of personal service at Troy, preferred a good mare to a bad man.[29] Now the Persians were surprised by the new force. When they caught up with the Greek army, it was on one side of the Pactolus river, with its followers scattered in search of loot. The Persians ordered their own baggage train to cross the river and make camp, and themselves fell upon the plunderers and killed many of them, evidently believing that Agesilaus's cavalry was ineffective and his infantry too slow-moving to catch them or threaten their camp. When Agesilaus sent his cavalry to the rescue, the Persians rallied their scattered men and took up the same formation, many ranks deep, that they had used with success the year before. But Agesilaus, realizing that they had no infantry with them, saw his opportunity and led on his phalanx, ordering the ten youngest age-groups of hoplites to run to close with the enemy, and the peltasts to follow at the double. To the cavalry he sent word that he himself was following with the whole army, and ordered them to charge. The Persians received the cavalry charge, but gave way before the threat of a combined onslaught of all arms.[30] Some fell in the river, which blocked their flight as the ravine had blocked that of Mithradates; the rest escaped, leaving their camp to be plundered, "and it was then that the camels were taken that Agesilaus carried off to Greece.

Here again the active support of charging hoplites enabled an inferior cavalry force to defeat a superior one. But the hoplites by themselves could have done nothing. It was because the Greek cavalry threatened to defeat them in detail that the Persians had to concentrate their forces and offer battle. If Agesilaus had only had infantry, the enemy would have been perfectly safe, however much they were dispersed.

This action is also remarkable for the fact that the younger hoplites (twenty to thirty-year-olds) led the charge. I suppose them to have been equipped in the manner described in Chapter II, that is, unarmoured, save for shield, *pilos,* and greaves. It is noteworthy that Plutarch, who follows Xenophon's account of the battle, omits this detail. He says that Agesilaus mingled his peltasts with the cavalry and followed up with the hoplites.[31] He is not of course interested in technical military details. Agesilaus had organized his enfranchised helots, mercenaries, and allies by age-groups, just as the regular Spartan army was organized,[32] which shows that this arrangement was not necessarily bound up with the whole structure of the State.

The part played by the mercenary peltasts in the battle did them little credit. After the capture of the Persian camp, "the peltasts, as one would expect, turned to looting." But Agesilaus threw a cordon of his other troops round them, and saw to it that the plunder reached his own war chest.

The Spartans continued to employ peltasts on a large scale.[33] They had a useful part to play in a strategy based on plundering raids. When Agesilaus returned to Europe in 394 B.C., his army included many more peltasts than that of the Thebans and their allies.[34] But they played no part in the battle of Coronea, and when Gylis the *polemarch* (no doubt the commander of the *mora* that had come from Corinth to join Agesilaus) led the army home through the mountains of Phocis and Locris, it was the Lacedaemonian hoplites that covered the rearguard, not the mercenaries, while the other soldiers carried off goods and provisions from the villages.

> When evening drew on, as the Lacedaemonians were the last to withdraw, the Locrians followed them up, throwing stones and javelins. When the Lacedaemonians turned and pursued them, and struck some of them down, they no longer followed from behind, but threw their missiles from the higher ground on the right [that is, against the unshielded side]. The Lacedaemonians attempted to pursue up to the brow of the hill also. But when darkness was coming on, and in their withdrawal some were falling because of the roughness of the ground, and others because they did not see what was in front of them, and some too under the missiles, there were killed the *polemarch* Gylis and Pelles, one of his aides, and in all about eighteen of the Spartiates, some overwhelmed by stones, and others wounded by javelins. And if the men who were making their evening meal in the camp had not come to their rescue, they would probably all have been killed.[35]

That Gylis should have kept his steadiest troops to cover the rear, and should have been with them himself, was to be expected. But he evidently let the rest of his men get out of hand, no doubt because he did not expect any serious opposition. He may also have misjudged the length of his march through the mountains, as it was usual to start early and reach camp early, not to go on stumbling in the dark. No doubt the peltasts could have fought as well as plundered, but Gylis did not try to use them to support his hoplites against their light-armed opponents.

Mercenary peltasts became still more important after the arrival at Corinth, some time before 392 B.C., of a large contingent in the Athenian service. The early history of this force is obscure, but has been convincingly reconstructed by H. W. Parke out of scraps of evidence. Probably they were raised near the Hellespont by Conon, with the help of the Persian satrap Pharnabazus, and brought in 393 B.C. to the Isthmus of Corinth, where they were left under the commander who later made them famous, Iphicrates.[36]

Iphicrates, an Athenian of humble origin, was probably still less than thirty years old, but had distinguished himself in action at sea.[37] He is represented as a strict—indeed a savage—disciplinarian, who killed with his own hand a sleeping sentry, saying only "I left him as I found him." [38] His men were not allowed to sink into idleness in the intervals between actions, but were constantly drilled, and taught to fall in upon the signal in a formation so exact that "each man appeared to have been posted by an expert general." [39] That light-armed troops, skirmishing individually, with wide intervals between each man, should be drawn up with the exactitude required of hoplites in close formation, was an important innovation. The Athenians must have kept these men well paid, for their discipline contrasts with the usual behaviour of mercenaries.[40] Some part of them may have been poor Athenian citizens like their general, but if the force is indeed that raised by Conon, most of the men probably came from the north. Twelve hundred peltasts, mostly from Corinth, went back with Iphicrates to the Hellespont in 389 B.C. But our sources do not call them Thracians, so perhaps many of them were Hellespontine Greeks.[41]

Xenophon first mentions "the mercenaries under Iphicrates" at the battle of 392 B.C. inside the Long Walls of Corinth. Iphicrates and his men were on the extreme right of the allied line, not because they were given the place of honour, but because peltasts and cavalry were always put on the flanks in battles between hoplite armies.[42] They were not expected to have much influence on the main struggle, but might make themselves useful in retreat or pursuit. Xenophon has nothing further to say about Iphicrates and his men in this battle, except that the Corinthian exiles on the Spartan left defeated their opponents and broke through to the upper ground. In the cramped space between the walls, peltasts could not display their proper tactics, but they seem to have escaped serious disaster. After Iphicrates had become famous, the battle was remembered as his defeat,[43] but Xenophon treats it as a battle of hoplites against hoplites.

After the storming of Lechaeum by the Spartans, both sides held fortifications in Corinthian territory and had allies round about. A war of raids and counter-raids followed, and in this the peltasts began to distinguish themselves. They inflicted such losses on Phlius that the people of the town handed over their citadel to the Spartans for a time, despite fears that the trust would be abused for political ends. By 390 B.C., Iphicrates was making repeated raids into Arcadia, wasting the country and attacking the forts, from which the Arcadian hoplites dared not come out to meet the peltasts. "But," says Xenophon, "the peltasts on their part were so afraid of the Lacedaemonians that they did not approach their hoplites within javelin-range."

For already, pursuing them even from that distance, the younger Lacedaemonians had caught and killed some of them. So the Lacedaemonians despised the peltasts, but despised their own allies even more. For once the Mantineans made a sortie against the peltasts from the Long Wall running down to Lechaeum, but broke under the javelins, and lost some men killed in their flight. So the Lacedaemonians had the effrontery to mock their allies for fearing the peltasts like children scared of bogies. But they themselves operated all round the city of Corinth from their base at Lechaeum, with a *mora* and the Corinthian exiles.[44]

The Spartan tactics against peltasts were not new for they had been employed by Brasidas.[45] Nor were they exclusively Spartan. Thucydides, in his account of the retreat of the Thracians after the sack of Mycalessus, says that they defended themselves not unskillfully against the Theban cavalry, running out in front and turning back again in accordance with "their native system of tactics," [46] so it is possible that the Spartans copied these tactics from the Thracians.

The confidence of the Spartans was increased when Agesilaus, at the head of the whole army and supported by a naval squadron under his brother Teleutias, recaptured the Long Walls to Lechaeum, which the Athenians had restored, and escorted the Corinthian exiles while they celebrated the Isthmian Games in defiance of the Argives and their friends. A bold stroke against the territory beyond the Isthmus was intended to complete the ruin of the Corinthians, and, having induced the enemy to recall Iphicrates to the defence of Corinth itself, Agesilaus was entirely successful in one of his favourite plundering raids. But his victory was outweighed by a disaster which was to befall the Lechaeum garrison, caused by the conceit of the Spartans and the king's own faulty dispositions. For while the main army was away beyond the Isthmus, the one *mora,* or regiment, that had been left in garrison at Lechaeum was marching across the Corinthian plain to Sicyon and back, regardless of the far stronger enemy forces in Corinth itself.[47]

The object of the march was not even military. It was the custom for the men of Amyclae to return home every year to celebrate the festival of the Hyacinthia, even if they were on active service abroad. The Amyclaeans from the whole army had therefore been left at Lechaeum, and the *polemarch* of the Spartan *mora* there was to escort them on the first stage of their homeward journey, leaving the allied units in the garrison to hold the walls. The Spartan force consisted of a *mora* of about six hundred hoplites, and the cavalry *mora* attached to it, probably about sixty men, though Xenophon does not specify its numbers.

On the outward march, cavalry and infantry stayed together, and they met no enemy. But two or three miles short of Sicyon, the *polemarch* ordered the cavalry to escort the Amyclaeans some distance further, and then catch up while he himself turned back with the *mora* of infantry.

> And that there were many men in Corinth, both hoplites and peltasts, they well knew. But they despised them because of their former good fortune, and thought that nobody would attempt anything against them. But the men in Corinth—Callias, the general of the Athenian hoplites, and Iphicrates, the commander of the peltasts—saw that they were few in number and unsupported either by peltasts or by cavalry, and considered that it was safe to set on them with the peltasts. For if they marched along the road, they would destroy them by throwing javelins at their unshielded side, and if they attempted to pursue it would be easy for the most active peltasts to escape the hoplites.

Accordingly Iphicrates attacked, while Callias drew up his men not far from the city to support him.

In the fight that followed, the Athenian hoplites were not directly engaged, but by their presence they frustrated the Spartan "running out" tactics and so made an important contribution to the victory. The Spartans suffered a few casualties in the first attack by the peltasts, and the *polemarch* ordered the men of the ten youngest age-groups to run out and give chase in the usual manner.

> But when they pursued they caught nobody, being hoplites chasing peltasts from the distance of a javelin's throw.[48] For he ordered them to fall back again before the hoplites came into contact. When they fell back they were scattered, each man having pursued at his own best speed. And then Iphicrates's men turned round again, and some threw at them from the front again while the others ran obliquely beside them and threw at their unshielded sides.

In the very first pursuit they shot down nine or ten of them, which made them press their attacks far more boldly.

A second attempt at pursuit by the fifteen youngest age-groups was attended by even greater losses.

The cavalry now arrived, and joined in the next attempt to give chase, but merely rode out and wheeled round together with the infantry, instead of pressing their attacks until they killed some of the peltasts. Xenophon criticizes them severely, but the presence of the Athenian hoplites may have been one reason for their timidity. As he himself observes elsewhere,

> If an army is drawn up opposite another, and the cavalry ride out against each other, and pursue their antagonists as far as the enemy phalanx and flee as far as their own, it is a good thing to understand in these circumstances that as long as one is beside one's friends, one can with honour and safety be among the first to wheel round and set on with all one's might, but when one comes near the enemy, one must keep one's horse in hand.[49]

Greek cavalry, mounted on ponies, either bareback or upon a simple saddle-cloth, and in any case without stirrups, were not expected to charge and break regularly formed hoplites. They were skirmishers, not shock troops, and Xenophon recommends that they should carry javelins instead of long spears.

Certainly it was the approach of the Athenian hoplites that made the Spartans finally give way and run, after a last stand on a small mound a quarter of a mile from the sea. Xenophon puts their total losses, in all the fighting and their final flight, at about two hundred and fifty dead, of whom probably not a single one was killed by the Athenian hoplites. But the lesson of the fight seems to be, not that the best peltasts could defeat the best hoplites even on level ground, but that even the best hoplites could not fight effectively against a skillful combination of heavy and light infantry unless they were themselves adequately supported by other arms. Iphicrates himself compared the light-armed troops to the hands, the cavalry to the feet, the phalanx to the trunk, and the general himself to the head, and this sums up very well his action against the Spartan *mora*.[50]

Iphicrates's tactics would not have succeeded if the Spartans had been strong enough to engage the Athenian hoplites in pitched battle. He and Callias did not make the mistake of coming out against Agesilaus when he laid waste the plain two days later.[51] But after the withdrawal of the main Spartan army, Iphicrates was able to capture their forts in Corinthian territory, except Lechaeum itself. Agesilaus had lost his chance of forcing a decision at the Isthmus and turned his attention to Acarnania in the north-west, to gratify his Achaean allies. Here his troops were harassed by light-armed antagonists with whom they could not get to grips, but could not be prevented from ravaging the enemy's fields and carrying off their cattle, so that the Acarnanians came to terms rather than face a second campaign.

Iphicrates's victory may be contrasted with the defeat of the Spartan Phoebidas at Thespiae in the winter of 378–377 B.C. Once again it was an action of peltasts supported by hoplites against hoplites and cavalry, and began to the advantage of the peltasts. Thespiae was at the time in not very willing alliance with Sparta against Thebes, and the Thebans invaded its territory with their whole army as a reprisal for raiding by the mercenaries under Phoebidas, the Spartan governor. But Phoebidas pressed upon them with his peltasts, and nowhere allowed them to scatter from the phalanx, until the Thebans were glad to return faster than they had come, abandoning such plunder as they had collected. During the retreat, he continued to attack them boldly with the peltasts, and ordered the hoplites, citizens of Thespiae with little heart for facing Thebans, to follow in good order. The retreat continued until the Theban cavalry, who were no doubt acting as rearguard to their infantry, came up against a ravine, which compelled them to bunch together, and then turn and fight because they could no longer get away. If Phoebidas had had hoplites of the same quality as the Ten Thousand in close support of his peltasts, they chould have charged and beaten the Thebans as Mithradates was beaten. But his hoplites were following timidly a long way behind, and he had allowed his peltasts to straggle in the pursuit, so that there were only a few of them to meet the cavalry when they turned. Those few ran away, and, as Xenophon puts it, by their flight taught the enemy to pursue. Phoebidas himself and two or three others were killed fighting; the fugitives spread panic to the rest of his army, and they never stopped running until they found shelter within the walls of Thespiae, though the lateness of the day prevented serious pursuit and few were killed.[52] Phoebidas's fault was that he allowed himself to be carried away by his first success and did not keep his men properly in hand, rather than that he did not understand the function of peltasts and expected them to do work for which they were unsuited. This action demonstrated clearly the importance to peltasts of support from reliable hoplites.

Phoebidas's defeat has been justly compared with that of Teleutias in 382 B.C. Teleutias was encamped near Olynthus, but with a river between himself and the city, and engaged in the favourite Spartan pursuit of ravaging the country. The Olynthian cavalry, which had for some time remained within the walls in consequence of a defeat, came out and quietly crossed the river, obviously hoping to draw some of the enemy to attack them. Teleutias lost his temper at their impertinence; and it is to this loss of temper rather than to any basic misunderstanding of the functions of peltasts that Xenophon ascribes the mistakes that followed. Tlemonidas, the commander of the peltasts—locally recruited mercenaries under a Spartan officer—was ordered to pursue the Olynthians at the double, no doubt in the hope that they would fall into confusion at the river crossing and that some of them would be overtaken there. But they did not wait to be closely pressed, and their withdrawal across the river was made in good order. Instead it was Tlemonidas's men who became disordered, pursuing as though the enemy were already in flight. The Olynthians allowed as many of their pursuers to cross as they thought they could deal with, and wheeled round and charged, killing Tlemonidas and more than a hundred of his men. Teleutias, more angry than ever, snatched up his own weapons and led on his hoplites, ordering the peltasts and cavalry to join him. Again he carried pursuit too far, going right up to the city walls, from which his men were driven back in disorder under fire from the towers. The Olynthians sallied out, first cavalry, then peltasts, and finally hoplites, and, falling upon the enemy while they were still in confusion, killed Teleutias himself and utterly scattered his army, with heavy losses.[53]

Iphicrates won a second great success with peltasts against hoplites in 389 B.C., after he had been withdrawn with twelve hundred of his men from Corinth to the Hellespont. His own base was on the European shore. Abydos in Asia had been secured for the Spartans by Dercylidas after the sea-fight at Cnidus, and was now governed by Anaxibius, who marched along the coast to establish a garrison in the friendly town of Antandrus, taking with him a small force of Lacedaemonians, a thousand mercenaries recruited in the cities of Aeolis, and two hundred and fifty hoplites from Abydos. Iphicrates crossed the straits by night and hid his peltasts along the route by which the enemy were expected to return. His ships then sailed up the European coast by daylight, leading Anaxibius to believe that Iphicrates himself had gone with them to collect tribute. Anaxibius therefore took no precautions—not even waiting for favourable omens—before his return march, and allowed his army to become strung out along the track, with the men of Abydos in front, the mercenaries next, and himself and the Lacedaemonians in the rear. Iphicrates had placed his ambush above a point where a steep descent led to a plain, and waited until the Abydenes had reached the level ground, most of the rest of the army was making its way down, and Anaxibius himself was beginning the descent. Then the peltasts burst out of ambush, and Anaxibius realized that there was no hope of escape, seeing his own army was strung out along a narrow track, and considering that the men who had gone on in advance would obviously be unable to come to his rescue against the slope. Seeing moreover that they were all terror stricken at the sight of the ambush, he said to those who were with him, "Gentlemen, honour demands that I die here. But do you save yourselves with all speed, before the enemy close with us." With these words he took his shield from his shield-bearer, and fell fighting in the spot. And the boy stood by him, and some twelve of the Lacedaemonian governors who had come together from the cities were killed fighting by his side. But the others fell in flight, and the pursuit lasted as far as the city. About two hundred of the others were killed, and of the Abydene hoplites about fifty.[54]

This action demonstrated the quality of Iphicrates as a commander, not the superiority of peltasts over hoplites. Indeed it is likely that the mercenaries who made up the greater part of Anaxibius's force were peltasts themselves, though Xenophon does not say so.

It is notable that Iphicrates himself seems to have become dissatisfied with the traditional armament of peltasts, and to have introduced, probably towards the end of his career, a new type of equipment, designed for hand-to-hand fighting. Unfortunately we have no contemporary accounts of it, and there are no certain instances of peltasts using it in action.[55] Diodorus Siculus, after giving an account of the unsuccessful Persian attack upon Egypt in 374 B.C., adds a digression upon the military abilities of Iphicrates, who had commanded the Greek mercenaries under Pharnabazus.[56] As a result of the experience gained in the Persian service, Iphicrates made changes in the equipment of the Greeks, replacing the big shields that had slowed down their movements with *peltae* of proper proportions, making their spears half as long again (or doubling them, according to Cornelius Nepos),

and almost doubling the length of their swords. I do not suppose
that this means that he gave them five-foot claymores; perhaps
he replaced short dirks of the Spartan type with swords of the
length that seems to have been more usual in Greece—about two
feet, six inches.[57] The spears were probably about twelve feet
long. "Iphicratean boots, easy to untie and light," sound like a
modification of the usual Thracian boots, which were already
well known in Greece (Plate 17).

It has been well pointed out that the long spears must have
been for hand-to-hand combat, and that soldiers armed with
them could not have been expected also to run in upon their
enemies, throw a pair of javelins at close quarters, and run away
again without letting the enemy come to grips. The long spear
is not mentioned in Xenophon's accounts of Iphicrates's victories,
and would have encumbered the peltasts to no purpose in their
encounters with the Spartans.[58]

A twelve-foot pike is not only a weapon for hand-to-hand
combat, but one more suited to infantry drawn up in close order
than to individual skirmishers, and this suggests that Diodorus
is right in putting the introduction of the new equipment at the
time of Iphicrates's service under the Persians. For light troops
armed with missiles were to be found in Asia, and the great
need of the Persians, which they sought to supply by recruiting
Greek mercenaries, was always, from before the time of the
younger Cyrus down to that of Darius III, steady infantry capable
of forming a solid line of battle. Moreover, long spears were, and
had been for over a century, the characteristic weapon of the
Egyptian heavy infantry,[59] which Iphicrates and his men had
been hired to fight. I believe that Iphicrates may have found in
Egypt that, though his peltasts were excellent soldiers, they were
not what was needed for that particular war. So he turned them
into pikemen, borrowing their weapons from the enemy, but
retaining their own characteristic shields, which gave adequate
protection without impairing movement. The long wooden shields
of the Egyptians themselves were too cumbrous to be of service, at

least in Xenophon's opinion.[60] The peltasts were in fact to perform, with different equipment, the function of hoplites, though Diodorus is not stating the case quite correctly when he says that "those who were formerly called hoplites from their shields now had their name changed to peltasts from their *peltae*." [61]

Certainly the new "Iphicratean" equipment did not replace the hoplite shield and spear in the citizen forces of the Greek states, or in later mercenary armies in the Persian service. But its importance in the history of warfare may have been far greater than can be proved from the scanty ancient evidence. Modern scholars have suggested that when Philip II created the Macedonian phalanx, he borrowed ideas from Iphicrates as well as from the Thebans, among whom he had lived as a hostage.[62] The Macedonian phalanx was equipped with round shields, perhaps something over two feet in diameter, and managed by a baldric, so that the bearer had both hands free for his pike.[63] When Alexander the Great was fighting the Triballi in Thrace, the enemy launched carts downhill against the Macedonian infantry, and some men who were unable to get out of the way escaped by lying flat and covering themselves with their shields, which must therefore have been more substantial than *peltae*.[64] The peltasts in the Macedonian service are regularly distinguished from the phalanx, not only in the time of Philip II,[65] but in the Hellenistic period. However, the Hellenistic peltast may have used the Iphicratean pike; Lucian tells, with picturesque details, the story of how a Thracian peltast killed Arsaces, Governor of Media (whoever he was), and his horse. Parrying his enemy's long lance with his *pelta,* the Thracian presented his own pike (*sarissa*) at the horse's chest, and the animal, in full career, impaled both itself and its rider.[66] Of course, the story may have no historical value whatever—and at least one detail, the cavalryman's twenty-cubit lance, must be exaggerated.

Xenophon does not describe the tactics and armament of peltasts in detail every time he mentions them, but nowhere in his writings is there any suggestion that those whom he encountered

were anything but javelin-men. Sparta continued to hire mercenary peltasts in considerable numbers, and usually enfranchised
more helots when in need of hoplites.[67] So in the *Cyropaedia,*
when the Persian commoners are invited to take up weapons
and armour suited for close combat, such as have already been
issued to the peers, instead of their former bows and javelins,
Cyrus concludes with the words: "Whoever is content with the
station of a mercenary, let him remain in arms fit for servants." [68]

Peltasts were of particular value in the Spartans' long unsuccessful struggle to crush Thebes, because both sides tried to use
them to secure the mountain passes through which the invaders
entered Boeotia. Thus when Cleombrotus first commanded the
Spartans, late in 379 B.C., Chabrias guarded the route through
Eleutherae against him with Athenian peltasts. But Cleombrotus
took the route through Plataea, and his own peltasts destroyed
the guard of a hundred and fifty men on the heights. He did
not, however, press the campaign against Thebes, but contented
himself with securing Thespiae under a Spartan governor, Sphodrias, with a garrison of allied troops and money for the hire of
mercenaries.[69]

Sphodrias, by his foolish and treacherous attempt to surprise the
Piraeus, and Agesilaus, by his disgraceful failure to punish him,
turned the Athenians from timid support of Thebes to whole-
hearted co-operation in the campaign of 378 B.C. This campaign
displays a new and interesting feature, the use of fortified lines
on an unprecedented scale to protect the agricultural land. The
Spartans were dissatisfied with the conduct of Cleombrotus and
again gave the command to Agesilaus, in spite of his age. Agesilaus
crossed the mountains without difficulty, having secured the
passes in advance with mercenaries borrowed from the allied
state of Clitor—presumably peltasts, though Xenophon does not
say so. He established his base at Thespiae, but "finding the plain
and the most valuable part of the country fenced off with ditches
and stockades round about, he moved his camp from place to
place, and led his men out after the morning meal to ravage as

much of the country as lay on his side of the stockade and ditch." [70] Polyaenus is probably referring to this campaign in his story of how Agesilaus shifted camp two or three times a day, so that his allies, who were unwilling to devastate Boeotia, should do the damage in spite of themselves, by cutting down the trees in order to make their bivouacs.[71]

Xenophon speaks of the lines as being "round about" the agricultural land, but in fact they seem to have run roughly from west to east, starting somewhere south-west of Thebes, and ending beyond Scolus where Agesilaus passed them in the campaign of 377 B.C. Scolus has been convincingly identified by Professor W. K. Pritchett[72] with a site on the north bank of the Asopus river, which may have been incorporated into the defensive system, though Xenophon mentions only artificial works.

The Theban lines sound much too substantial to have been improvised in a day or two when the news came that Agesilaus was over Cithaeron. But if they were prepared well in advance, it seems that the Thebans and Athenians deliberately chose this method of defence instead of trying to block the passes as Agesilaus had expected them to do. One reason was no doubt a reluctance to commit their whole force to the defence of one pass, when the enemy might come by another, or to divide it between the passes. Behind the lines, the whole force could move from one threatened point to another as required. They probably also preferred to conduct their campaign close to their base at Thebes, because of the difficulty of supplying a mixed army of citizens and mercenaries for any length of time in the middle of the mountains. Peltasts alone had failed to stop Cleombrotus the year before, though in 376 B.C. the Thebans and Athenians did secure the passes against Cleombrotus, who, after vainly trying to drive them from the heights with his peltasts, turned round and went home again. But he was suspected of half-heartedness towards the war, if no worse.[73]

At the beginning of the campaign of 378 B.C., the Thebans and their friends observed Agesilaus, and when he came out of his camp, after the morning meal, their own forces moved along the inside of the stockade opposite him. They were too weak to offer battle in the open, but even the Spartans preferred not to lead their hoplites against another phalanx drawn up on top of a steep hill,[74] or behind fortifications. It was presumably during this part of the campaign that Chabrias's mercenaries, by the smartness of their drill, deterred Agesilaus from attacking them.[75]

Entrenchments and stockades were of course no novelties. Lines round besieged cities and fortified camps[76] were familiar features of Greek warfare. But this use of fortified lines to cover whole territories, with one army moving up and down looking for an unguarded spot and another constantly covering it, is a new development reminding the modern reader of the wars in Flanders during Queen Anne's reign. But Agesilaus had less difficulty than the Duke of Marlborough in outwitting the enemy. "When he realized that the enemy always appeared after the morning meal, he sacrificed at daybreak and led on as quickly as possible, and passed within the lines through an undefended place. After this he ravaged and burnt the country within the lines as far as the city." [77]

The failure to hold the lines did not discourage the Athenians and Thebans from repeating the same strategy in the next campaign, and again being out-generalled by Agesilaus. And the construction of similar defensive lines in Attica became part of Athenian military policy, so that Plato in his *Laws* speaks slightingly of the young men of Athens, who, unlike the Spartans, are sent out every year into the country to dig trenches at this point and build walls at that, as though this were the only way to stop an enemy crossing the frontier.[78] Brilliant field-work, admirably supported by excavation,[79] has recently shown that one fragment of these fourth-century defences, dating probably from the generation of Demosthenes and Philip of Macedon, rather than from that of Chabrias and Agesilaus, is preserved on the pass that leads from the plain of Eleusis to Acharnae—the pass used by Archidamus at the beginning of the Peloponnesian War, and now familiar to all who travel by railway between Athens and the Peloponnese. The fortification known as the Dema has long been an object of curiosity, and has been assigned to various periods, from the prehistoric age onwards, but is now known to be a relic of the Athenians' last struggle to keep their place as an independent world power, and has been convincingly dated to 337–336 B.C. Built on a rocky hillside instead of deep agricultural land, it consists (unlike the Theban lines) not of a ditch and stockade, but of a series of short dry-stone walls, each with its right-hand end (from the defenders' point of view) slightly advanced, and overlapping the left-hand end of its neighbour, so that between each pair of walls is a passage about a metre wide, through which a man, or file of men, might issue obliquely, with the shielded left side turned towards an enemy advancing from the west. Fortified posts, from which the defence could be co-ordinated by signals, crown the neighbouring heights. The whole system of works has been rightly shown to be designed for a bold and active defence by mobile infantry.[80] Perhaps, in view of Plato's words, we can imagine not mercenary peltasts only, but the young Athenians themselves, hoplites lightly equipped in the manner described in Chapter II, being trained to take their part. Files of hoplites issuing simultaneously through each gap and wheeling together to the left could support the peltasts who would no doubt lead the sortie. But the plans of the designer were never put into practice, for after the fall of Thebes, Athens saw the wisdom of peaceful submission to Alexander the Great.

The Theban lines were also designed to allow the defenders to make sorties, but the nature of the ground encouraged the use of cavalry, in which Thebes was always strong. Xenophon mentions one such cavalry action in the campaign of 378 B.C.; one evening when Agesilaus was already retiring towards his camp,

the Theban cavalry, who had hitherto been unseen, suddenly galloped through the sally-ports constructed in the entrenchment. They charged just as the peltasts, who were going off to

their meal, were getting their things together, and when some of
the cavalry were still dismounted, and some were remounting.
And they struck down many of the peltasts, and of the cavalry
Cleas and Epicydidas, Spartiates, and one of the *perioeci,* Eudicus,
and some Theban exiles, who had not yet mounted their horses.
But when Agesilaus turned about with the hoplites and came to
the rescue, his cavalry rode to meet the enemy's cavalry and the
ten youngest age-groups of hoplites ran with them [just as they
had done against the Persians at Sardis]. But the Theban cavalry
were like men who had taken wine in the heat of the day. For
they waited for the men who were charging them so as to throw
their javelins [instead of at once appreciating the situation and
making off], but threw short, and when they wheeled round
from this range twelve of them were killed.[81]

After the defeat and death of Phoebidas, the Spartans had
garrisoned Thespiae with a *mora* of their own citizen army, and
Agesilaus opened the campaign of 377 B.C. by ordering the
polemarch in command to secure the road over Cithaeron.[82] He
also passed the Theban lines without fighting, by ordering supplies
to be prepared for his army at Thespiae and so leading the enemy
to suppose that he planned to attack from the south-west, and
then making a forced march to the east. "And so by covering with
his army two days' march in one, he crossed the palisade by
Scolus before the Thebans came from guarding the point at
which he had formerly entered." He was thus able to ravage
the territory to the east of Thebes, as far as the borders of
Tanagra. When he withdrew past Thebes on his way towards
Thespiae, the Thebans, with their Athenian allies, of whose part
Xenophon says as little as possible, determined to intercept his
retreat and hazard a battle in a strong position with the ditch
and stockade at their backs. But Agesilaus, instead of advancing
directly upon them, led his men obliquely towards the undefended
city, and the enemy did not risk an attack upon his flank, but
"ran towards the city by the Potniae road, which was the safer

one. Agesilaus's plan was admired, in that by leading away from the enemy he compelled them to withdraw at the double." Both armies were now racing towards Thebes in column, along converging routes. The Thebans and their allies still had the upper ground, but they were probably in some confusion after hurriedly abandoning their position, and the Spartans were on their unshielded right side. Accordingly, as the Thebans ran past, some of the *polemarchs* ran upon them with their *morai*. Xenophon does not say so expressly, but it seems that the *morai,* still in column, were wheeled to the left, to attack the flank of the Theban column "head-on like triremes." Such a manoeuvre would of course have been unsafe if the Thebans had been drawn up in a phalanx awaiting them. When the Spartans tried to break the Arcadian lines round Cromnus in 362 B.C., they attacked in double file up a wagon-track, and the Arcadians received them in massed formation, with locked shields, and, though fewer in numbers, repulsed them with heavy loss.[83] The Thebans were running, not standing fast. But the *polemarchs,* each at the head of his *mora,* were exposing themselves, so that when the Theban hoplites threw their spears from the hilltops (an act of desperation which left them weaponless except for their swords and so in no condition to make a proper stand), one of the *polemarchs* was killed.

> None the less, the Thebans were driven from this hill too. So the Sciritae and some of the cavalry got up it and struck the last of the Thebans as they ran past to the city. But near the wall the Thebans turned round, and when the Sciritae saw them they withdrew, faster than at a walk. And none of them was killed. All the same, the Thebans set up a trophy, because the men who had climbed the hill retreated.

On the next day, when Agesilaus drew off towards Thespiae, the mercenary peltasts in the Theban service followed him up, calling on Chabrias, the Athenian commander, to support them.

Chabrias had commanded the peltasts—who may have been Athenian citizens, not mercenaries[84]—against Cleombrotus two years earlier, and mercenary hoplites in the previous campaign. He may very probably have had both peltasts and hoplites under him, and it is not clear from Xenophon's account which he was being called to provide. Hoplite or cavalry support was, as it turned out, what the peltasts needed, for the Olynthian cavalry, who now served under Agesilaus, turned upon them and killed many of them, chasing them uphill. Xenophon justly remarks that going up a ridable hill, horsemen quickly overtake men on foot.

Xenophon's narrative, besides making clear once more the necessity for troops of all arms to support one another, shows clearly that the hoplite armies of his day were not ponderous masses of heavily-armoured men, edging crabwise towards each other on the flat, but were capable, if necessary, of rapid manoeuvre even on hilly ground.

Hoplites of Xenophon's time also showed themselves ready, though no more so than those of the previous generation, to assault fortifications. Here again the co-operation of light infantry armed with missile weapons was important. It was under cover of a general discharge of javelins, arrows, and stones that the Ten Thousand stormed the stronghold of the Drilae;[85] and when they attacked the Metropolis of the Mossynoeci, the hoplites were formed with the *lochoi* in parallel columns, with the archers in the intervals between them.[86] One of the scenes on the second frieze of the Nereid Monument[87] shows hoplites rushing forward to mount a scaling ladder planted against a fortress wall, while archers support them with covering fire (Plate 14A). These archers, to judge from their Greek helmets and *spolades,* might be Cretans, like those who accompanied the Ten Thousand or, later, entered the Spartan service.[88] Herein the scene differs from another representation, more than two hundred years older, of hoplite mercenaries storming a fort in the service of an Eastern ruler. On the British Museum's silver bowl from Amathus—

Phoenician work of the mid-seventh century B.C.[89]—a hoplite storming column has planted its scaling ladder against the walls of a fortress defended by other hoplites, just as on the Nereid Monument. But the archers who give covering fire are long-robed Asiatics.

Ladders and battering-rams were the siege-engines with which Xenophon was familiar. Siege-towers, such as had been used by the Assyrians, were brought against Motya by Dionysius I, as Xenophon was no doubt aware. In the *Cyropaedia,* he gives a description of mobile towers, drawn by eight yoke of oxen, which were intended in the first place for attacking fortresses, but were also brought upon the field of battle to support the phalanx. He seems however to be drawing upon his imagination rather than his experience.[90] He once mentions a wooden "tortoise," used by Thibron in an unsuccessful attempt to cut the water-supply of Larisa in Aeolis.[91] He frequently mentions the storm of small places, such as Lechaeum, where the Boeotian garrison was killed, some on the walls and some on the roofs of the ship sheds to which they had climbed, or Sidus and Crommyon, taken immediately after, or Creusis, stormed in Cleombrotus's last campaign.[92] When Thebes was liberated in 379 B.C., the Spartan garrison in the Cadmeia trusted neither in the fortifications nor in their own courage, but being few, and seeing the valiant zeal of all the attackers, and hearing great rewards proclaimed for the first to mount the walls, declared their willingness to capitulate.[93]

When immediate assault gave no prospect of success, the Spartans still sometimes resorted to the old expensive method of blockade by lines of circumvallation, as at Atarneus, Phlius, or Corcyra.[94] Neither Xenophon nor Aeneas Tacticus, his contemporary and perhaps his former comrade in arms, saw anything comparable with the siege of Plataea a generation earlier. Nor do they seem to have had any understanding of the new methods introduced by Dionysius I in his wars with Carthage. When the Athenian democrats were advancing from the Piraeus upon Athens, Xenophon notes with approval that great stones, each large enough to load a wagon, were thrown down at random in the way.[95] This was hardly the sort of obstacle that would have delayed Dionysius's engineers for very long.

One brilliant piece of military engineering the Spartans did achieve, the damming of the river that flowed through Mantinea, until the waters rose and brought down the mud-brick city walls. But this remained an unique achievement, that mankind by this example might know better than to build cities with rivers flowing through them.[96] Their inability to deal with major fortresses was one of the chief reasons why the Spartans neither secured a permanent hold on Greece nor made lasting conquests in Asia.

When Agesilaus withdrew after his first campaign in Acarnania (390 B.C.), the Achaeans, at whose instance he had made the expedition, "thought that he had achieved nothing, because he had not brought over a single city, either willingly or unwillingly, to his side." He had attacked a few towns, at their insistence, but unsuccessfully. His own strategy had been the traditional one of ravaging the enemy's agricultural land and carrying off their cattle, and in pursuing it in the face of constant attacks by light-armed troops he had shown great skill. Next year his policy was justified, and the Acarnanians submitted rather than let their fields be devastated again, "considering that since their cities were in the open country, they would be as much besieged by the men who were destroying the corn crop as if they camped round about and besieged them." [97] So against the small towns of Greece, Spartan methods justified themselves. Against the Persian Empire they were useless. Xenophon may have been thinking of Agesilaus when he made Cyrus tell his allies that, unless they fortified bases in the country that they overran, and captured the enemy's strongholds, they would be like men sailing over the sea, who sail on and on, and the waters that they have passed over are no more their own than those that lie ahead.[98]

VIII

HOPLITES AGAINST HOPLITES: FROM THE NEMEA TO TEGYRA

However important the use of hoplites against, or in support of, troops of other arms had become, their chief function was still to fight other hoplites, though the battles of the early fourth century were very different from the ponderous confrontations that had filled King Xerxes and his courtiers with contempt. In the new conditions of warfare, the Spartans showed not only valour and discipline, but a tactical skill that was perhaps un-looked-for. After their victory at Mantinea in 418 B.C., the verdict of Greece had been that in "experience"—that is, tactical skill—they had shown themselves far inferior to their enemies, but in courage they were as good as ever they had been. Rumours of their degeneracy, that had circulated since the surrender on Sphacteria, were silenced, but it was the Athenians who had the greatest reputation for skill.[1]

The next major battle in which the Spartan citizen army was engaged was that of the Nemea in 394 B.C. This was not, as has been maintained by some modern writers,[2] the last of the old-fashioned collisions of unintelligently led masses. The Spartans manoeuvred to bring about deliberately results that at Mantinea had been the product of accident, in a way which suggests that they had studied the earlier battle and were profiting by its lessons.[3]

At Mantinea, the Spartans had deployed hurriedly, being surprised by the appearance of the enemy several miles south of their expected position. Their dispositions had been faulty, and made worse by the last-minute efforts of King Agis to correct them. Their right wing had outflanked the enemy's left, not by design, but from the cumulative effect of hundreds of men each edging towards his right-hand neighbour in order to protect his own right side as much as possible. And the same process had brought the enemy's right outside the Spartan left. Both armies had been victorious on their right and beaten on their left, but Spartan discipline was such that the victorious part of their army did not fall into confusion and was still able to act effectively to restore the situation in the other part of the field.[4]

But at the Nemea, the armies were encamped over against each other for several days, and both sides had time to plan their dispositions—or at least, if Xenophon is to be believed, on the one side the Thebans made deliberate dispositions to which the Athenians and their other allies were compelled to conform. And the Spartans too seem to have acted with calculated selfishness, so that the victory was gained with as few casualties to themselves as possible.

Xenophon's account of the battle is as follows.[5] Seduced by Persian gold, Athens, Argos, Corinth, Boeotia and the lesser states of Central Greece had made war upon Sparta while Agesilaus was in Asia, and had gathered their army at Nemea. Here they had to decide how to fight the forthcoming battle. It was particularly necessary to agree on the depth of the phalanx, so that each contingent should have a fair length of front to hold and the line should not be too short and easily outflanked. It was obviously expected that the Thebans would mass their men to a great depth, as they had done at Delium a generation earlier, and their allies considered that such tactics would lead to an unfair division of the work, and of the danger. Delaying to discuss such matters, they lost the chance of smoking the Spartans out like wasps in their nest. By the time they were ready to move against Lacedaemon, the Spartans had already come out under Aristodemus, the kinsman and guardian of the young king Agesipolis, and, picking up the Tegeans and the Mantineans as they marched, had reached Sicyon and forced their way into the coastal plain. The enemy came back north to meet them and camped behind the water-course of the Nemea stream, from which the battle takes its name. The Spartans, when they had approached within ten stades (about a mile and a quarter), also encamped.

A delay now followed, which must have lasted for more than a day, for the Boeotians were waiting their turn to hold the right wing of the allied line and the chief command. Evidently the early quarrels had been resolved by giving each city in turn the command for one day. Xenophon makes a corresponding pause in his narrative, in order to list the forces on each side, which were far larger than those that had fought at Mantinea.[6] On the Spartan side he lists six thousand Lacedaemonian hoplites, who must have included five of the six citizen *morai,* as well as the Sciritae from the mountainous frontier district, and a large contingent of newly enfranchised helots.[7] Nearly three thousand came from Elis and the neighbouring small towns, fifteen hundred from Sicyon, and not less than three thousand from Epidaurus and its neighbours. There were also the Tegeans and Mantineans mentioned earlier, and a force of Achaeans whom Xenophon mentions in the battle but forgets to list here, so that twenty-three thousand, which Diodorus gives as the number of foot, may be close to the truth.[8] Six hundred Lacedaemonian cavalry, three hundred Cretan archers, and four hundred slingers from the hill villages that had revolted from Elis at the time of Agis's invasion six years earlier made up the auxiliary forces, but played no important part in the battle.

On the other side Xenophon reckons twenty-four thousand hoplites, six thousand Athenians, about seven thousand Argives, as was reported, five thousand Boeotians, three thousand Corinthians, and not less than three thousand from all Euboea. These figures may be rather too large, especially that for the Argives, about which Xenophon himself seems to feel doubtful, but it seems probable that the Spartans and their allies were slightly outnumbered. The enemy had also more than fifteen hundred cavalry, mainly from Athens and Boeotia, and light-armed troops from Corinth and the north-west, whose numbers Xenophon does not record. They had harassed the Spartan advance from Sicyon, but were of no importance in the main action.

The battle was brought on by the Boeotians.

> As long as they held the left wing they were in no hurry to join battle. But when the Athenians were opposite the Lacedaemonians and they themselves held the right wing and were stationed opposite the Achaeans, at once they said that the omens were good and gave the order to prepare for instant battle. And first they neglected the agreed depth of sixteen men and formed their phalanx altogether deep, and then they led to the right, so as to outflank the enemy. But the Athenians, to keep the line from being broken, followed the movement, though they knew they were in danger of encirclement.

Here there is no suggestion of the spontaneous, unregulated edging to the right that Thucydides describes. The Boeotians (at least in Xenophon's opinion) did deliberately what earlier armies had done with no set plan, and advanced obliquely to the right, forcing their allies to conform or allow the line to be broken. From the allies' point of view, the situation was made worse by the fact that the Boeotians were massed to a great depth and so holding an unfairly short front. No doubt their expectation was that the breaking of the left of the enemy's line would decide the battle before the Spartans had time to develop their own plans, especially as the rapidity of the attack seems to have surprised everybody, friend and foe alike (Fig. VI A).

For a while the Lacedaemonians did not perceive the enemy's advance, for the ground was wooded. But when they raised the paean, of course, the Lacedaemonians realized what was happening, and immediately gave their own orders to prepare for a general engagement. When each contingent had been drawn up as instructed by the Spartan officer attached to it, the order was given to follow the leader, and the Lacedaemonians too led off to the right. So far did they extend their wing that, of the ten Athenian regiments, six were opposite the Lacedaemonians and four opposite the men of Tegea.

(Again, this was a deliberate movement and probably planned beforehand, not improvised on the spur of the moment. Since Xenophon speaks of "following the leader," not just of conforming to keep the line unbroken, it seems that they actually moved to the right in column before turning back into line to face the enemy when they had taken enough ground to the right.) Six Athenian regiments should have amounted to thirty-six hundred men out of six thousand, and if their line was of the agreed depth, their front will have been two hundred and twenty-five men long. We are not told the depth of the Spartan line, but supposing it to have been twelve deep, as later at Leuctra, the whole front will have been five hundred men long, of whom more than half (about two hundred and seventy-five) will thus have extended beyond the Athenian left, with no enemy hoplites opposite them at all. Moreover this half will have been made up of the citizen *morai,* on the right of the line. We should probably allow about a yard for each man in calculating the actual distance covered by the front.

Xenophon's narrative continues: "When they were less than a stade [about two hundred yards] apart, the Lacedaemonians sacrificed the she-goat to the Goddess of the Wild, as the custom is, and led against their opponents, bending round the part of their line that extended beyond them in order to envelop them." How such a manoeuvre was to be carried out is briefly explained by

Xenophon in his account of the imaginary battle between Croesus and Cyrus and will be discussed in due course.[9] If it was completed without interference, the result would be that a second Spartan phalanx would be drawn up at right angles to the first, "like the letter gamma," facing inwards towards the exposed flank of the Athenians. Though Xenophon's language, here and later, literally implies "encirclement," it is evident, both from what he says in the *Cyropaedia* and from the actual event of the battle, that he does not in fact mean a ring surrounding the enemy on all sides. This second phalanx now advanced across the battlefield, cutting up the enemy contingents one after another.

> When the armies met, the allies of the Lacedaemonians were all beaten by their adversaries, except the men of Pellene [Achaeans on the far left of the Spartan army] who, being opposed to those of Thespiae, resisted them, and on both sides men died in their places. But the Lacedaemonians themselves defeated that part of the Athenians that was opposed to them, and, enveloping them with the extended part of their line, killed many of them. They themselves suffered practically no loss and advanced in good order [across the battlefield at right angles to the original axis of advance (Fig. VI B)] and passed the other four regiments of the Athenians before these regiments returned from the pursuit, so that none of them was killed, unless they lost one or two casualties in the encounter with the Tegeans. But the Lacedaemonians encountered the Argives withdrawing, and the story goes that when the first *polemarch* was about to meet them face to face [he would be on the right of the line, and apparently intended to wheel his *mora* round again, until it faced the original rear, to block the enemy's retreat] somebody shouted out to let the foremost pass [as other Spartan commanders are recorded to have done, to avoid dangerous frontal encounters, in accordance with advice shouted at the last moment by experienced veter-

ans].[10] When this was done, the Lacedaemonians struck at the unshielded sides of the enemy as they ran past, and killed many of them. And they also came upon some of the Corinthians as they retreated. And then the Lacedaemonians encountered some of the Thebans as they returned from the pursuit and killed many of them. After this, the defeated first of all fled towards the walls. But when the Corinthians barred them out they again bivouacked in their old camp. But the Lacedaemonians also withdrew, and set up a trophy where they had first joined battle with the enemy. Such was the issue of this battle.

Only eight of the Lacedaemonians are reported to have been killed,[11] and in the circumstances this may well be true. If, as Plutarch says, the Spartans sacrificed an ox to Ares when they out-generalled their enemies, but only a cock when they beat them in open fight,[12] this was clearly an occasion for the greater offering. They do not seem to have been greatly distressed by the heavy casualties of their allies, though Agesilaus played his part as champion of Greece against Persia, and when he was told that nearly ten thousand of the enemy had been killed (certainly an exaggeration) bewailed the loss to Hellas of enough men to have conquered all the barbarians, had they lived.[13]

Diodorus says that eleven hundred of the Lacedaemonians and their allies were killed, and twenty-eight hundred of the other side, and these figures seem reasonable.[14]

Xenophon, who was with Agesilaus at the time, must have heard the official Spartan account of the battle, and may also have had the chance to discuss it with Dercylidas, who had fought in it, and brought the news to Agesilaus as he was marching home from Asia. Perhaps Dercylidas himself, not Aristodemus, whose chief qualification for command seems to have been his royal blood, had suggested the Spartan plan of action. There seems to be no reason, therefore, to doubt that Xenophon gives a true account of the battle, from the point of view of the Spartan hoplites. But his story leaves us to guess the answers to a number of questions on which he might have enlightened us had he been present himself.

How were the armies (and especially the Lacedaemonians) able to manoeuvre in good order upon ground which was sufficiently wooded to conceal the first stage of the Theban advance? Why does the water-course, which lay between the camps, not appear in the account of the battle?

Apparently the Boeotians and their allies were encamped directly behind the water-course. The Spartans were therefore more than a mile away from it, and the battle took place entirely on the Spartan side. It would be a reasonable precaution against surprise for the Spartans to have encamped neither among, nor on the very edge of, woods, and the trees that covered the first stage of the enemy advance very probably grew close to the water. We may therefore imagine an open space several hundred yards wide in front of the Spartan position, upon which the battle took place. The defeated enemy were not driven into the water-course because the Lacedaemonians advanced parallel to it, across the battlefield from right to left, and so were not in a position to take advantage of the fugitives while they were re-crossing.[15]

Why did the Athenian cavalry not check the enveloping movement of the Spartan right wing, and give effective support to their beaten hoplites, as they had done at Mantinea in 418 B.C.?

Both sides may be presumed to have posted their cavalry on the wings. But perhaps the whole of the Spartan cavalry was on the right wing and was sufficient to hold the Athenians in check. Here especially we may regret that Xenophon, the cavalry expert, is not giving an eyewitness account.

Why did the four regiments of Athenians who had broken the Tegeans, and themselves suffered no serious losses, not fall upon the rear of the Lacedaemonians? Why did the victorious allies not attempt to re-form on a new front and offer an effective resistance to the Spartan progress across the battlefield?

The answer to both these questions is probably inadequate

discipline. After the combat and short pursuit, their ranks were broken and they were no longer under the effective control of their officers. They had chased the enemy for as long as there was a chance of catching him, but men who had thrown their shields away could run faster than men who kept them (again, where were the Boeotian cavalry during the pursuit?). They could, of course, occupy the enemy's camp and perhaps capture any slaves who had not chosen to run away with their masters, but there was probably little else in it worth taking, since they were not fighting Persian satraps. For the same reason the Spartans were not tempted to occupy the enemy's camp. The best thing for the allies to do was to fall back to the battlefield, re-form their ranks, set up a trophy and wait for the enemy to ask permission to bury his dead. The Spartans were on them before they could re-form. They were no longer armies but armed crowds, and were only interested in escaping along the ways left open for them.

Why did the Spartans not attempt a longer pursuit? Plutarch, who sometimes regarded the past too sentimentally, would have said that their own traditions forbade it. Lycurgus the Lawgiver had instructed them to pursue only as far as was necessary to confirm the victory, both in order to avoid the effusion of Greek blood (but this consideration does not seem to have weighed very heavily with the victors of the Nemea, whatever Agesilaus may have felt), and so that the enemy might learn that he had more to gain from flight than from resistance.[16] But in fact hoplites, however good they were, were not capable of prolonged pursuit. If they kept their formation and their shields, they were slowed down; if they abandoned either, they could no longer fight effectively should the enemy turn on them. Even light-armed troops were wise not to press pursuit too far.

Disciplined though the Spartans were, they were well advised not to try to cross the water-course and wooded ground that separated them from the enemy's camp. If the enemy should rally, they were now heavily outnumbered, as their own allies had disappeared from the scene, except for the Achaeans. And the enemy were greatly superior in cavalry. If Aristodemus had been as rash as Phoebidas and Teleutias, he would very probably have suffered the same fate, and the army that he would have imperilled consisted not of mercenaries and allies but of the irreplaceable Spartan citizen regiments. Moreover the Spartans may have thought that in gaining possession of the battlefield and of the dead they had done enough, not for that day only but for the whole war. After the battle of Mantinea. King Agis had not pressed the pursuit, but his victory had destroyed the coalition against Sparta. Many of the victors of the Nemea may have thought that the demonstration of Spartan superiority that they had just given would frighten their enemies back into good behaviour. But those enemies were now backed by Persian money and by the fleet which Persia had given to the Athenian Conon. "Good behaviour," which in 418 B.C. had seemed to mean acceptance of Spartan leadership, now meant submission to oligarchies supported by Spartan soldiers, and the oppressive rule of Spartan military governors.

The war therefore continued, and the first operations of both sides turned upon the march of Agesilaus from Asia,[17] bringing with him not only the best part of the army, with which he had vainly dreamed of conquering the western provinces of the Persian empire, but a large part of the treasure amassed in years of plundering those provinces—including the famous camels taken at Sardis. The news of the victory at the Nemea reached him at Amphipolis, on the border between Thrace and Macedonia, and he hurried on, defeating, as he passed through Thessaly, the famous Thessalian horsemen with the mercenaries that he had raised for the Persian Wars. The report of the naval defeat at Cnidus followed that of the victory of the Nemea, and Agesilaus entered Boeotia to find an army including contingents from all the enemy states waiting for him, but also a large reinforcement of Spartan citizens to stiffen his allies, mercenaries, and enfranchised helots. A *mora* had been sent from the army outside Corinth, and it was joined by half another, which was in garrison at Orchomenus, and to these were added local contingents from Orchomenus and Phocis. In addition to his hoplites, Agesilaus had a strong force of peltasts, far outnumbering those of the enemy, and cavalry equal to theirs, but the battle was once more settled by the hoplites, without the auxiliary troops playing any important part. Neither Xenophon nor any other ancient author commits himself to a definite statement of numbers, but the armies were probably smaller than those that fought at the Nemea, and evenly balanced in strength.[18]

The Thebans and their allies were waiting in the plain of Coronea, through which Agesilaus had to pass, drawn up facing north, with their backs to Mount Helicon. Again the Lacedaemonians and Thebans formed the right wings of their respective armies, and so did not meet face to face in the first shock, the Lacedaemonians being opposed to the Argives and the Thebans to the men of Orchomenus.

> As they advanced to the encounter there was at first deep silence on both sides. But when they were about a stade apart, the Thebans raised the war-cry and came on at a run to close with the enemy. When there were still three hundred feet between the armies, there ran out against them from Agesilaus's line the mercenaries under Herippidas [who included the remnants of the Ten Thousand whom Cyrus had raised][19] and with them Ionians and Aeolians and Hellespontine Greeks, and all these joined in the charge, came to spear thrusts, and routed their opponents. But the Argives did not receive the men who were round Agesilaus [the Lacedaemonians, including no doubt the "newly enfranchised" helots who had been in Asia, as well as the eight hundred and fifty-odd men from the citizen *morai*] but fled to Helicon.

That is to say, the Argives, unlike the opponents of the mercenaries and Asiatic Greeks, ran away without coming into physical contact with the Lacedaemonians at all. Some of the mercenaries were actually crowning Agesilaus with the victor's wreaths when the news, surely not wholly unexpected, came that the Thebans had broken through the men of Orchomenus and were among the baggage—the Persian plunder whose safe conveyance was one of the main objects of the campaign.[20]

> He immediately countermarched his phalanx and led against them. And the Thebans too, when they saw that their allies had fled towards Helicon, wishing to break through towards their men, closed their ranks and came stoutly on. For what happened next Agesilaus can unquestionably be called brave, but he did not choose the safest course. For he could have let the men who were breaking through pass, and then followed, and fallen upon those in the rear. But instead of doing so he closed with the Thebans face to face.

In fact, the Thebans, who had no doubt all fought at the Nemea, had learned their lesson, and kept together as a disciplined body despite the temptation of plunder. But Agesilaus had not learned from the reports brought to him, any more than he was to learn four years later from what the allies told him about Iphicrates and his peltasts.[21]

> And striking shield against shield they pushed, fought, killed, and were killed. At last some of the Thebans broke through to Helicon, but many were killed as they retreated. And when Agesilaus had gained the victory, and, being wounded, was being carried towards the phalanx, some of the cavalry rode up and told him that about eighty of the enemy, with their arms, were sheltering in the temple, and asked him what to do. But he, though he had received many wounds, did not forget what was due to the gods, but ordered them to be allowed to depart freely without any improper treatment. Thereupon, for it was already late, his men took their evening meal and went to sleep. But early in the morning he ordered Gylis the *polemarch* [no doubt the commander of

the *mora* from Corinth, later killed on the march through Locris[22]] to draw up the army in battle order and set up a trophy,
and for all the men to crown themselves in honour of the god and
for all the flute-players to play.

But though Agesilaus thus formally claimed the victory, and the
Thebans formally acknowledged defeat by requesting a truce for
the recovery and burial of their dead, they were encouraged by
the thought that their own men had not had the worst of their
own encounters with the enemy. So at least says Plutarch.[23]
Diodorus says that more than six hundred of the Boeotians and
their allies were killed, and three hundred and fifty of Agesilaus's
army.[24]

"Tactics," in the sense of drill, won the battle. Not only did
Agesilaus face his phalanx about, but his men later succeeded in
opening their ranks to let the Thebans through. Some of them
had already done the same thing against the Persian chariots at
Cunaxa,[25] but it was far harder for men who were actually locked
in close combat to carry out such an operation without falling
into confusion. Later military writers praised Agesilaus,[26] but in
fact he had done nothing but place his men where the enemy
would have to fight them or run away. In their campaigns against
Persia, he and his men had become used to enemies who broke
at the sight of Greek hoplites charging, and no doubt the conduct of the Argives encouraged them to believe that their Greek
opponents would be little more formidable than Asiatic infantry.
Even the Thebans had avoided a face-to-face encounter with the
Spartans at the Nemea. But now they were compelled to fight,
and the resulting battle was, in Xenophon's opinion, "like no
other in our time." [27] No doubt the men who had been at the
Nemea told him quite truthfully that the fighting there had not
been nearly as hard. Whether he would have repeated his judge-
ment (as he did) after the battle of Leuctra if he himself had
fought there is open to doubt.
After his victory, Agesilaus was able to dedicate at Delphi

the tithe of his Persian spoils, amounting to a hundred talents. Phocis and Orchomenus were secured for the Spartans. But both sides now transferred their main effort back to the Isthmus of Corinth, where the Spartans had a secure base in Sicyon, and their enemies in Corinth itself.

In 392 B.C., the Spartans were able to repeat on a smaller scale their victory of the Nemea.[28] Two of the aristocratic party at Corinth—driven to desperation by the ravaging of their land, the forced union of their city with Argos, and the impious murder of their own friends and leaders—admitted Praxitas, the commander of a Spartan *mora* in garrison at Sicyon, into the Long Walls that connected Corinth with its port of Lechaeum. Corinth itself stood some two miles from the sea, upon a series of terraces sloping down from the north side of the great fortress of Acrocorinth. Below the last of these terraces a steep scarp, up which the modern road zigzags with difficulty, falls into the coastal plain. The Long Walls ran north and south across the plain to the port of Lechaeum, not only securing communications between Corinth and the sea, but barring the movement of hostile armies between the western part of the Corinthian plain and the Isthmus.[29] Praxitas, having arranged for another *mora* to take over the garrison of Sicyon, was admitted by night through the gates where the conspirators were on guard, with his own men, some Sicyonians, and a hundred and fifty Corinthian exiles. His men were too few to form a line of battle across the space between the walls, and therefore entrenched themselves as best they could with a ditch and stockade, and waited for reinforcements. Their position, with a Boeotian garrison in the port at their backs,[30] was most insecure, but they were left undisturbed for the first day.

On the second, the Argives arrived in full strength, and Praxitas drew up his men for battle, with the Lacedaemonians on the right, the Sicyonians next them, and the Corinthian exiles on the left, with their flank resting on the eastern Long Wall. The mercenaries under Iphicrates were on the enemy right. In the cramped space between the walls, peltasts could not skirmish effectively, and they seem to have given way without much of a fight. The Argives were in the centre and the Corinthians from the city on the left, so that the Spartans were opposed to the least reliable of the enemy's troops.

Xenophon does not say how many men fought on each side, but as he gives the number of Sicyonians at the Nemea as fifteen hundred, and apparently not all of them took part in the attack on the Long Walls, Praxitas probably had no more than two thousand men, of whom less than six hundred were Lacedaemonians. The combined force of Argos and Corinth must have been far less than the ten thousand reported in 394 B.C.; quite apart from battle casualties, the strength of the Corinthians had been reduced by the massacre and exile of the "best" citizens. But Praxitas was very heavily outnumbered. The enemy had no doubt of their ability to overrun his "contemptible little army" and advanced immediately. They defeated the Sicyonians, and, breaking through the stockade, pursued them to the sea and there killed many of them.

There followed the death of Pasimachus, the commander of the Spartan cavalry, and his men, killed when they dismounted to fight on foot with shields taken from the Sicyonians[31]—an incident which reveals a good deal about the Spartan attitude to cavalry service, and to their allies. But meanwhile "the Corinthian exiles defeated their opponents and broke through to the upper ground and came close to the fortifications round the city. And the Lacedaemonians too, when they saw the defeat of the Sicyonians, came out to the rescue, with the stockade on their left hand." That is to say, having apparently disposed of their Corinthian opponents with an ease that rendered description unnecessary, the Spartans came out of their lines and, as they had done at the Nemea, re-formed their phalanx facing towards their original left, preparatory to sweeping the battlefield from side to side. The Argives remembered their earlier defeat, but, unlike the Thebans, had not learned how to avoid a repetition of it.

When the Argives heard that the Lacedaemonians were behind them, they turned and came tumbling out of the stockade again at a run. And those of them who were on the extreme right [as they retreated—the original left] were killed by the Lacedaemonians striking into their unshielded sides, but those who were towards the wall [the eastern Long Wall] retreated towards the city in a crowd with great confusion. When they encountered the Corinthian exiles and realized that they were enemies, they turned back again. But then some climbed up by the stairways and jumped down from the wall and perished, and some, pushing around the stairways, were struck down and killed, and some were even trampled underfoot by each other and suffocated.

The "wall" here is still the eastern Long Wall, not the wall of the city, from which the Argives had been driven by the Corinthian exiles. The "stairways" (whose presence is hard to account for on the *outside* of the city wall, even if one translates them as "ladders") are the regular permanent stairways on the *inside* of the Long Wall for gaining access to the rampart walk. Some of the Argives escaped as far as the ramparts, but there was no way of getting down on the other side, and some at least of those who tried to jump were killed.

But the Lacedaemonians had no difficulty in picking their victims. For God then gave them a work that they would not even have prayed for. For how could one disbelieve that it was by Divine Providence that a multitude of their enemies should be delivered into their hand, terrified, panic-striken, exposing their bare sides, not one turning to fight, but all in every way working for their own destruction? Indeed at that time so many men fell in a small space that, whereas men are accustomed to see heaps of grain or timber or stones, there they saw heaps of corpses.

So much for Spartan reluctance to shed Greek blood.

The victory was followed by the storming of Lechaeum and

the death of its Boeotian garrison, and it was a long time before any other hoplites dared to attack the Spartan citizens regiments, though Callias was prepared to support Iphicrates and his peltasts in 390 B.C.

The Corinthian War was ended by the "King's Peace" of 387 B.C., by which Persian rule over the Greeks of Asia was acknowledged, and in return the European Greeks were guaranteed an "independence" which for many of them meant government by oligarchies of "the best people" supported by Sparta. The terms of the peace also gave Sparta an excuse for preventing the Thebans from consolidating their rule over Boeotia, on the grounds that the freedom of the smaller Boeotian towns was guaranteed, and for interfering in the north to stop Olynthus from dominating the neighbouring Greek cities. In 382 B.C., the Spartan commander Phoebidas, on his way north with reinforcements for the Olynthian war, was persuaded by a party of Theban traitors to seize the Cadmeia, the citadel of Thebes. His action was supported by Agesilaus and the Spartan authorities. "If he has injured the interests of Sparta, it is right for him to be punished. If he has aided them, the ancient law allows freedom of initiative in such cases." This was too much even for Xenophon, who had been brought up to regard Sparta as the embodiment of the aristocratic ideal, was devoted to his old commander Agesilaus, and was tied by self-interest to the Spartans, who had established him in an estate that seems almost to have been a little principality.

One could give many examples, from the histories of Greece and of other nations, to show that the gods do not neglect impiety and sin. But now I shall speak of the present instance. The Lacedaemonians, who had sworn to allow the independence of the cities, seized the citadel of Thebes. And they were punished by none other than the victims of their injustice, they who had never yet been beaten by any one of mankind. As for the Theban citizens who brought them into the citadel and wished to enslave their country to the Lacedaemonians, so that they themselves could rule it as tyrants, no more than seven of the exiles sufficed to overthrow their government.[32]

The liberation of Thebes in 379 B.C. brought to the fore Epaminondas and Pelopidas, devoted friends, unselfish patriots, able statesmen, and soldiers of genius.[33] The career of Epaminondas is recognized as opening a new era in military history, and in Pelopidas he had not merely an efficient instrument but a true partner. No proper contemporary account of these great men survives, and nothing is more to be regretted in Xenophon's *Hellenica* than his neglect of them. To be fair, I believe that most of his omissions are due rather to want of system and faulty enquiry than to deliberate dishonesty and the wish to belittle the achievements of a rival to his own hero Agesilaus. The name of Epaminondas is omitted from his inadequate notes on the battle of Leuctra, but in describing the campaigns of Mantinea in 362 B.C., he pays due tribute to the skill of the Theban general, though he does not disguise his dislike of him.

Diodorus Siculus and Plutarch preserve material from writers favouring the Theban side, though we do not know for certain who those writers were, or how accurately their information has been transmitted, or how reliable that information was in the first place. My own belief (which I will try to justify insofar as the battle of Leuctra is concerned) is that Plutarch, in his *Life of Pelopidas,* transmits accurately information from an intelligent and reliable fourth-century source,[34] and I accept his account of the rebuilding of the Theban military strength in the years 379–371 B.C.

The military traditions of Thebes were in some respects distinct from those of the other Greeks. The plain of Boeotia had long produced good cavalry, and a still older tradition of chariot warfare was reflected in one of the most remarkable of the ancient institutions from which Epaminondas and Pelopidas created their new army. This was the Sacred Band of three hundred picked men. Every member of it was the sworn lover of another, and of these pairs one was known as the "charioteer" and the second as his "crew." But chariots had disappeared from the battles of European Greece before those battles began to be described in detail by historians. Xenophon, in the *Cyropaedia,* explains the disadvantages of the old-style chariotry, "used formerly at Troy and even at the present day by the Cyrenaeans," in which the chariot served to transport into and out of action a warrior who fought on foot. "It seemed to Cyrus that what ought to be the strongest part of his force, since the noblest men were on the chariots, was playing the part of skirmishers and making no great contribution to overcoming the enemy. For three hundred chariots provide three hundred fighting men, and they use twelve hundred horses." In fact two-horse chariots were the rule at Troy, according to the *Iliad.* But the waste of man and horse-power was of course a principal reason for the replacement of chariots by cavalry, when men had learned to control in battle sufficiently powerful ridden horses. "And the fighting men probably have as charioteers those whom they especially trust, the noblest. These are another three hundred men, who do no harm to the enemy whatever." [35]

It is not surprising therefore that chariotry of this type was in the classical age only a dim memory of the heroic past, or a curious survival in remote Cyrenaica. But the tradition of "the Sacred Band" is at least as likely to have been a genuine survival as a late romantic invention, and indicates that the force itself was ancient, unlike the picked citizen regiments who were enrolled for full-time military service at Argos and Syracuse in the late fifth century.[36]

Be that as it may, at Delium in 424 B.C., where they are first recorded, the Sacred Band all fought on foot as hoplites. At that time they formed the "cutting edge," the front ranks of the phalanx which were carried on by the mass of men behind. In forming this mass to a depth of twenty-five men, and concentrating their strength upon the right wing, the Thebans, or their general Pagondas, introduced a new concept into Greek warfare.[37]

Yet it is possible that the lesson that victory on one wing could decide the issue of a hoplite battle had been learned from the Athenians. In 457 B.C., the Athenian general Myronides defeated the Boeotians in the great battle of Oenophyta, of which no full account survives. He ordered the left wing to charge first when the signal was given, and then hurried to the right, where he encouraged his own men and disheartened the enemy by proclaiming the victory on the left.[38] But, since the story only comes to us from a late and unreliable source, not too much can be made of it.

The defeat of the Athenians at Delium marked the end of a long series of Theban reverses, going back to before the Persian wars, and including the great battle of Plataea, where they fought on the Persian side. For nearly a century the Boeotians had generally been beaten by the Athenians, except when they were fighting as part of armies led by the Spartans. At Delium, the Athenians, knowing that the Boeotians would have to fight without help from the Peloponnese, had deliberately provoked a trial of strength, and had been beaten. The deep mass of Theban infantry on the right wing was the instrument of victory.

The Thebans fought no pitched battles between Delium and the Nemea, thirty years later, but it is evident that they continued to drill and manoeuvre in their deep formation, so that at the Nemea their allies expected them to adopt it. At Coronea, they kept their formation and their discipline and showed themselves no less able than the Spartans and their mercenaries to reverse their front and fight a second action immediately after the first. They also showed that their deep formation could break through the Spartan line. But breaking through on a comparatively narrow front was not in itself sufficient to secure the victory, and some means had to be found of preventing the wings of the longer enemy line from closing in on the flanks and rear. However encouraged the Thebans may have been by the battle of Coronea, they did not risk another general engagement against the Spartans during the Corinthian War.

Nor did Epaminondas and Pelopidas at once hazard a pitched battle in their war of liberation. In the campaigns of 378 and 377 B.C., the Thebans and their Athenian allies only faced Agesilaus's army when they had the advantage of position, and then Agesilaus did not care to attack them. Boeotia was repeatedly laid waste, and at one time the Thebans were almost starved into surrender,[39] but later it was remembered against Agesilaus that by repeatedly making war on the Thebans, contrary to the precepts of Lycurgus, he had compelled them to become trained soldiers. When he came home wounded from Boeotia he was mockingly told that they had given him a good fee in return for the lessons that he had taught them. "But," says Plutarch, "the true teacher was not Agesilaus, but those who calculated their opportunities and skillfully set the Thebans like hounds upon their enemies, and when they had had a taste of victory and self-esteem brought them safely back again." [40]

During the Spartan occupation of the Cadmeia, Epaminondas had encouraged his countrymen to wrestle with the garrison, in order to learn for themselves that they were not inferior man to man. But now he declared that "the hoplites must train their bodies not just as athletes but as soldiers. He made war on fat men, and chased one away from the army, saying that three or four shields would hardly cover his belly." [41]

While Epaminondas was training the mass of the army, Pelopidas was entrusted with the re-building of the Sacred Band, which was henceforth to be used as an independent striking force. Plutarch's account[42] is as follows:

> The Sacred Band, as they say, was first formed by Gorgidas[43] from three hundred picked men, who were quartered in the Cadmeia and exercised and maintained by the city. For this reason they were called the City Band. For in those days men commonly called "citadels" "cities." Some say that this body consisted of lovers and their beloved.

After justifying this system with legendary examples, he describes how Philip of Macedon was moved by the sight of the bodies of the Sacred Band after their last fight at Chaeronea, and continues:

> This sacred band, then, was distributed by Gorgidas through the front ranks, and placed in front of the whole phalanx of hoplites. So the valour of these men was not displayed, nor was their strength used for a common purpose, since it was diluted and mingled with a greater quantity of inferior material. But Pelopidas, when in their action at Tegyra their valour blazed forth uncontaminated and conspicuous, no longer dispersed them nor broke them up, but, using them as a complete body, faced danger in the forefront of the greatest struggles.

He concludes with a comparison of noble natures, fired by generous emulation in a common struggle, with racehorses, which gallop faster when harnessed in a chariot team than when loose.

The action at Tegyra was in itself a minor affair, and Xenophon makes no mention of it. Living in retirement in the country, he seems to have been content to jot down the news that came to him, without pursuing his historical enquiries very seriously, or indeed having any very clear idea of the ultimate outcome of the events that he records. In his later books he is more of a chronicler than a historian, and if his chronicle misses an event which his informants doubtless preferred not to publicize, we need not accuse him of deliberate dishonesty. Plutarch, looking back over the centuries, sees the wars of Sparta and Thebes in historical perspective, and recognizes in the obscure action of Tegyra the forerunner of the decisive battle of Leuctra.

After the failure of Cleombrotus to invade Boeotia in 376 B.C., the Spartans had turned their main effort to the sea, in the hope of reducing Athens by famine and then making a descent upon the Boeotian coast. But the Athenians under Chabrias defeated the Spartan fleet and then themselves took the offensive by sea. So the Thebans were left free to complete the work that they had begun after the death of Phoebidas, and attack the oligarchies which still ruled the smaller Boeotian towns in the Spartan interest, though the common people had already fled to Thebes.[44] Plutarch mentions, besides the defeat of Phoebidas at Thespiae, successes gained by Pelopidas over the Lacedaemonians at Plataea and at Tanagra,

> where he routed many of them, and killed Panthoidas the governor. But these actions, though they encouraged the victors to self-esteem and boldness, left the conquered not wholly subjugated in their minds. For they were not properly drawn up, nor engaged in open and regular pitched battles, but their defeats occurred in raids made as opportunity offered, and when they set on the enemy and encountered them in flight or pursuit.[45]

It might have been added that the beaten men were allies and mercenaries, though under Lacedaemonian commanders.

But though the Spartans lost their bases in southern Boeotia as a result of Cleombrotus's failure to keep open the routes across Cithaeron, they were still able to secure Orchomenus, in the north-west, on the borders of Phocis, lying between the hills and Lake Copais, at that time a huge undrained swamp. The Phocians hated their Boeotian neighbours and so remained staunch allies of the Spartans, who were able to communicate with them by sea across the Corinthian gulf and so to supply or relieve their garrisons in Orchomenus.

In 375 B.C., the Spartan garrison consisted of two *morai*—a third of their own citizen army.[46] The *morai* seem to have taken this duty in turn, and when their relief arrived, the *polemarchs,* Gorgoleon and Theopompus, decided to make a raid into Locris before marching home, in the same way that Praxitas had captured the Long Walls to Lechaeum when his *mora* was relieved of its garrison duties at Sicyon. The raid was reported to Pelopidas at Thebes, but not the arrival of the relief garrison, and he marched on Orchomenus with the Sacred Band and some cavalry, hoping to find the city undefended. Finding that the relieving garrison had already arrived, he began to march home round the north side of Lake Copais, with the steep rocky hills close upon his left and the swamp upon his right, made impassable by the overflowing of the Melas river.

At Tegyra, a place sanctified by myths of Apollo, whose temple stood a little above the road, the Thebans encountered the Spartans returning from their raid. One of the scouts ran up with the words "We have fallen into the enemy's hands." "Why not they into ours?" replied Pelopidas, and ordered his cavalry (which had presumably been covering the rear in case of a sortie from Orchomenus) to come to the front and lead the charge, while his three hundred hoplites closed their ranks in order to break their way through the enemy, who outnumbered them by nearly four to one.[47] On their side the Spartan *polemarchs* advanced confidently, but Pelopidas attacked their line at the very point where they were themselves posted, and they fell at the first encounter. As the Thebans pressed on, striking down and killing their opponents, the Spartans were seized with fear and tried to open their ranks (as they had done at Coronea) for the enemy to pass through, evidently supposing that they still only wanted to escape. But Pelopidas used the path opened to him as a way into the heart of the enemy, instead of an escape route, and continued to attack them until their entire force was put to rout. He did not attempt a long pursuit, for fear of the garrison of Orchomenus, and did not apparently wait for the Spartans to request a truce for the recovery of the dead, remaining only long enough on the battlefield to strip the bodies and set up a trophy. The Spartan losses, for which no figures are given, were not large enough to reduce their fighting strength significantly, and they retained possession of Orchomenus. But, as Plutarch puts it, his secret was now out that it was not only the Eurotas and the ground between Babyce and Cnacion that produced good fighting men. The Spartans had "never before, in so many wars against Greeks and barbarians, been defeated by an enemy whom they outnumbered, or even by equal numbers in a pitched battle."

IX

THE "BATTLE OF THYMBRARA"

The armies of Thebes and Sparta, as they prepared for the decisive encounter that both sides must have expected, represented two distinct systems of tactics. The Spartans preferred a long line, so that their highly trained professionals could manoeuvre against the flank and rear of the enemy, as they had done at the Nemea and Lechaeum. The Thebans, the bulk of whose army, even after so many years of "schooling" by Agesilaus, was still unprofessional, counted on breaking through the Spartan line with a solid mass of men. The rival systems have been compared to the French column and British line at the beginning of the nineteenth century,[1] but Agesilaus's redcoats formed a deeper line than Wellington's, having no firearms. And in addition to the general citizen levy, the Thebans had their Sacred Band.

Xenophon examines the advantages and disadvantages of both tactical systems in the *Cyropaedia,* in the set-piece battle in which Cyrus defeats King Croesus of Lydia and his allies. Since there is only one pitched battle of this sort in the whole book, Xenophon has to arrange for Cyrus to be both "over-winged" and "overfiled" and to deal with both dangers in turn. In spite of the scythed chariots and other oriental trimmings that garnish the story, the tactics are essentially those of Thebes and Sparta, and, although the *Cyropaedia* was written many years after the battle of Leuctra,[2] I believe that its imaginary story may be examined before a discussion of the historical battle, for the light that it throws on the theory of Greek tactics.

The story in the *Cyropaedia* has nothing to do with the fate of the real historical King Croesus, who is believed by modern scholars, relying on a contemporary Babylonian chronicle, to have perished with his kingdom.[3] Xenophon does not even try to make his version agree with that of Herodotus, which probably passed for truth in fourth-century Greece, though he does borrow the story of the camels that frightened the Lydian cavalry horses —a detail which would have interested him personally and which may conceivably be historical. His Croesus is not saved from self-immolation by the miraculous intervention of Apollo, either to be carried off to the Earthly Paradise at the Back of the North Wind, as the Greeks first claimed when faced with the necessity of explaining what return the god had made for so many rich offerings, or to end his days as an honoured counsellor at the Persian Court.[4] Xenophon does not even make him climb onto the funeral pyre. He submits to his destiny, cheerfully greets Cyrus as his master, advises him on how to secure the wealth of Sardis for his army without giving the city over to sack, and gives a new version of his dealings with the oracle, saying that it is all his own fault for trying Apollo out to see if he spoke the truth—something that one should never do to a gentleman, let alone a god—and misunderstanding the advice to "know himself."[5]

Xenophon's story includes one detail which is sometimes supposed to be historical, and is in any case of great interest. This is the presence on the Lydian side of a large force of Egyptians. In actual fact King Amasis of Egypt, whom Xenophon does not mention by name, was a member of the coalition against the historical Cyrus, though he escaped the fate of his allies, and Egypt was not conquered by Persia until both Cyrus and Amasis were dead. Here again Xenophon departs from history, and extends the Persian Empire to its widest bounds in his hero's lifetime.[6] Amasis, like the other pharaohs of the Twenty-sixth

Dynasty, employed large numbers of Greek mercenaries, most of them from the coastal cities of Asia Minor, and the suggestion that some of these might have been sent home to help Croesus is a natural one.[7] But no ancient writer except Xenophon mentions this Egyptian aid, and Xenophon makes it clear that *his* Egyptians were not Greek mercenaries.

They were first reported to Cyrus by the Indian envoys, whom he had sent to spy on the enemy under cover of a pretended embassy, as "Egyptians, said to be twelve myriads in number, with shields that come down to their feet and great spears (such as they use even now) and slashing swords."[8] In saying that this equipment was "such as they use even now," Xenophon was remembering what he himself had seen at the battle of Cunaxa, where, near the left wing of the enemy, behind the scythed chariots, the Greeks had glimpsed, facing them, "hoplites with wooden shields coming down to their feet. These were said to be Egyptians."[9] Eighty years earlier the Egyptian marines who accompanied King Xerxes to Greece were distinguished by their huge spears and large shield-rims;[10] and in the first half of the fourth century, information from Egypt itself—once more temporarily independent—was available from men who had served under Agesilaus, Chabrias, or Iphicrates, on one side or the other, in the wars between Persia and the rebel kings. There is no doubt therefore that Xenophon's contemporaries would have recognized true Egyptians, not Ionian mercenaries, in the *Cyropaedia.*

In Xenophon's story, these Egyptians were the only troops in Croesus's army who distinguished themselves for gallantry, and after their surrender, Cyrus (who could recognize valour even in his enemies) rewarded them with the grant of certain cities, "some up country, which even now are called cities of the Egyptians, and Larisa and Cyllene beside Cyme near the sea, which their descendants hold to this day."[11] That a Larisa in western Asia Minor was indeed "Egyptian" in Xenophon's time and that its inhabitants remained true to the Persian cause is confirmed by an account of its unsuccessful siege by Thibron in the *Hellenica*.[12] Larisa was the name of several ancient cities, but "Egyptian" Larisa is mentioned only by Xenophon, and appears from the context to have lain in Aeolis. A Larisa is named by Herodotus immediately after Cyme in his list of Aeolian towns, but there is no reason to suppose that it was "Egyptian" in Herodotus's time, or in 425 B.C., when it appears to have paid tribute as a member of the Athenian League.[13] Nor is there any reason to believe that Larisa in Aeolis was "Egyptian" at any period later than Xenophon's lifetime. It would seem therefore that, unless Xenophon's "Egyptian" Larisa is a city unknown to any other writer, and unless the Larisa in Aeolis that existed both before and after his time was for some reason unknown to him, his "Egyptian" city is the same as Herodotus's "Aeolian" one, and the story that the Egyptians had been settled there ever since the time of Cyrus the Great is not true. But there is no reason to doubt that they were there in Xenophon's lifetime, and if he attributed their settlement to "Cyrus" it would be in the same spirit as that in which he makes "Cyrus" responsible for all the details of the armament and organization of the Persian army, or "Lycurgus" responsible for all Spartan institutions.

In actual fact, during Xenophon's lifetime a remarkable succession of Egyptian adventurers were active on the west coast of Asia Minor. In 412 B.C. the Persians, taking advantage of the Athenian disaster in Sicily, re-established their hold over Cyme and Phocaea, and probably Larisa as well, and very shortly afterwards Thucydides first mentions Tamos, at that time lieutenant-governor of Ionia under the satrap Tissaphernes.[14] This Egyptian from Memphis later commanded the fleet of the younger Cyrus, after whose death he fled to Egypt, expecting a friendly reception from Psammetichus, who had rebelled against the Persians and set himself up as king. But Psammetichus, forgetting past benefits, murdered Tamos and all his family, except for one son Glus, or Glos.[15]

This Glus had accompanied Cyrus to Cunaxa, but after the

battle he succeeded in making his peace with Tissaphernes, who used him to observe the movements of the Greeks. He was associated with Procles, who had inherited from his ancestor, the exiled Spartan king Demaratus, the lordship of Teuthrania, a small town not far from "Egyptian" Larisa.[16] There were many such little principalities under the Persian king and his satraps,[17] and it is at least possible that the towns that Xenophon knew as "Egyptian" had been granted to Tamos for his services and passed from him to Glus. Neither of them is actually named as the ruler of the towns, but no other Egyptian is known to have been a prominent figure in this area at this time.

It is unlikely that Tamos had himself inherited the "Egyptian" towns from ancestors established in them by Cyrus the Great, not only because the towns themselves are not called "Egyptian" before Xenophon's time but because Tamos himself is said by Diodorus to have been a Memphite by birth and to have had dealings with Psammetichus, the rebel king,[18] which would have been more likely if he had himself come from Egypt than if his family had been settled in Aeolis for a hundred and fifty years.

Glus later commanded the Persian fleet against Evagoras of Cyprus. The expedition assembled at Phocaea and Cyme; these are not the obvious bases for an attack on Cyprus and may have been chosen because the admiral had local connections. After Glus had changed sides and been murdered, another Egyptian adventurer, Tachos, established himself for a time on the crag of Leuce, near Cyme, but with him the line of Egyptians came to an end.[19]

If Xenophon gives to the Egyptians in the *Cyropaedia* a heroic part, Tamos and Glus seem better able to fill it than the fugitives from Cunaxa, who ran away before the Greeks even came to blows, or the native Egyptians in the service of their own kings, whom the Greek historians represent as far inferior to their own countrymen. If they are moved by prejudice, it was no doubt a prejudice that Xenophon shared.

There is, however, a special reason for the appearance of the

Egyptians in the *Cyropaedia*. In Cyrus and his nobles can be recognized an idealized representation of the Spartan kings and their peers, and in Cyrus's most formidable opponents can be seen the Thebans. Several arguments point towards this conclusion.[20] Even the name "Thebes" had its Egyptian associations. But I will here restrict myself to my proper subject—the part played by the Egyptians in the imaginary battle between Cyrus and Croesus, and the resemblance between their tactics and those of the Thebans as described by Xenophon in his historical works.

I shall, then, treat the battle in the *Cyropaedia* purely as fiction, written in order to teach certain tactical lessons, the fruits partly of Xenophon's own experience, partly of his study of contemporary battles at which he had not himself been present. I do not think that Xenophon imagined for one moment, or wished his readers to imagine, that the real battle between Cyrus and Croesus, or the forces engaged in it, bore any resemblance at all (except, as I have said already, in the matter of the camels) to what he describes.

In the *Cyropaedia,* then, Croesus did not "cross the Halys to destroy a mighty empire," but, after assembling his army on the banks of the Pactolus, advanced to Thymbrara, "where even now is the assembly of the barbarians of the lower provinces under the king." [21] Here, a little to the east of his capital, Sardis, he awaited the enemy.

Cyrus had meanwhile reorganized and improved his own army, encouraging his officers to see to their men's equipment, and the men themselves to practise the arts of war, by holding competitions for generous prizes, just as Xenophon had seen Agesilaus do in Asia.[22] He had already won a great victory over the Assyrian king, and had advanced almost to the walls of Babylon, but without making any permanent conquest of the country, though he had captured a few small forts and been joined by lesser kings and even Assyrian nobles who were glad to escape their master's cruelty. He had used the horses captured from the enemy to turn his Persian foot-soldiers into cavalry "so that from that day to this the Persians hold to this custom, and no Persian gentleman will be seen going anywhere on foot if he can help it." [23] He had replaced the light "Trojan and Libyan" chariots with huge armoured vehicles armed with scythes, and had constructed wooden towers, each drawn by eight pairs of oxen, primarily for assaulting enemy fortifications but also to support his infantry in the field. He had heartened his men by telling them to imagine the effect that the news of these preparations would have on the enemy, and by reminding them of the conduct of Croesus at the earlier battle, when, seeing his Assyrian allies defeated, he had not come to their help but made off as fast as he could. Now, after seeing that all was in readiness for the long march,[24] and having obtained favourable omens from the sacrifices, he advanced.

On the last stages of the march to Cunaxa, Xenophon had seen the discipline of the younger Cyrus's army slacken, and the men marching at-ease, leaving their shields to be carried with the baggage, while their leader relaxed in his chariot. There were, of course, cavalry patrols out ahead, and when, contrary to Cyrus's expectation, his brother's army appeared ahead in battle order, there was time for the men to get their weapons and deploy from a disorderly column into a regular line. But there was no opportunity to make the most favourable dispositions to meet the enemy, whose own order of battle seems to have been unknown until his army was actually in sight. The Greek mercenaries should have faced the king and his life-guards instead of the territorial infantry on his left, but when Cyrus ordered Clearchus to lead his men against the centre of the enemy's army, they had not yet finished their deployment; "the barbarian army continued to advance steadily, but the Greek army, still remaining on the same ground, was being formed in order from the men who were still coming up." Xenophon says that Clearchus was unwilling to uncover his right flank by leaving the river, but it would have been impossible to move ten thousand men while they were still in the act of deployment without falling into confusion, and to attempt to do so across the front of the advancing enemy would have been disastrous. Clearchus did the best he could, and does not deserve Plutarch's scornful comments. The real blame rests with Cyrus, who let himself be surprised.[25]

Xenophon takes good care not to let the hero of the *Cyropaedia* fall into the same errors.[26] This Cyrus had spies in the enemy's camp—Indian ambassadors, taking a most unfair advantage of their diplomatic status, and a pretended deserter from his own army, a young man whom Cyrus hoped to cure by absence and activity from the effects of an unhappy love affair. Cyrus also marched in good order, with patrols out in front. He therefore knew well in advance what forces Croesus had collected, and did not blunder into the enemy's position but was able to plan his approach and the battle that followed.

> The scouts in advance of the army thought that they saw in the plain men gathering fodder and wood, and pack-animals carrying loads of the same, and others grazing. And when they looked still further they seemed to perceive either smoke or dust rising in the air. From all these indications they were almost certain that the enemy's army was somewhere near.

Upon receiving this report, Cyrus ordered his scouts to remain in their posts of observation, and sent forward a regiment of horse to take prisoners. Meanwhile, the rest of the army was ordered to halt "in order to make those preparations that he thought needful before making close contact with the enemy." The first necessity was the morning meal. At Cunaxa, the Greeks had gone into action unfed, and most of them got no dinner that night either.[27] In the *Cyropaedia,* the men were to be fed and given a night's rest before the battle.

While the men were eating, Cyrus summoned his officers, including those of the auxiliary forces, to a conference. Some prisoners were brought in, who said that they had gone foraging beyond their outposts, for there was a shortage of everything because of the size of the army. The difficulty of supplying a large army which remained for any length of time in one position has already been mentioned [28] as a possible reason for the failure of the Greeks to make better use of the strong natural defences of their states.

Having learned that the enemy's army was two parasangs distant (generally rather over six miles, but the parasang is to be taken as an hour's march and the actual distance would vary)[29] and that his men were in poor heart at the news of the Persian advance, Cyrus next asked what they were doing, and was told that they were being drawn up in battle order, "and yesterday and the day before they did the same thing," and that Croesus himself drew them up, with the help of a Greek and a Mede, who was said to be a deserter from Cyrus's army. By bringing in the "Greek," Xenophon is no doubt hitting at Greek drillmasters in the service of Eastern princes, like Phalinus, who "was with Tissaphernes and held in honour, for he claimed to be an expert in matters of tactics and hoplite fighting." [30] The "Mede" was of course Araspas the spy, and Cyrus's prayer that he might "take him as I wish to do" was at once granted, for scarcely had the prisoners been dismissed than Araspas rode in to make his report.

From him Cyrus learned that the enemy was drawn up thirty deep, both foot and horse, except the Egyptians, and covered a front of about forty stades (roughly five miles). The Egyptians had insisted on following their native custom, and drawn up each myriad in a square, a hundred men deep on a front of a hundred. "And Croesus allowed them to adopt this formation, though most unwillingly. For he wished to outflank your army as much as possible." Here is an echo of the complaints of the allies at Nemea, when the Thebans "neglected the agreed depth of sixteen men, and formed their phalanx altogether deep." [31] When Cyrus asked why the enemy wanted to outflank him, the spy Araspas gave the expected reply, "In order to envelop you with the extra length of their line." Cyrus replied cryptically, "Let them see whether the envelopers may be enveloped." He ordered his officers to see to the equipment of the forces they commanded and on the next day to have both men and horses fed as soon as he sacrificed, and to give orders to the junior officers, *lochagoi,* and *taxiarchs* to draw the army out in line of battle (phalanx is, as always, Xenophon's word) with each *lochos* of twenty-four men in double file, to give a depth of twelve (compare Fig. I B).

One of the "captains of ten thousand" here asked whether Cyrus considered this depth sufficient against the deep formation of the enemy. Cyrus's answer no doubt represents the official Spartan doctrine. "When a phalanx is too deep for the men to reach the enemy with their weapons, what harm do you think they do to the enemy or good to their friends?" The reader may wonder at this point how the rear ranks of the imaginary Persian phalanx, twelve deep,[32] or the real Spartan or Athenian phalanx, eight, twelve, or sixteen deep, "reached the enemy with their weapons." Even the Macedonian pikes were only long enough for the spear heads of the first five ranks to project in front of the face of the phalanx.[33] Certainly no Greek hoplite could have reached the enemy from the rear ranks with his shorter spear, and Xenophon's imaginary Persians had no spears at all, only scimitars. So Cyrus, or Xenophon, was claiming too much when he implied that the twelve-deep formation allowed every man to bring his weapons into action at once. But it was obviously true that the deeper the formation, and the shorter its front, the fewer men were directly engaged with the enemy.

What function, then, did the men in the rear serve? Those in the very rear rank, closing each file, were picked men, preferably experienced veterans, chosen from among the oldest and most sensible, the foundation of the structure of the phalanx, to use Socrates's metaphor.[34] Their duty was to urge on their own files from the rear, to prevent any slackness or turning back. They might also on occasion be called on to lead them, should it ever be necessary to retire without countermarching the files to bring the leaders to the new front. But their main duty was to

provide the impetus that carried the leaders forward; "iron cuts
iron best when the cutting edge is well tempered and the weight
behind it is sufficient." [35] Xenophon makes Cyrus address his rear-
rank men as follows before the great battle against the King of
Assyria:

> Gentlemen, you are of the peers by birth, and have been picked
> because you seem in other respects to be equal to the stoutest fight-
> ers, but, owing to your age, to excel them in prudence. You have
> a place no less honourable than that of the front-rank men. For
> you, being at the rear, may see the good men and by your en-
> couragement make them even better, and if anyone plays the
> coward you will observe him too and prevent him. You are con-
> cerned in winning a victory, if anyone is, on account of your age
> and the weight of your equipment. Now if the men in front call
> to you and give the order to follow, see to it that not even in this
> are you inferior to them, but call back to them to lead more quickly
> against the enemy.

I would gladly (especially in view of the hint that the oldest
men will find it hardest to run away in the event of a defeat)
share General Boucher's opinion that these rear-rank men were
a purely Athenian institution: "Les Lacédémoniens estimaient
que les hommes d'une même file étaient des braves et ils plaçaient
à sa tête le plus brave de tous. Les Athéniens, eux, estimaient que,
si la plupart des soldats sont des braves, il peut s'en trouver qui
ne le sont pas." But since the Spartan army was not made up
entirely of Spartiates in Xenophon's time, and the Persian "peers,"
from whom Cyrus's rear-rank men were drawn, were certainly
modelled on those of Sparta, I do not think that we are justified
in saying that these picked men closing the files were found only
in the Athenian army. [36]

The rear ranks, then, gave weight and impetus to the "cutting
edge" in front. When the front ranks on either side met, the
men behind them did not stand waiting for their leaders to be

killed before taking their places; still less did the front-rank men fight for a time and then fall back to the rear to give some-one else a turn.[37] The rear ranks closed up, and when we read of one Greek army pushing another back,[38] or unable to bear the weight of another's attack,[39] the words are to be taken literally, not as mere figures of speech, as they would be in an account of a modern battle.

With reference to the later Macedonian phalanx, we are ex-pressly told that, though the rear-rank men do not come directly into action, they ward off missiles with their upraised pikes and "pressing on with the advance, by the actual weight of their bodies give force to their leaders' attack, and make it impossible for the front-rank men to turn about to the rear." [40] And the advice not to draw up cavalry in as many ranks as infantry, because not only do horses take up more space than men but they fall into confusion if they come into contact with each other,[41] might be taken to imply that infantry were expected to come into contact with their comrades. When, therefore, Xeno-phon, for instance, makes no express mention of the rear ranks in his account of the struggle at Coronea,[42] I believe it is because he assumed that everyone would understand what they were doing, not because they were disengaged while their leaders struck shield against shield, pushed, fought, killed, and were killed.

But the impetus of the leaders' advance was not of course always in direct proportion to the number of bodies behind them. Most of the force of a man shoving with fifty others in front of him would be absorbed by the bodies between him and the front rank, unless the effort of the whole mass was somehow co-ordinated. Resolute men, formed twelve deep could hope to struggle for some time against a far deeper formation. Critias and his men got no advantage of being massed fifty deep against Thrasybulus and the democrats in Munychia.[43]

Xenophon therefore had some reason to make his Cyrus wish

"that these hoplites were drawn up ten thousand deep instead of a hundred, for then we should have the fewest to fight with," and to claim that he himself was giving his phalanx a depth that would allow every part of it to do its duty in support of the rest.[44] But (perhaps because Xenophon remembered Thrasybulus's dispositions at Munychia) Cyrus next ordered javelin-men to be drawn up behind the men-at-arms, and archers behind the javelin-men.

> Who would post them in the front rank, when they themselves admit that they would never stand to fight hand-to-hand? But if they are screened by the armoured men they will stand fast, and the javelin-men will throw, and the archers shoot, over all those in front of them, and so injure the enemy.

(This had worked at Munychia, where the democrats were drawn up on a slope. But on level ground, light infantry drawn up behind the phalanx could only shoot blindly up into the air. Their missiles were not only unaimed but spent before they fell on the enemy, and did little damage.[45] In the first action against Mithradates during the retreat of the Ten Thousand, the Cretan archers had proved ineffective when compelled to shoot from behind the hoplites.[46]).

Last of all Cyrus posted the "rear-rank men, as they are called." [47] These were to play the same part as the file-closers of the phalanx in the earlier battle, but had to watch the light-armed troops as well, and were therefore instructed in their duties without mincing words. Xenophon makes Cyrus repeat his favourite metaphor of the house and its foundations, and continue as follows: "Do you [addressing the officers of the heavy-armed troops] draw up your men as I order, and you, the officers of the peltasts, in the same way draw up your *lochoi* behind them, and you, the officers of the archers, in the same way behind the peltasts." This passage makes it quite clear that Xenophon did not intend to incorporate a certain number of peltasts and archers in the *lochoi* of heavy infantry; the light-armed troops were in separate units under separate officers.

> But you, who are in command of the rear-rank men, keep your men behind and order them each to mark the man in front of himself and encourage those who are doing their duty and threaten strongly those who are playing the coward. And if any man turns round with a view to playing the traitor, let them put him to death. It is the duty of the men in the front ranks to encourage by word and deed those who follow them. But you who are posted behind everybody must make the cowards more frightened of you than of the enemy.

Having thus disposed his infantry, Cyrus next ordered the siege-towers to come behind them, with the oxen that drew them as close as possible to the line. After them were to come the baggage, then the coaches with the women. "For if all these follow us, they will give the appearance of numbers, and will give us the possibility of setting an ambush, and, if the enemy attempt to encircle us, will compel them to make their enveloping movement wider. And the more ground they cover, the weaker they must be" (Fig. VII A).

The reference to the possibility of "ambush," and Cyrus's earlier remark about "enveloping the envelopers" are then clarified. Cyrus had kept "two picked thousands" of foot and two of horse, for whose commanders Xenophon took the trouble to produce "Persian" names. He had earlier sometimes broken the rule that the general should know and use the names of his officers, but we may suppose that Xenophon's want of invention is to blame rather than a lapse on his hero's part.

Cyrus addressed them as follows:

> Do you, Artaozus and Artagerses, each keep your thousand of infantry behind the baggage and the coaches. And you, Pharnuchus

and Asiadatas, do not draw up the thousand of cavalry which each of you commands in the line with the others, but put them in array by yourselves behind the coaches. Then come to me with the other leaders. You must make your preparation in the expectation of being the first who will have to engage. And you, the commander of the men on the camels, draw them up behind the coaches, and do whatever Artagerses orders.

Cyrus next ordered the three divisions of scythed chariots, each a hundred strong, to be drawn up, one in column upon each flank and the third in line in front of the army. Abradatas, King of Susa and the husband of Panthea, whose beauty and faithfulness to her husband had caused the unhappiness of Araspas, was allotted the post of danger in the vanguard. Abradatas's chariot, with eight horses yoked in pairs to four poles,[48] is probably a product of Xenophon's imagination, but the others, with four horses yoked in pairs to two poles, are no doubt descriptions of what he had actually seen. They were not, however, Cyrus's invention, but Assyrian in origin.[49] They were far wider and heavier, and also far less manoeuverable than the Greek four-horse chariot, which had only one pole, to which the middle horses were yoked, those on the outside being attached to traces.

The Persian formation may thus be summed up as a line of heavily-armed infantry, twelve deep, backed up by a mass of light infantry, siege-engines, carts, baggage animals and coaches, behind which were concealed special detachments of cavalry and infantry, and also the camel corps. In front and on each flank were the scythed chariots, and it also appears from the narrative (though Cyrus inexcusably neglects them in his orders) that all the Persian cavalry, except the two "thousands" placed "in ambush," formed two wings, drawn up on each flank of the infantry, under Cyrus's trusted friends Chrysantas and Hystaspas (Fig. VII A).

At Amphipolis in 422 B.C., Brasidas had given Clearidas, his lieutenant, a picked detachment with which to follow up the main attack, "for the following-up force is more alarming to the enemy than that which is actually engaged in the fighting." [50] In the first battle before Syracuse, half the Athenian army had been in the line, the remainder being drawn up in the rear in hollow square, partly in order to protect the baggage but also so that they might support any part of the line that they observed to be in difficulties.[51] Xenophon himself, in the Ten Thousand's battle against the army of Pharnabazus in 400 B.C., placed three "guard companies" behind the centre, left and right of the phalanx, "so that, if need arises at any point, they may come to the support of the phalanx, and the enemy, themselves in disorder, may encounter fresh and unbroken troops." The generals did not however keep these reserves in their own hand, but trusted the commander of each detachment to act on his own initiative.[52]

But the special forces that Cyrus had "placed in ambush" behind his baggage train were clearly intended to serve a different purpose from any of these. They were not to follow up the first blow, but to be ready to begin the battle themselves. They were obviously not intended to push their way through the carts and carriages to support threatened sections of the front line. And, when the time came, Cyrus took command of them himself.[53]

On the next morning Cyrus sacrificed and his soldiers, after breakfasting and pouring drink-offerings, were arranged in their finest uniforms and armour. Xenophon dwells particularly upon Abradatas of Susa and his parting with Panthea, and then describes how Cyrus, having obtained favourable sacrifices and put out patrols, summoned his officers and made his final speech to them. He reminded them of the superiority of their equipment, and spoke especially of the Egyptians, the one part of the enemy army that they had not defeated already.

The Egyptians' armament is on a par with their formation. They have shields which are too big to permit them to do or see anything, and are drawn up a hundred deep, so that obviously they will prevent each other from fighting, all except a very few of them. If they count on pushing their way through they will have first to hold out against horses, and steel driven on by the strength of horses, and if any of them even holds his ground, how will he be able to fight at once against horses and infantry in line of battle and towers? For the men from the towers will support us, and their blows will bring the enemy from fighting to a state of helplessness.

And now, if any of you think that you still lack anything, tell me. For, with the help of the gods, we will deny you nothing. If anyone has anything to say, let him say it. If not, approach the holy offerings, make your prayers to the gods to whom we have sacrificed, and go to your posts. Let each one of you recall to his companions the matters of which I have reminded you, and make his own worthiness to command plain to his subordinates, by showing himself fearless in bearing, countenance, and words." [54]

After the departure of the commanders to their posts, Cyrus and his personal staff made their morning meal, which was followed by drink-offerings and prayers—answered by a propitious lightning-flash when Cyrus had mounted his horse and was about to move off at the head of his lifeguards. The advance began, with Cyrus riding between Chrysantas, the commander of the wing of cavalry on the right, and Arsamas, the commander of the infantry phalanx. The line was ordered to dress by the royal standard—the golden eagle that Xenophon had himself seen in the distance at Cunaxa. [55]

When the Persians had advanced about twenty stades (two and a half miles), the enemy came in sight, and Croesus began to carry out his carefully rehearsed plan.

When they were all in full sight of each other and the enemy realized that their line extended on either flank far beyond their opponents, they halted their own line (for there is no other way in which to carry out an enveloping movement) and bent it round to envelop the flanks,[56] making their own formation like a gamma on each side, so that they could fight from all sides at once. But though Cyrus saw this he did not hold back at all on that account but led on in the same way. And when he observed that they placed at a distance on either flank the marker round which they wheeled in extending their wings, he said, "Do you notice, Chrysantas, where they make their turning-point?"

"Certainly," said Chrysantas, "and I am surprised at it. For they seem to me to be detatching their wings a long way from their phalanx" [Fig. VII A].

"Indeed yes," said Cyrus, "and from ours too."

"Why are they doing it?"

"Obviously because they are afraid that if the wings are close to us while the phalanx is still a long way off we will fall on them."

"Well then," said Chrysantas, "how will one part of them be able to help the others, when they are so far apart from each other?"

"But obviously," said Cyrus, "when the wings in their advance come opposite the flanks of our army they will turn into line and advance in order to fight against us from all sides at once."

"Well," said Chrysantas, "do you think their plan is a good one?"

"Yes, against what they see. But against what they do not see, even worse than if they advanced in column." [57]

This passage explains how the manoeuvre by which the Spartans won their victory at the Nemea was carried out, though the Spartans had first to extend their line to the right to make the operation possible. It also indicates some of the dangers with which such a manoeuvre was attended. Croesus's army had been advancing in line, with its centre opposite the centre of the Persians. When the armies were fully in sight of each other it was clear that the Lydian line was considerably longer, and there was therefore no need to take additional ground to the right and left. The problem was how to bring the extended wings into action against Cyrus's flanks.

The centre ("the phalanx"; presumably all that part of the army that was directly opposed to the Persians) halted, facing the enemy. Obviously, if it was intended to bring the wings forward so as to enclose the enemy on three sides, the centre could not continue to advance, or the wings would be left behind, instead of brought forward. Nor could the wings be wheeled round in line, each pivoting on its inner flank where it joined the phalanx. Wheeling in line on a front of only twenty or thirty men, three deep, is difficult enough, and nowadays only practised as a cere-monial drill by highly-trained troops. To wheel a line several hundred men long and (on this imaginary occasion) thirty men deep was not possible, and if it had been, the outer flank of the wheel would have been brought close to the Persian front and exposed to attack.

There was, therefore, as Xenophon says, no other way to bring the wings round to enclose Cyrus's army than that which Croesus adopted. While the centre stood fast, both wings turned outwards into column and marched outwards to left and right. In so doing, they opened gaps between themselves and the main body, but, if the main body was long enough to cover the entire Persian front, there would be no unmarked Persian forces to penetrate those gaps, as the gap in the Spartan line at the battle of Mantinea in 418 B.C. was penetrated.[58]

When the wings had marched outwards to what was judged to be a safe distance, clear of the enemy's front, they were wheeled through ninety degrees, around markers—probably officers specially instructed for the purpose—still in column, and now marched parallel to the original axis of advance. The intention was that when Cyrus's army, which still came steadily on, was between them, the two columns should halt, and turn inwards into line. There would now be three separate bodies of men, all drawn up in line of battle, one directly facing the Persians, and one opposite each flank of the Persian line, ready to roll it up from both ends while it was held by the main body. But, as Cyrus said, the plan was only good against the part of his army that the enemy could see. The two wings had marched to what they considered a safe distance from the Persian front before wheeling round, but they did not know of the infantry and cavalry in the rear, waiting to attack their flanks when they turned into line.

Xenophon does not make the point here, but the halting of the main body in order to let the wings complete their manoeuvres was in itself dangerous, though more so when the opposing forces were cavalry than when they were infantry. At Cunaxa,[59] Artaxerxes had begun to bend his line round to encircle the smaller rebel army when his brother charged with his six hundred life-guards. It may have been because the "men drawn up before the king" were halted when they received the enemy's charge, in order to allow their own right wing to complete its encircling movement, that they gave way before the comparatively small number of rebels. The modern reader will recall Scarlett at Balaclava and Cromwell at Gainsborough breaking numerically superior cavalry who received their charges at the halt. But the younger Cyrus, less wise than Cromwell, charged at a gallop, not "a good round trot"; his men were scattered, and he himself perished obscurely at the very moment when victory and empire seemed to be within his grasp.[60]

In his "Battle of Thymbrara," Xenophon conceived a different plan.[61] His "Persians" were to deal tidily with the outflanking wings before tackling the centre of Croesus's army. After his conversation with Chrysantas, Cyrus gave him and Arsamas, the commander of the infantry, their final orders. They were to continue to advance steadily, while Cyrus went to his own position. He would himself make the first attack, and when they saw the enemy thrown into confusion by his onslaught, they were themselves to charge the centre, following as closely as possible behind Abradatas and his division of scythed chariots, who had already received their orders.

After giving the word, "Zeus, saviour and leader," Cyrus now passed along the ranks, encouraging his men and pausing for a short conversation with Abradatas, who expressed uneasiness about the flanks, which he saw threatened on each side by strong enemy wings of all arms and guarded only by chariots. Cyrus promised that he himself would deal with the enemy wings, and before Abradatas charged he would see the enemy forces that now alarmed him in full flight. Hystaspas, the commander of the cavalry on the left of the phalanx, was encouraged in similar terms, and told that, as long as any division of the enemy army stood fast, this was the part that they were to engage. Here again it is easy to see a remembrance of Cunaxa, and the Greek pursuit of the left of the Persian army while the issue was being decided elsewhere on the field. But this is perhaps not wholly fair to the Greeks, who did re-form their ranks once their immediate opponents were disposed of, and advance upon the large bodies of cavalry that they saw gathered round the royal standard.

From Hystaspas, Cyrus went on to the commander of the column of chariots on the left, and finally to his post behind the carts and carriages. Here he gave his final orders to Artagerses and Pharnuchus, the commanders of the cavalry and infantry "in ambush" behind the left of the baggage train. As soon as Cyrus himself with the other hidden troops attacked the outer flank of the enemy phalanx on the right, these were in the same way to attack the phalanx on the left.

> "You will fight against their flank, where an army is weakest, yourselves drawn up in line so as to be in the strongest formation. And, as you see, the men on the extreme wing of the enemy are cavalry. By all means send forward against them the camel corps, and you may be sure that before you fight the enemy you will have a laugh at them."

Cyrus now took his own post with the other half of the "ambush," having ridden almost completely round his own army, inspecting and encouraging it as he went. Meanwhile Croesus, considering that the phalanx with which he himself was marching was already closer than the extended wings to the approaching enemy, raised the signal to the wings to stop marching onwards, but to turn into line in the position where they were. [This] signal must have been pre-arranged for the occasion, some such device as the display of a white or red flag, upon which the wings were to carry out the movement in which they had already been instructed and rehearsed. There was no system of long-distance signalling by which Croesus, or any other ancient general, could transmit any but the simplest new orders over a distance.[62]] And when they halted opposite each other, looking towards Cyrus's army, he gave them the signal to march upon the enemy. And so there were advancing upon Cyrus's army three phalanxes, one against the front, and the other two one against the right and one against the left.

So far Croesus's plan seemed to be working, and there was great fear in all Cyrus's army when they saw themselves enclosed on all sides except the rear, and deep silence, for dread of what was to come. But when Cyrus gave the order they turned outwards to face the enemy. This order must have applied only to the columns of chariots on either flank, and to the detachments "in ambush"; the rest were already facing Croesus's centre. Cyrus raised the paean, and then the war-cry, which were taken up by his men, and then charged out with his concealed cavalry, "and, taking the enemy in flank, closed with them as soon as possible. And his infantry quickly followed behind him in good order, and enfolded the enemy on either side, so that Cyrus had very much the better of it. For he was attacking in line against their flank. And so the enemy were soon completely routed" (Fig. VII B).

Meanwhile Artagerses was dealing in the same manner with the other wing of Croesus's army, helped by the camels, whose effect on the Lydian cavalry horses was as Cyrus had predicted.

But Xenophon later[63] remarks that, whereas the improvements that Cyrus had introduced into the Persian cavalry and chariots had persisted until his own day,

> the camels merely scared the horses, but their riders neither killed anybody nor were themselves killed by the horsemen. For no horse came near them. And it seemed to be a useful device, but from that time on no gentleman has wanted to keep a camel for riding or to train for fighting from camel-back. And so the camels have got their proper place back again and continue among the baggage animals.

Herodotus,[64] who may here preserve a fragment of the true story, says that the Lydians, when their horses became unmanageable, dismounted and fought bravely on foot with their long spears.

In Xenophon's story, the destruction of the two wings of the Lydian army was completed by the charge of the two flanking divisions of scythed chariots. And now Abradatas with his divisions charged Croesus's centre, routing the "Trojan" chariots of the Lydians, which fled, "some taking up their crews [who had of course jumped down to fight on foot in the old style] and some abandoning them." But now came the great mass of the Egyptian infantry, into which Abradatas himself and the nearest charioteers on either side of him, the "companions who ate at his table," crashed headlong, while the others swerved aside from the solid mass of enemy infantry in pursuit of the fleeing Lydian chariots. The Egyptians were too densely massed to open their ranks and allow the chariots to pass through harmlessly, as the Ten Thousand had done at Cunaxa,[65] and many were crushed beneath the hooves and wheels or cut to pieces by the scythes. But at last the chariots were overturned on the heaps of their victims, and Abradatas and some of his companions were thrown out and killed fighting bravely, in spite of the efforts of the Persian infantry, who, following closely behind, cut down the Egyptians where they had been thrown into confusion by the chariot charge.

That Xenophon should represent the chariots as having such an effect is surprising. At Cunaxa "one man was caught by them, as though he had been knocked down on a racecourse. But they said that even he was not hurt." Pharnabazus once used two scythed chariots to break up a body of about seven hundred Greeks so that he and his cavalry could attack them, but they were not a regular force properly formed, but plunderers who had hurriedly run together when they were surprised. Agesilaus and his hoplites, to whom the survivors fled, were more than the Persians cared to tackle.[66] In the *Cyropaedia,* Xenophon was of course anxious to make as much as possible of the romance of Abradatas and Panthea and its tragic end, but he was no doubt convinced that the scythed chariot had real possibilities as a weapon for breaking the enemy's formation. Modern historians have the advantage of him, in knowing how the chariots failed at Gaugamela against the Macedonians and at Magnesia against the Romans. But we never had to face the possibility of a chariot charge ourselves, as he had done.

Most of the Egyptians were untouched by Abradatas's charge, and pressed on against the Persians.

Thereupon there was a terrible battle of spears and pikes and sabres. But the Egyptians had the advantage, both by their numbers and by their weapons. For even to this day they keep their long, strong spear, and their shields cover their bodies far better than cuirasses and wicker bucklers, and, being upon their shoulders, assist them in shoving. So, closing their shields together, they advanced and shoved. The Persians were unable to hold out against them, but fell back with their faces to the enemy, striking and being struck, until they were under the towers. [Here they were checked] and the rear-rank men allowed neither the archers nor the javelin-men to flee, but with uplifted sabres compelled them to shoot and throw their weapons. And there was great slaughter of men, and a great din of weapons and missiles of all sorts, and a great clamour of men, some calling on each other for help, others encouraging their friends, and others calling upon the gods.

To fall back with their faces to the enemy was an accomplishment of seasoned infantry. Xenophon later represents Cyrus as making his men, whom he had somewhat incautiously drawn up before Babylon, retire in this manner until they were out of range of the walls. In actual practice, the rearguard of the Ten Thousand accomplished the last stages of their retreat from before the stronghold of the Drilae in this way, and Polyaenus tells stories of how Clearchus drew on some enemy cavalry until they fell into a concealed ditch, and Gorgidas deceived Phoebidas by a feigned retreat.[67] This last story is inconsistent with Xenophon's account of Phoebidas's defeat; perhaps the Thebans put out this version to cover up their conduct in the earlier part of the action.

The struggle between the Persians and the Egyptians was decided when Cyrus himself and the Persian cavalry under Hystaspas and Chrysantas, having disposed of the Lydians, charged the Egyptians from all sides, "knowing that there was no quicker way of stopping the enemy's forward progress than by riding round his rear." Cyrus himself was for a moment in danger, when his horse was killed, but was rescued by the devotion of his friends and rode round to survey the battle from the towers. And now none of the enemy were attempting resistance any longer, except the Egyptians, and even they, being assailed on all sides, were crouching under their shields, suffering terribly and doing nothing in return. Cyrus offered them honourable terms, and they surrendered, agreeing to serve him against all his enemies except their former ally and commander, Croesus. Their story ends with the grant of cities for them to dwell in, which has already been discussed.

It was now already dark, and Cyrus led his army back and

encamped at Thymbrara, where his men, "after making their meal and posting the necessary sentries, went to sleep." Croesus and the remnants of his army meanwhile made good their escape to Sardis, and though they did not hold out very long in that great fortress, as the citadel was surprised the very next night, nothing illustrates more clearly the difference between classical Greek generalship and that of Alexander and his successors than the failure to pursue instantly and relentlessly immediately after victory.[68]

The lessons that Xenophon probably intended to convey may be summed up as follows:

The deep mass of men ("column" is the wrong word for the formation of the Egyptians, whose front was twelve times their depth) could push back and eventually break the shallower line. This, after all, was what Xenophon had himself seen at Coronea.

But the best way to check the mass was not simply to oppose to it an equal and opposite mass (or even a greater one if the extra force was available) but to attack its flanks and rear, and so compel the rear-rank men to turn outwards and fight, if they could, instead of continuing to support the advance of the front ranks. Even if the front-rank men were able to continue their advance unsupported, the result would be that the mass would break up. Perhaps best of all was to avoid any confrontation with the enemy mass, and only to assail its vulnerable sides. But this could only be done by skillful manoeuvre, and at the Nemea and Lechaeum, the Spartans were certainly helped by their enemies' mistakes.

Neither the siege towers nor the scythed chariots of Thymbrara are to be regarded as serious contributions to Greek tactical theory; they are merely properties suitable to an imaginary battle between Oriental monarchs. Nor need we suppose that Xenophon was actually recommending the adoption of either the Egyptian equipment, whose advantages and defects he describes, or the Persian scimitar and wicker shield; these too are Eastern fancy-dresses.

On the other hand, the use of light-armed troops armed with

missile weapons in support of a comparatively shallow phalanx was probably intended as a serious suggestion, prompted by the victory of Thrasybulus over the Thirty Tyrants at Munychia. But, except in the special circumstances of that action, when the slope of a hill allowed the archers and javelin-men to shoot effectively over the heads of their own phalanx, their support was unlikely to be of much practical value.[69]

The real way for the shallow line to deal with the mass was to use its greater length to attack the enemy's flank and rear, as the Spartans had done so successfully at the Nemea. But, as the end of the line was brought round to attack the enemy's flank, its own flank was exposed, should any part of the enemy's forces, through some miscalculation, have been left outside the enveloping movement. At Olpae in 426 B.C., the Peloponnesians had tried to outflank the left wing of the Athenian army, and been defeated by an ambush of four hundred hoplites and as many light-armed troops, previously concealed by Demosthenes in a hollow way.[70] In the "Battle of Thymbrara," it was the threatened army itself, not any feature of the ground, that screened the ambush until the proper moment came. Xenophon obviously approved of the idea. But I believe that it was not his own, nor was it, at the time that he wrote, unproved in the field.

X

THE BATTLE OF LEUCTRA

During the long war that followed the liberation of Thebes, the Spartans lost the pre-eminence throughout European Greece that had been left them by the "King's Peace" and seemed to have been secured by the seizure of the Cadmeia and the submission of Olynthus.[1] With their armies constantly engaged in Boeotia, they had been unable to retain their hold on the North, and had been compelled to advise their friends in Thessaly to make what terms they could with the rising power of Jason of Pherae.[2] At sea the Athenians had been able first to beat the Spartans in the Aegean and then to sail round the Peloponnese to Corcyra. Even in the main theatre of war the Spartans had lost ground, and the smaller Boeotian cities, with the exception of Orchomenus, had been brought under Theban control.

Theban rule over the rest of Boeotia could not have been established if most of the population had not thought it preferable to the rule of oligarchies acting in the Spartan interest. But when in 371 B.C. the exhausted combatants came to a treaty, Agesilaus made the Thebans' request that they should be allowed to take the oath on behalf of "the Boeotians" a pretext for excluding them from the general peace. The Athenians were concerned for the independence of their ancient ally Plataea, and also for that of Thespiae,[3] perhaps less for idealistic reasons than for fear of a strong power upon their northern frontier, and withdrew their support from Thebes. The Spartans, or Agesilaus and his friends, thought they saw their chance for a final settlement of scores.

Since 375 B.C., Phocis had provided the Spartans with a base of operations in Central Greece, and the other king, Cleombrotus, was in Phocis with an army consisting of four of the six Spartan *morai* and allied contingents.[4] He had never shown much enthusiasm for the Theban war, and now asked the home authorities for instructions. The forms of the newly concluded treaty and the observances of religion required that he should disband his army and that the allies and the gods should be consulted before any new move was made, but the Spartan Assembly, urged on, so Xenophon thought, by fate, rejected this course, and ordered him to act immediately against the Thebans, if they did not grant the cities their independence.[5]

Cleombrotus carried out the invasion of Boeotia with a skill that he had not displayed in his earlier campaigns, and was at first attended with marked success. His direct road to Thebes lay to the north of Mount Helicon, through Coronea, and he began by advancing along it. The Thebans, under Epaminondas, blocked the gap between the mountain and Lake Copais, and when Cleombrotus fell back again towards Phocis, they may have thought that he had given up as easily as in 376 B.C.[6] But, having deceived the enemy as to his intentions, he turned suddenly southward, and, marching through Thisbe "by a mountainous and unexpected road," destroyed a detachment that tried to oppose him and reached the Boeotian port of Creusis on the Corinthian Gulf, which he stormed, capturing twelve Theban triremes. From here he turned north-east towards the heart of Boeotia. Meanwhile the news of his movements had reached Epaminondas, who came back to meet him, and the two armies confronted one another across the plain of Leuctra.[7]

After the battle, tales were not wanting of divine warnings to the Lacedaemonians. Wolves had devoured the sacrificial beasts accompanying the army;[8] the very field of Leuctra was accursed to them, on account of an outrage committed long before against some maidens of the country.[9] But at this time it was the Theban prospects that looked desperate. They were deserted by Athens.

They were heavily outnumbered. Agesilaus was spitefully pursuing his old grudge against them, and, though he was not himself in the field, Cleombrotus was apparently carrying out his policy efficiently. Even if the Thebans did give in to the Spartan demands, they could not trust the enemy's good faith. No wonder that the soldiers were discouraged and ready to see unfavourable omens in every chance incident.

The resolution of Epaminondas kept the army in the field.[10] He reminded his men that

> One omen's best, our country to defend,

but also sought to put a favourable interpretation on incidents that had discouraged them. A ribbon from an officer's spear was blown onto the tomb of some Spartans who had been killed in one of Agesilaus's campaigns; this meant, not that the Thebans would lose their battle honours to the Spartans, but that they would soon crown the graves of their enemies.[11] Tricks which, to the modern reader, appear unworthy served their turn in the crisis. The soldiers were heartened by a supposed favourable response from the oracle of Trophonius, by a report that Heracles had taken up arms from his temple to come to their aid, and by the news that a venerated statue of Athena was no longer standing idly "at-ease" but had picked up the shield that had formerly rested against its knees.[12]

Pelopidas, who was in command of the Sacred Band, as he had been at Tegyra, supported his friend loyally. To his wife, who tearfully begged him to look to his own safety, he replied that this was proper advice for private soldiers, but officers must see to the safety of others.[13] His dream, in which the father of the outraged girls seemed to demand the sacrifice of a fair-haired maiden upon their tomb, drew general attention to the story of the Spartan's ancient guilt and the divine retribution that awaited them at Leuctra. A chestnut filly, running loose through the camp, offered itself as the appointed victim, and so the Thebans secured the favour of the gods without themselves incurring the guilt of human sacrifice,[14] and went into battle in as good heart as their commanders could give them.

The plain of Leuctra appears, to the modern eye, admirably suited to a pitched battle between hoplite armies, and seems to have been deliberately selected by Cleombrotus for the purpose. A level plain extends for rather over a mile between foot-hills that bound it on the north and south. To the west runs the Parmessus River; to the east are the head waters of the Asopus. No marked obstacle today divides the two river systems, and there is no reason to suppose that in antiquity armies operating on the plain would have been cramped by woods or other natural features.[15] Nor do the ancient accounts suggest that the battlefield was obstructed by the buildings of the village of Leuctra, whose site cannot now be determined and for whose existence there is only slight literary evidence.[16]

Cleombrotus seems to have reached the plain before the Thebans arrived, and halted to rest his men after their long and difficult march.[17] He encamped on the steep foot-hills to the south of the plain, and the Thebans "encamped on the opposite ridge, leaving no great distance in between." [18] Both sides were fully aware of each other's presence; the battle was deliberately fought, not an encounter action brought on by the collision between two armies marching in opposite directions. Though Xenophon does not say so, I think it probable that the Spartans, and perhaps the Thebans also, had spent at least one night in camp before the battle. If they had arrived in the morning, made camp and taken their meal, and fought the battle that very afternoon, they would have had little chance of resting. Cleombrotus was evidently not trying to race the enemy to Thebes, but to force them to fight a pitched battle on ground which he considered suitable to the Spartans.

The leaders on both sides, in Xenophon's opinion, had good reason to hazard a battle. The past actions of Cleombrotus had brought him under the suspicion of treacherously favouring the Thebans, and now, while his opponents looked to see his guilt established, his friends urged him to clear his name, and warned him that if he let the enemy go without a battle he was in danger of being put to death by the state. On the Theban side, the leaders were faced with the danger that, if they abandoned the field without fighting, the smaller cities would revolt from them and Thebes itself would be besieged. Cut off from provisions, the Theban people too would rebel. To those who had been banished at the time of the seizure of the Cadmeia, death on the battlefield seemed preferable to a second exile.[19] None the less, the odds were such that the Theban council of war was divided, and Epaminondas was barely able to carry his resolution for battle.[20]

Just what those odds were cannot be certainly determined. Xenophon gives no figure for the total strength of either side. Four of the six Lacedaemonian *morai,* or regiments, were present, each about five hundred and sixty strong, with a small number of supernumerary officers.[21] The king's personal life-guard is not mentioned by Xenophon as a separate body, and I believe, for reasons examined in the Appendix, that it was part of the first *mora,* and did not, as many scholars maintain, form an additional force of three hundred "knights."

Of the total of about 2,300 Lacedaemonians, only seven hundred were Spartiates.[22] There is no mention of the presence of the Sciritae[23] or of any contingents of newly enfranchised helots. There was a Spartan cavalry force, whose poor quality was one of the main reasons for the defeat. It probably amounted to rather over two hundred men—about one tenth of the strength of the infantry.

Of the rest of the army, Xenophon mentions "the mercenaries with Hieron and the peltasts of the Phocians and the contingents of cavalry from Heraclea and Phlius." [24] Certainly these mercenaries must have been peltasts, but equally certainly the allies must have supplied hoplites, as well as light-armed troops and cavalry. Which states had sent soldiers, and how big their forces were, we do not know.

Plutarch says that Cleombrotus's army consisted of ten thousand hoplites and one thousand cavalry, and this seems a reasonable figure, though we cannot accept it as certain since we do not know his source.[25] Other late writers exaggerate the Spartan numbers in order to make the most of the Theban achievement.[26]

Of the Theban force, Xenophon says only that they "had no allies except the Boeotians." [27] The very interesting contemporary account of the Boeotian constitution given by the *Hellenica Oxyrhynchia* says that Boeotia was divided into eleven districts, for each of which a *boeotarch* or general was elected annually. Each district provided one thousand hoplites and a hundred cavalry.[28] Four of the eleven districts at this time were Theban, so that on paper the Theban army alone should have amounted to four thousand foot and four hundred horse, and the allied Boeotians (Orchomenus, with two districts being excluded) should have provided a further five thousand hoplites and five hundred cavalry.

These figures certainly bear no relation to the actual strength of the army. In 424 B.C.,[29] there were about seven thousand Boeotian hoplites at Delium, and a thousand cavalry. There were also ten thousand light-armed infantry, so the manpower for the creation of a larger hoplite force was available, but the money presumably was not. In 371 B.C., Boeotia was no doubt considerably poorer, as a result of the Spartan invasions, than it had been half a century earlier. Moreover, many of the upper classes, especially in Thespiae and Tanagra, had taken the Spartan side and suffered accordingly. Diodorus Siculus says that the army at Leuctra amounted to "not more than six thousand men in all," [30] and this seems a reasonable figure either for hoplites and cavalry taken together, or for hoplites alone if we suppose the "in all" to be mistaken. At the Nemea in 394 B.C., Xenophon says that the Boeotians, without the men of Orchomenus, put into the field five thousand hoplites and about eight hundred cavalry.[31]

The figure of seven thousand hoplites recurs in accounts of other Theban campaigns; but this proves nothing about the number in the field at Leuctra. Diodorus says that after the liberation of Thebes an allied army of at least twelve thousand hoplites and more than two thousand cavalry assembled to meet the Spartans, including five thousand hoplites and five hundred cavalry from Athens, but these figures seem unreliable.[32] Plutarch speaks of Theban armies of seven thousand hoplites taking the field against Alexander of Pherae shortly after the battle of Leuctra,[33] but victory had certainly increased the resources of the state and the confidence of the citizens.

Perhaps it would not be far from the truth to suggest that Cleombrotus's whole army, including allies, outnumbered the Boeotians by something like three to two, but that the Thebans (whom we may suppose to have made up nearly half the Boeotian army) were probably at least equal in numbers to the Lacedaemonians. And it was between the Thebans and the Lacedaemonians that the battle was decided.[34]

We possess four ancient accounts of the battle. Only Xenophon's[35] is contemporary, and it is unsatisfactory because it is not a narrative of what happened but a list of reasons for the Spartan defeat. It is generally supposed that he is simply finding excuses for his friends, and indeed his opening sentence suggests as much: "As for the battle, everything went wrong for the Lacedaemonians, but for their opponents everything succeeded, even by chance." Yet Xenophon does not say that the Theban victory was the result only of luck; their plans went right, and they had luck too. Nor does he suggest that the Spartans were merely unlucky. They made mistakes, some of them discreditable, which he criticizes sharply and does not try to disguise. They were in the wrong, from the beginning of the war, as he makes perfectly clear. In this particular campaign, they had failed to abide by the rules.[36] A writer who wished merely to flatter King Agesilaus and to put the best face possible on the Spartan defeat would never have said that the Spartans were "punished by none other than the victims of their injustice." If he tells us not so much what happened at Leuctra as why, in his opinion, the Spartans lost, it is, I believe, because this was the first question that he asked himself. Nor are his answers dishonest: that is to say, he does not hide from his readers the answers that he himself believed to be the right ones, merely for fear of hurting Spartan feelings. He writes, in fact, as a critic of Sparta, not as a Spartan propagandist.[37] But this is not to say that he presents a balanced and impartial account. He is not hiding the truth as he sees it, but he makes no attempt to see more than one side of it. To a truly impartial historian, the chief reason for the Spartan defeat might have seemed to be that proclaimed by the inscription:

"The Thebans are mightier in war." [38]

Above all, Xenophon falls short of the truth in his failure to give credit to the generalship of Epaminondas. Yet here again his fault seems to be that he, and his Spartan informants, did not immediately realize the genius of the Theban commander. What Xenophon gives us is a collection of notes made shortly after the battle, and drawn from the Spartan side only, not a balanced narrative reviewed after the difference between Epaminondas and his fellow-*boeotarchs* had been made apparent in later campaigns.

Xenophon's account, then (with comments added), is as follows: "As for the battle, everything went wrong for the Lacedaemonians, but for their opponents everything succeeded even by chance. For in the first place Cleombrotus held his final council about the battle after the morning meal. And it was said that as they were drinking in the midday, the wine too set them on somewhat." I find no suggestion here that the Spartans issued a special drink ration to their men to keep up their courage before going into action.[39] Wine was a normal accompaniment of the morning meal—but on this occasion it would have been better to have withheld it, as it further inflamed the tempers of the king's advisers. The bitterness between those who supported Cleombrotus, and were urging him to act in order to clear himself of the charge of treason, and his opponents, who were waiting to see if he would "let the enemy off," has already been described.

Again, when both sides were arming and it was already evident that there would be a battle, at first, from the Boeotian army, those who had brought supplies, and some of the baggage train, and those who were unwilling to fight made a movement to leave. But the mercenaries with Hieron and the peltasts of the Phocians and the contingents of cavalry from Heraclea and Phlius made an encircling movement, and, setting upon the retreating men, turned them back and chased them to the Boeotian camp. In consequence, they made the Boeotian army much larger and more densely massed than before.

Pausanias says that Epaminondas, fearing that some of his men were going to desert and preferring that they should do so before the battle, had proclaimed that any who wished might go home. The men of Thespiae left in a body, "and any other of the Boeotians who felt ill will towards the Thebans." [40] Since Thespiae lay to the right rear of the Boeotian position, less than two miles from its probable centre, it is clear that the cavalry and light-armed troops who drove the would-be deserters back to the Boeotian camp were on the Spartan left wing, and were not drawn up with the Spartans' own cavalry.

Again, because the space between the armies was actually level ground, the Lacedaemonians drew up their cavalry in front of their own phalanx and the Thebans drew their cavalry up opposite them. The Theban cavalry was in good training because of the wars against Orchomenus and Thespiae, but the Lacedaemonians at that time had the most wretched cavalry. For it was the richest men who kept the horses. But when the army was called out, there came the man drafted for the purpose, and took the horse and whatever arms were given him and went on campaign on the spur of the moment. And those of the soldiers who were weakest in body and least desirous of distinction served on horseback. Such was the cavalry on both sides.

In the phalanx, it was reported that the Lacedaemonians formed the *enomotia* in threes. Consequently their depth was no more than twelve. But the Thebans were massed together not less than fifty shields deep, calculating that if they overcame the force about the king, all the rest would be easily dealt with. [Xenophon does not of course quote Epaminondas's famous demonstration of "crushing the head of the serpent." [41]]

When Cleombrotus began to lead towards the enemy, in the first place he did so before his own army even perceived that he was leading. [The king's ill-judged haste seems to have been a result of the angry council of war. The allies, left without clear orders and unenthusiastic for the battle, were glad enough to let the Spartans and Thebans fight it out.]

Furthermore, the cavalry engaged each other, and those of the Lacedaemonians were quickly beaten. In their flight they fell foul of their own hoplites, and then the Theban *lochoi* [42] were upon them. None the less, that the men around Cleombrotus were at first victorious in the battle can be recognized by this clear piece of evidence. They could not have taken him up and carried him living off the field, if those who fought in front of him were not winning at the moment. But when Deinon the *polemarch* was killed, and Sphodrias, one of those about the public tent, and Cleonymus his son, and the knights, [43] and the aides of the *polemarch* as they are called, the remainder, pushed by the mass of men, fell back. And those of the Lacedaemonians who were on the left wing, when they saw the right pushed back, gave way. [The left and right wings I take to be those of the Lacedaemonians themselves, forming a continuous line, without reference to the allies, who were merely lookers-on.]

None the less, though many were killed and they had been beaten, when they crossed the ditch which happened to be before their camp, they grounded their arms in the place from which they had started. However, the camp was not much on the plain, but rather towards the rising ground. [This last sentence seems to be an acknowledgement that the Spartans were driven from the battlefield, though the survivors retained their military formation and discipline.]

Thereafter there were some of the Lacedaemonians who, thinking that what had happened could not be endured, said that they must prevent the enemy from setting up the trophy, and must try to take up the dead, not under truce, but by battle. But the *polemarchs* saw that of the whole number of Lacedaemonians nearly a thousand were killed, and that of the Spartiates themselves, of whom about seven hundred were in the field, about four hundred had been killed. And they perceived that all the allies were in poor heart for fighting, but that some of them were not displeased at what had happened. So they assembled those who were best qualified and consulted on what was to be done. Since all agreed that the dead should be taken up under truce, they sent a herald accordingly. But the Thebans after this set up a trophy and also gave up the dead bodies under truce.

According to Pausanias, the herald was not sent until the day after the battle, and Epaminondas insisted on the Spartan dead being taken up separately so that the Thebans could count their number.[44] The high proportion of Spartiates killed must be allowed to be a strong argument for the existence of a separate royal body-guard, in addition to the men serving in the *morai*. But if three hundred Spartiates were serving in a special force of "knights," which was annihilated, or nearly so, one hundred would have been serving in each of the four *morai*, about one quarter of whom would have been killed, as against nearly a third (six hundred out of less than two thousand) of the *perioeci* and inferiors. I prefer the supposition that, while there was certainly a concentration of Spartiates about the king's person, in the part of the line that was the special object of the Theban attack, the Spartiates throughout the army, including, no doubt a high proportion of front-rank men, suffered more than their share of casualties.

Such are Xenophon's reasons for the Spartan defeat. They do not succeed in explaining the Theban victory. In particular they do not explain how the Thebans succeeded in killing so many Lacedaemonians. At Coronea in 394 B.C., the Theban column had broken through Agesilaus's line, but in doing so had suffered greater losses than it inflicted. At Leuctra, the Theban formation was more than four times as deep as that of the Lacedaemonians; therefore, unless there were actually many more Thebans than Lacedaemonians in the field, which hardly seems possible, their front was only about a quarter as long, and in this case, even if they killed every single man who was directly opposed to them, three-quarters of the Lacedaemonians should have survived. Clearly there was more to the Theban victory than the old device of massing men to a great depth on one wing. The attacking column had been transferred from the right wing to the left, so that the blow fell directly upon the Lacedaemonians before they could develop their own plans, and was not, as in earlier battles, wasted on their allies. But this was only part of Epaminondas's secret.[45]

The immediate consequences of the battle,[46] contrasted with its long-term results, seem surprisingly slight. The Spartans had lost the battle, and with it, as was to be seen, not merely the dominion that they had exercised over Greece for a generation, but the position that they had held for centuries in the Peloponnese. But there was no instant collapse of their power. There was not even an immediate pursuit of the beaten army. The *polemarchs,* to whom the command had passed upon the death of Cleombrotus, conceded the battlefield to the Thebans, but for some days they held the position along the edge of the hills, where the Thebans did not feel strong enough to attack them. Meanwhile both sides sent for reinforcements.

The news of the disaster was received at Sparta as befitted the traditions of the state. The festival that was in progress was not interrupted. The names of the dead were transmitted to their relatives with a warning to the women to make no lamentations, and next day the relatives of the killed could be recognized by their cheerful appearance in public, while few of the survivors' families were to be seen, and they were downcast.

Immediate steps were taken to support the beaten army. All soldiers under the age of sixty were mobilized, and Archidamus, son of Agesilaus, was sent out with the two remaining *morai,* the older men of the four *morai* that had been at Leuctra, and the office-holders who had previously been exempt. Allied contingents joined the Spartan force enthusiastically, according to Xenophon; ships were prepared for the crossing of the Corinthian Gulf, and Archidamus consulted the omens.

Before the new army reached the theatre of war, the situation had changed. The Theban messenger who brought the news of victory, and a request for help, to Athens was rudely dismissed. But Jason of Pherae acted swiftly to support his Boeotian allies. With the cavalry of his life-guard and his mercenaries (professional peltasts no doubt), he marched through the hostile territory of Phocis with such speed that the sight of his army was the first intimation of his coming and he was past long before a force could be assembled to resist him, "making it clear that in many situations results are achieved by speed rather than by force." The Boeotians proposed that his mercenaries should attack the Spartan position from above, while they themselves delivered a frontal assault, but he advised them to be content with their achievement rather than risk losing what they had gained by forcing the Spartans to fight for their lives. He also offered advice to the Spartans, reminding them of his hereditary friendship with them, and advising them not to attempt to engage a victorious army with a beaten one, or to count on their allies, many of whom were talking about going over to the winning side. Xenophon shrewdly observes that his true motive was perhaps to keep both parties at enmity with each other, but under obligation to himself. However, the *polemarchs* requested him to negotiate a truce, and when it had been arranged, immediately

> gave orders for every man to collect his baggage after the evening meal, saying that they were to march while it was still night in order to make the ascent of Cithaeron at daybreak. But when they had dined, before they slept, they gave the order to follow, and that very evening led along the road through Creusis, trusting in concealing their movements [by the false report that they had put out about their intended route and time of departure]

Fear and the difficulty of the road added to the troubles of their night march, but they got safely away to Aegosthena, where they encountered Archidamus with his reinforcements.

There was now clearly no question of restoring the situation by a second battle. Archidamus made no attempt to advance further, but merely waited until all the allied contingents had come in, no doubt fearing that if any of them arrived after he had left they would be exposed to attack, and led his army back to Corinth, whence he dismissed the allies and led the Spartans home.

Sparta had ceased to be the leading military power in Greece. But Greece did not at once realize the consequences. The oligarchies that had been kept in power by Spartan prestige did not collapse overnight. More than a year was to pass before the women of Sparta saw the smoke of their enemies' fires and the three-hundred-years' slavery of Messenia was ended. If the battle of Leuctra marks a revolution in the art of generalship, it is because of the way that it was won, not the way that it was followed up.

Though Xenophon does not give us the whole truth about the battle, I believe, as I have said already, that his account is truthful as far as it goes. The other ancient evidence, and any reconstruction of the battle that we may attempt in modern times, must therefore be believed only in so far as it can be reconciled with what Xenophon tells us.

For this reason, the narrative of Diodorus[47] cannot be accepted.

Some details are no doubt true, but they must be weighed separately; the story as a whole will not do. His account of the campaign begins in the same way as Xenophon's, though it is clearly not taken from him, being presented from the other side and differing in such details as the number of ships captured at Creusis. Cleombrotus turned the Theban position at Coronea by the difficult "shore road" and advanced to Leuctra, where he encamped. The Thebans marched to meet him, but were at first dismayed by the sight of the huge enemy army. The council of six *boeotarchs* was divided, but a late arrival gave his casting vote on Epaminondas's side.[48] The Thebans were heartened by pretended signs from heaven, and a deserter told the Thebans the story of the maidens whom the Spartans had outraged at Leuctra. So far, all is acceptable, and is confirmed by details found in Pausanias, who seems to be drawing independently on the same source, or a similar one.

But according to Diodorus, at this point, when battle was about to be joined, Jason arrived with his Thessalians, fifteen hundred foot and five hundred horse, to help the Thebans, and persuaded both sides to make an armistice and "beware the incalculable turns of fortune." Xenophon represents Jason giving similar advice to the Thebans. It is perhaps partly because Diodorus cannot imagine such words being said after fortune had declared itself on the Theban side that he places Jason's intervention before the great battle. Three and a half centuries afterwards, it was obvious that Leuctra had been decisive. But in the first few anxious days, when the Boeotians were still outnumbered by an enemy in position in the hills to the south, a reversal of fortune cannot have seemed impossible.

To resume Diodorus's narrative, Cleombrotus thereupon evacuated Boeotia with his army, but on his retreat met a second large army of Lacedaemonians and allies under Archidamus, son of Agesilaus. The combined Spartan force therefore returned to Leuctra, and both sides once more prepared for battle.

The suggestion that Archidamus was in fact at Leuctra, but that Xenophon removes him from the scene to preserve the reputation of the son of Agesilaus, has rightly been rejected by most modern scholars.[49] If it is rejected, Diodorus's narrative of the battle becomes unacceptable, as well as his account of the operations leading to it.

He says that one wing of the Spartan army was led by Cleombrotus and the other by Archidamus. But Epaminondas

> selected the best men from the whole army and posted them upon the one side, intending himself to settle the issue of the struggle with them. The feeblest men he posted upon the other wing and ordered them to make a running fight of it and fall back little by little before the enemy's attack. Accordingly, having formed his line *en echelon,*[50] he resolved to decide the battle with the wing which had the picked troops. When the trumpets sounded the war-note on either side and the armies raised their battle-cries at the first onset, the Lacedaemonians pressed forward on both wings, having made the formation of their phalanx crescent-shaped, but the Boeotians withdrew on one wing and on the other closed with the enemy at the double.

A desperate hand-to-hand struggle followed, in which the valour of the Thebans and the denseness of their formation at length prevailed. The Peloponnesians began to fall, all with their wounds in front. Cleombrotus was killed, fighting heroically, and a great mound of corpses was heaped about his body. Now his wing was left without a commander; the "heavy troops around Epaminondas" pressed on; the Lacedaemonians, fighting brilliantly about their king, recovered his body, but in the end gave way, and were at last completely routed, with the Thebans pursuing and slaying them.

Diodorus says that not fewer than four thousand of the Lacedaemonians fell in the battle, and about three hundred

Boeotians. The first figure is impossible; the second is probably also exaggerated. Pausanias says that forty-seven of the Thebans and other Boeotians were killed, which may be too few.[51]

Many details of this narrative—the trumpets sounding the war note, the Spartans dead with all their wounds in front, the mounds of corpses piled around the fallen king—read like rhetorical commonplaces. And the whole story is in fact a set-piece exercise, corresponding (as has not been generally observed) with the method recommended in Onesander's textbook for dealing with an enemy phalanx that advances in crescent formation with its horns towards you.[52] The crescent formation of the Lacedaemonians has been accepted by many modern scholars, but, as Wolter justly observes, is based on the story that two Heraclids, Cleombrotus and Archidamus, were in the field. The suggestion that the line of the Spartans and allies finally became crescent shaped when its centre gave way before the Theban attack neither saves Diodorus, who says that the attack was delivered against one of the horns, nor agrees with Xenophon.[53]

The attack delivered against one wing of the Spartan army by a dense mass of men agrees with Xenophon, though Diodorus does not give the depth of the formation on either side. He is clearly correct in saying that Epaminondas intended to settle the issue by the attack of his left wing upon the Spartan right, but it was probably not necessary for the Boeotian right to make the feigned retreat that Diodorus describes, nor is it likely that it could have done so in any order, if it had had to. It was apparently composed of the contingents from the smaller Boeotian cities, certainly less well trained than the Thebans and perhaps of doubtful loyalty. If they had begun to retreat, they would soon have been running in earnest. But they did not have to. They were not opposed to Archidamus and a second division of Lacedaemonians, but to the allies of the Spartans, who were unenthusiastic and had no very clear idea of what was happening because, as Xenophon says, Cleombrotus began his own advance "before his own army even perceived that he was leading." The Lacedaemonians moved off; the Boeotian left charged; the Boeotian centre and right and the allies of the Spartans were probably little more than spectators.

Diodorus says that Epaminondas "selected the best men from the whole army" to form his attacking wing. But the mass of men, drawn up fifty deep, that eventually bore down the Lacedaemonians, was clearly not a body of picked troops, but, as Xenophon says, the Thebans, fighting, as they were accustomed to, in a deep formation—not necessarily deeper than that in which they had been drawn up at the Nemea and Coronea.

Pausanias[54] gives us a third ancient account of the Leuctra campaign, preserving several interesting details. He seems to be making independent use of one of the sources used by Diodorus, but (perhaps because he is summarizing a single earlier account, not trying to reconstruct the battle out of several narratives) is more straightforward and avoids the error of making Cleombrotus invade Boeotia twice, accompanied the second time by Archidamus. He has little to say about the actual battle. The additional information that he gives us about the campaign has already been noted.

Plutarch's *Life of Pelopidas* preserves what I believe to be the best account of the action from the Theban side.[55] In this I follow Köchly and Rüstow's reconstruction of the battle, which was generally accepted until the end of the last century, but has since fallen into disfavour.[56] Wolter, in his learned and careful study,[57] found Plutarch full of obscurities and contradictions, but I believe that some of these difficulties can be resolved. We do not know for certain what sources Plutarch used,[58] but it is at least likely that they included good fourth-century material, and I believe that the *Life of Pelopidas* should be accepted as true, to the extent that it can be shown to make sense and is not contradicted by Xenophon.

It must also be remembered that in a *Life of Pelopidas* the author's purpose is to say what his hero did in the battle, not necessarily to give a full account of everything that happened. At Leuctra, Pelopidas was not commander-in-chief, nor even one of the *boeotarchs,* but commander of the Sacred Band.[59] Had Plutarch's *Life of Epaminondas* survived, he might have given us the full story. As it is, he only gives a part of it. If, for instance, he has nothing to say about the cavalry, this is because Pelopidas neither commanded the Theban horse nor engaged that of the Spartans. But if Plutarch leaves out things that Xenophon puts in, this does not prove that when he puts in things that Xenophon leaves out he is not to be trusted—provided always that his story can be reconciled with Xenophon's.

Plutarch's story, then, is as follows:

In the battle, Epaminondas drew his phalanx obliquely to the left,[60] so that the right wing of the Spartiates might be very far removed from the rest of the Greeks, and so that he might drive Cleombrotus from the field by falling in close order upon his flank and overwhelming him. But the enemy realized what had happened and began to rearrange themselves in their formation, and were unfolding their right wing and leading it round,[61] in order to encircle Epaminondas and envelop him by their number. But at this moment Pelopidas charged out in front, turned the three hundred [the Sacred Band] together at the double, and anticipated Cleombrotus, before he could extend his wing or bring it back again into the original position and close up the formation. Pelopidas attacked the Lacedaemonians when they were not properly drawn up, but falling foul of one another; and yet the Spartiates were supreme craftsmen and professors of the warlike arts, and educated and drilled themselves in nothing so much as in not becoming lost or confused when their formation had been broken, but each using every one, wherever and with whomsoever danger might overtake them, as his comrade in rank and file, and forming up and fighting regardless. But then Epaminondas's phalanx, bearing down upon them alone and passing by the others [that is, their allies], and Pelopidas, displaying incredible speed and daring in arms, so confounded their science and their skill that there was such a rout and slaughter of Spartiates as had never been before. Therefore, though Epaminondas was a *boeotarch* and Pelopidas was not, and though the one commanded the whole army and the other a small part of it, Pelopidas gained an equal share of glory for that victory and achievement.

When Plutarch says that the Lacedaemonians "were unfolding their right wing and leading it round," and that Pelopidas charged "before Cleombrotus could extend his wing or bring it back into the original position and close up the formation," I take it that the Spartans were attempting the manoeuvre by which they had won the battle of the Nemea, and which Xenophon makes Croesus try to use against Cyrus in the romance. That is, they turned into column and marched to the right before wheeling left in order to form up at right angles to their original front (Fig. VIII A). "Extending the wing" in this manner was a necessary part of the enveloping movement, not inconsistent with it, and I therefore do not accept the arguments brought against Plutarch by Wolter, who supposed that Plutarch's source spoke of "extension" by bringing up the rear half of each file in order to double the number of men in each rank. Wolter considered that not only had Plutarch misunderstood his source but the source itself must be in error, as this kind of "extension" would have to be carried out at the halt and Xenophon says that Cleombrotus "began to lead towards the enemy." Moreover since the Spartans and their allies outnumbered the Boeotians and the Theban formation was four times as deep as the Lacedaemonian phalanx, Wolter could see no need for Cleombrotus to make his line longer. But, as the *Cyropaedia* makes clear, a turning movement could not be attempted in front of the enemy. Croesus's army also had a considerably longer line than that of Cyrus, but his wings marched out a long way to either flank and were widely separated from his centre before they began to wheel round.

These arguments against Plutarch, then, are based on a misunderstanding of what he says. His story makes sense if we suppose his words to bear the significance that one would expect an author of the fourth century B.C. to give to them, and do not try to make them the equivalent of Hellenistic technical terms. This in itself is a reason to suppose that Plutarch is drawing upon a source contemporary with the battle, or nearly so. There remains the further argument, that Xenophon does not say that the Spartans were attempting to outflank the Thebans. But Xenophon does not tell us what the Spartans were trying to do, only why they lost. If the supposition that they were trying to outflank the Thebans can be shown to be consistent with the reasons Xenophon gives for the Spartan defeat, it need not be given up. And in any case what were the Spartans trying to do? Even if they thought of Delium as ancient history and Tegyra as an unimportant skirmish, they cannot have forgotten the Nemea and Coronea. Cleombrotus must have expected the Thebans to be drawn up in a deep formation, and, since he deliberately sought battle, he must have been confident that he had the answer to the Theban tactics. He did not choose to draw up his army "altogether deep" as King Pausanias had done against the Athenian democrats in the Piraeus,[62] and meet mass with mass. He proposed to meet the Theban column in line, and presumably he did not wish three quarters of his army to stand idle while one quarter fought against odds. As at the Nemea, the Spartans must have intended to use the extra length of their line to outflank and envelop the enemy.[63]

It has been objected[64] that an outflanking movement cannot stop a column from breaking through a line. Whether this is true or no (and Xenophon certainly thought that the quickest way for Cyrus and his friends to stop the forward progress of the Egyptians at Thymbrara was to attack their rear[65]), it is quite possible that the Spartans did not intend to stop the Thebans "breaking through." At the Nemea and at Coronea, they had "broken through," but had then had to come back again across the battlefield, where the Spartans were waiting for them. At the Nemea, the Spartans had not tried to oppose the front ranks of the returning enemy directly, but had speared them from the side as they ran past. At Coronea, Agesilaus would, in Xenophon's opinion, have been wise to adopt the same tactics.[66] The Spartan camp at Leuctra was not full of the plunder of Asia, as Agesilaus's had been, and the Thebans, even if they had reached it, would have gained little by it. I believe therefore that the Spartans may not have intended to stop the Thebans, or even to oppose them directly, but to sweep the battlefield from side to side.

The supposition that the Spartans began the battle by moving off to the right provides an explanation for one of the strangest features of Xenophon's narrative—the part played by the Spartan cavalry. He says that it contributed to their defeat not just because it was inferior in quality and soon beaten by the Theban horse, but because it had been drawn up in front of its own phalanx, and so in its rout threw the Spartan hoplites into disorder, "and then the Theban *lochoi* were upon them."

The usual position of the cavalry in the Greek battle was of course on the wing, where it might play a part in retreat or pursuit, once the lines were broken by the clash of hoplite against hoplite, or perhaps threaten the flank of the enemy line. The Spartan dispositions at Leuctra were exceptional. At Crannon in 322 B.C., the Greeks (with the Thessalians on their side) had the advantage in cavalry, but were far inferior to the Macedonians in infantry, and therefore placed their cavalry in front of the infantry phalanx, hoping that it would decide the battle.[67] Obviously the Spartans did not entertain such hopes. It was their infantry upon which they relied; they despised their cavalry. If they had planned to advance straight forward, they must have known that their cavalry would be in the way, even if it were not attacked. And they can hardly have expected it to do any better than it did in fact do if the Theban cavalry attacked it. Major Bellenden's remarks upon Sir James Turner spring to mind: "He wants to draw up the cavalry in front of a stand of pikes, instead of being upon the wings. Sure am I, if we had done so at Kilsythe, instead of having our handful of horse upon the flanks, the first discharge would have sent them back among our Highlanders." [68]

The Thebans might have counted upon their cavalry to defeat that of the Spartans, but hardly to break the enemy phalanx by charging it "in face, contrary to the custom of the service." But Xenophon is quite clear that the Theban dispositions were made in answer to those of the Spartans. In placing their cavalry where they did, the Spartans must therefore have intended that it should play some part in their plan of operation (whatever it was) and not simply have attempted to counter a Theban move.

Xenophon[69] says that the Spartans placed their cavalry in front of the phalanx because the space between the armies was actually level ground. This has been interpreted to mean that there was something other than level ground on the flank of the armies; that there existed some natural obstacle which prevented the Spartans from extending their line further to the right, either during the battle or when they were originally drawing their army up. Delbrück suggested [70] that Epaminondas had drawn up his army with his left flank resting upon this supposed obstacle, but with the cavalry in its usual position on the wings. There was thus a gap between the "obstacle" and the Theban infantry, which the cavalry filled. The Spartans drew up their own infantry with its right flank resting on the "obstacle," and sent their cavalry forward to defeat that of the Thebans and so open the gap for the following infantry, who were then to attack the left flank of the main body of the Thebans. But there is no trace of any such obstacle on the ground today,[71] and it is only to be found in Xenophon by turning his meaning inside out. Besides, as has been said already, the Spartans can hardly have hoped that their cavalry could attack the Thebans' cavalry successfully. There is no suggestion in Xenophon that the Spartan cavalry charged the Thebans. We cannot even suppose that the Spartans miscalculated the space available, found they had left no room for their cavalry between the "obstacle" and the phalanx, and so were compelled to place it in front. If they had made such a mistake, they would surely have placed the cavalry behind the phalanx, to follow up and help in the pursuit, not in front of it, to get in the way.

A different explanation, offered by Wolter, comes, I believe, close to the truth.[72] One function of the cavalry, including Spartan cavalry,[73] was to patrol in front of the army when it was on the line of march, and also before the camp, in order to guard against surprise. Accordingly, Wolter supposes that on the day of the battle both sides pushed their cavalry forward into the plain in order to screen the deployment of their infantry. The Spartans had intended to draw their cavalry back to its usual position on the wings before the main action, but Epaminondas was too quick for them. Before they were ready, his cavalry drove in theirs, and it was followed directly by the charging column of heavy infantry. The Thebans advance was so rapid that the Spartans had no time to develop an outflanking movement, and besides, the victorious Theban cavalry could have protected the flanks of the infantry column.

This reconstruction of the battle does not altogether explain the heavy Spartan casualties—more killed than, on any probable reckoning of numbers, were opposed to the front of the Theban phalanx.[74] Even if we allow three thousand Theban hoplites, which seems an outside estimate, in the main body, this would give them a front of only sixty men, and their phalanx would have been directly opposed to only 720 Lacedaemonians. Nor is it altogether clear what sort of protection the Spartans expected their cavalry to give them. Their army was not feeling its way forward towards an enemy of whose exact position it was unaware. Even if the two camps were not in sight of each other, as they probably were, the Thebans could not come into the plain without being seen, at well over a mile's distance, from the Spartan position. Watchposts on the hills to the south could have kept the battlefield under observation more effectively than horsemen riding in the middle of the flat ground. Nor is it likely that the Spartans expected their despised cavalry to be able to fight off the Thebans if they attacked while the hoplites were still deploying.[75]

I therefore turn to the view of Köchly and Rüstow[76] that Cleombrotus intended his cavalry to screen his movements, not in the sense of observing, and if necessary opposing, the movements of the enemy, but in that of concealing what the Spartans were doing themselves. "The space between the armies was actually level ground," and the Thebans were no less favourably placed to observe it than the Spartans. Cleombrotus proposed to march in column to the right and, when he was well clear of the Thebans, wheel left and form up at right-angles to his original front. He did not want the Thebans to realize what he was doing; and therefore interposed his cavalry between himself and the enemy. Not only the men and horses but the dust that they raised would effectively screen the Spartans from direct observation. At the battle of Mantinea in 362 b.c., Epaminondas did in fact move the Theban infantry to the left in column of route, and then form it up to charge the enemy's right wing, behind a screen of cavalry manoeuvering in order to raise a protective dust cloud;[77] the enemy realized that he was drawing off to the west, but thought that he was going to encamp and did not understand his true intention until too late.[78] At Leuctra, it would have been obvious to the Thebans that some movement to the right was in progress, but Cleombrotus may have hoped that it would be interpreted as a raid like that earlier carried out by the allied cavalry and mercenaries on the left wing. But Epaminondas must have studied the battle of Nemea too, and had his own plans for dealing with the Spartans if they tried to repeat their success.

The function of the Sacred Band remains to be considered, and the feat that won its commander Pelopidas glory equal to that of Epaminondas himself. At Delium, this picked body served, not as an independent force, but as the front ranks, the "cutting edge," of the mass of Thebans, drawn up twenty-five deep,[79] and after the liberation of Thebes, its first commander, Gorgidas, did not change the old tradition.[80] Most recent scholars have believed that the Sacred Band was used in the same way at Leuctra, as seems to be implied by Cornelius Nepos's statement that Pelopidas "in the battle of Leuctra under the command of Epaminondas was the leader of the picked body that first overthrew the phalanx of the Spartans." [81] If this view is correct, Pelopidas had no independent command in the battle, and the Sacred Band did not take part as a single unit, since they must have been distributed throughout the army in order to take their position at the head of the separate *lochoi* that, brought up side by side, were to form the files of the phalanx. That the Thebans, like the Spartans, and the imaginary Persians in the *Cyropaedia,* formed their phalanx by bringing one file up beside another, not by bringing one rank up behind another, is stated quite clearly in Xenophon's account of the second battle of Mantinea.[82]

Plutarch's evidence is quite definite, that Pelopidas did not break up the Sacred Band as Gorgidas had done, but, after it had proved its quality at Tegyra, "using it as a complete body, encountered danger in the forefront of the greatest struggles." Moreover, he says that Epaminondas himself led the phalanx (as he did later at the battle of Mantinea), and indeed it is hard to conceive of his doing anything else.[83] Pelopidas's speed and dash would not have called for special praise, if he had been acting merely as an officer of the phalanx under Epaminondas's command. To have trained the men who formed the front ranks and led on the rest would have been a notable service, but not one that deserved honours equal to those of the commander-in-chief.

If the Sacred Band formed an independent unit, and if Pelopidas exercised his own initiative in commanding them, the likeliest explanation is again that advanced by Köchly and Rüstow.[84] The Sacred Band was held behind the main phalanx, like the "ambush" that Cyrus kept under his personal command at Thymbrara in the romance. At the beginning of the battle, the Lacedaemonians under Cleombrotus moved off to the right, as they had done at the Nemea, using a screen of cavalry to hide their movements and leaving their allies standing (Fig. VIII A). Ill-judged haste following the last angry council of war was no doubt one reason why the allies were not properly informed of the king's intentions, but perhaps the Spartans would have cared as little as they did in 394 B.C. if the Thebans had fallen upon their friends and broken them, provided they themselves succeeded in their purpose.

But Cleombrotus, marching with his hoplites in his proper place, between the first and the second *morai*,[85] could no longer observe the enemy's movements. The cavalry screen that hid him from them also hid them from him. And Epaminondas had realized what was going on behind the dust. Instead of advancing straight across the field, he advanced diagonally. This would be more easily done by his deep formation than by an extended line. He sent his cavalry in front, to drive in the enemy screen and disorder their hoplites, and followed straight up with the main mass of Theban infantry, which charged the part of the Lacedaemonian line where the king himself was. A bitter fight followed; as Xenophon points out, the recovery of the king's body is proof that the men about him were at first able to hold their own and something more. Meanwhile only about a quarter of the Spartan line was engaged, and those on the right, who extended beyond the Thebans, thought that they could still turn Epaminondas's flank, in conformity with the original plan (Fig. VIII B). As Plutarch says, they "were unfolding their right wing and leading it round in order to encircle Epaminondas and envelop him by their number." That is, they were forming up at right-angles to the original line of advance in order to attack the Theban flank. But before they could put their plan into effect they were themselves taken in flank by Pelopidas, charging, like the Persian "ambush" in the *Cyropaedia,* from behind the mass of his own army. Nepos correctly says that the Sacred Band was the first to overthrow the phalanx of the Spartans, because, just as in the imaginary "Battle of Thymbrara," the men who had thought they were outflanking the enemy but were themselves caught by a flank attack broke at once. But if Pelopidas had not charged in the nick of time, the Spartans would either have completed their movement and inflicted heavy losses on the flank of the main Theban column before they were driven off, or been able to "bring their wing back again into the original position and close up the formation." In that case the Theban column would no doubt have broken through the Spartan line in the end, as it did at Coronea, but perhaps with no more decisive results. The extraordinarily heavy Spartan losses at Leuctra were the result, not only of the crushing of a quarter of the Spartan line by the Theban column under Epaminondas, but of the destruction of another quarter by Pelopidas's flank attack. Epaminondas, who was leading the main mass of infantry, could not also direct the charge of the Sacred Band. Pelopidas had to be trusted to act on his own initiative, and won his equal share of glory by the manner in which he discharged his trust.

The Spartans who were directly opposed to the main body of the Theban infantry gave way at last when Epaminondas, calling for "one pace forward to please me," combined the efforts of his mass of men into a single gigantic heave that bore the Spartans backwards.[86] Once they had begun to go they could not recover. Those on the left of their line "when they saw the right pushed back, gave way," but reached the camp in sufficiently good order to "ground their arms in the place from which they had started" and even to talk of renewing the battle. They had not in fact been heavily engaged. The *polemarchs* in command of them did not attempt to wheel round and attack the right flank of the Theban column. They would have had to begin the movement by marching off to the left, with their unshielded sides turned to the Boeotian allies and to the Theban cavalry, and if they had succeeded in forming their line at right-angles to its original front, their own left flank and rear would have been completely exposed. Moreover, though they could see that the original plan had gone wrong because the Thebans had attacked before it could be carried out, they could not from their places in the ranks form a true picture of the general situation, or consult together to form a new plan, or learn what the king (if he was not already dead) wanted them to do. Like Croesus at Thymbrara, Cleombrotus had made a good plan against what he could see of the enemy's dispositions. But once he had committed himself and his army to it there was no way of altering it to meet the unexpected.

EPILOGUE:
THE SECOND BATTLE
OF MANTINEA

The battle of Leuctra broke not only the Spartan power but the old order that it supported. The aristocrats in the Peloponnese, who had been prepared to humble their cities before Sparta in order that they themselves might be free of the inconveniences of popular rule, were massacred or exiled. Xenophon lost the pleasant barony that Agesilaus had found for him near Olympia. Epaminondas and Phoebidas used the power of Thebes in the south to liberate Messenia after centuries of enslavement to Sparta, and in the north (where Phoebidas was killed in 364 B.C.) against the Thessalian tyrants. But they did not succeed in unifying Greece under Theban leadership. Agesilaus, whose "lame reign" had at last brought the prophesied disaster, refused to recognize what Sparta had lost, in spite of repeated Theban invasions of the Peloponnese, and the Athenians sided with him to preserve the balance of power. The Arcadians, whose federation might have been the noblest result of the Spartan overthrow, quarrelled among themselves, and in 362 B.C., Mantinea broke with the other Arcadian states and went over to the Spartan side.[1] Epaminondas led a Boeotian army, together with strong Euboean and Thessalian contingents, into the Peloponnese to support the remaining states of the Arcadian Confederation, headed by Tegea. Sparta, Athens, Elis, and Achaea prepared to help Mantinea, but Epaminondas reached Arcadia and sheltered his army within the walls of Tegea before his enemies had assembled their forces. "For my part," says Xenophon, "I would not say that his generalship was fortunate. But of all things that are the work of forethought and of daring, this man seems to me to have omitted not one." Learning that the greater part of the Spartan army, under Agesilaus, was on its way north to the general rendezvous at Mantinea, he struck directly at Sparta itself, and would have found the city "as defenceless as a nest of young birds" if "by some Divine Providence" a Cretan mercenary had not brought Agesilaus the news and enabled him to return to the city in the nick of time. The Thebans failed to take Sparta, but as a result of their raid, Agesilaus himself and nine of the twelve Spartan *lochoi* were absent from the great battle that followed.

Epaminondas now marched north again with such speed that he surprised the Mantineans before they could bring in their stock from the fields. But the Athenian cavalry, who had just arrived after a forced march from Eleusis, saved the situation, though they had neither fed themselves nor baited their horses. Xenophon's two sons were serving in this force, and he shows a proper pride in the Athenian achievement against superior numbers of Thebans and Thessalians, the finest cavalry in Greece.

The Mantineans and their allies, including the three Spartan *lochoi* who were not with Agesilaus, now took up a defensive position where the central plain of Arcadia narrows, south of the city of Mantinea. Epaminondas saw that he must win a victory before returning home, for the sake of his Peloponnesian allies and of his own reputation. He drew up his army, and then appeared to change his mind and marched westwards, towards his left, as though to encamp under the hills. But behind the dust cloud created by a screen of cavalry,[2] the companies of hoplites, marching in column, were brought up and halted side by side to form a strong front.[3] Once again the Thebans, in their deep formation, were to break the enemy right, consisting of the Mantineans and the three Spartan *lochoi,* before the weaker allied contingents came into action at all. The cavalry, in a similar deep formation and accompanied by light-armed auxiliaries, were to break through the cavalry on the enemy right, who were drawn up in a line of the same depth as their hoplite phalanx, and without supporting infantry. If the Thebans cut their way through, the whole force opposed to them would give way. "For it is very hard to find men who will be willing to stand fast, when they see some of their own side in flight." The defeat of the enemy right wing was to decide the battle. The Athenians on the enemy left were to be contained by a force of hoplites and cavalry placed opposite them on "certain hillocks,"[4] who would fall upon their rear if they attempted to attack the right flank of the Theban assault column.

This elaborate plan succeeded, up to the breaking of the enemy line. When Epaminondas's army marched westwards, halted and grounded arms, the enemy believed that there would be no battle that day, relaxed their screwed-up courage, and broke ranks. When the Thebans suddenly picked up arms and charged, some of their opponents were scurrying to their places in the ranks, others bridling their horses, others arming themselves, "and all seemingly more ready to suffer than to act."

But to "crush the head of the serpent" was no longer sufficient, as it had been at Leuctra. The enemy was not merely a Spartan army accompanied by a train of unwilling allies. What plans Epaminondas had made to follow up his initial success, or whether, as at Leuctra, he would have been content with the possession of the battlefield and the dead bodies, we do not know. In the confused fighting that followed the breakthrough, he was mortally wounded, "and when he fell the rest of them were no longer even able to use the victory properly, but though the hostile phalanx fled before them, the hoplites killed none of them and did not advance from the spot where the encounter had taken place. And though the cavalry also fled before them, the (Theban) cavalry did not pursue and kill either horsemen or hoplites, but like beaten men passed in fear through the fleeing enemy. Moreover the auxiliaries and peltasts who had shared in the victory

of the cavalry reached the left wing (of the enemy), acting as
victors, and there most of them were killed by the Athenians."

At some point in the fighting, one of Xenophon's own sons was
killed, and he concludes his history with a comment on the
futility of the action, in which both sides set up trophies as victors
and both sent heralds as though vanquished to ask back the bodies
of their dead. The general expectation that the battle would settle
the affairs of Greece, one way or the other, was disappointed. The
Spartans had failed to reverse the verdict of Leuctra, but after the
death of Epaminondas, Thebes had no chance of becoming the
undisputed leader of Greece. Within a generation, the power
of the free city states had been broken by Macedonia, and Thebes
itself destroyed. The Greeks consoled themselves with the reflection that it was in the school of Pelopidas and Epaminondas
that Philip of Macedon had learned the art of war, when in his
youth he was detained in Thebes as a hostage. That Pelopidas and
Epaminondas in their turn had been schooled by Agesilaus is
generally forgotten.

APPENDIX

THE ORGANIZATION
OF THE SPARTAN ARMY
IN THE
CLASSICAL PERIOD

The ancient evidence for the organization of the Spartan army is obscure and has been variously interpreted in modern times. In the body of this book, I have taken the position that Xenophon's *Hellenica* and *Constitution of the Lacedaemonians* are consistent with one another and correct for the early fourth century, but that their information is not necessarily applicable to other periods. I believe that the Spartan army was reorganized more than once, and that much of the information that has come down to us applies only to earlier or later periods.[1] The following notes are intended to explain my reasons for choosing this solution to the problem.

In the *Hellenica,* Xenophon offers no description of the organization of the Spartan army, but he frequently mentions units and the officers commanding them. In the period before the battle of Leuctra, the unit most often mentioned is the *mora,* not only because the *morai* were the largest divisions of the army when it went on campaign as a whole, but because single *morai* were often employed independently. Each *mora* was commanded by a *polemarch,* and had a strength of about six hundred officers and men,[2] though the exact number in the field would vary slightly, as the whole strength was not called out for every campaign. There were six *morai* of infantry,[3] and to each was attached a much smaller cavalry unit, also called a *mora*.

The internal organization of the *mora* is nowhere explicitly described in the *Hellenica*. On two occasions during the Corinthian War, Xenophon says that *"polemarchs and pentekonteres"* were summoned to receive orders from the king,[4] which seems to imply that at this time the largest unit within the *mora* was the *pentekostys*. But the *Constitution of the Lacedaemonians,* while confirming the existence of six *morai,* adds that each had "one *polemarch,* four *lochagoi,* eight *pentekonteres,* and sixteen *enomotarchs."* [5] This is not inconsistent with what we are told in the *Hellenica* about the Spartan army at the battle of Leuctra, and rather than assume that the *Constitution of the Lacedaemonians* is wrong, it seems preferable either to suppose that the organization was changed after the Corinthian War[6] or not to insist on the letter of the evidence from the *Hellenica,* where Xenophon is more interested in telling his story than in giving details of organization.

After the battle of Leuctra, the Spartan army was almost certainly reorganized, as Xenophon twice writes of "the twelve *lochoi"* of which it consisted and never mentions the *morai* again. This is the more striking because "three of the twelve *lochoi"* are employed in the sort of work—as garrison of a fortified outpost—for which a *mora* was often used in the earlier period.[7] The most probable explanation is that the loss of men at Leuctra, and of territory soon after, had greatly reduced the size of the Spartan army.[8] The six *morai,* according to the *Constitution of the Lacedaemonians,* had been organized in twenty-four *lochoi.* Now there were only enough qualified men to make up twelve *lochoi,* and so the *morai* were done away with and the *lochoi* became the major units of the Spartan army.

But Xenophon does not expressly mention this reorganization, and, since we know very little about the population of ancient

Sparta, it cannot be proved that there were not reserves of manpower from which the losses of Leuctra were made good. Some scholars therefore believe that "the twelve *lochoi*" were the lasting basis of the Spartan organization. An easy textual emendation gives "two *lochoi*" instead of four to each *mora* in the *Constitution of the Lacedaemonians,* and the "twelve *lochoi*" are thus made as old as the *morai,* which are first mentioned by Xenophon in his account of the fighting against the democrats in the Piraeus just after the Peloponnesian War.[9]

The evidence of Thucydides has been ingeniously manipulated to carry the origin of the "twelve *lochoi*" back still farther. Thucydides calls the largest units of the Spartan army *lochoi,* and never uses the word *mora,* which is also unknown to Herodotus. That the major units in the Spartan army at the time of the Persian War, and probably considerably earlier, were called *lochoi,* not *morai,* appears not only from Herodotus, but from a number of statements in the scholiasts and lexicographers, all of which seem to refer to an earlier period, though their immediate source is no older than Aristotle. They will be noted in due course. In the meantime, it must be observed that though Thucydides agrees with them in calling the major units *lochoi,* he is not describing the same system, as Aristotle spoke of five *lochoi,* which are not to be found in Thucydides, though they can be reconciled with the information provided by Herodotus.

Thucydides says that the Spartan force landed on Sphacteria in 425 B.C. consisted of 420 men, "taken by lot from all the *lochoi.*"[10] It has been suggested, very reasonably, that the ballot would have been simplified, and the force made more efficient, if the draw had been by units rather than by individuals. The smallest unit, the *enomotia,* was generally about thirty-five men strong. Thirty-five multiplied by twelve equals four hundred and twenty, and so it is supposed that "the twelve *lochoi*" formed the basis for the ballot, one *enomotia* being taken from each.[11]

If Thucydides had no more to say on the *lochoi,* this would be acceptable, though unverifiable. But it is contradicted by his

evidence on the battle of Mantinea in 418 B.C. Here, he says, the
Spartan army consisted of "seven *lochoi* exclusively of the Sciritae." This allows the supposition that fourteen *enomotia* of
thirty men each were landed on Sphacteria;[12] be that as it may,
the whole Spartan army took part in the battle of Mantinea,
except the oldest and youngest men, who had been called out at
the beginning of the campaign but later sent home,[13] so it
cannot be argued that Thucydides means "seven of the twelve
lochoi." Unfortunately, his authority does not make it certain
that the full Spartan army at that time was divided into seven
major units called *lochoi*, not because his "seven" are not found
in lesser authors writing about different periods, but because his
account of the Spartan organization is ambiguous and hard to
reconcile with his own narrative of the battle.

When the Spartans at Mantinea learned that their enemies
were approaching, they were themselves drawn up by Agis the
king.

> For when the king leads, everything is ordered by him, and he
> himself gives orders by word of mouth to the *polemarchs,* they to
> the *lochagoi,* they to the *pentekonteres,* they again to the *enomo-
> tarchs,* and they to the *enomotia*. . . . On this occasion the
> Sciritae formed the left wing, who alone of the Lacedaemonians
> have this post as their particular charge. Beside them were the
> soldiers who had fought under Brasidas in Thrace, and newly
> enfranchised men with them. [Brasidas's men had also been
> "newly enfranchised," so that this whole contingent consisted of
> helots who had been freed from agricultural labour and enlisted
> for military service.] Then the Lacedaemonians themselves mar-
> shalled their *lochoi* in order, and by them the Arcadians of
> Heraea; after them the Maenalians; and on the right wing the
> men of Tegea, and a few of the Lacedaemonians, holding the
> extreme end of the line. Their cavalry were posted on each
> wing.[14]

After describing the order of battle of the Mantineans and their allies, Thucydides attempts an estimate of the strength of the Lacedaemonian army. Their numbers had been concealed as a state secret, but

> by calculating along the following lines one can form an idea of the number of Lacedaemonians then present. There took part in the battle seven *lochoi,* apart from the Sciritae, who were six hundred men. In each *lochos* were four *pentekostyes,* in each *pentekostys,* four *enomotiai.* Of the *enomotia* four men fought in the front rank. In depth they were drawn up not all alike but as each *lochagos* wanted. But over all they were drawn up eight deep. Along the whole line except for the Sciritae, the first rank consisted of four hundred and forty-eight men." [15]

Did the "seven *lochoi*" include the Brasideans from Thrace and other newly enfranchised? It is arguable [16] that "the number of Lacedaemonians" means "Lacedaemonians themselves," distinguished by Thucydides from both Sciritae and newly enfranchised in the previous passage. The newly enfranchised had been settled at Lepreum, on the border between Laconia and Elis, and it has been maintained that they no longer counted as Lacedaemonians, and that their numbers were too large for them to have formed a single *lochos.* But the Spartans certainly had not granted them complete independence, and the Sciritae, though distinguished from the "Lacedaemonians themselves," are yet said to be "of the Lacedaemonians" when their special place is mentioned. Thucydides may have been wrong in his assumption that all seven *lochoi* were identically organized.

If Thucydides thought that "Lacedaemonians" plainly excluded all except the "Lacedaemonians themselves," there was no need for him to emphasize twice over that his calculations did not include the Sciritae. Alternatively, if he considered the name "Lacedaemonians" ambiguous and wished to exclude the newly enfranchised as well as the Sciritae, he could have said so. "Along the whole line except for the Sciritae," should mean what it says, and not pass over a large contingent posted between the Sciritae and the "Lacedaemonians themselves." Probably, therefore, the army included only six *lochoi* of "Lacedaemonians themselves," the seventh being the newly enfranchised,[17] but the matter cannot be settled beyond the possibility of doubt.

A further question arises as to whether Thucydides is consistent in his use of the word *lochos*. The Mantineans and their friends could no doubt count seven distinct bodies of troops, apart from the Sciritae, coming at them, all clearly recognizable as Lacedaemonians by their red uniforms and the lambda on their shields.[18] An eyewitness in the allied army could have told Thucydides of the "seven *lochoi*," but that any of the allies calmly counted off the number of shields in the Lacedaemonian front rank I do not myself believe. The "448 men" in the front rank are, as Thucydides says, a calculation from the number of *lochoi* and the information available to him on the strength of the *lochos,* not an independent observation confirming it.[19]

If the "Lacedaemonians themselves" were actually organized in six *lochoi* at the time, one possible explanation of the appearance of the *morai* at the end of the Peloponnesian War could be a change in the function of the *polemarchs*, without a fundamental reorganization of the whole army. Thucydides implies that the *polemarchs* had no body of troops under their personal command in 418 B.C., but received from the king's mouth orders which they passed on to the *lochagoi*. Senior officers can hardly have served merely as message-bearers, and so the *polemarchs* would in fact have been a standing council of war.[20] But the Spartans may have felt that they were not giving enough scope to their best officers. Accordingly, at some time between 418 and 404 B.C., the *lochagoi* were done away with and the *polemarchs* were given direct command of the largest units. To avoid confusion, the name *lochos* was also dropped and *mora* was substituted.[21] This would account for the mention of only *"pole-*

marchs and *pentekonteres,"* not *lochagoi,* during the Corinthian War. But it would not explain why the *pentekostys* should have consisted of four *enomotiai* in 418 B.C. and only two at the time of the *Constitution of the Lacedaemonians.*

Another possibility is that Thucydides made a mistake, and that the *polemarchs* were in 418 B.C. in the same position that they held a generation later—in other words, the *morai* already existed, and in the form known to Xenophon. On this hypothesis, Thucydides was correctly informed as to the Spartan chain of command and the names of the officers who composed it (perhaps as a result of conversations with prisoners taken at Sphacteria),[22] but was unfamiliar with the word *mora.* For the largest unit in the Spartan army he used the word *lochos,* which, like the English "company," could either have a precise technical meaning or be used indefinitely of bodies of troops of different sizes. So he was led to give the Spartan *lochagoi* the command of the units that properly belonged to the *polemarchs.*

This possibility must be considered because his account of the battle itself seems to imply a much smaller *lochos* than the 512 men of his preliminary calculations. He describes how each army edged towards its own right as it approached, not by any set design, but because each individual soldier, beginning with the leader of the right-hand file, tried to put his unshielded right side out of harm's way. As a result, the right wing of each army overlapped its enemy's left, but since the Lacedaemonian line was longer, it overlapped by a greater amount. King Agis, at the last moment, decided to equalize his own left wing with the enemy's right, calculating that he could do so and still have enough troops left over on his own right wing to outflank the enemy's left. Accordingly, he ordered the Sciritae and Brasideans to lead off from the main body and cover the Mantineans on the enemy's right. This created a gap between the right of the "Brasideans" and the left of the "Lacedaemonians themselves." Accordingly, Agis "ordered from the right wing Hipponoidas and Aristocles of the *polemarchs,* having two *lochoi,* to come along the line and throw their men into the gap and fill it, thinking that his own right wing would still have an advantage, and that the wing opposite the Mantineans would be more strongly formed." [23]

This appears to mean that Agis intended to transfer troops from the part of his right wing that overlapped the enemy's left in order to extend his own left. To reduce the amount of ground that they had to cover, and also no doubt so that they should fight side by side with the rest of the "Lacedaemonians themselves" and not on the left of the Sciritae, he did not bring these men round to his extreme left wing, but ordered the units on his left to move out and leave a gap into which the troops transferred from the right were to come. But these troops are said to be "two *lochoi*," that is, well over a thousand men according to the reckoning of the Lacedaemonian numbers, whereas in the order of battle only "a few" of the Lacedaemonians were said to be on the extreme right, beyond the Tegeans. Here is the chance for those who believe that twelve Lacedaemonian *lochoi* (or ten, for reasons to be discussed presently) took part in the battle. If, instead of "a few," Thucydides wrote "the rest of the Lacedaemonians," [24] this could be taken to cover the desired three, or five, *lochoi* that are to be added to the seven that he mentions. But, even if the emendation were allowable, it is not sufficient to produce the desired result. For if Thucydides really wrote "the rest," and knew or believed that another fifteen or twenty-five hundred Lacedaemonians were on the far right, it was unpardonably careless of him to forget to add them to the reckoning when he was trying to calculate the total number. Unless he was completely misinformed, there cannot have been more than a very few hundred Lacedaemonians on the extreme right; and therefore, if the two *lochoi* who were to fill the gap were to be taken from this body, they cannot have been *lochoi* of five hundred men each. Here again it is tempting to suppose that the organization of the army may not have been as Thucydides describes it but as it is described in the *Constitution of the Lacedaemonians,* and that the word *lochos* is here being used of a body of four *enomotiai,* or, in this battle, 128 men and the supernumerary officers. Two hundred and sixty Lacedaemonians might be counted "a few." We might suppose that the condemnation and exile of Hipponoidas and Aristocles made it notorious throughout Greece that the commanders of two Spartan *lochoi* had played the coward at Mantinea, and that as this story came ultimately from a Spartan source the word *lochos* was here used in its technical sense.

It may be argued that two hundred and sixty Lacedaemonians would have been too few to close a gap through which "the Mantineans and their allies and the thousand picked men of the Argives" penetrated the line. But Thucydides obviously does not mean that the gap was wide enough for all these enemy contingents to pass through at once. Once the Lacedaemonian left wing was encircled and gave way, the gap will have increased rapidly enough.

If we are to assume that the *lochos* consisted of four *enomotiai,* we must suppose that Thucydides was wrong in saying that four *enomotiai* formed a *pentekostys.* A *pentekostys,* or "fifty," of a hundred and twenty-eight men is hard to explain in any case, whereas one of sixty-four men (two *enomotiai,* as in the *Constitution of the Lacedaemonians*) would be more intelligible. Discrepancies between the names and actual numerical strength of ancient military formations are found elsewhere, the best known being the Roman *centuria* of sixty men. The Macedonian *pentekostys* and *pentekontarchia* of sixty-four are also noteworthy.[25] It has been suggested that the *pentekostys* may have been a "fiftieth," not "a fifty," [26] and certainly in an army of six *morai,* each with eight *pentekostyes,* it would be approximately a fiftieth. But fifty *pentekostyes* cannot be found in the Spartan army at Mantinea without assuming errors in Thucydides as great as or greater than, those that have been suggested above.[27] Moreover, the *pentekostys* is certainly a "fifty" in the one passage in which Xenophon uses the word in connection with the organization of the Ten Thousand.[28] Here he is speaking of six *lochoi* of one hundred men, each consisting of two *pentekostyes* and four *eno-matiai,* organized for special duty by the generals at a time when Chirisophus the Lacedaemonian was still the chief commander. Presumably Chirisophus knew how the various technical terms were actually used at Sparta, and this is not therefore a case of professional soldiers wanting to sound like Spartans but not really understanding the Spartan military vocabulary.

If there were really 128 men in each *pentekostys* in 418 B.C., a possible explanation, which receives some support from the proportion of Spartiates to *perioeci* among the prisoners taken at Sphacteria, is that seventy-odd *perioeci* were added to each "fifty" of Spartiates.[29]

Since the "few" Lacedaemonians on the extreme right cannot have provided two *lochoi* of 512 men each, scholars have looked for these *lochoi* elsewhere in the line. Were they not Lacedaemonians at all, but Tegeans?[30] In that case, Thucydides should have said so. Moreover, Spartan officers attached to allied contingents were *xenagoi,* not "of the *polemarchs,*" and one was sent to each allied town,[31] not one to each regiment in the allied army. The statement that two of the *polemarchs*[32] were in command of *lochoi* makes difficulties in any case. *Lochoi,* whatever their size, should have been commanded by *lochagoi,* but Thucydides speaks of Hipponoidas and Aristocles as "having" the two *lochoi,* that is, as being in command of them, not as being sent to take them over for one particular operation.

Were the two *lochoi* taken from the right, not of the whole line, but of the main Lacedaemonian body? Were they, in fact, the first and second *lochoi* of the "Lacedaemonians themselves" in the centre? This suggestion also presents difficulties, for if Agis had taken a thousand men from the line at this point to close the gap between the left of the "Lacedaemonians themselves" and the Sciritae and the Brasideans he would have opened a new gap, and an even more dangerous one, uncovering the shieldless side of the centre. How was this gap to be closed? The remaining Lacedaemonian *lochoi* could have continued to edge to the right while the Arcadians stood fast; the units on either side of the gap could have extended their front and decreased their depth,[33] but Thucydides has nothing to say on the matter. Of course, it may be said, this second gap was never opened because Hipponoidas and Aristocles disobeyed orders, and therefore the plans that Agis had doubtless formed for closing it were never put into effect and so Thucydides never learned anything about them. None the less, the breaking of the centre of the line (leaving the extreme right as far extended as before) seems to be dangerous and ill-calculated to bring about the desired result,[34] whereas to transfer men from the overlapping right to the overlapped left makes sense. And if Hipponoidas and Aristocles were on the right, so that the king's order reached them by messenger, their disobedience is less astonishing than if the king had addressed them personally, as he probably could have done if they were the commanders of the right-centre.[35]

The choice is, in fact, between Thucydides's account of the battle, which is clear and straightforward,[36] and his account of the Spartan military organization, whose details he frankly acknowledges to have been hard to discover. Most of the recent British general historians take the former course, no doubt rightly.[37] The troops who should have filled the gap were to have been brought from the extreme right of the whole line; therefore either there were more than "a few" Lacedaemonians in this position, or Thucydides uses the word *lochos* in two different ways, and one of them is wrong.

If we assume that Thucydides made mistakes, the hypothesis that the Spartan army was organized in the manner described in the *Constitution of the Lacedaemonians* at least assumes fewer mistakes than some other conjectures that have been made. On this hypothesis, the Spartan line consisted of the Sciritae and seven other large bodies of men. Thucydides calls all seven of these *lochoi,* but in fact one consisted of the Brasideans and other newly enfranchised, and may have been about a thousand strong, and the other six were the six *morai,* each between five and six hundred strong. That Thucydides should have used the word *lochos* for these large units, if he was not familiar with the technical Spartan term for them, as well as for the smaller units from the right wing, is natural enough. The word *lochos* carried in itself no indication of number, and Xenophon in the *Anabasis* applies it to bodies of about four hundred men, each commanded by a "general," [38] though more usually to formations of about a hundred under a *lochagos*.

Two smaller units had been detached and posted on the extreme right, beyond the Arcadian allies. Thucydides calls them *lochoi* too, this time using the word in a different sense, perhaps because he is here drawing on a different source. But their commanders should not, on this assumption, have been "of the *polemarchs*." The chain of command, from the king through the various officers to the rank and file, is correctly stated, but the *polemarchs* were in fact regimental commanders, not senior staff officers. The most serious errors are in the account of the Lacedaemonian organization upon which the numerical estimate is based, the name *lochos* being applied to the *mora*, four *pentekostyes* being given to the *lochos*, and the size of the *pentekostyes* being doubled. But these errors cancel each other to a certain extent, and the conclusionn that the major unit contained sixteen *enomotiai* is correct.

Thucydides makes no comment upon the result of his estimate —600 Sciritae + (8 × 448), or 4184 hoplites in all—from which we may suppose that he found the answer reasonable. He does not profess to do more than "give an idea" of the numbers, and his estimate is very probably low, especially if there were more newly enfranchised than he allows for. Combining six hundred Sciritae with one thousand "newly enfranchised" and six *morai* of between five and six hundred men each, would give a total of nearly five thousand Lacedaemonians. But it is surprising that not more than seven or eight thousand hoplites to a side (three thousand Arcadians on the Spartan side seems a high estimate, and their army appeared the bigger) should have been engaged in a battle which Thucydides himself describes as the greatest of the time in respect to the magnitude of the armies and the importance of the cities engaged.[39] Some scholars therefore conclude that both Thucydides and Xenophon were mistaken, that their accounts of the Spartan organization must be rejected because they lead to impossible results; but that the true system can be pieced together, using some scraps of information that Thucydides, Xenophon, and other authors give us, rejecting information that does not fit, and filling in the gaps in order to reach the desired result.[40]

The supposition is that the six *morai* were already in existence in 418 B.C., but that each consisted of two *lochoi,* one of Spartiates and one of *perioeci,* about six hundred strong. The argument is developed along the following lines: Herodotus says that the Lacedaemonian army in 479 B.C. consisted of five thousand Spartiates and five thousand picked hoplites of the *perioeci.*[41] This is probably a round-figure estimate, and may be too high, but it is not obviously wildly exaggerated, like Herodotus's account of the Persian numbers. The figures for the Spartan strength cannot be checked, and scholars generally accept them. Spartiates and *perioeci* seem to have been brigaded separately, though this is not certainly established by the ancient testimony, and the basis for Herodotus's calculation may have been that at the time of the Persian War, the Spartiates were organized in five large bodies called *lochoi,* which were perhaps territorial in origin.

That there were at some period five *lochoi* at Sparta is known from several sources, all of which seem to go back to Aristotle's lost *Constitution of the Lacedaemonians.*[42] The evidence is as follows:

(1) In the *Lysistrata* of Aristophanes,[43] the women of Athens seize the Acropolis. When the police try to drive them out, they call out that they have within four *lochoi* of women fully armed. There is a pun here on *lóchos,* a company, and *lochós,* a woman in childbed. There is nothing in the text to show that the women

in question are Lacedaemonians, but it is possible that in the
original production the Lacedaemonian hostages who had been
left behind by Lampito, the Spartan delegate to the conference
that opens the play, were indicated by a gesture. A scholiast[44]
comments that "there are women in childbed among the women.
He says this because among the Lacedaemonians too there are four
lochoi, which the king uses." A second scholiast[45] corrects him,
saying that there were not four *lochoi* at Sparta but five: Edolus,
Sinis, Arimas, Ploas, Messoages. But Thucydides says seven, not
counting the Sciritae.

(2) The scholiast on Thucydides iv, 8.9[46] (where the men
landed on Sphacteria are said to have been "taken by lot from
all the *lochoi*") says, "There were five *lochoi* of Lacedaemonians:
Aedolius, Sinis, Sarinas, Ploas, Mesoates."

(3) Hesychius[47] says that Edolus was the name of a *lochos* at
Sparta, and that Aristophanes says that there are four *lochoi*
of Lacedaemonians, wrongly, for there are five, as Aristotle says.
Aristophanes here seems to be blamed for the mistake of the
scholiast on the *Lysistrata.*

(4) Photius[48] says, "Four (*lochoi*) of Lacedaemonians, says
Aristophanes. But Thucydides says five, and Aristotle seven."
No doubt he has mixed up the testimony of Thucydides and
Aristotle in his notes. Aristophanes is again blamed for his
commentator's mistake.

(5) Harpocration[49] says, "Aristotle says that there are six
morai, as they are called, and all the Lacedaemonians are distributed into the *morai.*"

(6) Herodotus names a Pitanate *lochos,* which is not in the
lists given by the scholiasts, and whose existence is denied by
Thucydides.[50] It is impossible to be certain which is right; the
undoubted existence of a Pitanate *oba,* or administrative district,
might be taken either as the reason for Herodotus's mistake or
as evidence for his accuracy. Perhaps a Pitanate *lochos* existed
at the time of the Persian War, but disappeared in a later reorganization, or changed its name to one of those listed by the

scholiasts. Or the *lochos* was recruited in the Pitanate *oba,* but bore its own regimental name. But it is not certain that there were five *obai,* or, if there were, that they had anything to do with the *lochoi.*[51] (The suggestion that the Pitanate *lochos* was a "young soldiers' battalion" and so not included in the regular lists[52] is interesting but unverified.)

If the five thousand Spartiates of Herodotus represent the five *lochoi* of Aristotle, the five thousand *perioeci* might be supposed to make up another five *lochoi.* No ancient author speaks of ten *lochoi* of Lacedaemonians, and there is no evidence that the *lochoi,* if there were ten of them, were coupled in pairs, one of Spartiates with one of *perioeci.* But the suggestion that they were so coupled is taken up by those who believe the "twelve *lochoi*" to have been a permanent feature of the Spartan organization, and that each *mora* consisted of two *lochoi.* "Spartiate *lochoi*" for five of the *morai* are found in the list of *lochoi* derived from Aristotle, and for the sixth, or rather the first, the "three hundred knights," who, according to Thucydides, formed the royal body-guard at Mantinea. There is no ancient evidence for any of this. The "five *lochoi*" are said to have been of Lacedaemonians, not of Spartiates. We do not even know whether Aristotle said that the "five *lochoi*" and "six *morai*" existed at the same time, or, if they did, how they were fitted into the same organization. It certainly seems easier to suppose that they belong to different evolutionary stages.[53] From at least 425 B.C. onwards, the *perioeci* seem to have outnumbered the Spartiates in the army,[54] and in the fourth century Spartiates and *perioeci* fought side by side in the same units.[55] To say that this must mean that *perioeci* were drafted into the "Spartiate *lochoi*" to make up numbers is to force the evidence to fit the theory.

If the "three hundred knights" formed the royal body-guard and fought as a single contingent, and if that contingent was called a *lochos,* and if there were two *lochoi* to the *mora,* it is possible to fit the "knights" into an army of six *morai* of six hundred men each. But we are invited to believe in six *morai* of more than a thousand men each,[56] in the face of the ancient testimony,[57] on the grounds that five *morai* (one being in garrison at Orchomenus) took part in the battle of the Nemea in 384 B.C., where, according to Xenophon[58] (who was not present), there fought about six thousand Lacedaemonian hoplites. Xenophon's statement that the *mora* defeated by Iphicrates was about six hundred strong is explained as follows: "The perioikic λόχος of the μόρα had returned to their homes in the autumn of 391 and not rejoined the colours again, so that in May 391 only the Spartiate λόχος of the μόρα was present at Lechaion."[59] There is no hint of this in Xenophon, who surely would not have wished to exaggerate the Spartan disaster by saying that a whole *mora* was defeated if in fact it was only half a *mora*. If the *mora* really consisted of two *lochoi* of six hundred men each, the *Constitution of the Lacedaemonians* must be altered to give thirty-two *enomotiai*, but only two *lochoi*, to the *mora*. And the "three hundred knights" can no longer be fitted neatly in as half a *mora*. Where then is the "Spartiate *lochos*" of the sixth *mora* to be found? This simply will not do. The six thousand Lacedaemonians at the Nemea must have included (besides five *morai* of about six hundred men each and the Sciritae) more than two thousand "newly enfranchised." This may seem a surprisingly large number, in view of the fact that another two thousand were serving abroad with Agesilaus at the time,[60] but Xenophon says that Agesilaus's men were only part of the total, without saying how many were left behind.

To sum up, Xenophon's evidence on the Spartan military organization does not contradict itself, and I believe that it is better not to tinker about with it in order to force it to fit other pieces of information (for example, the list of five *lochoi*), which should be referred to other periods, or to multiply the Spartan numbers. Thucydides cannot have got the Spartan organization right, because his evidence does not fit his own account of the battle of Mantinea, but we cannot say with certainty what is wrong, or how it is to be corrected. I have tried to indicate what mistakes must be assumed if we are to suppose that the Spartan army in 418 B.C. was in fact organized in the same units as in the early fourth century, and how some of these mistakes might have arisen. Two reorganizations of the Spartan army, one between the Persian and Peloponnesian Wars, probably as the result of the earthquake of 464 B.C., and one after the disaster at Leuctra, need to be assumed on this hypothesis, and I do not pretend that it is more than a hypothesis.

It is also necessary to assume either that the number of Spartan fighting men decreased greatly in the fifth century,[61] presumably as a result of the earthquake of 464 B.C. and the wars that followed it, or that Herodotus is wrong about the numbers at Plataea. But Thucydides's estimate of the Spartan numbers is consistent with Xenophon's evidence on the strength of the *mora,* and if he did not find it absurd, we are not justified in doing so. No doubt he failed to penetrate the secrets of the Spartan army, but he was in a better position to reach the truth than we are. The division of the *mora* into a Spartiate and a *perioecic lochos* is a modern invention and must be rejected. In any case, it does nothing to solve the problem of Thucydides's account of the battle of Mantinea. We must still ask ourselves either why Agis proposed to open a second gap in his line between the "Lacedaemonians themselves" and the Arcadians, or why Thucydides believed that two *lochoi,* amounting to more than a thousand men, could be drawn from the "few" Lacedaemonians on the extreme right.

The name *enomotia* implies a group of sworn companions, but in Xenophon's time, when Spartiates and *perioeci* served in the same units, it is unlikely that the bond was much closer than it was among the Ten Thousand. In the field, members of the same *enomotia* shared the same messes and billets, no doubt so that they, like the Persians of the *Cyropaedia,* might become familiar with their comrades in arms. But the system had its drawbacks. A story is told of how Epaminondas, after an action in which both Thebans and Spartans suffered heavily, ordered his men to take the evening meal and bivouac as they were, without trying to re-form their units. So it was at once obvious to the Spartans how many of their friends were missing, but the Thebans were not confronted with their losses, and gained courage accordingly.[62]

No ancient author suggests that in peace time some part of the *perioeci* was kept permanently in Sparta, in order to drill with the Spartiates with whom they were to serve in the field,[63] or that the Spartiate peers opened their messes to outsiders. In the distant age when the Spartan military institutions were established, the *enomotiai* may have been closely connected with the *triecades* (whatever they were) and *syssitia*,[64] and the men who were to serve together in war probably lived and trained together in peace. But in the late fifth and fourth centuries this was no longer so. There was only time to call up the nearest of the *perioeci* to accompany the Spartiates in the first hurried move against the Athenians at Pylos.[65] When the army returned to Laconia at the close of a campaign, the king "let the Spartiates go to their homes, and dismissed the *perioeci* to their own cities." [66] Men from a single town seem to have been distributed throughout the army, perhaps because the formation of local attachments within particular units was deliberately discouraged, and members of families were also separated.[67]

The slowness with which the Spartans mobilized may have been due in part to the need for telling off the men to the proper units after they had assembled. And units made up for the campaign must have been less efficient than permanently constituted ones, though the Spartans claimed that even those whom chance brought together in the confusion of battle could fight effectively, if they had been brought up under the Lycurgan laws.[68] But there is no reason to suppose that the two thousand five hundred *perioeci* (more or less) who served in the *morai* were not efficient full-time soldiers. When Agesilaus wanted to silence his allies, who said that Sparta did not contribute enough men to the army, he ordered all those who followed various professions, as potters, smiths, and carpenters, to stand up, one trade after another, until at last almost all the allies were standing, "but of the Lacedaemonians not one. For they were forbidden to work at a craft and to learn servile occupations." [69] Perhaps not too much should be made of the fact that this story speaks of the Lacedaemonians, not just the Spartiates, as full-time soldiers. But Xenophon notes the separate mobilization of the craftsmen, to act as a service corps, not as soldiers, when the Spartan army was called out.[70] We have practically no information on the internal organization of the *perioecic* towns, but it seems not improbable that each had its group of privileged citizens, who preferred submission to Sparta to an independence which might upset the social order.

That the Spartan army was called out by age groups is securely established.[71] These groups were defined with reference to the age of qualification for full military service (twenty), and at the beginning of the campaign, the order was given for "thirty-five from military age," or "forty," or whatever number was judged necessary, to serve. For each number there would be a group of soldiers who had reached the appropriate year and so the calling up of "thirty-five from military age" would cover thirty-five such age groups.

It has been well observed that, since the Spartans met the attacks of light-armed troops by ordering the youngest men to run out and catch the enemy, the youngest men must have been evenly distributed throughout the army. It has further been proposed that, since the number of year-groups called out for the battle of Leuctra corresponds to the number of men serving in each *enomotia,* and a similar correspondence seems likely for other campaigns, such as that of 418 B.C., each *enomotia* consisted of one man from each of the year-groups mobilized.[72] This is probably right as regards the theoretical organization of the Spartan army, but in practice such a rigid scheme cannot have been strictly enforced.[73] In the field, when the younger men were ordered out to pursue light-armed troops, the order was given to "five from military age," "ten from military age," and so on, implying that for the distribution of the younger men, five year-groups were taken together, so that, although the number for any one year might not be exactly right, there was a chance of averaging out over a period. Not even at Sparta can the authorities have been able to count on the right number of boys being born every year, or reared to maturity, in an age of high infant mortality. But they doubtless had lists of qualified men of military age, just as the Athenians had, to help them in the work of mobilization.

There was at Sparta a large class of "inferiors," apparently men equal in birth to the "peers," but, because no lots of land had been provided for them, unable to become members of the regular Spartiate messes and to share in the privileges of the ruling class. We do not know their numbers, or whether as children they underwent the same education as the "peers." Cinadon, who conspired against the state at the beginning of Agesilaus's reign, seems to have been of their number, and he had been employed on Secret Service duties against the helots. Whether he had done any other military service, and whether the "inferiors" as a class did normally serve in the army, is not established by the ancient evidence. I believe that they did, since it was apparently upon members of this class that the "peers" thrust cavalry service at the time of Leuctra, and since it is clear that more than one brother from the same family could serve in the army simultaneously. Two brothers could not both *inherit* the family lot, and though another lot, whose owner had died without an heir, might be found for the second, the arrangements seem to have been faulty, as in fact the land passed into fewer and fewer hands through the marriage of heiresses with land-owners. Large families, in Aristotle's opinion, increased the number of landless.

Again, if there had been a large pool of unemployed men eagerly waiting their chance to serve in the ranks, the Spartans would have been able to draw from it replacements not only for battle casualties but for men who had been disgraced and deprived of their rights for misconduct. Yet such men were not disqualified from military service, which suggests that replacements for them were not in fact immediately available.[74]

I do not believe therefore that the "inferiors" formed a large reserve of freeborn and fully trained, but unemployed, men, from whom a replacement of exactly the right year-class could be produced for every casualty. This supposition is inconsistent with the Spartans' anxiety to recover the prisoners taken at Sphacteria and with the decrease in the proportion of Spartiates to *perioeci* in the army. Agesilaus was able to organize his army in Asia, which did not include any of the regular *morai,* by year-groups, which proves, if proof were needed, that the Spartan system did not depend on each man being assigned to his *enomotia* when he came of military age and remaining in it all his life. The Ten Thousand were also organized by age-groups, but more roughly, the "under thirties" being sometimes employed on particularly active service,[75] and the older men being conveyed on shipboard when the opportunity offered, or left behind to guard the camp.[76]

The fact that the different age-groups were distributed throughout the Spartan army does not prove, therefore, that the distribution was not made anew as required.

A further detail given by Thucydides raises difficulties, but has only a slight bearing upon the main problem and may be considered separately. This is his mention of the "three hundred knights" who fought around Agis himself.[77]

That the Spartan kings had a picked body-guard is well established. Herodotus, describing the kings' privileges, says that they had "a hundred picked men to guard them in the field." [78] He does not use the word *hippeis* or "knights," in connection with them, though he is one of the main sources of information about the corps of three hundred picked "knights." Nor does he suggest that the three hundred picked men who died with

Leonidas at Thermopylae were the "knights." They were men specially chosen for what was recognized to be a dangerous mission, with children to leave behind them.[79]

That "three hundred picked Spartiates, those that are called knights," formed a guard of honour for Themistocles upon his visit to Sparta[80] does not prove that they formed the royal body-guard upon the battlefield.

In the fourth century, the royal body-guard did not accompany the kings on distant expeditions in which the citizen *morai* did not take part. Thirty Spartiates went with Agesilaus to Asia, and thirty with Agesipolis to Olynthus, besides many noble volunteers from among the *perioeci,* foreigners educated at Sparta, and bastards of the Spartiates,[81] but these men seem to have served as a staff rather than as a life-guard. According to Plutarch,[82] Agesilaus at Coronea was surrounded by fifty volunteers who had come from Sparta to serve as his life-guards in the battle. Xenophon says only that a *mora* and a half of the home forces had joined the army that the king had brought back from Asia.[83]

The royal body-guard is mentioned several times in the *Hellenica,* but without any account being given of its numbers. When Agesilaus hurried back to Lechaeum after the defeat of the *mora* by Iphicrates in 390 b.c., the *doryphori,* "spear-bearers," accompanied him.[84] This is the word usually used for the armed guards of great men, like tyrants. It does not seem to have had for Xenophon the unpleasant associations that it may have had for some other Greeks,[85] but if Agesilaus had been guarded by a special force of "knights," it seems likely that Xenophon would have mentioned it as a mark of distinction.

The death of noble Spartans "fighting before the king," both at Leuctra and in a skirmish at Cromnus in 364 b.c., where King Archidamus was wounded,[86] is noted. In his account of the battle of Leuctra, Xenophon refers to "those about the king" and "those about Cleombrotus." [87] There is perhaps a reference to the "knights" in the list of picked men whose death was followed by the defeat of the others. We should probably read, "When

Dinon the *polemarch* was killed and Sphodrias, of those about the public tent, and Cleonymus his son [whose death fighting 'before the king' is mentioned elsewhere] and the knights and the aides of the *polemarch,* as they are called. . . ." But the manuscripts actually say "horses," not "knights," and the emendation is not certain.[88] In any case, since Xenophon described the Lacedaemonian contingent in the army of Cleombrotus as consisting of four *morai,*[89] not "four *morai* and the body-guard," it is likely that the body-guard was incorporated into the structure of one of the *morai,* and did not form an entirely separate body. That it was not a separate body in 418 B.C. either might be inferred from the fact that Thucydides does not mention it in the Spartan order of battle at Mantinea or take it into account in his numerical computation.[90]

The institution of the "knights" was certainly very ancient. Though their name properly means "horsemen," they had nothing to do with the actual Spartan cavalry in the late fifth and early fourth centuries, a body whose history only went back to 424 B.C.,[91] and which was generally despised.[92] There is no doubt at all that in historical times the Spartan kings and their attendants fought on foot, and the "knights" must therefore have been instituted at a very early period, and were perhaps originally a select corps of hoplites who rode to battle but dismounted to fight.[93]

The *Constitution of the Lacedaemonians* describes the selection of the knights at some length, without having a word to say about their employment as a royal body-guard.[94] They were instituted by Lycurgus, who wished to stir up a spirit of noble emulation among the young men. The ephors chose three men "from those in the flower of their age," who were called *hippagretai,* marshals of the knights, a title that was not given to the officers of the actual cavalry.[95] Each of these three then selected a hundred men, stating clearly why he chose or rejected each candidate, and the rejected were thereafter at enmity with those who had dismissed them and with those who had been chosen—an enmity which was carried to blows when they met, though the fights were not allowed to proceed far before being stopped by the bystanders. In addition, the chosen three hundred were jealously watched for any slip from the path of honour.[96]

The *hippagretai* were apparently appointed annually, and it may be that in practice they only chose men to fill the places of those who had died, reached the age limit, or disgraced themselves. We may well suppose that re-nomination of men who were still qualified was automatic. What the age limit was we are not told, but it seems likely that it was thirty.[97]

If these three hundred really formed the royal body-guard, it is strange that they are nowhere mentioned as such in the chapters of the *Constitution* that describe the functions of the kings and the Spartan military organization. Here[98] we are told, "Whenever the king leads the army, if no enemy is in sight, nobody goes before him on the march, except the Sciritae and the advance patrols of cavalry. But if they ever think there will be a battle, the king takes the *agema* of the first *mora,* turns to the right and leads until he is between two *morai* and two *polemarchs.*" That is, the first *mora,* which is in column with the king and its own *polemarch* at its head, countermarches to the right, until its head, with the king and the first *polemarch,* reaches the head of the second *mora,* where the second *polemarch* is. Presumably the first *mora* then turns about, and the march is resumed with the original rear of the first *mora* at the head of the army. But what is meant by "the *agema* of the first *mora*" is not known. It is simplest to translate it as "the lead," [99] but the form of the word suggests that it should be a body of troops, and in this context presumably the royal body-guard. But this passage affords no additional evidence for the composition of that body-guard; we cannot say for certain either that the *agema* means "the three hundred knights" [100] or that "the leading *enomotia* of a division in column of route" was called the *agema.*[101] The word *agema* is also used by Xenophon when he is talking of countermarching the phalanx by ranks in order to transfer the commanders from one flank to the other,[102] but this passage does not help to make the meaning clear either. It can at least be taken to mean the unit (whatever that unit was) that would have been at the head if the army had been in column.

Whatever the precise meaning of *agema*, it is at least clear that it was "of the first *mora*." This passage therefore strengthens the view that, in the fourth century at least, the life-guards were incorporated into the organization of the *morai* and the king was not at the head of an entirely distinct body of troops. The "three hundred knights" could have formed half a *mora* of six hundred, but their organization in three bodies of one hundred under the three *hippagretai*, could not have been fitted into the internal organization of the *mora*.[103] It seems the more doubtful therefore that the royal life-guards consisted of "the three hundred knights" as such. But even if the life-guard was not "the knights" collectively, all its members individually may have been "knights." If Herodotus is right as to its numbers and Thucydides wrong, it was an even more select body than the "knights," and we may suppose that no young man who had been refused the lesser honour had much chance of being chosen for the greater. How highly the body-guard was honoured is shown by Plutarch's story of a Spartan wrestler who preferred the right to fight by the king's side, which he earned as an Olympic victor, to the large bribe that was offered him to lose his match.[104]

But if the knights no longer fought as a single corps on the battlefield, they still had important functions as a police and intelligence service. When the state was threatened by Cinadon's conspiracy at the beginning of Agesilaus's reign, it was to "the oldest of the *hippagretai*" that the ephors turned for reliable men to arrest the arch-plotter.[105] And Herodotus says that the five senior "knights" discharged from the corps at the end of each year spent the next year travelling abroad for the good of the state.[106]

The nature of the *lochos* of the Sciritae that formed the Lacedaemonian left wing at Mantinea in 418 B.C. is also disputed.

Thucydides distinguishes them, as has already been noted, from the "Lacedaemonians themselves," though he counts them as "Lacedaemonians," and I believe that the simplest explanation is the right one, namely that this force was actually raised in the mountainous district of Sciritis, on the frontier between Sparta and Tegea, which had been conquered by the Spartans in their early wars, but was apparently never absorbed into "Lacedaemon." Xenophon says that the Hyrcanian light horse were used by the Assyrians "as the Lacedaemonians use the Sciritae, unsparingly in toil and danger." [107] His meaning I take to be that both Sciritae and Hyrcanians were the oppressed subjects of a warlike master race, and used for dangerous and unpleasant work, rearguards, outpost duty, and the like. Some scholars push the parallel still further, and believe that Xenophon means that the Sciritae sometimes served on horseback too,[108] but nothing else that we are told about them suggests this. After Leuctra, the Spartans lost control of Sciritis (just as in the romance the Assyrians lost Hyrcania when they were defeated) and we hear no more of Sciritae in the Spartan army. At the time of the first Theban invasion of Laconia, the Spartan Ischolaus still treated Oeum in Sciritis as an ally, but with disastrous results.[109] A few years later, Archidamus ravaged Sciritis as hostile territory.[110]

Diodorus Siculus says that the "Scirites *lochos*" amongst the Spartiates was not drawn up with the others, but formed a special reserve of picked troops, stationed with the king, who went to the rescue of any part of the line that was in danger and often decided the fate of battles.[111] This is quite inconsistent with the evidence of Thucydides and Xenophon. Possibly Diodorus misunderstood, or was misled by somebody else who had misunderstood, the passage in the *Constitution of the Lacedaemonians* in which only the Sciritae and the cavalry are said to precede the king on the march.[112] If the "cavalry" was taken to be the picked "knights," a careless reader might confound the two and suppose that the Sciritae were "the picked knights who went before the king."

The suggestion that the Sciritae had no connection at all with Sciritis and that they were "skin wearers" as contrasted with fully armoured men is ingenious but improbable.[113] They are mentioned together with, but distinguished from, the "newly enfranchised and the *perioeci*" at the time of the first Spartan expedition against Olynthus, under Eudamidas,[114] which seems to confirm that they were not a specially equipped body of Spartans, but simply the inhabitants of a frontier district subject to Sparta.

NOTES AND SELECT BIBLIOGRAPHY

ABBREVIATIONS USED IN THE NOTES

ABV	Sir John Beazley, *Attic Black-Figure Vase-Painters*. Oxford: Clarendon Press, 1956.
AJA	*American Journal of Archaeology*
Annal. dell' Inst.	*Annali dell' Instituto di correspondenza archeologica*
ARV²	Sir John Beazley, *Attic Red-Figure Vase-Painters*. 2nd ed. Oxford: Clarendon Press, 1963.
BCH	*Bulletin de Correspondence Hellénique*
BSA	*Annual of the British School at Athens*
CQ	*Classical Quarterly*
CVA	*Corpus Vasorum Antiquorum*
FGH	*Fragmenta Graecorum Historicorum*
JdI	*Jahrbuch des Deutschen Archäologischen Instituts*
JRS	*Journal of Roman Studies*
REG	*Revue des Études Grecques*

For special abbreviations, see the Bibliography.

NOTES

CHAPTER I

1. Herodotus vii, 9.2. Professor L. A. Mackay reminds me that the words that Herodotus puts, for dramatic reasons, into Mardonius's mouth, do not necessarily reflect the opinion of any section of the Persian High Command, and that the Persian Wars did in fact provide, in the Battle of Thermopylae, the outstanding instance of the defence of a strong natural position by a Greek army.

2. Polybius xiii, 3.

3. Strabo x, 1, 12.

4. Herodotus i, 82—a fight between champions, not a general battle.

5. The inferior position of the bow in the *Iliad* (H. L. Lorimer, *Homer and the Monuments,* pp. 389 ff.) does not reflect upon missiles as such; spears are regularly used as missiles by the greatest heroes. But see F. E. Adcock, *The Greek and Macedonian Art of War,* pp. 15–16.

6. G. B. Grundy, *Thucydides and the History of His Age,* pp. 240–266. Grundy's ideas are examined by A. W. Gomme, *A Historical Commentary on Thucydides,* I, 10–14, especially p. 12, n. 1. See also F. E. Adcock, *op. cit.,* pp. 1–13.

7. Polyaenus i, 45.5; ii, 3.5.

8. Plutarch *Moralia* 215 B; 231 E.

9. Compare Plutarch, *Agis and Cleomenes* 47 (26).1.

10. Gomme, *op. cit.,* I, 12–14.

11. Thucydides ii, 22.2.

12. Thucydides iv, 44.

13. Karl Woelcke, "Beiträge zür Geschichte des Tropaions," *Bonner Jahrbücher,* 120 (1911), 127–235; A. Reinach, in Daremberg-Saglio, *Dictionnaire des Antiquités,* s.v. *Tropaeum.* Sir J. D. Beazley, in L. Caskey and J. D. Beazley, *Attic Vase-Paintings in*

the Museum of Fine Arts, Boston, III, 66–67, gives a list of trophies represented upon Greek vases, none before the middle of the fifth century B.C. The trophies shown to Pausanias as erected by Heracles and other legendary heroes are obviously concoctions of a late age, and Woelcke (*op. cit.,* p. 135) holds that even the trophy for Solon's victory over Megara (compare Demosthenes lxi, 49), is a projection of fourth-century custom back into the early sixth century. For the circumstances in which a trophy might or might not be demolished, Thucydides viii, 24.1; Vitruvius ii, 8; Woelcke, *op. cit.,* p. 138.

14. See the interesting article by William C. West, III, "The Trophies of the Persian Wars," *Classical Philology,* LXIV, No. 1 (January 1969), 7–19, especially p. 10 for the Theban trophy at Leuctra. (Cf. Cicero *De Invidia* ii, 23.69.)

15. Thucydides ii, 92.4–5; Xenophon *Hellenica* vii, 5.26.

16. Described by L. Chandler in *JHS,* XLVI (1926), 1–21, and U. Kahrstedt, "Die Landgrenzen Athens," *AM,* LVII (1932) 8–28. These are cited by Gomme, *op. cit.,* I, 14, n. 1. See also James R. McCredie, *Fortified Military Camps in Attica,* Supplement XI: *Hesperia* (1966), for a list of less permanent defensive works of various dates.

17. Xenophon *Memorabilia* ii, 1.13.

18. Compare Thucydides ii, 23.3; iii, 1.3; iii, 26.4, for Spartan invasions of Attica lasting as long as the invaders' supplies held out, and iv, 6.1–2 for living off the country. For convoys bringing supplies to armies detained in positions where they had looked for an immediate battle, Herodotus ix, 39; Diodorus Siculus xi, 79–80.

19. This point is made by Gomme, *op. cit.,* II, 67. See also C. Hignett, *Xerxes' Invasion of Greece,* p. 67, on the passes leading out of the plain of Marathon; and Adcock, *op. cit.,* pp. 68–69.

20. Plutarch *Moralia* 210 E, 217 E.

21. Thucydides i, 10.2.

22. Xenophon *Anabasis* iii, 4.8–12. For the names given by Xenophon to these cities, R. D. Barnett, *JHS,* LXXXIII (1963), 25–26.

23. Compare E. Delebecque, *Essai sur la vie de Xénophon*, pp. 18–19.

24. Xenophon *Hellenica* vii, 2.

25. Xenophon *Hellenica* vi, 5.6 ff.

26. Thucydides v, 65.

27. Xenophon *Hellenica* vi, 5.18–19.

CHAPTER II

1. This subject has recently been excellently treated by A. M. Snodgrass, *Arms and Armour of the Greeks,* chapters 3 and 4. Snodgrass does not, however, examine fully the evidence here presented for hoplites without body armour and wearing the *pilos* in place of the helmet.

2. Tyrtaeus frag. 7 (Diehl), lines 1–2; Plato *Laches* 190 E. A similar spirit appears in the Oath of the Ephebes, republished and discussed by Georges Daux, "Deux steles d'Acharnes," in ΧΑΡΙΣΤΗΡΙΟΝ ΕΙΣ ᾿ΑΝΑΣΤΑΣΙΟΝ Κ. ᾿ΟΡΛΑΝΔΟΝ, pp. 78–90.

3. H. L. Lorimer, *Homer and the Monuments,* chapter 5, especially p. 167; *BSA,* XLII (1947), 89. Snodgrass, *op. cit.,* p. 55. Kromayer, *Heerwesen,* pp. 65–66 shows from [Demosthenes] *In Neaeram* 94 that in the mid-fifth-century Painted Stoa at Athens, the Boeotian (Plataean) hoplites were distinguished from the Athenians by their helmets, but not by their shields. T. B. L. Webster, "Homer and Attic Geometric Vases," *BSA,* L (1955), 38–50, and A. M. Snodgrass, *Early Greek Armour,* pp. 58–60, argue that the "Dipylon" shield too is a piece of fantasy, but I am not convinced.

4. I have noted the following red-figure examples in the *CVA: ARV²,* p. 28, no. 1 (Nikosthenes Painter); *ARV²,* p. 72, no. 21 (Epiktetos); *ARV²,* p. 149, no. 14 (Manner of the Epeleios Painter); *ARV²,* p. 333, "Compares with the work of the Oinophile Painter": Heroic nudity, and in the first example a chariot.

On the famous cup by Douris (ARV^2, p. 429, no. 26) the shield of Achilles, presented by Odysseus to Neoptolemus, is "Boeotian" in the old tradition, and Achilles uses a "Boeotian" shield against Memnon on the Tyszkiewcz Painter's vase in Boston (ARV^2, p. 290, no. 1). Miss Lorimer (*Homer and the Monuments,* p. 167) suggests that the Attic artists lost their models in 480 B.C.

5. Lorimer, *Homer and the Monuments,* p. 195; J. Delorme, *Gymnasion,* p. 475; Snodgrass, *Early Greek Armour,* pp. 61, 84, 203.

6. Plutarch *Philopoemen* 9; Pausanias viii, 50.1. For the *thyreos* as a Celtic shield, Polybius ii, 30.3; as a Roman shield, Polybius vi, 23.2. On the question of whether the Romans adopted it from the Celts or vice versa, Quentin F. Maule and H. R. W. Smith, *Votive Religion at Caere; Prolegomena,* pp. 6 and 121 ff. See A. S. F. Gow and D. L. Page, *Hellenistic Epigrams,* II, 344. Terracotta model *thyreoi* of the period of the later "Achaean" League have been found at Corinth (Gladys Davidson, *Corinth,* Vol. XII: *The Small Finds,* 20, 340, no. 2926: "dated to about 250 B.C." by the associated coins and lamps).

7. Especially Xenophon *Hellenica* iv, 4.10. The Achaean mercenaries of Cyrus are closely linked to the Arcadians in the *Anabasis,* and stated to have been hoplites. (*Anabasis* vi, 2.16). For the round shield of Arcadian mercenaries in Asia a few years before Cyrus's expedition, Pierre Demargne, and Pierre Roupel, "Towards a reconstruction of the inscribed pillar of Xanthus," *Illustrated London News,* October 5, 1963, p. 512; Demargne, *Fouilles de Xanthos,* Vol. I: *Les Piliers Funeraires,* 79–105, especially 87–90; M. N. Tod, *Greek Historical Inscriptions²,* pp. 226–228.

8. Plutarch *Moralia* 220A. Snodgrass, *Early Greek Armour,* pp. 197 ff., and *JHS,* 85 (1965), 111, rightly notes examples of "multi-handled" shields that were used in other tactical systems than the phalanx. But these other shields to which might be added some representations of the *pelta*) do not have their handles arranged to give the overlap on the bearer's left, whose im-

portance is made clear by Thucydides v, 71. The close connection between the *aspis* and the phalanx is taken for granted by the ancients in general (e.g., Xenophon *Memorabilia* iii, 9.2; Diodorus Siculus xxiii, 2.1). I share the opinion of A. H. M. Jones, *Sparta,* p. 33, that the comparatively late appearance in vase-painting of warriors fighting in close formation "is probably because the hoplite phalanx is more difficult to portray and less effective artistically than two or four warriors."

9. Lorimer, *BSA,* XLII, 76.

10. Xenophon *Anabasis* vi, 5.16 speaks of slinging the shield on the back in retreat. Snodgrass, *Arms and Armour of the Greeks,* p. 95, notes that many studs of the type illustrated have been found at Olympia. He holds that the cord is simply spare material in case the first handgrip should break.

11. The surviving Greek examples (mostly from Olympia) and others from Italy and elsewhere, are conveniently collected by Snodgrass, *Early Greek Armour,* pp. 63–65; with references on pp. 231–232. Snodgrass notes the remarkable similarity between the Archaic shields, the late fifth-century example from Pylos, and a still later one from Olynthus (probably 348 B.C.). For the Spartan shields, Xenophon *Lac. Pol.* 11.3.

12. Xenophon *Agesilaus* 2.7.

13. T. L. Shear, "A Spartan Shield from Pylos," *Ephemeris Archaeologike* (1937), Part I, pp. 140–143, and, more briefly, *Hesperia,* VI (1937), 347–349. This discovery makes it unnecessary to follow F. Ollier, *Xénophon: La République des Lacédémoniens,* p. 54, in removing the words καὶ χαλκῆν ἀσπίδα from the text of Xenophon *Lac. Pol.* 11.3. The Pylos shield is oval, but not so markedly as to justify the distinction between round and oval shields drawn by P. Coussin, *Les Institutions Militaires et Navales,* pp. 47–48.

14. Plutarch *Moralia* 219C.

15. Sir Charles Fellows, *An Account of the Ionic Trophy Monument Excavated at Xanthus,* p. 8.

16. R. H. Cook, "A List of Clazomenian Pottery," *BSA,*

XLVII (1952), 139, no. 19. Compare Cook, *CVA, Great Britain,* XIII, 54 of text.

17. O. Benndorf, *Das Heroön von Gjölbaschi-Trysa,* Pl. xxiv B, block 3, and Pl. xiii A, block 10–11. Also on the Nereid Monument, A. H. Smith, *Catalogue of Greek Sculpture in the British Museum,* II, 14.

18. The following list is not a complete one, but I believe it to be representative:

Berlin Painter	*ARV²*, p. 207, no. 138.
Eucharides Painter	*ARV²*, p. 227, no. 11; p. 231, no. 76.
Syriskos Painter	*ARV²*, p. 263, no. 43.
Troilos Painter	*ARV²*, p. 296, no. 6.
Foundry Painter	*ARV²*, p. 402, no. 16.
Douris	*ARV²*, p. 441, no. 184.
Alkimachos Painter	*ARV²*, p. 530, no. 23.
Pan Painter	*ARV²*, p. 553, no. 33.
Leningrad Painter	*ARV²*, p. 571, no. 77.
Altamura Painter	*ARV²*, p. 590, no. 12.
Niobid Painter	*ARV²*, p. 599, no. 2; p. 600, no. 17.
Geneva Painter	*ARV²*, p. 615, no. 1.
Oinokles Painter	*ARV²*, p. 649, no. 47.
Related to the Charmides Painter	*ARV²*, p. 654, no. 2.
Telephos Painter	*ARV²*, p. 818, no. 17.
Sabouroff Painter	*ARV²*, p. 837, no. 2.
Penthesilea Painter	*ARV²*, p. 881, no. 29.
Heimarmene Painter	*ARV²*, p. 1173, no. 3.

19. A. Michaelis (*Annal. dell' Inst.,* X, 78; followed by A. H. Smith, *Catalogue of the Scultures in the British Museum,* II, 14) suggested that the στρώματα tied to Lamachus's shield in Aristophanes *Acharnians* 1136, may be a shield-apron. But (1) the

shield-apron is very rare on Attic works of art of the Peloponnesian War period (only the last example of the list above); (2) it is not tied to the shield but fastened with studs or rivets; (3) Lamachus next picks up his knapsack and orders his servant to carry his shield. It seems best to take στρώματα in the more usual sense of bedding, tied to the shield for convenience in carrying.

20. George Daux, "Chronique des Fouilles, 1958" *BCH,* 83 (1959), 675–679; compare *BCH,* 85 (1961), fig. 4 on p. 743.

21. Sir J. D. Beazley, *Antike Kunst,* IV (1961), 49–67, and Beazley in L. Caskey and J. D. Beazley, *Attic Vase-Paintings in Boston,* II, 79; Erika Simon, *AJA,* 67 (1963), 50. Aeschylus *Seven Against Thebes* 374 ff. dates from 467 b.c., but is obviously heroic in style and subject.

22. Bacchylides frag. 21 (Snell) (Scholiast on Pindar *Olympian* xi [x], 83).

23. Xenophon *Hellenica* vii, 5.20; *Hellenica* ii, 4.25. For Argive white shields, Sophocles *Antigone* 106, and other references in the tragic poets. "Boeotian" shields with the club blazon appear on Theban coins. C. M. Kraay and M. Hirmer, *Greek Coins,* No. 458 (p. 337).

24. Pausanias viii, 11.8. In this matter, I follow L. Lacroix, "Les 'Blasons' des villes Grecques," *Études d'Archéologie Classique* (*Annales de 'L'Est*), 1955–1956, pp. 89–115, especially pp. 93–103, 367. Lacroix and R. J. Hopper—"A Note on Aristophanes, *Lysistrata,* 665–670," *CQ* (New Series), X, No. 2 (November 1960), 242 ff.—refute C. Seltman's attempt in *Athens: Its History and Coinage before the Persian Invasion* to establish the existence of family blazons in ancient Greece. G. H. Chase, "The Shield Devices of the Greeks," *Harvard Studies in Classical Philology,* XIII (1902), 61–127, classifies (pp. 91–92) Greek blazons under twelve headings, including

4. Devices intended to indicate country or nationality.

(a) Devices carried by individuals.

(b) Devices carried by whole armies.

5. Devices chosen with reference to family or descent.

25. Plutarch *Alcibiades* 16; Athenaeus xii, 543e.

26. Eupolis frag. 359 (Kock) (Eustathius, *in Iliada* Bk. I, 293) referring to the conduct of Cleon, probably at Amphipolis in 422 B.C.

27. Xenophon *Hellenica* iv, 4.10.

28. Eustathius, *loc. cit.* citing Theopompus frag. 91 (Kock). Shields marked with initial letters are shown on the coinage of several Greek states (Lacroix, *op. cit.,* p. 104).

29. Chase, *op. cit.,* p. 110, nos. 147, 152. Mr. D. E. L. Haynes has very kindly examined the vases in the British Museum for me and dispelled my unworthy doubts as to the genuineness of the inscriptions. For a fuller list of examples, see J. De la Genière, *CVA, France,* XX, text p. 25, who suggests that the letters may stand for Athena, not Athens.

30. Herodotus v, 77.

31. See C. Hignett, *A History of the Athenian Constitution,* p. 157, on the importance of the hoplite class under the constitution of Clisthenes.

32. Cf. Herodotus ix, 74 (the anchor of Sophanes); Aristophanes *Acharnians* 574 (Lamachus's gorgon); Plutarch *Alcibiades* 16 (cited above).

33. Plutarch *Moralia* 243C.

34. A. Hagemann, *Griechische Panzerung,* corrected and improved by Ljuba Ognenova, "Les cuirasses de bronze trouvées en Thrace," *BCH,* 85 (1961), 501–538. Miss Lorimer, *BSA,* XLII (1947), 79, maintained that the plate cuirass was introduced with the hoplite shield as its essential complement. But the discovery of a plate cuirass earlier than any known to her reopens the question (P. Courbin, "Une Tombe géometrique à Argos," *BCH,* 81 [1957], II, 322 ff.). Snodgrass, *Early Greek Armour,* pp. 81, 84, justly holds that the wearer of this cuirass was probably not a hoplite in "the fullest sense, that of a heavy-armed infantryman operating in massed close formation."

35. Hagemann, *op. cit.,* pp. 17–19, "Verbesserte Glockenpanzer." The type perhaps appeared slightly earlier than he supposed; there is a doubtful representation by the Lysippides Painter (c. 525 B.C.) on the back of a "Bilingual" amphora in Boston (*ABV*, p. 254, no. 2; *ARV²*, p. 4, no. 7). But I believe that this picture probably shows leather corslets to which the painter has unthinkingly added engraved pectoral muscles proper to a plate cuirass. The unimproved type is usual on red-figured vases of the last quarter of the sixth century (e.g., the Andokides Painter's picture on the front of *ARV²*, p. 4, no. 7; four examples on a bilingual cup by the Andokides and Lysippides Painters, *ARV²*, p. 5, no. 14; compare also *ARV²*, p. 3, no. 2; p. 4, no. 10; and by other hands, *ARV²*, p. 8, no. 9 Psiax; p. 61, no. 72 Oltos). I would myself assign Hagemann's fig. 25a (Temple F in Selinus) to the unimproved type. *ARV²*, p. 27, no. 3 by Euthymides (Hagemann, p. 19, fig. 24) though without *pteryges,* is given by Hagemann to the improved type. Compare the outside of *ARV²*, p. 47, no. 151. Perhaps the latest picture of the unimproved type is *ARV²*, p. 186, no. 51 (Amazonomachy by the Kleophrades Painter). Vase-paintings of the "improved" form, generally with *pteryges* (Hagemann's list, supplemented by a search through the *CVA*) are of the Late Archaic and Early Classic periods:

Berlin Painter	*ARV²*, p. 207, no. 137 (Hagemann, p. 18, fig. 23) (Epic fight).
Foundry Painter	*ARV²*, p. 402, no. 23 (Achilles pursuing Hector).
Douris	*ARV²*, p. 429, no. 26 (Hagemann, p. 17, fig. 22); and p. 445, no. 256 (Hagemann, p. 17, fig. 21).
Deepdene Painter	*ARV²*, p. 499, no. 11 (Arming —of Achilles?).
Kaineus Painter	*ARV²*, p. 511, no. 1 (Kaineus).

Altamura Painter	*ARV²*, p. 595, no. 65 (Hagemann, p. 19, fig. 25) (Armour of Dionysus).
Sabouroff Painter	*ARV²*, p. 851, no. 272 (without *pteryges* and with projecting rim: Sleep and Death with warrior's body on white ground).

The improved bell cuirass also occurs in Late Attic black-figure (*CVA, USA*, X, Pl. 12, no. 1) and in Late Etruscan black-figure (*CVA, Deutschland*, XXIII, Pls. 1090–1091). Contrast the unimproved form on the earlier *CVA, Great Britain*, XII, Pls. 563–564.

One rider on the Parthenon frieze (Hagemann, p. 17, no. 4) is apparently wearing a bell cuirass of the improved form, but the figure on the Nereid Monument (*ibid.*, no. 5) seems to be wearing a *muskelpanzer* of the later form. Mlle. Ognenova (*op. cit.*, note 34 *supra*) shows that Hagemann exaggerated the persistence of the improved type of bell cuirass.

36. This type appears in Late Archaic vase-painting. In the Early Classic period it outnumbers the improved bell cuirass, and replaces it completely thereafter. I add a list of examples in Attic red-figure vase-painting, based on Hagemann, p. 20, n. 1 but with additions made after a search through the *CVA* and other publications.

Late Archaic

Douris	*ARV²*, p. 434, no. 74 (Hagemann, p. 20, fig. 26) (Epic fight).

Early Classic

Painter of Bologna 228	*ARV²*, p. 511, no. 4 (Charioteer).

Painter of London 95	*ARV²*, p. 583, no. 1 (Marpessa).
Altamura Painter	*ARV²*, p. 590, no. 12 (Achilles and Memnon).
Altamura Painter	*ARV²*, p. 591, no. 13 (Achilles and Memnon).
Niobid Painter	*ARV²*, pp. 598–599, no. 1 (Iliupersis).
Niobid Painter	*ARV²*, p. 599, no. 2 (Hagemann, p. 22, figs. 30–31) (Amazonomachy).
Niobid Painter	*ARV²*, p. 600, no. 12 (Amazonomachy).
Niobid Painter	*ARV²*, p. 600, no. 17 (Fight).
Niobid Painter	*ARV²*, p. 601, no. 18 (Iliupersis).
Niobid Painter	*ARV²*, p. 602, no. 24 (Gigantomachy).
Niobid Painter	*ARV²*, p. 604, no. 56 (Warrior leaving home).
Painter of Bologna 279	*ARV²*, p. 612, no. 3 (Amazonomachy).
Geneva Painter	*ARV²*, p. 615, no. 1 (Amazonomachy).
Painter of the Berlin Hydria	*ARV²*, p. 616, no. 3 (Hagemann, p. 23, fig. 32) (Amazonomachy).
Near the Penthesilea Painter	*ARV²*, p. 891 (Calyx crater with Amazonomachy).
Painter of Berlin 2536	*ARV²*, p. 1287, no. 1 (p. 1689) (Warrior leaving home).

Classic

Polygnotus	*ARV²*, p. 1027, no. 1 (Kaineus).

| Ariana Painter | ARV^2, p. 1101, no. 2 (worn by mounted Amazon, not hoplite). |
| Kadmos Painter | ARV^2, p. 1186, no. 30 (Arms of Heracles on pyre). |

Fourth Century

ARV^2, p. 1518, no. 4 (Arms of Achilles).

Sculptured examples, from the Parthenon to the Roman period, are given by Hagemann, p. 20, n.1. This type of cuirass is also found in Italiote fourth-century vase-painting (e.g., the Darius Painter's Funeral of Patroclus, in Naples), but I have not attempted to draw up a list.

37. Lorimer, *BSA*, XLII (1947), 132. She refers to the work of the Amasis painter (e.g., S. Karouzou, *The Amasis Painter,* p. 36, no. 62). For the early literary evidence for the linen corslet (*Iliad* ii, 529, 830; Alcaeus frag. Z 34 [Page]; *Palatine Anthology* xiv, 73), see D. L. Page, *Sappho and Alcaeus,* pp. 215–216. In sculpture, the stele of Aristion in the National Museum at Athens is an excellent late sixth-century example (G. M. A. Richter, *The Archaic Gravestones of Attica,* p. 47, no. 67: compare also nos. 46, 68).

38. I have not attempted to supply a full list of vase-paintings of corslets (but see also note 54 *infra*). The following table gives the numbers of examples illustrated in Attic red-figure vases published in the *CVA* (fascicles issued before August 1964). I have indicated by periods the number of examples, the number of those vases in which those examples are shown, and how many of those vases illustrate subjects which can be definitely identified as legendary. It is not certain, of course, that *all* the others were intended to portray scenes of contemporary life.

	Corslet without metal reinforcement	Corslet with scale or other metal reinforcement
Early Red-figure	11 examples on 8 vases (4 epic subjects)	2 examples on 1 vase (epic subject)
Late Archaic	69 examples on 42 vases (19 epic subjects)	24 examples on 16 vases (8 epic subjects)
Early Classic	55 examples on 35 vases (16 epic subjects)	21 examples on 16 vases (9 epic subjects)
Classic	17 examples on 16 vases (7 epic subjects)	5 examples on 4 vases (all epic subjects)
Late Fifth Century	1 example	1 example (epic subject)

The decline in numbers at the end of the fifth century reflects the altered tastes of the vase-painters and their clients, who turned to escapist subjects at the time of the Peloponnesian War.

39. *ARV²*, p. 615, no. 1.

40. On *ARV²*, p. 602, no. 24.

41. *ARV²*, pp. 598–599, no. 1; *ARV²*, p. 599, no. 2 (Hagemann, p. 22, figs. 30–31).

42. Plutarch *Alcibiades* 7.3–5.

43. Hagemann, pp. 44 ff and 142–145, lists and discusses examples known in 1919. But see also Ognenova, *op. cit.* (note 34 *supra*), and for the Early Archaic period, Snodgrass, *Early Greek Armour,* pp. 72 ff., with interesting parallels from Central Europe.

44. Xenophon *Anabasis* iii, 3.20; iv, 1.18. The *spolas* of Aristophanes, *Birds* 933 ff., is apparently some sort of weather-proof jerkin, not a piece of armour.

45. Pollux *Onomasticon* vii, 70, quoting Sophocles (frag. 10).

46. For Persian armour, Anne Bovon, "La Représentation des Guerriers Perses," *BCH*, 87 (1963), 579–602. Her fig. 3 (*ARV²*, p. 1656, bottom of the page) has a corslet, apparently of normal Greek type. Her fig. 2 (*ARV²*, p. 399, Painter of the Oxford Brygos), fig. 7 (*ARV²*, p. 417, no. 4), fig. 10 (*ARV²*, p. 646, no. 7) show the possibly quilted type. The Egyptian origin of the Persian corslet is noted in Herodotus i, 135; Persian scale-armour in Herodotus vii, 61; ix, 22.

47. Pausanias i, 21.7.

48. A. W. Kinglake, *Invasion of the Crimea,* VII, 200 (Leipzig, Tauchnitz: 1868).

49. Aeneas Tacticus 29.4—practical advice from a professional soldier; Cornelius Nepos *Iphicrates* 1.4.

50. Xenophon *Anabasis* iv, 7.15; v, 4.15; *Cyropaedia* vi, 4.2.

51. Plutarch *Alexander* 32.8.

52. Snodgrass, *Early Greek Armour,* pp. 84–86.

53. Lorimer, *Homer and the Monuments,* pp. 197–199.

54. Compare note 38 *supra.* Scale-pattern is commonly used by black-figure artists to indicate hair on hides (or on the aegis of Athena), or even as a pattern on cloth. I have not noted any certain representations of scale armour before the red-figure period. In the Early period, see *ARV²*, p. 21, no. 1 (Sosias). In the Late Archaic period, there are several fine examples: e.g., *ARV²*, p. 427, no. 3; p. 429, no. 26 (Douris); p. 458, no. 1; p. 460, no. 15 (Makron), and scales are found through the Early Classic and Classic periods, with one late fifth-century example (*CVA, Berlin,* III, Pl. 121.4). Laminated armour (small square plates sewn side by side onto the backing, instead of overlapping scales) is perhaps indicated by chequer pattern, or by a grid pattern with the squares filled with dots. I note examples from the Early Classic and Classic periods: *ARV²*, p. 585, no. 24 ("Earlier Mannerists: Undetermined"); p. 842, no. 118 (Sabouroff Painter); p. 1011, no. 16 (Dwarf Painter).

55. Lorimer, *BSA,* XLII (1947), 132. For the survival of arm-guards as cavalry armour, Xenophon *De Re Equestri* 12, 5, and A. Rumpf, Κράνος Βοιωτιουργές, p. 16. The thigh-guards which Xenophon recommends for cavalry cannot be the same as the infantry thigh-guards shown on black-figure vases.

56. The greaves of classical Greece are similar to those of the Archaic period (Snodgrass, *Early Greek Armour,* pp. 86–88, with a good list of preserved examples on pp. 239–240)

57. Cf. *Iliad* iii, 330–331; xv, 131–132; xix, 369.

58. The *chitoniskos* without body armour appears in the early

red-figure period (e.g., *ARV²*, p. 30, no. 1, Hypiss—Amazons arming; p. 59, no. 57, Oltos—Centauromachy) and is found in all periods down to the late fifth century. The subjects are often heroic (*ARV²*, p. 203, no. 101; p. 445, no. 265; p. 458, no. 1; p. 571, no. 77; p. 601, no. 24; p. 1044, no. 1), but not always (*ARV²*, p. 402, no. 15; p. 512, no. 15; p. 529, no. 4; p. 649, no. 47; p. 837, no. 2). Also on white-ground *lekythoi* (*ARV²*, p. 999, no. 185; p. 1384, New York, ex Gallatin collection, no. 41:162.11). A count through the *CVA* gave the following figures:

Early Red-figure	8 on 4 vases (2 epic subjects)
Late Archaic	29 on 19 vases (7 epic subjects)
Early Classic	19 on 12 vases (7 epic subjects)
Classic	11 on 11 vases (5 epic subjects)
Late Fifth Century	2 on 2 vases

59. For an early example of nudity (subject unidentified but marked as heroic by a Boeotian shield), see *ARV²*, p. 149, no. 14. Two fourth-century Amazonomachies, *ARV²*, p. 1464, no. 61; p. 1473, no. 1. A count through the *CVA* gave the following figures:

Early Red-figure	38 on 13 vases (no epic subject certainly identified)
Late Archaic	75 on 34 vases (11 epic subjects)
Early Classic	25 on 21 vases (12 epic subjects)
Classic	28 on 14 vases (all epic subjects, including the Eretria Painter's Amazonomachy in New York: *ARV²*, p. 1248, no. 9, except *ARV²*, p. 1207, no. 18 —Greek and Persians)
Late Fifth Century	8 on 2 vases (1 epic subject)
Fourth Century	5 on 4 vases (3 epic subjects)—also on Apulian funeral craters

60. ARV^2, p. 84, no. 16; p. 85, no. 23 (Skythes); p. 1565 ("vaguely akin to Douris"); p. 1135 (Pelike in Laon by a follower of the Washing Painter); sometimes with loin-cloths, *CVA*, Deutschland, XVIII, Pl. 837, no. 1.

61. ARV^2, p. 34, no. 14 ("The Pioneer Group—Sundry"); p. 1060, no. 144 ("The Group of Polygnotus: Undetermined"). On the Pyrrhic dance, see E. K. Borthwick, "Trojan Leap and Pyrrhic Dance in Euripides, *Andromache* 1129–1141," *JHS*, 87 (1967), 18–23, with references to earlier literature.

62. An early example, ARV^2, p. 72, no. 21. Found at all periods (e.g., ARV^2, p. 653, "Related to the Nikon Painter"; p. 1030, no. 35; p. 1344, no. 2). With *pilos* instead of helmet, ARV^2, p. 1041, no. 11, and three times in the fourth century, ARV^2, p. 1471, "Near Group G: Delicate Style," nos. 3 and 4; "Not so close to Group G," no. 2. Results of a count through the *CVA*:

Early Red-figure	4 on 4 vases (none epic)
Late Archaic	14 on 13 vases (1 epic subject)
Early Classic	10 on 9 vases (1 epic)
Classic	6 on 6 vases (3 epic)
Late Fifth Century	1 on 1 vase
Fourth Century	7 on 4 vases (1 epic)

63. One early red-figure (ARV^2, p. 150, "In the Manner of the Epeleios Painter"—Tarquinia No. RC 1130). Other good examples, ARV^2, p. 220, no. 4; p. 231, no. 76; p. 653, no. 1; p. 818, no. 17. Result of count:

Early Red-figure	1 on 1 vase
Late Archaic	22 on 15 vases (5 epic subjects)
Early Classic	3 on 3 vases (no epic subjects)

64. ARV^2, p. 402, no. 16 (Foundry Painter).

65. Compare ARV^2, p. 227, no. 11 (Eucharides Painter): p. 263, no. 43 (Syriskos Painter); p. 451 (Oedipus Painter no. 2).

66. Sir J. D. Beazley briefly discusses patterns on "blanket"

material (without special reference to its use for hoplites' tunics) in "Prometheus Fire-Bringer," *AJA,* 43 (1939), 622. I have noted hoplites wearing tunics of heavy patterned stuff (not always "blanket pattern") on the following vases:

Alkimachos Painter	*ARV*², p. 529, no. 6; p. 530, no. 25; *CVA, Italia,* XXXI, Pl. 1391, no. 1 (lower edge of tunic only is visible below shield).
Niobid Painter	*ARV*², p. 599, no. 8 (Figure of Menelaus; the tunic though patterned, is of apparently quite light material); p. 600, no. 17 (diamond pattern; patterned tunic worn by light-armed attendant as well as by hoplite).
Achilles Painter	*ARV*², p. 994, no. 105.
Westreenen Painter	*ARV*², p. 1006, no. 6. Described in *CVA, USA,* text p. 12, as wearing a "jerkin covered with fish-scale armoured plates," but I think it more probable that a heavy patterned cloth is intended.
"Group of Polygnotus: Undetermined."	*ARV*², p. 1058, no. 120 (only lower edge visible below shield).
Kleophon Painter	*ARV*², p. 1157, nos. 22, 37; *CVA, Great Britain,* XI, Pl. 504, no. 2b. Also worn by a light-armed attendant on a hoplite.
Curti Painter	*ARV*², p. 1042, no. 4.

Also in South Italian red-figure, e.g., *CVA, Great Britain,* IV, Pl. 196; XII, Pl. 578, no. 1.

67 The apron is shown on vases by the:

Peleus Painter	*ARV*², p. 1038, no. 1.
Kleophon Painter	*ARV*², p. 1143, no. 2.
Also worn by a hoplite Amazon over oriental dress,	
Shuvalov Painter	*ARV*², p. 1207, no. 16;
and by a Persian fighting a heroically nude Greek,	
Chicago Painter	*ARV*², p. 631, no. 38 [Bovon, *BCH,* 87 (1963), 589, no. 13].

For the Mossynoeci, Xenophon *Anabasis* v, 4.1. For their dress, *Anabasis* v, 4.13.

68. Lorimer, *Homer and the Monument,* pp. 245 ff.; Page, *Sappho and Alcaeus,* pp. 220–221.

69. Polybius vi, 25.3.

70. E.g., *CVA, Italia,* XI, Pl. 518, no. 1; XVIII, Pl. 889, no. 2.

71. I am indebted to Miss Edith Rutter, formerly of the Art Department of the University of California, for a discussion of this garment.

72. Four *exomides* on large vases of the Early Classic period, portraying epic subjects—Amazons or Giants—with a variety of hoplite equipment.

Niobid Painter	*ARV*², p. 602, no. 24.
Painter of the Woolly Satyrs	*ARV*², p. 613, no. 1.
Near the Penthesilea Painter	*ARV*², p. 891, Calyx Crater, Bologna 289.
Polygnotus	*ARV*², p. 1031, no. 38.

One of the Classic period, showing a hoplite with sword defending himself against a light-infantryman with a spear, *ARV*², p. 1083, Nolan amphora in Madrid, No. 11108. The sculptured examples are discussed below.

73. Aristophanes *Wasps* 444.

74. Aelian *Varia Historia* ix, 44.

75. Xenophon *Anabasis* i, 2.15–16. Professor Page cites Anacreon frag. 388.4, as the oldest reference to shield-bags, and also notes Caesar *Bellum Gallicum* ii, 21. Cf. Aristophanes *Acharnians* 574. I have not noted any pictorial representations as early as Anacreon (*ARV²*, p. 793, no. 78, by the Euaion Painter).

76. Xenophon *Anabasis* iii, 3.20.

77. Xenophon *Anabasis* iii, 4.47–48.

78. Xenophon *Anabasis* iv, 2.20. Compare Plutarch *Pelopidas* 32.3.

79. Xenophon *Anabasis* iv, 1.18; for the length of the arrows, iv, 2.28.

80. Diodorus Siculus xiv, 43.2–3.

81. H. Droysen, *Heerwesen*, p. 24 noted the evidence of the *Anabasis* as indicating that the Spartans wore no body armour, but did not distinguish between Xenophon's contemporaries and the Spartans of Tyrtaeus's time, or use archaeological evidence. His opinion was dismissed by H. Delbrück, *Geschichte der Kriegskunst*, I, 25, n. 2. More recently Miss K. M. T. Chrimes, *Ancient Sparta,* pp. 359 ff. especially p. 368, has independently suggested, after considering some of the archaeological material, that the Spartans developed a lightly-equipped type of hoplite before the Peloponnesian War.

82. E. Künze, *Deutsches Archaelogisches Institut*, Vol. VII: *Bericht über die Ausgrabungen in Olympia*, 56–128; Snodgrass, *Early Greek Armour*, pp. 20–28, with remarks on other early types, pp. 28–34.

83. For the "Thracian" helmet, and its descendants in the Macedonian period, see Bruno Schröder, "Thrakische Helme," *JDI*, XXVII (1912), 317–344; Snodgrass, *Arms and Armour of the Greeks*, p. 95.

84. Chrimes, *Ancient Sparta*, pp. 359 ff. But see Thucydides v, 70 for the steady Spartan advance.

85. Hesiod *Works and Days* 544 (also 540, of a felt lining for boots). See note 88 *infra* for examples in vase-painting.

86. Kreis-von Schaewen, *RE*, 20 (2), col. 1339 ff. s.v. *Pilos;* the cap of Patroclus, on *ARV²*, p. 21, no. 1, is explained in this manner. Rolf Blatter, "Rüstungsszene auf einer attischen Schale," *Antike Kunst,* 7 (1964), Part 1, 48, and Pl. 14, fig. 2, rightly distinguishes between this tight under-cap and the thick *pilos* worn by the attendants of the hoplites, which could not go under a helmet. Cf. also *Iliad* x. 265.

87. Kromayer, *Heerwesen*, p. 50 and Pl. 4, figs. 18–19.

88. Good pictures of such attendants:

Niobid Painter	*ARV²*, p. 598, no. 1 (Damophon).
Phiale Painter	*ARV²*, p. 1016, no. 42.
Curti Painter	*ARV²*, p. 1042, no. 4.
Guglielmi Painter	*ARV²*, p. 1043, no. 4.

In sixth-century black-figure, a light-armed horseman on an amphora in Bonn, Gerhard, *Auserlesene Vasenbilder,* III, 213: W. Helbig, *Les Hippeis Athéniens,* p. 178, fig. 9. Cf. Helbig, p. 198. Eurytion on *ABV*, p. 136, no. 49 wears a *pilos*, but as a herdsman rather than as a warrior or an attendant on one. Odysseus probably wears a *pilos* as a traveller, as well as a Sacker of Cities; Hermes journeys on his errands; the *pilos* that characterizes both of them is probably usually of felt. The rougher cap of Charon the Ferryman is in a different category. The *piloi* of the Dioscuri are probably often metal helmets.

89. *ARV²*, p. 605, no. 64 (attendant with plain pilos); *ARV²*, p. 600, no. 13 (Gigantomachy). Cf. also Munich 2359 (*ARV²*, p. 1661).

90. C. Carapanos, *Dodone et ses Ruines,* Pl. 54, no. 7 and examples exhibited in Athens, National Museum, no. 138 (from Dodona) and no. 7598 from Haghios Kosmas in Kynouria.

91. Aristophanes *Lysistrata* 562.

92. Thucydides iv, 34.3.

93. *Scholia in Thucydidem,* ed. C. Hude (Leipzig: Teubner, 1927), p. 248.

94. Beazley, *Attic Vase-Paintings in the Museum of Fine Arts, Boston,* III, 36, 61. Gomme, Commentary on Thucydides, III, 475, takes the *pilos* to be "the regular Laconian round steel cap," but I do not know his authority for saying that it was steel. He adds, "We may still agree that the javelins that were broken had struck the cuirasses." Droysen's suggestion, *Heerwesen* (1889), 8.4, that a sort of felt shield is meant, is refuted by the actual bronze shield from Pylos. Miss Chrimes, *Ancient Sparta,* p. 362 calls the *pilos* "a pointed leather cap." It is impossible to be certain of the material intended in vase-paintings. In *RE,* 20 (2), col. 1333 s.v. *Pilos,* the hats worn by Odysseus in the foot-washing scene (*ARV²,* p. 1300, no. 2) and Polynices bribing Eriphyle (*ARV²,* p. 629, no. 23) are said to be metal, but in both cases a felt traveller's hat would seem more appropriate and I suggest that the lines painted on these *piloi* may represent draw-strings rather than engravings on metal.

See also Stephen V. Grancsay, "A Sassanian Chieftain's Helmet," *Bulletin of the Metropolitan Museum of Art* (April 1963), p. 255, on the derivation of certain shapes of metal helmet from prototypes of "padded or quilted fabric."

95. Sir J. D. Beazley "Stele of a Warrior," *JHS,* 49 (1929), 1–2. See also Hans Diepolder, *Die Attischen Grabreliefs,* pp. 21–22.

96. Arrian *Tactica* 3.5; Dio Chrysostom xxxv, 433.

97. I have not noted any hoplites with *piloi* earlier than those by the Niobid Painter noted above (note 89). Other examples from Classic vase-painting:

Westreenen Painter	*ARV²,* p. 1006, no. 6 (note 66 *supra*).
Manner of the Peleus Painter	*ARV²,* p. 1041, no. 11 (naked except for *chlamys*).

Dwarf Painter	*ARV*², p. 1011, no. 16 (corslet with overlapping metal plates).
Shuvalov Painter	*ARV*², p. 1207, no. 18 (naked: battle of Greeks and Persians).
Codrus Painter	*ARV*², p. 1270, no. 14 (unreinforced corslet).

One crested *pilos* for this period:

Polygnotus	*ARV*², p. 1028 no. 3 (Achilles in Amazonomachy; "half-heavy armed" with loincloth).

Late Fifth Century

Reed Painter	*ARV*², p. 1381, no. 112 (unreinforced corslet).

Fourth Century

Group G	*ARV*², p. 1464, no. 61 (naked).
"Near Group G: Delicate Style"	*ARV*², p. 1471, no. 3 (naked except for *chlamys*).
"Not so close to Group G"	*ARV*², p. 1471, no. 2 (naked except for *chlamys*).

Cf. also *ARV*², p. 1473, no. 1 (naked).

Crested *piloi* from South Italy:

CVA, Italia, XI, Pl. 549, no. 6.
CVA, Great Britain, II, Pl. 88, no. 3 (and no. 8 for *piloi* without crest).

98. Carl Blümel, *Staatliche Museen zu Berlin: die Griechischen Skulpturen der V und IV Jahrhunderts v. Chr.,* III, Pl. 38; K. Friis Johansen, *The Attic Grave Reliefs,* figs. 16 on p. 33, 17 on p. 34, 79 on p. 155 (with further references). And on Attic gravestones of later date (e.g., A. Conze, *Die Attischen Grabreliefs,* nos. 627, 912, 1009, 1059, 1148, 1117, 1139).

99. G. M. A. Richter, *Bulletin of the Metropolitan Museum of Art,* xxxvi (1941), 67–70; *Catalogue of the Greek Sculptures in the Metropolitan Museum of Art,* No. 82 (pp. 55–56 and Pl. LXVIb); No. 81 (Pl. LXVIa) also shows the combination of *pilos* and hoplite shield.

100. For the Boeotian monuments, E. Pfuhl, *Malerei und Zeichnung der Griechen,* figs. 633, 634; W. Vollgraff, "Deux Steles de Thebes," *BCH,* XXVI (1902), 554 ff., and Pls. 7–8; A. D. Keramopoulos, *Ephemeris Archaeologike* (1902), pp. 1 ff. Miss Chrimes, *Ancient Sparta,* pp. 362–368, argues that these are the monuments of Spartans who died at Thebes, comparing Frontinus *Strategemata* i, 12.5. But the fact that monuments showing this equipment are more widespread than she supposed reduces the importance of the question.

101. Athens, Acropolis Museum, no. 3173. Karl Woelcke, *Bonner Jahrbücher,* 120 (1911), 149, fig. 3, publishes drawings in which the corslets are not apparent, and I therefore formerly believed that this piece proved that they were not worn. They are however apparent in the photographs kindly supplied by the German Archaeological Institute in Athens which I publish as Plate 11 in order to save others from my own error.

102. Pierre Demargne, *Fouilles de Xanthos I: Les Piliers Funéraires,* pp. 79–105, and especially Pls. XXX–XXXII; Pierre Demargne and Pierre Roupel, "Towards a reconstruction of the inscribed pillar of Xanthos," *Illustrated London News,* October 5, 1963, p. 512. For the Greek inscription (with commentary and earlier references), M. N. Tod, *Greek Historical Inscriptions,* I (Oxford: 1933), 226–228 (no. 93).

103. A. H. Smith, *Catalogue of Greek Sculpture in the British Museum,* II, 46–52, and Plates IX and X.

104. Herodotus vii, 92. For Attic and South Italian crested *piloi,* note 97 *supra.* For Cypriot crested piloi, J. D. Beazley and B. Ashmole, *Greek Sculpture and Painting,* fig. 220.

105. Snodgrass, "Carian Armourers: the Growth of a Tradition," *JHS,* 84 (1964), 107–118, has questioned the view that the Carians invented hoplite armour and tactics. But they certainly used them from an early period (Herodotus ii, 152; vii, 93).

106. The fullest illustrations of the friezes of the Nereid Monument are still the drawings published by A. Michaelis, *Mon. dell' Inst.,* X. See also A. H. Smith, *op. cit.,* pp. 8 ff.; and (for the date, c. 400 B.C.) G. M. A. Richter, *The Sculpture and Sculptors of the Greeks,* pp. 44, 131.

107. Called "peltasts" by Smith, *op. cit.,* pp. 20–21, nos. 866, 867; also p. 24, no. 879.

108. Michaelis, *op. cit.,* Pl. XV, no. 15, Smith, *op. cit.,* no. 869.

109. I am indebted to Mrs. Marian Sagan for her comments upon the equipment of these figures. For shield-aprons, the further hoplite leading the sortie, Smith, *op. cit.,* no. 869 (my Plate 13 A); more clearly on one of the ruler's body-guards, Smith, *op. cit.,* no. 879.

110. For long Thracian *chitons,* Xenophon *Anabasis* vii, 4.4. For Italiote Greeks, Hans Klumbach, *Tarentiner Grabkunst,* Beilage F, no. 11 (an Apulian crater in the Museo Gregoriano). Also see my Plate 17. In Attic vase-painting, it seems to be a distinguishing mark of orientals (*ARV*^{2}, p. 1038, "near the Hector Painter," no. 5; Persian?).

111. Richter, *Sculpture and Sculptors of the Greeks,* p. 125.

112. With *pilos,* hoplite shield, and corslet, O. Benndorf, *Das Heroön von Gjölbaschi-Trysa,* Pl. ix B, block 3, right-hand figure; Pl. x B, block 4, second figure from right. Other figures on these blocks have *pilos,* hoplite shield, and tunic. The Attic helmet is shown twice with and once without the corslet on Pl. ix A, block

2. Shield-aprons, Pl. xxiv B, block 3, and Pl. xiii A, blocks 10–11.

113. Benndorf, *op. cit.,* Pls. xi B, block 8; xvi A, block 3.

114. Benndorf, *op. cit.,* Pls. xxv–xxvi, blocks A 2, B 2–4.

115. Benndorf, *op. cit.,* Pls. xiii A, blocks 10–11; Richter, *Archaic Gravestones of Attica,* figs. 421–422.

116. Benndorf, *op. cit.,* Pl. xiii B, block 12. Another gate, to the left of this group, is assailed by soldiers in Attic helmets.

117. Aeschylus *Persae* 239–240. Compare 817.

118. "Etwa einhalbmal so hoch wie der Hoplit," is Kromayer's estimate (*Heerwesen,* p. 51). He allows for the possibility that the artists may sometimes have reduced their spears to fit them into the space available.

119. On the early development of Greek spears, Snodgrass, *Early Greek Armour,* pp. 115 ff.

120. Miss Richter (*Catalogue of Greek Sculptures in the Metropolitan Museum of Art,* p. 55, no. 82) notes several representations of this action.

121. Homer *Iliad* x, 153.

122. Homer *Iliad* v, 66; xix, 390; xxii, 225, etc.

123. Theophrastus, *Historia Plantarum,* iii, 12.2 (the long Macedonian pike). Xenophon *De Re Equestri* 12.12 advises cavalry to use two javelins of cornel wood rather than a long lance. But see Arrian, *Anabasis* i, 15.5, on the advantage of the long Macedonian lance (of cornel wood) over the Persian javelin.

124. Xenophon *Hellenica* iii, 5.20; iv, 6.11; v, 4.52; also the democratic party defending the Piraeus, ii, 4.15. Snodgrass (*Early Greek Armour,* pp. 138–139) argues convincingly, on the evidence of seventh-century vase-painting, that the earliest Greek hoplites continued to use the pair of spears—one to throw, one for close quarters—that had been used in the skirmishing warfare of the preceding age.

125. C. Carapanos, *Dodone et ses Ruines,* Pl. 57, no. 2; H. Weber, *Olympische Forschungen,* I, 164 and Pl. 71a. For Greek swords in the early Iron Age, Lorimer, *Homer and the Monuments,* pp. 267–270; S. Foltiny, "Athens and East Hallstatt:

Cultural Interrelations," *AJA*, 65 (1961), 289; Snodgrass, *Early Greek Armour*, 92–113.

126. Xenophon *De Re Equestri* 12.11. For actual examples, *British Museum: Guide to the Exhibition Illustrating Greek and Roman Life*, p. 100; Coussin, *Institutions Militaires et Navales*, p. 51 and Pl. XV, no. 1. Horace Sandars, "The Weapons of the Iberians," *Archaeologia*, 64 (1912–1913), 231 ff.

127. Plutarch *Moralia* 191 E, 216 C; *Lycurgus* 19.2

128. Plutarch *Moralia* 217 E.

129. Plutarch *Moralia* 241 F.

130. Plutarch *Dion* 57–58 (for the description of the sword, 58.3) and *Moralia* 553 D.

131. Chrimes, *Ancient Sparta*, p. 363 (but the mention of Demades shows that Plutarch's story must refer to Agis III, not Agis II).

132. References, Chrimes, *Ancient Sparta*, p. 255, n. 4.

133. Xenophon *Anabasis* iv, 7.16, 8.25. He also uses the word *xyele* of a spokeshave used in trimming the shafts of spears; *Cyropaedia* vi, 2.32.

134. Plutarch *Moralia* 233 F.

135. Though Chrimes, *Ancient Sparta*, p. 255 and H. Michell, *Sparta*, p. 269 hold otherwise. Kromayer (*Heerwesen*, p. 39, n. 3) equates the *xyele* with the short sword, and therefore concludes that the latter was not used for stabbing.

136. References, Chrimes, *Ancient Sparta*, p. 87, n. 2.

137. Xenophon *Lac. Pol. 11, 3*. F. Ollier, *Xénophon: La République des Lacédémoniens*, p. 54, suggests that red is a colour of magical potency and virility.

138. Plutarch *Lycurgus* 27.

139. Aristophanes *Lysistrata* 1140 (written in 411 B.C., but perhaps here repeating old tradition).

140. Plutarch *Moralia* 193 B; Pausanias ix, 13.11–12.

141. Xenophon *Agesilaus* 2.7.

142. E. Friederici, *Das Persische Idealheer des Xenophon*, p. 45, makes the same point for the imaginary army of the *Cyropaedia*.

143. Aristophanes *Peace* 1172–1178; cf. *Acharnians* 965. Kromayer, *Heerwesen,* p. 51; Ollier, *Xénophon: la République des Lacédémonians,* p. 54. Cf. also M. Bieber, *History of the Greek and Roman Theatre,* p. 259 fig. 351, and fig. 370.

144. Herodotus vi, 112.3. G. B. Grundy, *The Great Persian War,* p. 188, translates the key word δρόμῳ as "quick-step." But it seems better, and more in accordance with the general usage of the word δρόμος, to follow Delbrück (*Geschichte der Kriegskunst,* I, 45, 49, 55, n. 7) who supposes that they did indeed charge at a run, but perhaps only at the last moment, after coming within bowshot. See also Snodgrass, *Arms and Armour of the Greeks,* pp. 91, 102–103.

145. Herodotus vii, 211.3; Grundy, *op. cit.,* p. 297; Hignett, *Xerxes' Invasion of Greece,* p. 144.

146. Herodotus, ix, 59–63.

147. Chrimes, *Ancient Sparta,* pp. 360–361.

CHAPTER III

1. Xenophon *Lac. Pol.* 11.2; F. Ollier, *Xénophon: La République des Lacédémoniens,* pp. 53–54.

2. Xenophon *Cyropaedia* vi. 2.25–3.4; Kromayer, *Heerwesen,* p. 40. H. Michell, *Sparta,* p. 261. For the cavalry screen in front of the Spartan army on the march, cf. Xenophon *Lac. Pol.* 13.6.

3. Thucydides vi, 44.1 (and vi, 22, for the advice of Nicias). On the whole question of the supply of Greek armies, see K. Tänzer, *Das Verpflegungswesen der Griechischen Heere,* to whom I am indebted for many references, and the short but clear account by Kromayer, *Heerwesen,* pp. 76–78.

4. Aristophanes *Peace* 312; *Acharnians* 197.

5. Aristophanes *Peace* 1182–1184.

6. Μάζα Archilochus frag. 2 (Diehl); Plutarch *Moralia* 230 E–F.

7. Plutarch *Moralia* 349 A; Tänzer, *Verpflegungswesen,* p. 40.

8. Aristophanes *Peace* 1129.

9. Γυλιός, Aristophanes *Peace* 527; *Acharnians* 1099–1101. W.

Helbig. *Les Ἱππεῖς Athéniens,* p. 208, notes three illustrations from Attic vase-painting.

10. Xenophon *Cyropaedia* ii, 1.31. Cf. E. Friederici, *Das Persische Idealheer des Xenophon,* p. 19.

11. Theophrastus, *Characters,* xxvii (xxv).

12. Thucydides vii, 75.5.

13. Isaeus v, 11.

14. Compare Chapter Two, note 88, *supra.*

15. The crowd of light-armed and unarmed men that accompanied both sides at Delium in 424 B.C. had no influence on the battle (Thucydides iv, 94.1). Compare the distinction drawn by Arrian, *Tactica* 2.1, between the fighting troops, and "what is brought together to support the fighting troops, such as the servants, the medical corps, the merchants, and the hucksters."

16. Xenophon *Lac. Pol.* 12.1–4.

17. Athenaeus xiv 657 b–c.

18. Aristophanes *Acharnians* 1099–1101 and 1136–1137.

19. Plutarch *Moralia* 187 C.

20. Xenophon *Lac. Pol.* 15.4; *Agesilaus* 5.1. Cf. Herodotus vi, 57.3. Ollier, *Xénophon,* p. 72, suggests that not all kings may have set such good examples as Agesilaus.

21. Xenophon *Cyropaedia* ii, 1–30.

22. Note 4 *supra;* also for a picked advance guard making a forced march, Xenophon *Cyropaedia* v, 3.35. Cf. Tänzer, *Verpflegungswesen,* pp. 43–44.

23. Thucydides vii, 73.2; Plutarch *Phocion* 24.3; Polyaenus iii, 12.2.

24. Xenophon *Hellenica* vii, 1.41.

25. Xenophon *Hellenica* v, 1.18.

26. Aristotle *Rhetoric* 1411a.

27. Thucydides v, 47.6.

28. Diodorus Siculus xiii, 95.3.

29. Compare Thucydides iii, 17.4 on the allowance of the Athenian army at Potidaea—a drachma a day for each hoplite and the same for his servant.

30. Frontinus *Strategemata* iv, 1.6; Plutarch *Moralia* 178A (*Philip* 13).

31. Thucydides ii, 101.5.

32. Demosthenes xviii, 157.

33. Polyaenus iv, 2.10.

34. Demosthenes liv, 3–6.

35. On the whole question, see L. A. Moritz, *Grain Mills and Flour in Antiquity*.

36. Polybius vi, 38.2–3.

37. Thucydides ii, 78.3.

38. G. M. Trevelyan, *England in the Reign of Queen Anne,* (London, Longmans, Green and Co.: 1948) II: *Ramillies,* 101 (footnote).

39. Thucydides iv, 16.1.

40. Thucydides vii, 87.2.

41. A. W. Gomme, *Commentary on Thucydides,* III, 453.

42. Athenaeus iv, 131c.

43. Plutarch *Lycurgus* 12.2. Plutarch's figures for barley and wine differ from those of Athenaeus, but he seems to be using a different system of measures.

44. Tänzer, *Verpflegungswesen,* pp. 35–38, tries to calculate the loaf that could be baked from this ration, but his figures are irrelevant if the ration was consumed in the form of μάζα. H. Michell, *Sparta,* pp. 287 ff., discusses the difficulties raised by these ancient figures, which seem improbably large for one man.

45. Athenaeus iv, 131c.

46. Xenophon *Hellenica* iv, 5.4.

47. Xenophon *Lac. Pol.* 15.3. For the herds accompanying the army, Herodotus vi, 56.1; Pausanias ix, 13.4.

48. Xenophon *Lac. Pol.* 13.4–5. For the distribution of meat after sacrifice, *Hellenica* iv, 3.14.

49. Tänzer, *Verpflegungswesen,* p. 38.

50. Xenophon *Anabasis* i, 5.6.

51. Xenophon *Anabasis* vi, 2.3–4.

52. Xenophon *Anabasis* v, 3.3; vi, 2.16.

53. Xenophon *Anabasis* vi, 1.15.

54. Xenophon *Hellenica* v, 1.17.

55. Cf. Xenophon *Hellenica* ii, 1.1–2.

56. Thucydides vi, 44.1–3.

57. Xenophon *Hellenica* i, 6.37.

58. Aristotle *Oeconomicus* ii, 1350b 10; Polyaenus iii, 10.10; H. W. Parke, *Greek Mercenaries,* pp. 108–109.

59. Xenophon *Cyropaedia* vi, 2.38; *Anabasis* i, 5.6; for the reserve wagons, *Anabasis* i, 10.18; Tänzer, *Verpflegungswesen,* pp. 45 ff. Friederici, *Das Persische Idealheer des Xenophon,* pp. 18 ff., perhaps overlooks the "Lydian" market when he says that the supply system of the army in the *Cyropaedia* is arranged in the Greek manner.

60. Xenophon *Anabasis* v, 7.21–29; Tänzer, *Verpflegungswesen,* p. 47.

61. Thucydides viii, 95.4; Xenophon *Hellenica* ii, 1.25.

62. Thucydides viii, 100.2; Diodorus Siculus xii, 68.5.

63. Xenophon *Hellenica,* iii, 4.11; v, 4.48–49; Polyaenus ii, 1.11.

64. Xenophon *Hellenica* iii, 2.11 (cf. Kromayer, *Heerwesen,* p. 78, n. 2); *Cyropaedia* ii, 4.18.

65. Herodotus ix, 39.2. Tänzer, *Verpflegungswesen,* pp. 16–17, supposes that the animals were drawing 250 carts, but they were more probably pack-animals.

66. Diodorus Siculus xi, 80.3–4.

67. Cf. G. F. Hill, *Historical Greek Coins,* pp. 57–60; C. M. Kraay and Max Hirmer, *Greek Coins,* nos. 621–623 (pp. 358–359).

68. Xenophon (*Anabasis* i, 3.21; vii, 2.36; vii, 6.1) records the different monthly rates of pay offered the Ten Thousand at different times by Cyrus, Seuthes of Thrace, and the Spartans. Thucydides, iii, 17.4, gives the very generous daily allowance of the Athenian hoplites at Potidaea; viii, 29.1–2 and 45.2, the bargaining over the maintenance of the Spartan fleet by the Persians; v, 47.6, the terms of the quadruple alliance between Athens, Argos, Elis, and Mantinea; vii, 27.2, the pay of Thracian peltasts in Athenian service. Aristophanes *Acharnians* 153 ff. is,

of course, comic exaggeration. For the Ten Thousand and Anaxibius, Xenophon *Anabasis* vii, 1.7–17.

69. Xenophon *Hellenica* v, 1.13–24.

70. Xenophon *Hellenica* vi, 2.16. Cf. *Hellenica* v, 2.20–21 for the rate at which they were allowed to commute.

71. Xenophon *Hellenica* vi, 2.5–26.

72. Xenophon *Hellenica* vi, 2.27–39.

73. Xenophon *Hellenica* ii, 1.1.

74. Demosthenes xx, 75–77.

75. Plutarch *Timoleon* 24 (Tänzer, *Verpflegungswesen,* p. 58); Xenophon *Anabasis* i, 1.9–11; *Hellenica* iii, 1.2.

76. Cf. Xenophon *Hellenica* v, 4.54; also his criticism of the way in which the Spartan cavalry was mishandled against Iphicrates' peltasts, *Hellenica* iv, 5.16.

77. Thucydides i, 111; Diodorus Siculus xv, 71.4–5.

78. Xenophon *Hellenica* iii, 4.22–24; *Agesilaus* 1.30–32. Xenophon's account cannot be reconciled with that in the *Hellenica Oxyrhynchia* xi (vi), and Diodorus Siculus xiv, 80. After careful reflection, I accept the view of W. Kaupert (in Kromayer, *Schlachtfelder,* IV, 262 ff.) that Xenophon is to be preferred.

79. Xenophon *Hellenica* iv, 8.17–19.

80. Thucydides ii, 23.3; iii, 1.3; iii, 26.4.

81. Thucydides ii, 57.2.

82. Thucydides iv, 6.1–2.

83. Xenophon *Memorabilia* iii, 4.

84. Xenophon *Anabasis* vii, 3.33–41.

85. Compare the description of Ephesus when Agesilaus was mustering his army there; Xenophon *Hellenica* iii, 4.16–17.

86. Diodorus Siculus xiv, 43.2–3; cf. Plutarch *Timoleon* 13.3 for the arms stored in the citadel of Syracuse. The veteran mercenaries who accompanied Dion to Sicily perhaps provided their own arms, but Dion himself took a large additional supply. (Plutarch *Dion* 22.5; 25.1).

87. Xenophon *Hellenica* iv, 2.5; *Anabasis* vii, 2.3.

88. Frontinus ii, 1.14.

89. E.g., L. W. King, *Bronze Reliefs from the Gates of Shalmaneser,* Pls. 12, 13, 18, 19, 30.

90. Herodotus ix, 15; 65; 70.

91. Plutarch *Moralia* 187A; Polyaenus iii, 9.17.

92. Xenophon *Lac. Pol.* 12, on which see Ollier's commentary, *Xénophon,* pp. 62–65.

93. Ollier, *Xénophon,* p. 62.

94. Xenophon *Hellenica* vi, 4.14.

95. Polybius vi, 41–42.

96. See Appendix.

97. Herodotus ix, 10 and ix, 29, says that each Spartan at Plataea in 479 B.C. was accompanied by seven helots. This may be a mistake, or a gloss by a commentator, or it may have been due to the special circumstances of the campaign, or conceivably the men may have been employed in the lines of communication bringing up supplies. (Cf. W. V. How and J. Wells, *Commentary on Herodotus,* II, 298; Hignett, *Xerxes' Invasion of Greece,* pp. 282, 437.)

98. Xenophon *Anabasis* v, 7.35.

99. Polyaenus ii, 30.3.

100. Polyaenus ii, 1.20.

101. Note 18 *supra.*

102. Plutarch *Moralia* 177 E (*Philip* 8)

103. Thucydides vi, 64.3; 75.2.

104. Xenophon *Cyropaedia* ii, 1.25; *Anabasis* v, 8.5 ff.; vii, 3.15.

105. Polyaenus iii, 9.19. Στιβάδες the word translated "bivouacs," is used by Plutarch, *Moralia* 237B, for the reed-filled pallets of the Spartan boys, but Polyaenus must mean some sort of shelter which concealed the men.

106. Xenophon *Hellenica* vi, 5.30. Cf. Thucydides vi, 66.2.

107. Polybius xviii, 18.

108. Polyaenus ii, 4.2; Frontinus *Strategemata* i, 5.2.

109. Xenophon *Anabasis* vi, 1.1.

110. Cf. Xenophon *Anabasis* iii, 32–33.

111. Xenophon *Anabasis* vii, 4.12 ff.

112. Xenophon *Cyropaedia* iii, 3.26–27.

113. E. Delebecque, *Essai sur la vie de Xénophon,* p. 423, n. 401, comparing *Anabasis* iii, 4.35; *Hipparchicus* 7.12; *Hellenica* vii, 5.22; add also *Anabasis* vii, 16–22.

114. Xenophon *Cyropaedia* iii, 3.47.

115. Xenophon, *Cyropaedia* iii, 3.56 ff.

116. Plutarch *Agesilaus* (also Polyaenus ii, 1.22, who gives similar stories about Brasidas and Clearchus, i, 38.2; ii, 2.5).

117. Xenophon *Agesilaus* ii, 28–31.

118. Xenophon *Hellenica* iii, 2.2 ff. Cf. Polybius ii, 69.6.

119. Polybius x, 39.5.

120. Thucydides iii, 112.3–4.

121. Xenophon *Hellenica* ii, 4.4–6.

122. Xenophon *Hellenica* iv, 6.7. Delebecque, *Essai sur la vie de Xénophon,* p. 18, suggests with probability that Xenophon's account may be that of an eyewitness. It must at least come directly from eyewitnesses. E. Friederici, *Das Persische Idealheer des Xenophon,* p. 52, is obviously surprised at Xenophon's attitude to fortified camps as expressed in the *Cyropaedia,* and adds "Sein Abgott Agesilaus befestigte das Lager unter Umstanden (*Agesilaus* 1.32)." This passage however says nothing express about fortification. Friederici follows G. Gilbert, *Handbuch des Griechischen Staatsaltertums,* in supposing that the Spartan camp could not have been described as circular unless it was surrounded by at least a palisade, but this does not seem a necessary conclusion.

123. By Alexander's time there seems to have been no excuse for generals who left their camps unfortified. Cf. Arrian *Anabasis* i, 6.9.

CHAPTER IV

1. Maps like that shown to the Spartans by Aristagoras (Herodotus v, 49.1) or used in the Socratic *phrontisterion* are unlikely to have contained enough accurate detail to have been useful in

the conduct of tactical operations. A. E. M. Johnston, "The earliest preserved Greek map: a new Ionian coin type," *JHS,* 87 (1967), 86–94, convincingly interprets a strange pattern on the reverse of certain coins struck probably in Ionia under Persian rule as a relief map of the hinterland of Ephesus, and connects this issue with the operations of Memnon of Rhodes. This may be evidence for the use of maps by fourth-century generals, but such relief maps would not be easily transported. A single copy at headquarters, for use in planning strategy, is not improbable. I do not believe that every regimental commander had a map with him in the field.

2. Thucydides (v. 58–59) believed that Agis had the enemy where he wanted them, but makes it clear that many of the Argives thought that the Spartans were trapped.

3. Thucydides iv, 76.4; 89.1. Xenophon *Hellenica* iii, 5.25, where Pausanias's failure to be at Haliartus on the appointed day is given as the reason for Lysander's defeat.

4. Cf. Xenophon *Anabasis* i, 2.9 (where the total reported present at Cyrus's review agrees only approximately, as the editors point out, with the separate figures reported for the different contingents); v, 3.3 (another general review after regaining civilization); thereafter (cf. vi, 2.16) steady reduction by wastage, but no exact tally seems to have been kept from day to day.

5. Xenophon *Hellenica* iii, 3.8–9; v, 2.34, 38.

6. The mechanics of the σκυτάλη are described by Aulus Gellius, *Noctes Atticae* xvii, 9; Plutarch *Lysander* 19, and other sources, collected by J. Oehler in the Paully-Wissowa *Realencyclopädie,* Zweite Reihe, Band III A. cols. 691–692, sv σκυτάλη. The suggestion that it was originally a token comes from Leopold, "De Scytala Laconica," *Mnemosyne,* XXVIII (1900), 365 ff., and is favored by H. Michell, *Sparta,* pp. 273–274. Other methods of conveying messages secretly were, as Professor Page points out to me, used in antiquity (e.g., those recommended by Aeneas Tacticus 31), but these did not call for a staff specially trained in ciphering.

7. Called by Xenophon (*Hellenica* i, 1.23; iv, 8.11; vi, 2.25) ἐπιστολεὺς or ἐπιστολιαφόρος. Hippocrates, the ἐπιστολεὺς of i, 1.23, reappears as a *harmost* at i, 3.5. In Thucydides viii, 99 he appears as second secretary with Philippus. On the office, see Michell, *Sparta,* pp. 279–280.

8. Xenophon *Hellenica* iii, 4.2; v, 3.8.

9. Xenophon *Hellenica* iv, 1.39.

10. Xenophon *Hellenica* v, 3.18–20.

11. Xenophon *Lac. Pol.* 13.11. *Agesilaus* 1.17–19.

12. οἱ περὶ δαμοσίαν (Xenophon *Hellenica* iv, 5.8; *Lac. Pol.* 13.7. Σκηνήν is to be understood (Liddell and Scott, *Greek Lexicon,* s.v. δημόσιος). The δορυφόροι mentioned immediately afterwards in *Hellenica* iv, 5.8 I believe to be the body-guard, not (as Kromayer, *Heerwesen,* p. 40) the shield-bearers of the king and his staff. Cf. F. Ollier, *Xénophon: La République des Lacédémoniens,* p. 68; also the use of δορυφορία in *Cyropaedia* ii, 2.10. For volunteers, cf. *Hellenica* v, 3.9.

13. Xenophon *Lec. Pol.* 13.1.

14. Herodotus vi, 57; Xenophon *Lac. Pol.* 15.5.

15. See Harold Popp, *Die Einwirkung von Vorzeichen, Opfern und Fester auf der Kriegführnng der Griechen in 5 und 4 Jh. vor Chr.* for a recent examination of the problem

16. E.g. Xenophon *Anabasis* vi, 6.35–36; ii, 1.10.

17. Xenophon *Hellenica* iii, 1.17. Compare the manner in which the omens changed at the battle of Plataea, at the very moment when Pausanias saw that the time was ripe for the decisive charge (Herodotus ix, 61–62).

18. Xenophon *Hellenica* iv, 3.13–14.

19. Similar charges were brought against Alexander the Great —Plutarch *Moralia* 214F; Frontinus *Strategemata* i, 10.3; Polyaenus iii, 9.9—for Iphicrates.

20. E.g., Xenophon *Anabasis* vi, 1.31; vi, 2.15; vii, 6.44.

21. Xenophon *Anabasis* vii, 8.20–22.

22. Xenophon *Anabasis* vii, 8.1–16.

23. Xenophon *Cyropaedia* i, 6.15–19.

24. Xenophon *Anabasis* iii, 4.30.

25. Compare F. E. Adcock, *The Greek and Macedonian Art of War,* p. 6.

26. Thucydides v, 66.3. See Appendix on the organization of the Spartan army.

27. Παραγγέλειν (Thucydides v, 71.3).

28. Xenophon *Anabasis* i, 8.16; vi, 5.25; *Cyropaedia* iii, 3:58; vii, 1.10.

29. Onasander 25.

30. E.g., Herodotus ix, 60; Xenophon *Hellenica* iv, 5.7.

31. Xenophon *Anabasis* i, 8.15; iii, 1.4; *Agesilaus* 2.2; *Hellenica* iv, 3.4.

32. Xenophon *Anabasis* v, 2.8–12.

33. Compare Xenophon *Anabasis* vi, 6.30; vii, 7.2.

34. Xenophon *Cyropaedia* iv, 2.27.

35. Xenophon *Lac. Pol.* 11.5 (but neither the text nor the meaning of the second half of the passage quoted is certain).

36. Xenophon *Lac. Pol.* 11.6.

37. Xenophon *Cyropaedia* viii, 1.14.

38. Xenophon *Cyropaedia* viii, 4.29–30.

39. Xenophon *Lac. Pol.* 11.4–5. On the organization of the Spartan army, see Appendix.

40. See Appendix.

41. This seems to be the required sense. Marchant refers to *Cyropaedia* vi, 3.21, where Cyrus orders his officers to draw up the line of battle εἰς δύο ἔχοντας ἕκαστον τὸν λόχον, and suggests that *Lac. Pol.* 11.4 should read εἰς β'ἔχοντες τὰς ἐνωμοτίας. But a unit drawn up in two files cannot be re-formed in three without departing from the principle that the file is a complete unit. For εἰς ἐνωμοτίας, compare κατ' ἐνωμοτίας in Xenophon *Anabasis* iv, 3.26, but the text still seems incomplete. Kromayer, *Heerwesen,* p. 79, n. 4, reads καθίστανται τότε μὲν εἰς ⟨ἕνα αἰ⟩ ἐνωμοτίαι, τότε δὲ εἰς τρεῖς, τότε δὲ εἰς ἕξ.

42. Xenophon *Cyropaedia* v, 3.46–50.

43. Xenophon *Lac. Pol.* 11.6.

44. Xenophon *Cyropaedia* iii, 3.34–42; 56–63.

45. Xenophon *Hellenica* iv, 3.17.

46. Thucydides v, 69.2.

47. Xenophon *Lac. Pol.* 13.8–9 (accepting Marchant's κεχριμένῳ for the manuscripts κεκριμένῳ). For the sacrifice of the goat, *Hellenica* iv, 2.20.

48. φαιδρὸν εἶναι; cf. *Cyropaedia* iii, 3.59.

49. Despite encouragement from Professor D. L. Page, I do not feel confident that I have rendered this sentence correctly. ἔξω appears to be misplaced: I would suggest ἔξω ἀφ᾽ ἑκάστου ⟨τοῦ⟩ ἐνωμοτάρχου. Ollier, *Xénophon: la République des Lacédémoniens,* p. 17, translates: "En outre, les exhortations sont transmises à l'énomotarque, car chaque énomotarque placé à l'extérieur de sa troupe, ne se fait pas entendre à travers son énomotie tout entière." This translation seems to require the emendation ἀφ᾽ ἑκάστου τοῦ ἔξω ἐνωμοτάρχου, proposed by Weiske, which Ollier notes but does not adopt in his text. The supposition that the *enomotarch* was posted outside his *enomotia,* to the right of the leading man of the right-hand file, is taken from A. Boucher, "La Tactique Grecque à l'origine de l'histoire militaire," *REG,* XXV (1912), 306. I believe it to be incorrect (cf. Chapter Six, note 18). Marchant, in the Loeb edition, translates: "Moreover, the men shout words of encouragement to the subaltern, for it is impossible for each subaltern to make his voice travel along the whole of his section to the far end." He adds, "These detached notes are not clearly expressed." Surely it should be possible to make oneself heard by thirty-six men drawn up closely together, even on a battlefield with other voices to contend against?

50. E.g., Xenophon *Anabasis* ii, 2.30; iii, 1.36; *Hellenica* iv, 5.7.

51. E.g., Xenophon *Anabasis* v, 2.18.

52. Xenophon *Anabasis* i, 2.17; vi, 5.25–27.

53. Xenophon *Hellenica* v, 1.9. For visual signals at sea, Diodorus Siculus xiii, 77; Polyaenus i, 48.2.

54. Diodorus Siculus xiv, 52.1–5.

55. Xenophon *Anabasis* iv, 3.14 ff., especially 29–34.

56. Thucydides v, 10.3. See also J. K. Anderson, "Cleon's Orders at Amphipolis," *JHS*, LXXXV (1965), 1 ff., where this passage is discussed further and more examples of signalling are given.

57. Polybius xii, 261.

58. Xenophon *Anabasis* ii, 2.4; *Cyropaedia* v, 3.44, 52. Compare Vegetius *De Re Militari* iii, 5.

59. Xenophon *Anabasis* vii, 4.16.

60. Xenophon *Hellenica* iv, 8.18–19.

61. Thucydides v, 70.

62. Xenophon *Hellenica* iv, 3.1.

63. Polyaenus i, 10.

64. Plutarch *Moralia* 238B, 1140C. Perhaps in the Archaic period more hoplite armies marched to flutes. It has often been noted that the finest picture of a military flute player is on a vase made at Corinth (the Chigi vase).

65. Polyaenus i, 10.

66. Thucydides i, 63.2 (Kromayer, *Heerwesen,* p. 84) seems to me clearly to refer to the use of visual signals to direct the detachment that had been placed in Olynthus (sixty stades away) to fall upon the Athenian rear.

67. Polyaenus ii, 5.2.

68. Polybius ii, 66.11; Plutarch *Philopoemen* 6.

69. Xenophon *Anabasis* i, 10.12. See also Anne Bovon, *BCH,* 87 (1963), 596. The standard shown on her fig. 1 (*ARV²*, p. 433, no. 62), saltires within squares, is clearly not royal.

70. Xenophon *Cyropaedia* vii, 1.4.

71. Xenophon *Cyropaedia* viii, 5.13. At sea, admirals seem to have flown their flags (Polyaenus i, 48.5).

72. Livy xxxvii, 7; Arrian *Tactica* x, 4; *Anabasis* viii, 14.10. But see Kromayer, *Heerwesen,* pp. 132–133, who observes that the unity of the phalanx as a whole was of more importance than that of its individual units.

I have found no evidence that the δόκανα, emblems of Castor and Pollux (Plutarch *Moralia* 478A) were carried into action in front of the Spartan kings (Michell, *Sparta,* p. 107). Pairs of beams linked by crosspieces would make awkward standards. Perhaps the emblems stood over the grave where Castor and Pollux were supposed to lie: the lexicographers (*Etymologicon Magnum,* s.v.) believed that the δόκανα were "certain tombs in Lacedaemonia" which in their time had "the appearance of opened tombs."

CHAPTER V

1. Xenophon *Cyropaedia* ii, 1.9, 16.
2. Xenophon *Cyropaedia* ii, 1.15–16.
3. Xenophon *Cyropaedia* ii, 3.7 ff.
4. J. Delorme, *Gymnasion,* p. 27.
5. Plato *Laches* 181 E–183 D.
6. B. B. Shefton, "Some Iconographic Remarks on the Tyrannicides," *AJA,* 64 (1960), 173–179.
7. Vegetius *De Re Militari* i, 12.
8. Xenophon *Anabasis* i, 2.17.
9. Xenophon *Anabasis* vi, 5.25–27.
10. E.g., the Chigi vase (on which see A. M. Snodgrass, *Early Greek Armour,* pp. 138–139); the Pan Painter's charming Athena, *ARV²,* p. 555, no. 96; Euphronios's Amazons on the back of *ARV²,* p. 15, no. 6.
11. E.g., the tombstones from Thebes, Chapter Two *supra,* note 100; but also earlier, especially in single combats; e.g., Achilles fighting Memnon and Hector, by the Berlin Painter, *ARV²,* p. 206, no. 132.
12. H. L. Lorimer, *BSA,* XLII, 83, 99, 103. The underhand thrust is still used defensively on the *kantharos* by Douris in Brussels (*ARV²,* p. 445, no. 256) by an Amazon who tries to protect a fellow comrade: she faces the enemy but has probably just turned round. But already the Berlin Painter's Achilles, on *ARV²,* p. 206, no. 132, uses it in the attack. There is no absolute rule: on a *kylix* by the Euergides Painter (*ARV²,* p. 90, no. 35) the turning fugitive thrusts overarm, the pursuer underhand.
13. Plutarch *Moralia* 229C (Lysander 22).
14. The amount of disarming implied in the phrase Θέμενοι

τὰ ὅπλα will no doubt have varied according to the circumstances. The Thebans who surprised Plataea (Thucydides ii, 2.4), to take one example, were no doubt glad to put down shield and spear when they halted in the market-place, but are not likely to have removed body armour and greaves in darkness and a hostile city. The shield would have been grounded whenever possible; Thrasybulus, addressing his men at Munychia in the actual presence of the enemy, ordered his men Θέσθαι τὰς ἀσπίδας καὶ αὐτὸς θέμενος, τὰ δ' ἄλλα ὅπλα ἔχων.

15. Diodorus Siculus xv, 32–33 (to be preferred to Cornelius Nepos *Chabrias* 1). See also J. K. Anderson, "The Statue of Chabrias," *AJA,* 67 (1963), 411–413, where reasons are given for rejecting the interpretation proposed by Bernhard Müller, *Beiträge zür Geschichte des griechischen Söldnerwesens bis auf die Schlacht von Chaeronea,* p. 46, followed by H. W. Parke, *Greek Mercenaries,* pp. 77 ff.

16. Xenophon *Anabasis* i, 5.13.

17. Xenophon *Anabasis* vi, 6.25.

18. Thucydides v, 10.5–6.

19. Polyaenus iii, 9.8.

20. Compare Xenophon *Anabasis* vi, 5.16.

21. Xenophon *Anabasis,* vii, 4.17.

22. Asclepiodotus xii, 11 (p. 194 in Köchly and Rüstow's *Griechische Kriegsschriftsteller*); Arrian *Tactica* xliii, 1; Aelian *Tactica* xlii, 1 (both Köchly and Rüstow, *op. cit.,* p. 466). Köchly and Rüstow's "Schild gefasst! Aufgenommen!" for the ὑπόλαβε τὴν σκευήν. ἀνάλαβε of Asclepiodotus seems to me better than the "Take up arms! Shoulder arms!" of the Loeb edition, p. 333. Aelian has here ὑπόλαβε. ἀνάλαβε without any expressed object, and Arrian Ἄνω τὰ δόρατα. κάθες τὰ δόρατα. Aelian and Asclepiodotus place Ἄνω τὰ δόρατα after "Take distance" (διάστηθι).

23. Arrian *Anabasis* i, 6.2–3.

24. Athenaeus iv, 631a.

25. Xenophon *Cyropaedia* ii, 3.17–20.

26. Xenophon *Hellenica* iv, 4.17.

27. Xenophon *Anabasis* vi, 1.1–13.

CHAPTER VI

1. Aristotle *Politics* ii, 1297b 17.

2. Polybius x, 22.

3. Diodorus Siculus xxiii, 2.1.

4. Xenophon *Hipparchicus* 2.7 (of cavalry).

5. J. Delorme, *Gymnasion,* pp. 19–30, especially 24–25, with further references at p. 24, n. 5.

6. *Iliad* iv, 297–300. "The manner of our Modern Training, or Tactick Practise," by Clement Edmonds, *Remembrancer of the City of LONDON,* p. 326 (appendix to his translation of Caesar's *Commentaries*), London: "Printed by *Tho. Newcombe* for *Jonathan Edwin,* at the Three Roses in Ludgate street," 1677.

7. Xenophon *Memorabilia* iii, 1 (Socrates's figure is repeated in *Cyropaedia* vi, 3.25). Compare Plato's *Euthydemus,* where Dionysodorus and his brother Euthydemus are described as teachers of forensic, as well as military, arts. Cf. also Kromayer, *Heerwesen,* p. 9, and H. W. Parke, *Greek Mercenaries,* p. 39, for these professional instructors.

8. Xenophon *Memorabilia* iii, 4.

9. Thucydides vi, 96.3; Xenophon *Anabasis* ii, 1.7.

10. Polybius, i, 26–34.

11. A. Boucher, "La Tactique Grecque à l'origine de l'histoire militaire," *REG,* XXV (1912), 300 ff., especially 311 ff. "La Tactique Athénienne"; also (with special reference to the hollow-square formation, since we know this to have been used by the Athenians—Thucydides vi, 67.1) *Les lois éternelles de la guerre,* pp. 66, 81, cited by F. Ollier, *Xénophon: la République des Lacédémoniens,* p. xxxiii. But though the hollow square is not mentioned in the brief sketch of Spartan tactics given in *Lac. Pol.* 11, it was used by Brasidas (Thucydides iv, 125) and Agesilaus (*Hellenica Oxyrhynchia* xii, [vii], 2; Xenophon *Hellenica* iv, 3.4;

Agesilaus 2.2), and there is therefore no reason to suppose that the formations adopted by Cyrus in the *Cyropaedia,* or by the Ten Thousand in real life (and before Xenophon came to the chief command), were Athenian in origin.

12. Aristophanes *Acharnians* 575; Plutarch *Moralia* 186F.

13. Xenophon *Hellenica* i, 2.3 (410 B.C.). The dramatic date of the conversations recorded in *Memorabilia* iii, 1.5 and iii, 4.1 must be about this period.

14. Cf. Thucydides iv, 4.1 (*taxiarchs* at Pylos); vi, 98; Kromayer, *Heerwesen,* p. 49.

15. Xenophon *Hellenica* iii, 1.28; iii, 2.16; iv, 1.26; vi, 2.18; *Anabasis* vi, 5.11.

16. Xenophon *Lac. Pol.* 11.5. For πεμπάδες at Phlius, *Hellenica* vii, 2.6.

17. An obvious example is λόχος; in Xenophon's *Anabasis,* a company of up to 100 men: in Thucydides or Herodotus (when speaking of the Spartan army), a still larger unit: in Arrian's *Tactica,* a file of 16 men. This use seems to be foreshadowed in the use of λόχος for a sub-unit of 20–24 men in Xenophon, *Cyropaedia* ii, 3.21; 4.4.

18. Xenophon *Cyropaedia* ii, 2.6–9. This passage seems in itself sufficient to refute Boucher's view (*REG,* XXV (1912), 306) that the subaltern officers were posted outside their units, and not each at the head of the first file of his men. Besides, such an arrangement would have left a blank file, consisting only of a single officer, between every three or four files of the phalanx, which would thus have been riddled with weak spots.

19. Xenophon *Cyropaedia* ii, 3.21.

20. Arrian *Tactica* 25. For the intervals between the files, Polybius xii, 19.7; Kromayer, *Heerwesen,* p. 135.

21. On the open and close order of the Macedonian phalanx, Asclepiodotus 4.1–4 and 12.8–9. Kromayer, *Heerwesen,* pp. 114, 135–136, notes Arrian *Anabasis* v, 17.7; Polybius xviii, 24.8; Livy xxxiii, 8.14, as examples of the actual use of the close order in the

field. For the Ten Thousand at Cunaxa, Xenophon *Anabasis* i, 8.20; i, 10.7. For Coronea, Polyaenus ii, 1.19; Frontinus *Stratege-mata* ii, 6.6.

22. Thucydides v, 70.

23. Xenophon *Cyropaedia* ii, 3.22–24.

24. Here again it is evident that the officer was at the head of his troops, not to one side of them. Cyrus himself, however, was outside the formation, on the right of the front rank. The manuscripts read "two hundred," which is emended to "three hundred" to agree with what Xenophon says elsewhere about the strength of the Persian army, but he is not always consistent.

25. Xenophon *Cyropaedia* ii, 4.1–6.

26. Xenophon *Lac. Pol.* 11.4 ff.

27. This information is here assumed to be correct. I believe the *Lac. Pol.* to be the work of Xenophon himself, and the chapters in military organization to refer to the period shortly before the battle of Leuctra. A. Momigliano, "Per l'unità logica della *Lakedaimonion Politeia* di Senofonte," *Rivista di Filologia e d'Istruzione Classica,* New Series 14, fasc. 2 (1936), 170–173—conveniently reprinted in *Storia e Letteratura,* 108 (1966), 341–345—shows that it is possible, contrary to the opinion of most editors, to trace a logical sequence through the whole work on the assumption that it was all written in 378 B.C. and that the chapters are in their correct order. For further discussion of the section on military organization, see my Appendix.

28. See Chapter Four, note 41.

29. Xenophon *Hellenica* vi, 4.12.

30. Plutarch *Pelopidas* 23.5.

31. The (coincidental) resemblance between Spartan and American infantry drill will have occurred to many readers; cf. especially *Department of the Army Field Manual,* FM 22–5: *Drill and Ceremonies* (Headquarters, Department of the Army: August 1958), pp. 91–92, 137–138, and fig. 47 on p. 129).

32. Ollier, *Xénophon, le République des Lacédémoniens,* p. 57, who suggests, citing L. Gautier, *La langue de Xénophon,* pp.

40–41, that Xenophon may have borrowed this usage from the Spartans.

33. Thucydides v, 66.

34. Xenophon *Hellenica* iv, 3.17–18.

35. Xenophon *Lac. Pol.* 11.8, ἐξελίττεται—literally unwinds." For the meaning, cf. Ollier, *Xénophon,* p. 59; Kromayer, *Heerwesen,* p. 81.

36. Asclepiodotus 10.13; Arrian *Tactica* 27.2–28.1; Aelian *Tactica* 27.2–28.1.

37. Ollier, *Xénophon: la République des Lacédémoniens,* p. 59, following Boucher, *REG,* XXV (1912), 306. But they make every Spartan officer particularly vulnerable, by placing *enomotarchs* and higher officers, not at the head of their units, but in "blank files" on the right.

38. Kromayer, *Heerwesen,* p. 82. In this interpretation, τὰ γυμνὰ and τὰ ὡπλισμένα become little more than synonyms for "left" and "right," which is an argument against it.

39. See Appendix.

40. Xenophon *Lac. Pol.* 11.10.

41. Xenophon *Hellenica* iv, 8.35 ff.

42. Notably by Demosthenes at Olpae (Thucydides iii, 107.3). Also by Agesilaus at Sardis, if *Hellenica Oxyrhynchia* xi (vi) is to be preferred to Xenophon (*Hellenica* iii, 4.23–24; *Agesilaus* 1.31–32). But see the discussion by W. Kaupert in Kromayer, *Schlachtfelder,* IV, 262–289, especially 265–275.

43. I have discussed this passage, and modern interpretations of it, in *Classical Philology,* LIX (1964), 175–178.

44. Xenophon *Anabasis* iv, 8.9–13. Compare *Anabasis* iv, 2.12; iv, 3.17; v, 4.22; *Cyropaedia* iii, 2.6.

45. E. Friederici, *Das Persische Idealheer des Xenophon,* pp. 62–63 (arguing against Köchly and Rüstow, *Griechische Kriegsschriftsteller,* II, 49).

46. See Appendix.

47. Xenophon *Hellenica* iv, 3.22–23 (where, however, there is no mention of the younger men running out). When Iphicrates,

starting from Corinth, attacked the Spartan *mora* marching from Sicyon to Lechaeum, he must have been on its right side, and the younger men were sent out against him (Xenophon *Hellenica* iv, 5.11 ff.).

CHAPTER VII

1. Xenophon *Hellenica* vii, 5.26–27.

2. W. W. Tarn, *Hellenistic Military and Naval Developments,* pp. 119–120; F. E. Adcock, *The Greek and Macedonian Art of War,* pp. 58–61.

3. Aristotle frag. 498 (Rose).

4. H. W. Parke, *Greek Mercenaries,* pp. 17–18. Περιτεταμένη might be taken to imply a round shield. Kromayer, *Heerwesen,* p. 88, says that the peltasts had "einen kleinen runden oder augeschweiften Schild," and suggests that certain figures on Thessalian coins (British Museum, *Catalogue of coins: Thessaly,* Pl. II, 1–5) have a small round shield slung over their backs. This is however more usually, and I believe correctly, taken to be a *petasos.* The oval shield of the Amazon on the metope of the Temple of Zeus at Olympia has a rim, and so is probably not to be classed as a *pelta.*

5. Xenophon *Anabasis* vii, 4.17.

6. Xenophon *Anabasis* v, 2.29.

7. Eg., D. von Bothmer, *Amazons in Greek Art,* Pl. 75 (ARV^2, p. 613, no. 1), or the Solokha comb (see note 9 *infra*). The improvisation of wicker shields for hoplites is mentioned by Xenophon *Hellenica* ii, 4.25; Aeneas Tacticus 29.11–12.

8. Plutarch *Pompeius* 35.

9. Note in particular the fine example carried by the dismounted horseman of the Solokha comb—M. Rostovtzeff, *Iranians and Greeks in South Russia,* Pl. 19; A. Mantsevitch, *Peigne provenant du Tumulus Solokha* (Leningrad: 1962). I am indebted to Mrs. M. Littauer for knowledge of this valuable monograph, with its fine enlarged photographs.

10. Until late in the sixth century, Amazons nearly always

fight on foot, usually with hoplite equipment, to which a few barbarian touches are sometimes added. The hoplite Amazon does not disappear thereafter (being found most notably on the works of art derived from the shield of Pheidias's Athena Parthenos) but the barbarian horsewoman becomes increasingly common, her popularity increased from the middle of the fifth century onwards by the influence of Micon's Painted Stoa. These developments are easily followed in von Bothmer's handsome illustrations *Amazons in Greek Art.*

11. Xenophon *Anabasis* vii, 4.4; identical with the equipment of the Bithynian Thracians, who had settled in Asia and were subject to Persia; Herodotus vii, 75.

12. *ABV*, p. 297, no. 15 (amphora in Munich by the painter of Berlin 1686); also a Little Master cup with the signature Epilinos in Copenhagen, *CVA, Danemark*, VIII, Pls. 324, 325.1,e,f, showing on each side a Greek skirmishing with a Thracian. Snodgrass, *Arms and Armour of the Greeks*, p. 79, suggests that the tyrant Pisistratus may have brought Thracian mercenaries to Athens.

13. Von Bothmer, *op. cit.*, Pl. 72, no. 5 (*ARV²*, p. 66, no. 120; Oltos).

14. *CVA, USA*, VI, Pl. 253 Ib.

15. Easily found in the "Mythological Index" of *ARV²*; but see also G. M. A. Richter, *Attic Red-Figure Vases*, pp. 125–126 and fig. 93.

16. Parke, *Greek Mercenaries*, pp. 17–18.

17. Thucydides vii, 28.

18. Xenophon *Hellenica* i, 2.1 ff.

19. Parke, *Greek Mercenaries*, p. 18, note 3.

20. Note the distinction between peltasts and ψιλοί in Xenophon *Hellenica* i, 2.3.

21. Parke, *Greek Mercenaries*, pp. 23–42.

22. Xenophon *Anabasis* iii, 3–4.

23. Xenophon *Anabasis* iii, 4.34–35.

24. Xenophon *Anabasis* iii, 4.13–17.

25. Thucydides iii, 98.1.

26. Tarn, *Hellenistic Military and Naval Developments,* pp. 89–92, comments upon the camel train that brought arrows to the Parthian horse-archers attacking Crassus. But what did Xenophon's cavalry, or Iphicrates's peltasts, do when they had thrown their javelins?

27. Xenophon *Hellenica* iii, 4.20–24; *Agesilaus* 1.28–32. For the different version, *Hellenica Oxyrhynchia* xi (vi) (cf. Diodorus Siculus xiv, 80).

Most modern scholars reject Xenophon, and I may well be wrong to oppose them. W. Kaupert, in Kromayer, *Schlachtfelder,* IV, 268, is his chief champion, but perhaps exaggerates the difficulties presented by the other version. Thus, in view of the Persian custom of retiring to a considerable distance each evening to avoid night attacks on their cavalry, Agesilaus would have run less risk in setting his ambush than Kaupert allows. I. A. F. Bruce, in his admirable *Historical Commentary on the Hellenica Oxyrhynchia,* Appendix I, pp. 150 ff., maintains the superiority of the anonymous historian, suggesting (p. 153) that Xenophon, superseded by Herippidas in command of the Cyreans, had remained at Ephesus and knew little about the campaign or the battle, owing to "his lack of first-hand knowledge and the uncertain memory of his informants." For conjectures on the sources of the *Hellenica Oxyrhynchia,* cf. Kaupert, *op. cit.;* Bruce *op. cit.,* pp. 5–8 and 155. If a conjecture may be allowed on the other side, I wonder whether Xenophon did not have more to do with the reform of Agesilaus's cavalry and its subsequent successes in Asia and Thessaly than he tells us, in his desire to do honour to the king. In any case, some of the difficulties that Bruce finds in his story are unreal. The presence of the Persian's baggage train does not necessarily imply that their infantry were close at hand. The aristocratic and luxurious Persian cavalry (cf. *Cyropaedia* viii, 8.19) would not move without tents and other conveniences, loaded on baggage animals (the famous camels) which could outpace the infantry. Xenophon's battle was not, as Bruce says

(p. 156), "of considerable duration." The Greek infantry were following their cavalry at top speed, and the Persians gave way as soon as they arrived.

Bruce ably refutes the desperate suggestion that Xenophon and the *Hellenica Oxyrhynchia* are describing two entirely separate actions.

28. It is arguable (cf. Kaupert, *op. cit.,* pp. 288–289; N. G. L. Hammond, *History of Greece,* pp. 452–456) that Tissaphernes was in fact guarding the true danger point, and that it was Agesilaus's duty, instead of indulging in plundering expeditions, to conquer Caria and so deny the Persian fleet under Conon a a base. But Agesilaus had no siege train with which to capture the coastal fortresses, and so could hardly have done what Alexander did sixty years later. The invasion of Caria by Dercylidas in 397 B.C. was only another plundering raid, designed to force Tissaphernes to make peace by devastating his homeland (Xenophon *Hellenica* iii, 2.12). There is no reason to suppose that Agesilaus could have done more than repeat it on a larger scale. The fact is that the Spartans had no effective strategy against the Persians, and should have made peace with them and secured their own position in European Greece.

29. Xenophon *Hellenica* iii, 4.13–15. Plutarch *Moralia* 209 B–C.

30. ἐπεὶ δ᾽ ἅμα πάντα τὰ δεινὰ παρῆν, ἐνέκλιναν. (Xenophon *Hellenica* iii, 4.24; *Agesilaus* 1.32).

31. Plutarch *Agesilaus* 10.3.

32. See Appendix.

33. For the earlier use of Thracian peltasts and cavalry by Dercylidas in Bithynia, Xenophon *Hellenica* iii, 2.2. His lieutenant, Dracon of Pellene, is said by Isocrates (*Panegyricus* 4.144) to have gathered three thousand peltasts and devastated the Mysian plain from his base at Atarneus (on which see Xenophon *Hellenica* iii, 2.1). But the number is very probably much exaggerated, and there is some doubt as to whether Isocrates uses the word peltast in its strict sense (Parke, *Greek Mercenaries,* p. 44). The "Dercylidean mercenaries" who, according to *Hellenica Oxyrhynchia*

16.3, served Agesilaus so well on his march through the Mysian Olympus in 395 B.C., are more likely, in my opinion, to have been members of this force than "veterans who had served under Cyrus" (Bruce, *Historical Commentary on the Hellenica Oxyrhynchia*, p. 136, following B. P. Grenfell and A. S. Hunt).

34. Xenophon *Hellenica* iv, 3.15.

35. Xenophon *Hellenica* iv, 3.22–23.

36. Parke, *Greek Mercenaries*, pp. 48–53.

37. Parke, *Greek Mercenaries*, p. 52.

38. Frontinus *Strategemata* iii, 12.2, who repeats the same story, less probably, of Epaminondas.

39. Polyaenus iii, 9.35; Cornelius Nepos *Iphicrates* 2.1; Parke, *Greek Mercenaries*, pp. 77–78.

40. B. Müller, *Beiträge zur Geschichte des Griechischen Söldnerwesens bis auf die Schlacht von Chaeronea*, pp. 107 ff., noting Jason of Pherae and Philip of Macedon as other commanders who were able to discipline their mercenaries because they paid them properly.

41. Xenophon *Hellenica* iv, 8.34. Demosthenes iv, 24 speaks of the Athenians serving side by side with the mercenaries in Corinth, but this surely refers to cooperation between the citizen hoplites and the peltasts, as in the action against the Spartan *mora* (Parke, *Greek Mercenaries*, p. 50).

42. Xenophon *Hellenica* iv, 4.9; compare iii, 2.16.

43. Diodorus Siculus xiv, 86.3. Compare Andocides iii, 18 for the battle as an Athenian defeat (Parke, *Greek Mercenaries*, p. 53, n. 3).

44. Xenophon *Hellenica* iv, 4.15–17.

45. Thucydides iv, 127 (Cf. iv, 34.1). Compare G. B. Grundy, *Thucydides and the History of his Age*, pp. 272–273.

46. Thucydides vii, 30.2.

47. The following narrative is from Xenophon *Hellenica* iv, 5.11 ff.

48. I do not know the effective range of a javelin in action.

H. A. Harris, *Greek Athletes and Athletics,* pp. 95–97, suggests on admittedly scanty evidence that in athletic events "the best Greek throwers could achieve well over 300 feet," but I imagine that Iphicrates's men attacked from a far shorter distance.

49. Xenophon *De Re Equestri* 8.12 (and Chapter 12, for his recommendations on cavalry armament).

50. Plutarch *Pelopidas* 2.1. Cf. Kromayer, *Heerwesen,* p. 89, where the part played by the Athenian hoplites on Sphacteria is also noted (Thucydides iv, 31–38).

51. Xenophon *Hellenica* iv, 5.10.

52. Xenophon *Hellenica* v, 4.42–45.

53. Xenophon *Hellenica* v, 3.3–6. Cf. Parke, *Greek Mercenaries,* pp. 84–85, where, however, the Spartan commanders are misjudged in my opinion.

54. Xenophon *Hellenica* iv, 8.33–39.

55. I have given elsewhere ("The Statue of Chabrias," *AJA,* 67 (1963), 411–413) my reasons for supposing that the action of 378 B.C., described by Diodorus Siculus, xv, 32–33, and, less well, by Cornelius Nepos, *Chabrias* 1, has nothing to do with "new style" peltasts, as some modern scholars believe (see Chapter Three, note 15, supra).

56. Diodorus Siculus xv, 44; cf. Cornelius Nepos *Iphicrates* 1.3–4. Parke, *Greek Mercenaries,* pp. 79–81, accepts Diodorus's description of the innovations, but rejects his account of their introduction.

57. See Chapter Two.

58. Parke, *Greek Mercenaries,* p. 80, following O. Lippelt, *Die griechische Leichtbewaffneten bis auf Alexander dem Grossen* (Jena: 1910), p. 62. Kromayer, *Heerwesen,* p. 89, takes the view that Iphicrates's men had both javelins and the long lance as early as the Corinthian War, but this seems hard to reconcile with Xenophon's account of the defeat of the Spartan *mora.*

59. Xenophon *Anabasis* i, 8.9; *Cyropaedia* vi, 2.10; vii, 1.33. Cf. Herodotus vii, 8.1, on the Egyptian marines in the time of Xerxes.

60. Xenophon *Cyropaedia* vi, 4.16. But at vii, 1.33 their use in pushing when the Egyptians close up in a dense mass is described.

61. Parke, *Greek Mercenaries,* pp. 79–81.

62. Parke, *op. cit.,* pp. 155–156, with earlier references. On Philip at Thebes, see also A. Aymard, "Philippe de Macédoine, ôtage à Thèbes," *Revue des Études anciennes,* LVI (1954), 15–36.

63. Kromayer, *Heerwesen,* pp. 108, 133, reckons the diameter of the Macedonian shield as only a little over half a metre. But the authorities whom he quotes (Asclepiodotus *Tactica* 5.1; Aelian *Tactica* 12) seem to indicate a rather larger size. Ὀκτωπάλαιστος—eight palms' width—would be about two feet on the reckoning of C. H. and W. A. Oldfather (p. 271 of the Loeb edition of Aeneas Tacticus, Asclepiodotus, and Onasander). The Macedonian had to have both hands free to manage his large pike, but the freedom of the left hand was secured by slinging the shield to a baldric, not by using a shield small enough to be managed by an arm ring only, without a handgrip (Plutarch *Agis and Cleomenes* 32 [11].3; *Aemilius* 19.1; in the latter passage, Plutarch writes of *peltae,* but seems not to be using the word in its original sense, as he is referring to the "other Macedonians" of the phalanx, not the peltasts proper). The monument of Aemilius Paullus at Delphi shows large round shields, scarcely smaller than hoplite shields, and the later Macedonian coinage (e.g., Barclay V. Head, *British Museum Catalogue of Coins: Macedon* etc., pp. 7 ff.) confirms that they are of Macedonian type.

64. Arrian *Anabasis* i, 1,9.

65. Demosthenes ix, 48 ff.

66. Lucian *Dialogi Mortuorum* 22(27).439–440; a dialogue between the ghosts of the Cynics Diogenes, Antisthenes, and Crates, so the dramatic date is presumably the third century B.C. Lucian, who preserves (*Zeuxis* 8) details of the "Elephant Victory" over the Gauls which are not given by any other surviving writer, may have been drawing upon some vividly written history of the time.

67. Parke, *Greek Mercenaries,* pp. 83 ff. But he is not correct in saying that Sparta ceased to employ mercenary hoplites after the King's Peace. Mnasippus's mercenaries at Corcyra in 374 B.C. were clearly hoplites, being drawn up in a phalanx eight deep (Xenophon *Hellenica* vi, 2.21).

68. Xenophon *Cyropaedia* ii, 1.18.

69. Xenophon *Hellenica* v, 4.14–16.

70. Xenophon *Hellenica* v, 4.37–38.

71. Polyaenus ii, 1.20.

72. W. K. Pritchett, *Topography,* pp. 107–109.

73. The routes over Mount Cithaeron have been repeatedly studied in connection with the Plataea campaign of 479 B.C. See especially Pritchett, *Topography,* pp. 119–121, and "New Light on Plataea," *AJA,* 61 (1957), 9–28, especially 16–22. For the repulse of Cleombrotus, Xenophon *Hellenica* v, 4.59.

74. As in the first part of the campaign of Mantinea in 418 B.C. (Thucydides v, 65.1–3).

75. Diodorus Siculus xv, 22–23.

76. See Chapter One *supra.*

77. Xenophon *Hellenica* v, 4.41.

78. Plato *Laws* 778D ff. Cf. Lycurgus *In Leocratem* 44, referring to the aftermath of Chaeronea. Xenophon, *Memorabilia* iii, 5.25–28, proposes arming the young men lightly for the defence of the mountain passes into Boeotia, copying the example of the Mysians and Pisidians (*Anabasis* iii, 2.25).

79. J. E. Jones, L. H. Sackett, and C. W. J. Eliot, ΤΟ ΔΕΜΑ. A Survey of the Aigaleos-Parnes Wall," *BSA,* LII (1957), 152–189, especially 175 ff. Note especially the comparison with the lines of Boeotia in 378 B.C. (pp. 175, 180). See also J. E. Jones, L. H. Sackett and A. J. Graham, "The Dema House in Attica," *BSA,* LVII (1962), 75–114.

80. Jones, Sackett, and Eliot, *BSA,* LII, 180.

81. Xenophon *Hellenica* v, 4.39–40.

82. Xenophon *Hellenica* v, 4.47–55. I am not clear what "the wall" (τὸ τεῖχος) was that Agesilaus had on his left hand (para.

49) when he began his withdrawal from Tanagra. Certainly not the Theban lines, as I once supposed, since Xenophon calls them the "stockade" (σταύρωμα) not the "wall." Moreover, as Professor Page points out to me, this supposition leads to impossible results when we try to imagine the position taken up by the Thebans "with the stockade at their backs." Perhaps the "wall" is that of Tanagra, as E. C. Marchant (Loeb edition) supposed, but Agesilaus can only have had this on his left at the beginning of the retreat.

83. For the affair at Cromnus, Xenophon *Hellenica* vii, 4.23.

84. Parke, *Greek Mercenaries,* p. 76.

85. Xenophon *Anabasis* v, 2.12.

86. Xenophon *Anabasis* v, 22–26.

87. A. H. Smith, *Catalogue of the Sculptures of the British Museum,* II, 22, no. 872.

88. Xenophon *Anabasis* i, 2.9, etc.; *Hellenica* iv, 2.16; iv, 7.6; vii, 5.10.

89. J. L. Myres, "The Amathus Bowl," *JHS,* LIII (1933), 25–39.

90. "Engines" (μηχαναί) in the *Cyropaedia* are not always fully defined (e.g., vi, 1.20), but towers of the type described at vi, 1.52–55 seem generally to be meant. *Cyropaedia* vii, 4.1 speaks of "engines" and "rams"; "Engines" and "ladders" are used against Sardis (*Cyropaedia* vii, 2.2).

91. Xenophon *Hellenica* iii, 1.7.

92. Xenophon *Hellenica* iv, 4.12–13; vi, 4.3.

93. Xenophon *Hellenica* v, 4.11.

94. Xenophon *Hellenica* iii, 2.11; v, 3.16–25; vi, 2.4 ff.

95. Xenophon *Hellenica* ii, 4.27.

96. Xenophon *Hellenica* v, 2.1–7.

97. Xenophon *Hellenica* iv, 6.1–7.1.

98. Xenophon *Cyropaedia* vi, 1.16.

CHAPTER VIII

1. Thucydides v, 72.2; 75.3; vi, 72.3.

2. E.g., M. Cary in *Cambridge Ancient History,* V, 47, "a typical

encounter of the pre-scientific age of Greek warfare." W. Kaupert, in Kromayer, *Schlachtenatlas,* IV, text to Blatt V, col. 29, "noch ganz im alten Stil." These criticisms are certainly just, to the extent that both sides limited their objectives to breaking the enemy's phalanx and driving him off the battlefield. But the same is true of Leuctra.

3. Compare Vegetius *De Re Militari* III, 1, where the Spartans are said to have been the first to have written of the military art, *experimenta pugnarum de eventibus colligentes,* with the result *"ut rem militarem, quae virtute sola, vel certe felicitate, creditur contineri, ad disciplinam peritiaeque studia revocarint.*

4. Thucydides v, 64 ff.

5. Xenophon *Hellenica* iv, 2, 9–23.

6. See Appendix.

7. Appendix.

8. Diodorus Siculus xiv, 83.1. He gives the cavalry as 500, but makes no separate reckoning of light infantry. His 15,000 for the infantry on the Boeotian side seems to be a mistake, rather than deliberate distortion.

9. Xenophon *Cyropaedia* vii, 1.5. See pp. 181–184 *infra.*

10. Thucydides v, 65.2.

11. Xenophon *Hellenica* iv, 3.1; *Agesilaus* 7.5.

12. Plutarch *Moralia* 238F.

13. Xenophon *Agesilaus* 7.5; Plutarch *Agesilaus* 16.4.

14. Diodorus Siculus xiv, 83.1.

15. W. Kaupert, in Kromayer, *Schlachtenatlas, IV,* col. 31 (Cf. Blatt V, Maps 1 and 2), considers it impossible to fix the exact battlefield. It must have been somewhere near the edge of the foot-hills, where the Nemea stream enters the coastal plain between Sicyon and Corinth.

16. Plutarch *Moralia* 228F; Polyaenus i, 16.3. We need not of course suppose that these sentiments were really current in classical Sparta.

17. Xenophon *Hellenica* iv, 3 (especially paragraphs 15–20 for the battle of Coronea). See also Kaupert, *op. cit.*

18. Xenophon *Agesilaus* 2.7–9, twice says that Agesilaus had brought into the field a force equal to the enemy's, and insists that in doing so he showed himself a prudent and capable general. Kaupert, *op cit.,* col. 32 (Cf. Blatt V, Map 3), reckons the armies at 20,000 men each.

19. Xenophon *Hellenica* iii, 4.15; H. W. Parke, *Greek Mercenaries,* pp. 46–47.

20. Though not all the fruits of the Persian wars were with the army (Xenophon *Anabasis* v, 3.4–13).

21. See pp. 122–123 *supra.*

22. Xenophon *Hellenica* iv, 3.22–23.

23. Plutarch *Agesilaus* 18.4.

24. Diodorus Siculus xiv, 84.2.

25. Xenophon *Anabasis* i, 8.20.

26. Polyaenus ii, 1.19; Frontinus *Strategemata* ii, 6.6.

27. Xenophon *Hellenica* iv, 3.16; *Agesilaus* 2.9. E. Delebecque, *Essai sur la vie de Xénophon,* p. 10, points out that since the phrase is repeated in the *Agesilaus,* we cannot use it as evidence that the passage in the *Hellenica* was written early in Xenophon's literary career.

28. Xenophon *Hellenica* iv, 4.1–13.

29. Henry S. Robinson, *The Urban Development of Ancient Corinth* (Athens, American School of Classical Studies: 1965), pp. 1–4 and fig. 4.

30. Diodorus Siculus xiv, 86.3 says that the Spartans stormed Lechaeum before the main battle. I follow Xenophon's account.

31. Xenophon *Hellenica* iv, 4.10.

32. Xenophon *Hellenica* v, 4.1.

33. The friendship of Epaminondas and Pelopidas attracted legendary material: for example, the story that Epaminondas saved Pelopidas at the battle of Mantinea cannot be true unless it refers to some incident (otherwise unattested) in the campaign of 385 B.C., when a Theban contingent might have been present on the Spartan side (Marcello Fortina, *Epaminonda,* p. 9, with references, n.45).

34. Callisthenes, according to Jacoby, s.v. *Kallisthenes* (2), in Paully-Wissowa, *Realencyclopädie,* X, col. 1707; *FGH,* II D, pp. 417, 419 commentary on Kallisthenes frag. 11. See also Fortina, *op cit.,* p. 13, n.62, and (for other possibilities) H. D. Westlake, "The Sources of Plutarch's *Pelopidas,*" *Classical Quarterly,* XXXIII (1939), 11 ff.

35. Xenophon *Cyropaedia* vi, 1.27–28. Few scholars would, I suppose, allow that chariots could have been used in warfare after the end of the Geometric period (700 B.C. or earlier), and some might say that the tradition of the Sacred Band had no foundation in actual fact, but was derived entirely from epic poetry. But the "Cyrenaic" chariots are attested by other authors (Diodorus Siculus xviii, 19; xx, 41; Aeneas Tacticus 16.14). Perhaps a select aristocratic band of Theban hoplites continued to be conveyed to the battlefield by chariot even as late as the sixth century B.C., but evidence that might confirm this is lacking. The National Museum at Athens has a fine late archaic Boeotian terracotta group of a four-horse chariot carrying a driver, with a "Boeotian" shield slung over the driver's back, and a hoplite standing beside him (E. von Mercklin, *Der Rennwagen in Griechenland,* No. 49, p. 43 and Pl. 3, with further references, dated too early). But even if this is taken from life, it probably represents part of a ceremonial parade (cf. the Parthenon frieze) rather than a fighting unit in the contemporary army. Though it is not possible to find a portrayal of a particular epic legend in every Archaic vase-painting, in which chariots appear in battle, the presence of a chariot is generally sufficient in itself to label the scene as heroic, and some sixth-century Attic vase-painters place their figures in impossible conventional attitudes (discussed by Mrs. M. Littauer, "A Nineteenth and Twentieth Dynasty Heroic Motif on Attic Black-Figured Vases?" *AJA,* 72 (1968) 150–152) which suggests that chariot fighting was only a poetical and artistic tradition in their day. J. A. O. Larsen, *Greek Federal States: Their Institutions and History* (Oxford: 1968), pp. 106 ff., accepts the view that chariots continued to be used in warfare

down to the Homeric period, and supposes the "Sacred Band" to have been derived from an ancient institution.

36. Thucydides v, 67.2; vi, 96.3. Diodorus Siculus (xii, 70.1) is the authority for the Sacred Band at Delium. This is contrary to Plutarch's evidence (*Pelopidas* 18.1) that it was first raised by Gorgidas. I suppose that Gorgidas was its first commander when it was re-formed after the liberation of Thebes. Στόμα (mouth, or cutting edge of blade) is used by Xenophon both for the front of a phalanx and the head of a column (cf. *Hellenica* iii, 1.23; *Anabasis* iii, 4.42; v, 2.26; v, 4.22; *Cyropaedia* vi, 3.24). For the soft mass of the blade following the hardened edge, Arrian *Tactica* 12.2.

37. For the battle of Delium, Thucydides iv, 93–96. See also the discussion by J. Beck in Kromayer, *Schlachtfelder*, IV, 177 ff.

38. The battle of Oenophyta is mentioned by Thucydides, i, 108.3. Polyaenus, i, 35.1, tells the story of the charge beginning on the left wing. Frontinus, *Strategemata* ii, 4.11, reports only that Myronides encouraged his right wing with reports of victory on the left. He also says (*Strategemata* iv, 7.21) that before the battle, he pointed out to his men that they were in the middle of a plain and could only escape the Theban cavalry by standing fast.

39. Xenophon *Hellenica* v, 4.56–57.

40. Plutarch *Lycurgus* 13.6; *Agesilaus* 26.3; *Pelopidas* 15.4.

41. Plutarch *Moralia* 192C-D.

42. Plutarch *Pelopidas* 18–19.

43. Cf. note 37 *supra*.

44. Xenophon *Hellenica* v, 4.46; 60–63.

45. Plutarch *Pelopidas* 15.6–8. Polyaenus, ii, 5.2, gives Gorgidas the credit for the defeat of Phoebidas, saying he lured him on by a feigned retreat.

46. The date is from Diodorus Siculus, xv, 37, who speaks of an expedition against Orchomenus with five hundred picked men. He does not mention the battle of Tegyra by name except at xv, 81.2, where he recounts the achievements of Pelopidas after describing his death. For the narrative, Plutarch *Pelopidas* 16–17.

47. On the strength of the *mora,* for which Plutarch quotes different figures from various authorities, see Appendix.

CHAPTER IX

1. F. Cousin, *Kyros le jeune en Asie Mineure,* p. 155, compares the British and Spartan system for the additional reason that both got foreigners to do their fighting for them.

2. E. Delebecque, *Essai sur la vie de Xenophon,* pp. 384 ff., suggests a date between 365 and 358 B.C.—later than the *Evagoras* of Isocrates.

3. A. R. Burn, *Persia and the Greeks,* pp. 42–43 (especially n.9).

4. Bacchylides *Epinikion* 3; Herodotus i, 86 ff.

5. Xenophon *Cyropaedia* vii, 2.9 ff.

6. Xenophon *Cyropaedia* viii, 6.19–21.

7. K. Schefold, in J. Boehlau and K. Schefold, *Larisa am Hermos,* I, 26, gives insufficient credit to the native Egyptians, who had beaten the Greeks at the beginning of Amasis's reign, and later fought stoutly against Cambyses.

8. Xenophon *Cyropaedia* vi, 2.10.

9. Xenophon *Anabasis* i, 8.9. Delebecque, *Essai sur la vie de Xénophon,* p. 400 ff., notes the important part played by the Egyptians in the *Cyropaedia* and rightly emphasizes the interest aroused by Agesilaus's last campaigns. On p. 423, n.58, he rejects the suggestion that the Egyptians briefly glimpsed at Cunaxa could have inspired those of the *Cyropaedia,* and no doubt this memory would not by itself have moved Xenophon to describe the Egyptians as he did.

Professor Klaus Baer informs me that he knows no contemporary Egyptian works of art that illustrate Xenophon's description. The monuments of the Eighteenth and Twentieth Dynasties show a different type of armament. The national peculiarities of Egyptians are sometimes portrayed, not without humour, in Greek vase-painting (e.g., the Pan Painter's Heracles and Busiris, *ARV²*, p. 554. no. 82), but I know no Greek pictures of Egyptian soldiers.

10. Herodotus vii, 8.1.

11. Xenophon *Cyropaedia* vii, 1.45.

12. Xenophon *Hellenica* iii, 1.7. By the name "Egyptian," he distinguishes this Larisa from the Larisa in the Troad mentioned in iii, 1.13. The ancient testimonia are collected by Schefold, *op. cit.* A third, but insignificant, Larisa stood near Ephesus. Larisa in Aeols was regarded by Strabo (xiii, 3.2) as that mentioned in the *Iliad* (ii, 840; xvii, 301). Whether the remarkable excavations published under the name of *Larisa am Hermos* have in fact disclosed the site of this city or of another is doubted; cf. J. M. Cook, *BSA,* LIII (1958), 20 n. 47. Objects discovered by Boehlau and Schefold are neither more nor less "Egyptianizing" than those from other "East Greek" sites. Since I do not believe in the reality of Xenophon's sixth-century Egyptians, I do not think that this is relevant to the identification of the site.

13. Herodotus i, 149; Merritt, Wade-Gery, and Macgregor, *The Attic Tribute-Lists,* Vol. I, 511; Vol. III, 199. Along with Cyme and Phocaea, Larisa probably fell again under Persian rule in 412 B.C. (Schefold, *Larisa am Hermos,* I, 36–37, citing Thucydides viii, 18.1–3). The architectural remains of the excavated site are consistent with the supposition that a tyranny had been replaced by a democracy in the second half of the fifth century B.C. Of course this does not establish the excavated site as the "Larisa" of the ancient documents.

14. Thucydides viii, 31.2; 87.1–3.

15. Xenophon *Anabasis* i, 2.21; i, 4.2; Diodorus Siculus xiv, 19.6; xiv, 35, 3 ff.

16. Xenophon *Anabasis* i, 4.16; i, 5.7; ii, 1.3; ii, 4.24. For Procles see also *Anabasis* vii, 8.17; *Hellenica* iii, 1.6.

17. Cf. the story of the adventure with Asidates, Xenophon *Anabasis* vii, 8.9 ff.; on the rule of Zenis and Mania in Dardania, *Hellenica* iii, 1.10 ff.

18. Cf. note 15 *supra.*

19. Diodorus Siculus xv, 2.2; 3 ff.; 9.3 ff.; 18.1 ff.

20. Cf. P. Lévêque and P. Vidal-Naquet, "Épaminondas Pythagoricien," *Historia,* IX (1960), 296, n. 15.

21. Xenophon *Cyropaedia* vi, 2.11. The manuscripts give different versions of the name, but at vii, 1.45, Thymbrara seems to be confirmed. Diodorus Siculus (xiv, 80) says that Agesilaus's victory over the Persians outside Sardis in 395 B.C. was at "Thybarna," but Xenophon seems to have imagined his battle as taking place further to the east. Since it seems to take place on perfectly level ground without any natural obstacles to the manoeuvres of either side, the topography of the real Thymbrara makes little difference.

22. Xenophon *Cyropaedia* vi, 2.4–6. Cf. *Hellenica* iii, 4.16–18.

23. Xenophon *Cyropaedia* iv, 3.23. That Xenophon makes Persian horsemanship date only from the time of Cyrus is typical of his treatment of the past.

24. Chapter Three *supra*.

25. Xenophon *Anabasis* i, 7.20–8.14. Cf. Plutarch *Artoxerxes,* 7.

26. Xenophon *Cyropaedia* vi, 3.5 ff

27. Xenophon *Anabasis* i, 10.19.

28. Pp. 53–54 *supra*.

29. Cf. J. Kromayer, "Cunaxa," in Kromayer, *Schlachtfelder,* IV, 224–225.

30. Xenophon *Anabasis* ii. 1.7.

31. Xenophon *Hellenica* iv, 2.18.

32. Xenophon *Cyropaedia* vi, 3.21; εἰs δύο ἔχοντας τὸν λόχον must mean "having the *lochos* in twos," and we are then reminded that there were twenty-four men in each *lochos* so that we can calculate the depth. Cf. *Hellenica* vi, 4.12; τοὺς μὲν Λακεδαιμονίους. ἔφασαν εἰs τρεῖs τὴν ἐνωμοτίαν ἄγειν. τοῦτο δὲ συμβαίνειν αὐτοῖς οὐ πλέον ἢ εἰs δώδεκα τὸ βάθος. Compare *Lac. Pol.* 11.4, and for εἰs followed by a number meaning "in twos," "in threes," etc., *Hellenica* iii, 1.22; iii, 4.13; vii, 4.22.

Had Xenophon wished to say that the phalanx was to be "two deep" he might have said simply εἰs δύο (cf. εἰs ὀκτώ, *Hellen-*

ica iii, 2.16) but he would not have added ἔχοντας τὸν λόχον, because the depth would apply to the whole line, as well as to the *lochoi* of which it was formed. He might have added some word to indicate that it was the depth of the line that he meant, cf. *Hellenica* ii, 4.12; iv, 2.18.

εἰς followed by a number is in itself ambiguous. Cf. *Cyropaedia* viii, 3.9–11.

In *Hellenica* iii, 4.13, εἰς with the accusative is used for the number of files, ἐπί with the genitive for the depth. But ἐπί with the genitive is also used in either sense; for the number of files, *Cyropaedia* ii, 3.21; v, 3.36; viii, 3.18; for the number of ranks, *Hellenica* i, 6.29, 31; ii, 4.34; vi, 4.12; vi, 5.19; *Anabasis* i, 2.15; sometimes qualified with a word indicating "depth," *Hellenica* ii, 4.12; *Cyropaedia* vi, 3.19.

Compare also the description of "Persian" drill; *Cyropaedia* ii, 2–4; pp. 99–100 *supra*. The depth of twelve does not include the archers and javelin-men stationed behind the phalanx.

33. Polybius xviii, 29. Cf. Kromayer, *Heerwesen*, pp. 134–135.

34. Xenophon *Memorabilia* iii, 1. 7–8.

35. As at the crossing of the Centrites river, Xenophon *Anabasis* iv, 3.27–32. Cf. *Cyropaedia* ii, 3.22. For the importance of having sensible and experienced men at the rear of cavalry formations, cf. *Hipparchicus* 2.

36. Xenophon *Cyropaedia* iii, 3.41–42. Cf. A. Boucher, *REG*, XXV (1912), 311.

37. As has been suggested by A. D. Fraser "The Myth of the Phalanx-Scrimmage," *Classical Weekly,* 36, No. 2 (1942), 15–16.

38. E.g., Thucydides vi, 70.2; Herodotus ix, 62.2; Xenophon *Hellencia* ii, 4.35.

39. E.g., Diodorus Siculus xviii, 17.4.

40. Polybius xviii, 30.4; cf. Asclepiodotus v, 5.2.

41. Asclepiodotus 7.5. Xenophon, *Hipparchicus* 2, recommends that the Athenian cavalry should be formed ten deep, but it is clear that he expected many of them to be poor riders and ill practiced in their weapons.

42. Xenophon *Hellenica* iv, 3.19.

43. Xenophon *Hellenica* ii, 4.10–19.

44. Xenophon *Cyropaedia* vi, 3.23 ff.

45. Onasander 17.

46. Xenophon *Anabasis* iii, 3.7.

47. τοὺς ἐπὶ πᾶσι καλουμένους (Xenophon *Cyropaedia* vi, 3.25). The file-closers of the phalanx (note 36 *supra*) are οὐραγοί.

48. Xenophon *Cyropaedia* vi, 1.51.

49. The gold models from the Oxus Treasure (O. M. Dalton, *Treasure of the Oxus,* No. 7, pp. 3–4), confirm the yoking of four horses to a two-pole vehicle in Achaemenid Persia. Mrs. M. Littauer points out to me that four-horse chariots with two poles were also known in Cyprus from about 700 B.C., presumably as the result of Assyrian influence. Several of the terracotta models of war chariots from Ayia Irini, dating from the "Cypro-Archaic I" period, have four horses yoked to two poles (e.g., Einar Gjerstad, *The Swedish Cyprus Expedition,* II, Pls. CCXXXIV, CCXXXV, nos, 1046, 1124, 1780, 1781 + 1778, 2000. The one-poled type is also found; no. 1125. Actual examples of two-poled chariots have been recovered by V. Karageorghis, "Chronique des fouilles a Chypre en 1966," *BCH,* XCI, Part 1 (1967), 338–343, especially fig. 140. Chariots shown in Assyrian works of art are depicted in profile, so that it is difficult to establish the method of harnessing or even the number of horses without a minute examination of the evidence, upon which Mrs. Littauer is at present engaged.

50. Thucydides v, 9.8.

51. Thucydides vi, 67.1.

52. Xenophon *Anabasis* vi, 5.9–11.

53. Cf. E. Friederici, *Das Persische Idealheer des Xenophon,* p. 62. He cites, in addition to the examples given in notes 50–52 *supra,* Xenophon, *Anabasis* iii, 4.14, which, however, I understand in a different sense: Tissaphernes was placing some of his men *behind the Ten Thousand* while he led others to harass the flank of their column.

54. Xenophon *Cyropaedia* vi, 4.17–20.

55. The narrative of the battle is in Xenophon *Cyropaedia* vii, 1.

56. ἐπέκαμπτον εἰς κύκλωσιν (Xenophon *Cyropaedia* vii, 1.5) repeats the phrase used of Artaxerxes's turning movement at Cunaxa and the Spartans at the Nemea (Xenophon *Anabasis* i, 8.23; *Hellenica* iv, 2.20).

57. Xenophon *Cyropaedia* vii, 1.6–8.

58. Thucydides v, 71–72. See also Appendix.

59. Xenophon *Anabasis* i, 8.23–24.

60. Plutarch's account (*Artoxerxes* 7–13) preserves the narrative of Ctesias, the Greek physician who accompanied Artaxerxes on the battlefield. Xenophon, on the other side of the field saw nothing of Cyrus's fate and did not even learn that he was dead until the next day.

61. Xenophon *Cyropaedia* vii, 1.19–22.

62. Compare Chapter Four *supra*.

63. Xenophon *Cyropaedia* vii, 1.48–49. The cavalry equipment of the *Cyropaedia* (vii, 1.2) corresponds closely with that worn by the younger Cyrus at Cunaxa (*Anabasis* i, 8.6–7), but in one respect follows the pattern recommended by Xenophon for Greek cavalry (*De Re Equestri* 12). The trousered Persian himself wore thigh-armour, but for the Greek, Xenophon recommends fitting the horse with armour that protected his sides and his rider's thighs (J. K. Anderson, *Ancient Greek Horsemanship*, p. 149).

64. Herodotus i, 80.

65. Xenophon *Anabasis* i, 8.20.

66. Xenophon *Hellenica* iv, 1.17–19.

67. ἐπὶ πόδα. Xenophon *Anabasis* v, 2.22; *Cyropaedia* vii, 1.34; vii, 5.6; Polyaenus ii, 2.9; ii, 5.2.

68. E. Friederici, *Das Persische Idealheer des Xenophon*, p. 67.

69. But Alexander the Great seems to have thought the idea worth serious consideration (W. W. Tarn, *Hellenistic Military and Naval Developments*, p. 13, citing Asclepiodotus 6).

70. Thucydides iii, 107–108.

CHAPTER X

1. Cf. Xenophon *Hellenica* v, 3.27; Diodorus Siculus xv, 24.1, for Spartan power just before the liberation of Thebes.

2. Xenophon *Hellenica* vi, 1.2 ff.

3. Xenophon *Hellenica* vi, 3.1. Cf. Diodorus Siculus xv, 45, 4–6, on the Plataean appeal to Athens against Thebes.

4. Cleombrotus is said by Xenophon to have taken an army by sea into Phocis in 375 B.C. and is not mentioned again until 371 B.C. (*Hellenica* vi, 1.1; 4.2 ff.). It is disputed whether he was continuously in Phocis from 375–371 B.C.; most probably not; cf. R. E. Smith, "The Opposition to Agesilaus's Foreign Policy," *Historia,* II (1954), 284, n.6, and T. T. B. Ryder, "Athenian Foreign Policy and the Peace-Conference at Sparta in 371 B.C.," *CQ* (New Series), XIII, No. 2 (November 1963), 238, n.1, with references to earlier literature on the other side.

5. Xenophon *Hellenica* vi, 5.2 ff.

6. J. Wolter, "Leuctra," in Kromayer, *Schlachtfelder,* p. 293.

7. Cleombrotus's route is discussed by A. R. Burn, "Helikon in History," *BSA,* XLIV (1949), 313–323, and by W. K. Pritchett, "The Battle of Leuctra," in *Topography,* pp. 49–58, especially pp. 52–57. They correct Wolter, "Leuctra," on important points, notably the route from Creusis to Leuctra. For the destruction of the Theban detachment under Chaereas, the only authority is Pausanias ix, 13.3.

8. Pausanias ix, 13.4.

9. This story was known to Xenophon (*Hellenica* vi, 4.7); cf. Plutarch *Pelopidas* 20.4–8; Diodorus Siculus xv, 54.2–3.

10. Diodorus Siculus xv, 52.1–7; 53.4.

11. The interpretation is given by Frontinus *Strategemata* i, 12.5. Diodorus (xv, 52.6) says that Epaminondas made no reply to those who cried out that this was an unfavourable omen.

12. Xenophon *Hellenica* vi, 4.7; Polyaenus ii, 3.12.

13. Plutarch *Pelopidas* 20.2.

14. Plutarch (*Pelopidas* 21) represents the Thebans as seriously

contemplating a human sacrifice, and citing not merely legendary but historical precedents as late as the time of Themistocles. But the story of the sacrifice before Salamis is unknown to Herodotus. More probably the Theban leaders at Leuctra had secretly arranged in advance for their substitute victim. Xenophon (*Hellenica* vi, 4.7) knew only that the Thebans adorned the girls' monument before the battle.

15. See Pritchett, *Topography,* especially p. 57, Pl. 51a, and fig. 4 on p. 50. Cf. also Kromayer, *Schlachtenatlas,* IV, Blatt V, fig. 5.

16. Pritchett, *Topography,* pp. 49–52.

17. This is expressly stated by Diodorus Siculus xv, 53.2, but he is not the best of witnesses. Xenophon *Hellenica* vi, 4.4, also strongly suggests that the Spartans arrived first, but his text could be reconciled with the supposition that the armies arrived more or less simultaneously. See Pritchett, *Topography,* pp. 57–58.

18. Xenophon, *loc. cit.*

19. Xenophon *Hellenica* vi, 4.9–7.

20. Plutarch, *Pelopidas* 20.3, gives the credit to Pelopidas. But he was not a *boeotarch.* Diodorus Siculus xv, 53.3; Pausanias ix, 13.6–7 seem to give the true story of the council.

21. See Appendix. Pritchett, *Topography,* p. 58, n.47, reckons 2,300 Lacedaemonians; N. G. L. Hammond, *A History of Greece,* p. 661, is on the low side with 2,100. If 300 of the 700 Spartiates were taken out of the ranks to serve as the king's body-guard, there were only 100 left in each *mora,* out of nearly 600. G. Busolt, "Spartas Heer und Leuktra," *Hermes,* XL (1905), 387–449, concludes that these figures are to be accepted and that the dilution of the Lacedaemonian army by "inferiors" was a major reason for the Spartan defeat. Wolter, "Leuctra," p. 300, considers that the 300 knights are probably to be added to about 2,300 men in the four *morai.*

The suggestion (examined in the Appendix) that each *mora* was about 1,200 men strong is unsupported by ancient evidence.

22. Xenophon *Hellenica* vi, 4.15.

23. On whom see the Appendix.

24. Xenophon *Hellenica* vi, 4.9.

25. Plutarch *Pelopidas* 20.1; generally accepted as a reasonable figure for the whole army.

26. Polyaenus ii, 3.8 says that there were 40,000 of the Spartans and their allies at Leuctra. His 6,000 (ii, 3.12) for the Thebans is acceptable, and agrees with Diodorus. Frontinus, *Strategemata* iv, 2.6, says that the Lacedaemonians had 24,000 foot and 1,600 horse against 4,000 Thebans, of whom 400 were cavalry. This last figure may have come from a misunderstood version of the system described by the *Hellenica Oxyrhynchia* (note 28 *infra*), under which Thebes should have supplied 4,000 hoplites and 400 cavalry.

27. Xenophon *Hellenica* vi, 4.4.

28. *Hellenica Oxyrhynchia* 11.4.

29. Thucydides iv, 93.3.

30. Diodorus Siculus xv, 52.2. Hammond, *loc. cit.*, suggests that this is just the number of hoplites.

31. Xenophon *Hellenica* iv, 2.17

32. Diodorus Siculus xv, 26. But his account does not wholly agree with that of Xenophon, who says (*Hellenica* v, 4.19) that the Athenian generals acted on their own initiative, and were punished for it.

33. Plutarch *Pelopidas* 31.4; 35.2.

34. Busolt, *Hermes,* XL (1905) pp. 444–445, concludes that the strength of the Thebans was about 3,000 hoplites and some hundreds of cavalry, out of a total Boeotian army of about 6,000–6,500 hoplites, 600–800 horse, and an unknown number of light-armed troops. Some other scholars have made no separate estimate of the Theban strength. Wolter, "Leuctra," accepting Diodorus's 6,000 as the basis for calculation, but making extra allowance for infantry detachments and the cavalry, concludes that the Boeotian infantry can be reckoned at probably not more than 8,000 men at the most, with not more than 800 cavalry. W. Judeich, "Athen und Theben vom Königsfrieden bis zür schlacht bei Leuktra," *Rheinisches Museum,* 76 (1927), 193–194,

calculating along similar lines, concludes that the Lacedaemonians had about 11,000 men against about 8,000 Boeotians.

35. Xenophon *Hellenica* vi, 4.8–15.

36. Cf. especially Xenophon *Hellenica* v, 4.1; vi, 4.1–3.

37. But for a different estimate of Xenophon, cf. Wolter, "Leuctra," especially pp. 301–302 and 306.

38. M. N. Tod, *Greek Historical Inscriptions,* II (Oxford: 1944), no. 130 with references.

39. As is maintained by Hammond, *op. cit.* (note 21 *supra*), p. 493.

40. Pausanias ix, 13.8.

41. Polyaenus ii, 3.15.

42. The heavy infantry, as in the account of the battle of Mantinea (Xenophon *Hellenica* vii, 5.22). The temptation to read into Xenophon the original meaning of *lochos,* "men placed in ambush," which survives in, for instance, Polyaenus iii, 9.24, must be resisted.

43. This translation depends upon a doubtful emendation. The generally accepted view is that Cleombrotus was guarded by a corps if three hundred "knights," organized separately from the *morai.* This may be right, though for reasons given in the Appendix I do not myself believe it, and suppose that (if the emendation is correct) the "knights" referred to were a smaller select group within the first *mora.*

44. Plutarch *Moralia* 193B; Pausanias ix, 13.11–12.

45. Though a most important part. Cf. F. E. Adcock, *The Greek and Macedonian Art of War,* p. 25, for Epaminondas getting his blow in first. I do not believe that Epaminondas placed his deep column on the left for metaphysical reasons, but see Pierre Lévêque and Pierre Vidal-Naquet, "Epaminondas Pythagoricien," *Historia,* IX (1960), 294–308.

46. Xenophon *Hellenica* vi, 4.16–26.

47. Diodorus Siculus xv, 52–56.

48. Pausanias ix, 13.6–7 gives the same story, with more cir-

cumstantial detail, including the names of the *boeotarchs*. The seventh *boeotarch,* Brachyllides, had been guarding the way over Cithaeron; perhaps Chaereas, who had been killed earlier, was also a *boeotarch.* Orchomenus should have provided two more, who were of course absent, but this still only accounts for ten out of the eleven.

49. Wolter, "Leuctra," p. 301.

50. Diodorus Siculus xv, 55.2. A *"loxe phalanx"* according to Arrian, *Tactica* 26.3, is one which has "one wing, whichever the general wishes, approaching the enemy, and fights with it alone, reserving the other by holding it back." But the word could also imply an oblique, diagonal march, as it seems to in Plutarch *Pelopidas* 23.

51. Pausanias ix, 13.12. Diodorus's figure might be reconciled with Pausanias's if we supposed that the former included men killed in Chaereas's defeat, the storming of Creusis, and other actions before the main battle. But that the Thebans did in fact suffer heavily is suggested by Polyaenus ii, 3.11, which (if it is true) seems more likely to refer to Leuctra than to any other action of which we know.

52. Onasander 21.5 ff., especially para. 8.

53. Wolter, "Leuctra," p. 309, criticising in particular the reconstruction of the battle by Köchly and Rüstow, *Geschichte des Griechischen Kriegswesens,* pp. 171 ff. The suggestion that the Lacedaemonian line "finally" formed a half-moon is from Judeich, *Rheinisches Museum,* 76 (1927), p. 196.

54. Pausanias ix, 13.3–12.

55. Plutarch *Pelopidas* 23.

56. Köchly and Rüstow, *loc. cit.* Cf. Wolter, "Leuctra," pp. 308–309 for further references. While not fully accepting their reconstruction of the battle, I believe that they were right in the main point—the function of the Sacred Band.

57. Wolter, "Leuctra," pp. 302–306.

58. See Chapter Nine, note 34 *supra.* I do not understand why

Busolt, *Hermes* XL (1905) p. 435, believed that Plutarch's source for the battle used as a model Thucydides's account of the battle of Mantinea.

59. Plutarch *Pelopidas* 20.3.

60. τοῦ 'Επαμεινώνδου τὴν φάλαγγα λοξὴν ἐπὶ τὸ εὐώνυμον ἕλκοντος. This does not seem to mean the same thing as the apparently similar phrase in Diodorus (note 50 *supra*). I believe that Plutarch may be keeping more closely to the original sense, and that in Diodorus the sense has been changed to make it fit the technical meaning given to *loxe phalanx* by the later tacticians.

61. τὸ δεξιὸν ἀνέπτυσσον καὶ περιῆγον. The word ἀναπτύσσειν has two distinct meanings in military contexts. Xenophon uses it for "bending back" a phalanx that has been already deployed, either (as at Cunaxa; *Anabasis* i, 10.9) in order to form a second front at right angles to the first, or (as in the imaginary account of Cyrus's withdrawal from before Babylon, *Cyropaedia* vii, 5.3, with which cf. *Hellenica* vi, 5.18–19) in order to bring the wings round behind the centre of the phalanx and so double its depth. In neither case can the wing that was to be "bent back" have wheeled in line until it reached its new position. It must have been first turned outwards into column and then been wheeled in column, either through ninety degrees (at Cunaxa), or through one hundred and eighty degrees (at Babylon). The manoeuvre is similar to that which the wings of Croesus's army execute in *Cyropaedia* vii, 1.5 ff., though Xenophon does not here use the word ἀναπτύσσειν, perhaps because the wings are being "folded forward," not "back."

Arrian uses the word to mean deploying from column into phalanx, by leading up successive files beside each other (Arrian *Anabasis* ii, 7.3) or extending the phalanx (*Anabasis* iii, 12.2; cf. *Tactica* 9.5). Compare its normal sense, to unroll a parchment scroll.

I agree with Wolter, "Leuctra," pp. 302–306, that Plutarch is using the word as Xenophon does. I believe that this shows that he is drawing upon a fourth-century source in which some words have not yet acquired the technical meanings given them by the later tacticians, and interpreting it rightly, not that he has invented the "turning" movement through misunderstanding a source that spoke only of "extending." But Wolter mistakes the nature of the "extension." The ἀνατεῖναι τὸ κέρας of Plutarch, *Pelopidas* 23.3, is to be taken in the same sense as that in which the Lacedaemonians ὑπερέτεινον τὸ κέρας at the Nemea before turning the Athenian flank (Xenophon *Hellenica* iv, 2.19). It has nothing to do with the διπλασιασμός of Arrian (on which see Wolter, p. 304, n.1).

62. Xenophon *Hellenica* ii, 4.34, παντελῶς βαθεῖαν—the same phrase that he uses (iv, 2.18) of the Thebans at the Nemea. K. M. T. Chrimes, *Ancient Sparta,* p. 497, appears to overlook the former passage when she argues that the Spartans at Leuctra were unable to achieve a depth of more than twelve because their system of tactics was inadequate.

63. Judeich, *Rheinisches Museum,* 76 (1927), pp. 194–195.

64. H. Delbrück, *Geschichte der Kriegskunst,* I³, 134.

65. Xenophon *Cyropaedia* vii, 1.36.

66. Xenophon *Hellenica* iv, 2.22; 3.19.

67. Diodorus Siculus xviii, 17.3.

68. See Sir Walter Scott, *Old Mortality,* Note VII.

69. Xenophon *Hellenica* vi, 4.10, ἅτε καὶ πεδίου ὄντος τοῦ μεταξύ.

70. Delbrück, *op. cit.,* pp. 160 ff.

71. Wolter, "Leuctra," p. 311. See also Pritchett, *Topography,* p. 49, for references to more recent archaeological work, especially the reconstruction of the trophy, and for an excellent view of the battlefield. (Pl. 51a).

72. Wolter, "Leuctra," pp. 311–312, 314.

73. Xenophon *Lac. Pol.* 12.2.

74. P. 203 *supra.* For the figures, cf. Busolt, *Hermes,* XL (1905), pp. 444–445, who has given more attention to the question of the relative lengths of the two front lines than most modern scholars.

75. The cavalry of the Hellenistic age from which Wolter (p. 312) draws examples to illustrate his argument was, of course, far more efficient.

76. Köchly and Rüstow, *loc. cit.* Cf. Judeich, *Rheinisches Museum* 76 (1927) pp. 194–195.

77. Polyaenus ii, 3.14; Frontinus *Strategemata* ii, 2.12. Epaminondas also used smoke-screens upon occassion; Polyaenus ii, 3.13.

78. Xenophon *Hellenica* vii, 21–22.

79. Diodorus Siculus xii, 70.

80. Plutarch *Pelopidas* 19.3

81. Cornelius Nepos *Pelopidas* 4.2.

82. Xenophon, *Hellenica,* vii, 5.22.

83. Plutarch *Pelopidas* 19.4, 23.1; Xenophon *loc. cit.*

84. Köchly and Rüstow, *Geschichte des Griechischen Kriegswesens,* pp. 171 ff. But they do not make full use of the evidence of the *Cyropaedia* to support their argument.

85. Xenophon *Lac. Pol.* 13.6.

86. Polyaenus ii, 3.3 (but compare iii, 9.27 where a similar story is told of Iphicrates).

EPILOGUE

1. Xenophon *Hellenica* vii, 5 is the main source. Diodorus Siculus xv, 82–88 also gives an account of this campaign, which adds some supplementary details, but seems definitely to be wrong on several important matters in which it differs from Xenophon, notably the events leading to the secession of Mantinea and the part played by Agesilaus. His account of the battle is another confused rhetorical exercise.

2. This detail is from Polyaenus ii, 3.14; Frontinus *Strategemata* ii, 2.12.

3. Xenophon *Hellenica* vii, 5.22 (and again of the cavalry, para. 24) uses the word ἔμβολον of the Theban formation. This word is used by later writers (e.g., Polybius i, 26.13, of the Roman

fleet; Asclepiodotus 11.5) for a wedge-shaped formation, the equivalent of the Latin *cuneus*. Arrian (*Tactica* 16.1, 16.6, 29.5) uses the word in this sense. But he also says that Epaminondas formed his hoplites in an ἔμβολον at Leuctra and Mantinea (*Tactica* 11.2), and is here speaking of deepening the phalanx and not of a wedge; perhaps also Arrian *Anabasis* i, 6.3 (cf. Alexander the Great) though the meaning of "wedge" cannot be ruled out in this passage. I believe that this is another instance of a word acquiring in later tactical authors a precise technical sense unknown to Xenophon. Arrian uses it in its old sense when writing of fourth-century battles. Many recent authors (e.g., N. G. L. Hammond, *A History of Greece,* pp. 507–509; Fortina, *Epaminonda,* p. 97) believe that Epaminondas used a wedge formation. But Xenophon talks of Epaminondas leading the Thebans "head on like a trireme" (not, as Hammond takes it, "like the bow of a ship"), which is the phrase he uses of the Spartan *lochoi* wheeling in parallel columns to the right to meet an attack on the line of march (*Lac. Pol.* 11.10). Cf. Kromayer, *Heerwesen,* p. 94. Kromayer seems to me to have been mistaken in the conclusion that he evidently reached (*Schlachtfelder,* IV, 317 ff.) that it was the *whole* army that Epaminondas formed up in his column of assault. No doubt the whole army moved off to the left (with the exception of the covering force of cavalry and hoplites posted to prevent the Athenians from intervening); as Kromayer justly observes (*op. cit.,* p. 321), if part of the army had remained drawn up in phalanx facing them, the enemy would not have supposed that Epaminondas was moving off to a camping ground. But Epaminondas charged when enough men had come up to make strong "the striking force about himself" (τὸ περὶ ἑαυτὸν ἔμβολον). This seems to mean that he waited only for a sufficient part of his army (i.e., the Thebans, who were in a special sense "about himself") not that he formed the *whole* army in one deep mass.

4. See Kromayer, *Schlachtfelder,* I, 124–125. *Schlachtenatlas,*

IV, Map 5, figs. 7–8. I do not pretend to offer a proper study of the battle, for which a full examination of the topography is of course essential.

APPENDIX

1. J. Beloch, *Bevölkerung der griechisch-römischen Welt,* p. 130 maintains that Spartan conservatism was too strong to allow any major change; but this is begging the question.

2. The *mora* is first mentioned in the account of the campaign against the democrats in the Piraeus; Xenophon *Hellenica* ii, 4.31. Other references include *Hellenica* iv, 3.15; iv, 4.7; iv, 4.18; iv, 5 *passim;* v, 1.30. *Polemarchs* are mentioned expressly as commanders of *morai* at iv, 5.7 and v, 4.46, and in other contexts (e.g., ii, 4.33; iv, 2.22) it can be inferred that they commanded *morai.* For the strength of the *mora, Hellenica* iv, 5.12, confirmed by the information in *Lac. Pol.* 11.4 (sixteen *enomotiai* to a *mora*) and *Hellenica* vi, 4.12 (36 men to an *enomotia* at Leuctra). To the 576 men that this implies should be added supernumerary officers—probably the *polemarch* himself and the *lochagoi* (cf. *Cyropaedia* iii, 3.11) but perhaps also the *pentekonteres.*

3. Xenophon *Hellenica* vi, 1.1 and vi, 4.17, taken together.

4. Xenophon *Hellenica* iii, 5.22; iv, 5.7.

5. Xenophon *Lac. Pol.* 11.4. W. G. Forrest, *History of Sparta,* p. 134, holds that "there can be no doubt that Xenophon in *Lac. Pol.* believes that he is writing about a purely Spartan army, not an army contaminated with *perioikoi.*" I find no grounds for this; indeed Xenophon repeatedly calls the army that he is describing "Lacedaemonian," and I believe that he is more careful to distinguish Spartiates from the general body of Lacedaemonians than Forrest allows. Nor do I agree that the *perioeci* were necessarily amateurs; we know nothing about the internal organization of their cities, but those who served in the army may well have been drawn from a privileged military upper class.

6. G. Busolt, "Spartas Heer und Leuktra," *Hermes,* XL (1905), 426.

7. Xenophon *Hellenica* vii, 4.20; vii, 5.10.

8. This view is taken by Busolt, *op. cit.,* pp. 425–426; H. Michell, *Sparta,* pp. 243–245, and others.

9. δύο is supposed to have been corrupted into δ'.

10. Thucydides iv, 8.9.

11. Beloch, *Bevölkerung* . . . , p. 135; Arnold J. Toynbee, "The Growth of Sparta," *JHS,* XXXIII (1913), 264.

12. Thucydides v, 68.5; Busolt, *op. cit.,* p. 408.

13. Thucydides v, 64.2–3.

14. Thucydides v, 66.2–67.1.

15. Thucydides v, 68.2–3.

16. Busolt, *op. cit.,* p. 397; J. Kromayer, "Die Wehrkraft Lakoniens und seine Wehrverfassung," *Klio,* III (1903), 190 ff.; *Heerwesen,* p. 34 (especially n. 3); *Schlachtfelder,* IV, 213. For the settlement at Lepreum of a thousand hoplites, Thucydides v, 34.1; v, 49.1, though we cannot be certain how many came to Mantinea.

17. So Beloch, *Bevölkerung* . . . , p. 140.

18. At Cunaxa, Xenophon (*Anabasis* i, 8.9) noticed the distinctive equipment of the different contingents drawn up against the Greeks, but his estimate of the Persian numbers was wildly inaccurate.

19. Compare Chrimes, *Ancient Sparta,* pp. 384–386.

20. "Sie fungirten nicht als ταξίαρχοι, sondern als στρατηγοί" (Busolt, *op. cit.,* p. 419).

21. *"Lochos"* cannot mean the Spartan contingent in the *mora* without the *perioeci,* as has been suggested (references, Michell, *Sparta,* p. 244) if we are to accept the statement (Thucydides iv, 8.9; 38.4) that the men of Sphacteria, who included a majority of *perioeci,* were taken by lot from all the *lochoi.*

22. A. W. Gomme, "Thucydides and Sphakteria," in *Essays in Greek History and Literature,* pp. 125 ff., considers that Spartan prisoners supplied Thucydides with much of the material for his account of the fighting on the island. Cf. Chrimes, *Ancient Sparta,* p. 386.

23. Thucydides v, 71.3.

24. οἱ λοιποί for ὀλίγοι in Thucydides v, 67.1; proposed by Ringnalda, *De Exercitu Lacedaemoniorum* (Groningen: 1893), pp. 19 ff., and properly rejected by Busolt, *Hermes* XL (1905), p. 399. Nor does the suggestion that there were seven *lochoi*, of which five fought in the centre, two on the extreme right, agree with the text of Thucydides. Apart from the objection that two *lochoi* were more than "a few" men, Thucydides says that the order of the seven *lochoi* was continuous (ἑξῆς). (Busolt, *loc. cit.*, arguing against Köchly and Rüstow, *Geschichte des Griechische Kriegswesen*, p. 146; H. Delbrück, *Geschichte der Kriegskunst*, I, 97.9).

25. For the *centuria*, cf. A. Monigliano, "An Interim Report on the Origins of Rome," *JRS*, LIII (1963), 120, with further references. For the *pentekontarchia* and Macedonian *pentekostys*, Arrian *Tactica* 14.3, 32.2, quoted by Chrimes, *Ancient Sparta*, p. 357, n. 4.

26. H. T. Wade-Gery, "The Spartan Rhetra in Plutarch *Lycurgus* VI," *CQ*, XXXVIII (1944), 123–126.

27. Wade-Gery (*op. cit.*) holds that at Mantinea there were, besides the Sciritae and Brasideans, six Lacedaemonian *morai*, in each of which were two *lochoi* of more than five hundred men. Michell, *Sparta*, pp. 239–240, accepts Thucydides's statement that there were seven *lochoi* of four *pentekostyes* each, but, since four sevens are twenty-eight, maintains that the *pentekostys* was a fiftieth of the whole army, Sciritae, Brasideans, and all. He makes two arithmetical errors ($448 \times 8 = 3,840$, and $3,840 - 3,584 = 266$), from which he conjures a royal guard of 266 men. He gives 5,584 as the total number of Lacedaemonians (counting seven *lochoi* in addition to the Brasideans, which is not necessarily wrong but is inconsistent with what he says on p. 241), reduces this to a round figure of 5,550, adds "about 975" for the oldest and youngest who had gone home, being about one sixth of the whole army (here again his reckoning is very rough and seems to assume that the "oldest and youngest" formed separate *pentekostyes*) and concludes that "the entire Lacedaemonian army in 418

amounted to 6,475 men." Fifty multiplied by one hundred and twenty-eight equals 6,400 and so the *pentekostys* of four *enomotiai* is a fiftieth.

28. Xenophon *Anabasis* iii, 4.21–22.

29. Busolt, *Hermes* XL (1905), p. 414.

30. Kromayer, *Klio,* III (1903), 196, rejected by Busolt, *op. cit.,* p. 400.

31. Compare Xenophon *Hellenica* v, 2.7.

32. Professor D. L. Page doubts my suggestion that τῶν πολεμάρχων in Thucydides v, 70.3 might be a mistaken gloss, on the grounds that a commentator would have been unlikely to have used a partitive genitive. The words are not to be construed as qualifying δύo λόχους: in any case, what would *"lochoi* of the polemarchs"* mean?

33. Busolt, *op. cit.,* p. 403, arguing that by "the right wing," Thucydides means the whole Spartan-Tegean army except for the Sciritae and Brasideans.

34. W. J. Woodhouse, "The Campaign of Mantinea in 418 B.C.," *BSA,* XXII (1916–1918), 51–84, and (more fully) *King Agis of Sparta and his Campaign in Arkadia in 418* B.C., tries to show that Agis had contrived an elaborate plan whereby different units of the opposing armies should be destroyed or spared to suit the king's opinion of their politics. This is sufficiently refuted by A. W. Gomme, "Mantinea," in *Essays on Greek History and Literature,* pp. 51–84.

35. And as Busolt, *op. cit.,* p. 402 supposes he did.

36. Kromayer (*Schlachtfelder,* IV, 217) says: "Der Gang der Schlacht ist bei Thukydides (v, 71–73) so klar geschildert, dass kaum etwas hinzuzufügen ist." He does not however discuss the details examined here, saying (p. 218) simply that Agis, in order to close the gap, "gab deshalb 2 Lochen Befehl, vom rechten Flügel abzurücken." But he over-simplifies. The "few Lacedaemonians" on the extreme right of the line are not even marked on his plan.

37. W. S. Ferguson, in the *Cambridge Ancient History,* V, 273;

J. B. Bury, *History of Greece,* p. 461 (third edition, revised by Russell Meiggs), "two captains on his right"; N. G. L. Hammond, *History of Greece to 322 B.C.,* pp. 385–386, "two battalions on his right wing." The precise meanings of "captains" and "battalions" are not discussed.

38. Xenophon *Anabasis* vi, 3.2 ff.

39. Dr. W. G. Forrest has shown me, in private correspondence, reasons for believing that there must have been many more Lacedaemonians present than Thucydides reckons, if their line matched that of the enemy in the way that he says it did. These reasons, and a possible solution to the problem, will be presented in Dr. Forrest's forthcoming work on Sparta.

According to Herodotus (ix, 28.3) there were 1,500 Tegeans at Plataea in 479 B.C. Maenalus and Heraea were small places. Thucydides (iv, 93.3; 94.1) says that there were about 7,000 Boeotian hoplites at Delium (besides 10,000 light armed and 1,000 cavalry) and the Athenian hoplites were about equal in numbers. According to Thucydides (vi, 43), 5,100 hoplites, Athenian, allied and mercenary, sufficed to defeat the whole force of Syracuse in the field.

40. Arnold J. Toynbee, "The Growth of Sparta," *JHS,* XXXIII (1913), 264–270, developing ideas put forward by Beloch, *op. cit.,* pp. 131 ff. He is followed by Wade-Gery, *op. cit.* A.H.M. Jones, *Sparta,* pp. 61–62, properly rejects the suggestion that there were separate *lochoi* of Spartiates and *perioeci,* but agrees with Toynbee and Wade-Gery that both Thucydides and Xenophon are probably mistaken; Thucydides "conflates the *morae* with the *lochoi*"; Xenophon "should have said four *enomotiae* to a *pentecostys.*" Xenophon's statement that the *mora* destroyed by Iphicrates was about six hundred strong is not explained, though accepted (p. 112) without comment. Jones remarks (p. 174, Additional Note v) that "it is curious that Xenophon should by another error get the same total" as Thucydides.

W. G. Forrest, *History of Sparta,* pp. 133–134 very reasonably finds it "hard to believe that Thucydides and Xenophon should make the same mistake about the size of the largest unit." He suggests that Thucydides, in his account of Mantinea, mistakenly gave "the numbers and the units of the Spartans alone, ignoring the *perioikoi*" and that the text of Xenophon should be amended to give 1,700 Spartiates at Leuctra. This would give a fairly steady decline in the Spartiate population from 479–371 B.C., with a sharp drop thereafter, due not so much to the casualties at Leuctra as to the subsequent loss of Messenia.

41. Herodotus ix, 10–11.

42. Aristotle frag. 541 (Rose). Cf. also Chrimes, *Ancient Sparta,* p. 315; Jones, *op. cit.,* p. 32.

43. Aristophanes *Lysistrata* 453.

44. F. Dübner, *Scholia Graeca in Aristophanem,* p. 254; W. G. Rutherford, *Scholia Aristophanica,* II, 185.

45. Dübner, *loc. cit.*

46. C. Hude, *Scholia in Thucydidem,* p. 230.

47. Hesychius, s.v.v. Ἔδωλος, λόχοι.

48. Photius, s.v. λόχοι.

49. Harpocration, s.v. μόρα; Aristotle frag. 540 (Rose).

50. Herodotus ix, 53; Thucydides i, 20.3.

51. Wade-Gery, *op. cit.,* pp. 120–121. Jones, *op. cit.,* pp. 31–32 considers that as late as the Persian Wars, each *obe* probably raised a *lochos,* though *obai* and *lochoi* bore different names. But, as Dr. W. G. Forrest points out to me, it is probable that there were at least six *obai,* perhaps more; cf. A. J. Beattie, "An early Laconian Lex Sacra," *CQ,* 45 (1951), 46–58, especially 47–50. M. A. Levi, "Phylai e obai," in *Quattro studi spartani e altri scritti di storia greca,* suggests that the *obai* may be survivals of pre-Hellenic village organization, with Anatolian connections. For another theory, Forrest, *History of Sparta,* pp. 42–46.

52. Chrimes, *Ancient Sparta,* p. 318.

53. Michell, *Sparta,* pp. 234 ff.

54. Thucydides iv, 40.2 (and at Leuctra: Xenophon *Hellenica* vi, 4.15).

55. Isocrates *Panathenaicus* 176–181; Aristotle frag. 540 (Rose).

Kromayer, *Heerwesen,* p. 37, n. 1, also cites Xenophon *Hellenica,* vii, 4.20 and 27, for Spartiates and *perioeci* fighting side by side in the "twelve *lochoi*" in the period after Leuctra, though, as Dr. Forrest points out to me, Xenophon does not say that they fought in the same *enomotiai.*

56. Toynbee, *op. cit.,* pp. 264–269, accepted by Wade-Gery, *op. cit.,* p. 118.

57. Apart from Xenophon's "about 600" (*Hellenica* iv, 5.12), the following testimony on the strength of the *mora* is given by ancient authors:

(1) Diodorus Siculus xv, 32.1 says 500.

(2) Plutarch *Pelopidas* 17.3. "Ephorus says that the *mora* is 500 men, but Callisthenes 700, and some others 900, of whom Polybius is one." Busolt, *op. cit.,* p. 420 is probably right in applying Polybius's testimony to the time of Cleomenes III. Plutarch wishes to magnify Pelopidas's victory by making the *mora* as large as possible, but is too honest not to give all the evidence he knows.

(3) Photius (s.v. μόρα) says 1,000 men. Busolt, *loc. cit.,* supposes, probably correctly, that he simply divided the 6,000 men at the Nemea by six (as does Wade-Gery, *op. cit.,* p. 123), neglecting the Sciritae and the "newly enfranchised," and the absence of one *mora* at Orchomenus.

58. Xenophon *Hellenica* iv, 2.16. Orchomenus had been brought over to the Spartan side by Lysander (*Hellenica* iii, 5.6) though it is not absolutely certain that it had had a Spartan garrison ever since.

59. Toynbee, *op. cit.,* p. 266.

60. Xenophon *Hellenica* iii, 4.2. Note the partitive genitive (εἰς δισχιλίους δὲ τῶν νεοδαμώδων). A thousand "newly enfranchised" were already serving in Asia. I believe that Xenophon means that the number was to be brought up to 2,000, but some scholars (e.g., W. Kaupert, in Kromayer, *Schlachtfelder,* IV, 284) hold that Agesilaus's 2,000 were to be added to those already there.

Beloch, *Bevölkerung* . . . , reckons that there were 1,800 "newly enfranchised" at the Nemea, but on the assumption that all six *morai* took part in the battle.

61. Compare G. L. Huxley, *Early Sparta,* pp. 146–147, n. 661.

62. Polyaenus ii, 3.11.

63. As is proposed by Toynbee, *JHS,* XXXIII (1913), p. 268. This would of course have been desirable, from the military point of view. Cf. Onasander 10.2.

64. Herodotus i, 65.

65. Thucydides iv, 8.

66. Xenophon *Hellenica* vi, 5.21. Admittedly this is in the period after Leuctra. In earlier campaigns (e.g., *Hellenica* iv, 4.91; v. 3.25) the king is said to dismiss the allies and lead the citizen army home, without Spartiates and *perioeci* being separately mentioned.

67. Xenophon *Hellenica* iv, 5.11, shows that the men of Amyclae were distributed through the army, not that they formed a "bataillon d'Amyclées" (E. Delebecque, *Essai sur la vie de Xénophon,* pp. 183–184). Cf. Kromayer, *Heerwesen,* p. 38. From *Hellenica* iv, 5.10 it appears that "sons and fathers and brothers" of the dead were serving in the other *morai.*

68. Xenophon *Lac. Pol.* 11.7.

69. Plutarch *Agesilaus* 26.5.

70. Xenophon *Lac. Pol.* 11.2. Cf. Busolt, *op. cit.,* pp. 390–391.

71. Xenophon *Lac. Pol.* 11.2; *Hellenica* vi, 4.17.

72. Busolt, *Hermes* XL (1905), p. 416; Toynbee, *JHS,* XXXIII, (1913), pp. 263–264; Chrimes, *Ancient Sparta,* p. 389. Xenophon (*Hellenica* vi, 4.17) says that thirty-five year-groups fought at Leuctra, and (vi, 4.12) that the Spartan *enomotiai* were formed in threes, with a depth of "not more than twelve."

73. Toynbee, *op. cit.,* p. 264.

74. On Cinadon and his conspiracy, Xenophon *Hellenica* iii, 3, 4–11, where the under-privileged classes are listed, apparently in ascending order (iii, 3.6), as helots, newly enfranchised, inferiors, and *perioeci.* The seer Tisamenus, who played such a strange

part in the conspiracy, seems to have been an "inferior," presumably because the grant of citizenship to his famous ancestor did not carry a lot of land with it. He was certainly liable to military service, of a special sort. For the social class of the cavalry, Xenophon *Hellenica* vi, 4.10–11. For the encouragement of large families and its consequences, Aristotle *Politics* ii, 1270b and for the simultaneous service of several members of a family, Xenophon *Hellenica* iv, 5.10; Plutarch *Moralia* 241 B,C. See Beloch, *Bevölkerung* . . . , p. 137, who also cites Plutarch *Agis* 5.14, and Xenophon *Cyropaedia* ii, 1.18. But though this last passage certainly seems to represent Spartans in Persian dress, it may have more connection with the "newly enfranchised" than with the "inferiors." For arguments on the other side, Toynbee, *JHS*, XXXIII (1913), p. 260. Busolt, *Hermes* XL (1905), p. 409 makes the point that disgrace did not involve discharge from military service, citing Thucydides v, 31; Herodotus vii, 231; ix, 71; Plutarch *Agesilaus* 5.

75. Xenophon *Agesilaus* 1.31; *Hellenica* iii, 4.23; *Anabasis*, ii, 3.12; vii, 3.46. H. W. Parke, *Greek Mercenaries,* p. 29, notes that most of the Ten Thousand were probably fairly young.

76. Xenophon *Anabasis* v, 3.1; vi, 5.4.

77. Thucydides v, 72.4.

78. Herodotus vi, 56. Isocrates (*Epistolae* ii, 6) says that "the most distinguished of the citizens" formed the royal guard, without mentioning the number or calling them "knights."

79. Herodotus vii, 205.2.

80. Herodotus viii, 124.3.

81. Xenophon *Hellenica* iii, 4.2; v, 3.9.

82. Plutarch *Agesilaus* 18.2–3.

83. Xenophon *Hellenica* iv, 3.15.

84. Xenophon *Hellenica* iv, 5.8. τὰ ὅπλα ἔχοντες I take to mean that they were themselves armed, not that they were carrying the shields of Agesilaus and the senior officers.

85. E.g., Herodotus v, 92.7 (on Periander's guards); Thucydides vi, 55.3. (those of Hippias at Athens).

86. Xenophon *Hellenica* v, 4.33; vii, 4.23–24.

87. Xenophon *Hellenica* vi, 4.12–13.

88. Xenophon *Hellenica* vi, 4.14. cf. vi, 4.17.

89. Xenophon *Hellenica* vi, 1.1; cf. vi, 4.17.

90. But many scholars take a different view: Busolt, *Hermes,* XL (1905), pp. 403–405 and 422–423; Toynbee, *JHS,* XXXIII, (1913), p. 271; M. Cary, "Notes on the ἀριστεία of Thebes," *JHS,* XLII (1922), 185–186; F. Ollier, *Xénophon: La République des Lacédémoniens,* p. 34, commenting on Xenophon *Lac. Pol.* 4.3–6 (where Xenophon describes the organization of the "knights" at some length without mentioning their function as a royal body-guard); Michell, *Sparta,* p. 249.

91. Thucydides iv, 55.2.

92. Xenophon *Hellenica* vi, 4.10.

93. Compare Strabo x, 4.81, who argues that the Cretan "knights," who had horses, must have been an older institution than the Spartans, who did not.

94. Xenophon *Lac. Pol.* 4.1–6.

95. Xenophon *Hellenica* iv, 4.10; v, 2.41 uses the titles ἵππαρχος and ἱππαρμοστής for Spartan cavalry officers.

96. Cf. Plutarch *Moralia* 191F; 231B, for the story of the rejected candidate who smiled to think that Sparta had three hundred men better than himself.

97. Busolt, *Hermes,* XL (1905) p. 404.

98. Xenophon *Lac. Pol.* 13.6. ἱππεῖς in this passage clearly means "cavalry," not "knights," as they are said to be patrolling in advance, not escorting the king.

99. So Marchant, in the Loeb edition of Xenophon's *Opuscula.* Professor Page suggests to me that ἄγημα means "contingent" τῆς πρώτης μόρας, being a genitive of definition. The whole phrase would then mean only "the first *mora,*" of which the royal body-guard would then be a part.

100. So Beloch, *Bevolkerung . . . ,* p. 134. Busolt, *Hermes* XL (1905) expresses doubts. Ollier, *op. cit.,* p. 67, believes that it was an advance-guard, "ce que Xénophon appelle dans l'*Anabase*

τὸ ἡγούμενον" and on p. 68 accepts the view that it was the "three hundred knights."

101. So Toynbee, *JHS*, XXXIII (1913), p. 263 n.69.

102. Xenophon *Lac. Pol.* 11.9.

103. For this reason Busolt, *Hermes*, XL (1905), pp. 404–405 considers that they must have formed a separate body at Mantinea, and also (pp. 422–423) at Leuctra.

104. Plutarch *Lycurgus* 22.

105. Xenophon *Hellenica* iii, 3.9.

106. Herodotus i, 67.5.

107. Xenophon *Cyropaedia* iv, 2.1.

108. But see the useful account of the Sciritae in Ollier, *Xénophon: la République des Lacédémoniens*, pp. 62–63.

109. Xenophon *Hellenica* vi, 5.24.

110. *Ibid.*, vii, 4.21.

111. Diodorus Siculus xv, 32.1.

112. See note 69 *supra*.

113. Chrimes, *Ancient Sparta*, pp. 378 ff.

114. Xenophon *Hellenica* v, 2.24.

SELECT BIBLIOGRAPHY
With Special Abbreviations

Adcock, Sir F. E. *The Greek and Macedonian Art of War*. Berkeley and Los Angeles: University of California Press, 1957.

Beazley, Sir J. D. and B. Ashmole *Greek Sculpture and Painting*. Cambridge: University Press, 1932.

Beloch, J. *Die Bevölkerung der griechisch-römischen Welt*. Leipzig: Dunker und Humblot, 1886. (= Beloch, *Bevölkerung*).

Benndorf, O. and G. Niemann *Das Heroön von Gjölbashi-Trysa*. Wien: A. Holzhausen, 1889.

Bieber, M. *History of the Greek and Roman Theatre*. 2nd ed. Princeton: Princeton University Press, 1961.

Boehlau, J. and K. Schefold *Larisa am Hermos,* Vol. I. Berlin: W. de Gruyter, 1940.

von Bothmer, D. *Amazons in Greek Art*. Oxford: Clarendon Press, 1957.

Bruce, I. A. F. *An Historical Commentary on the "Hellenica Oxyrhynchia."* Cambridge: University Press, 1967.

Burn, A. R. *Persia and the Greeks*. London: Edward Arnold, 1962.

Carapanos, C. *Dodone et ses Ruines*. Paris: Hachette, 1878.

Caskey, L. D. and Sir J. D. Beazley *Attic Vase-Paintings in the Museum of Fine Arts, Boston*. Boston: Museum of Fine Arts, Part I, 1931; Part II, 1954; Part III, 1963.

Chrimes, K. M. T. *Ancient Sparta: A Re-examination of the Evidence*. Manchester: University Press, 1949. (= Chrimes, *Ancient Sparta*).

Conze, A. *Die Attischen Grabreliefs*. Berlin: W. Spermann, 1893.

Cousin, G. *Kyros le jeune en Asie Mineure.* Paris: Berger-Lerrault, 1905.

Delbrück, H. *Geschichte der Kriegskunst im Rahmen der politischen Geschichte,* Vol. I. Berlin: G. Stilke, 1920.

Delebecque, E. *Essai sur la vie de Xénophon.* Paris: C. Klincksieck, 1957.

Delorme, J. *Gymnasion.* Paris: E. de Boccard, 1960.

Demargne, P. *Fouilles de Xanthos,* Vol. I: *Les Piliers Funeraires.* Paris: C. Klincksieck, 1958.

Diepolder, H. *Die Attischen Grabreliefs.* Berlin: Heinrich Keller, 1931.

Droysen, H. *Heerwesen und Kriegführung der Griechen.* Freiburg: J. C. B. Mohr, 1888 (= Droysen, *Heerwesen*).

Fellows, Sir C. *Account of the Ionic Trophy Monument Excavated at Xanthus.* London: John Murray, 1848.

Forrest, W. G. *A History of Sparta, 950–192 B.C.* London: Hutchinson University Library, 1968.

Fortina, M. *Epaminonda.* Torino: Societa editrice internazionale, 1958.

Friederici, E. *Das Persische Idealheer des Xenophon.* Berlin: 1909.

Gomme, A. W. *Essays on Greek History and Literature.* Oxford: B. Blackwell, 1937.

——. *A Historical Commentary on Thucydides.* Oxford: Clarendon Press, 1945.

Grundy, G. B. *The Great Persian War.* London: J. Murray, 1911.

——. *Thucydides and the History of his Age.* London: J. Murray, 1911.

Hagemann, A. *Griechische Panzerung.* Leipzig: 1919. (= Hagemann).

Hammond, N. G. L. *A History of Greece to 322 B.C.* Oxford: Clarendon Press, 1959.

Harris, H. A. *Greek Athletes and Athletics.* London: Hutchinson, 1964.

Hignett, C. *A History of the Athenian Constitution to the End of the Fifth Century* B.C. Oxford: Clarendon Press, 1952.

———. *Xerxes' Invasion of Greece.* Oxford: Clarendon Press, 1963.

Hill, G. F. *Historical Greek Coins.* London: Constable, 1906.

How, W. and J. Wells. *Commentary on Herodotus.* Oxford: Clarendon Press, 1928.

Huxley, G. L. *Early Sparta.* Cambridge, Mass.: Harvard University Press, 1962.

Johansen, K. Friis *The Attic Grave Reliefs.* Copenhagen: Ejnar Munksgaard, 1951.

Jones, A. H. M. *Sparta.* Oxford: Basil Blackwell, 1967.

Karouzou, S. *The Amasis Painter.* Oxford: Clarendon Press, 1956.

King, L. W. *Bronze Reliefs from the Gates of Shalmaneser.* London: British Museum, 1915.

Klumbach, H. *Tarentiner Grabkunst.* Reutlingen: Gryphius, 1937.

Köchly, H. A. T. and W. Rüstow. *Geschichte des Griechischen Kriegswesens.* Aarau: 1852.

———. *Griechische Kriegsschriftsteller,* Vols. I–II. Leipzig: 1853–1855.

Kromayer, J. and G. Veith. *Heerwesen und Kriegführung der Griechen und Römer.* München: C. H. Beck, 1928 (= Kromayer, *Heerwesen*).

———. *Schlachtenatlas zür antiken Kriegesgeschichte,* Parts I–V. Leipzig: H. Wagner and E. Debes, 1922–1929 (= Kromayer, *Schlachtenatlas*).

———. *Antike schlachtfelder in Griechenland,* Vols I–II. Berlin: Weidmann, 1903–1907 (= Kromayer, *Schlachtfelder*).

Levi, M. A. *Quattro studi spartani e altri scritti di storia greca.* Milano: Instituto editoriale cisalpino, 1967.

Lorimer, H. L. *Homer and the Monuments.* London: Macmillan, 1950.

Maule, Quentin F. and H. R. W. Smith. "Votive Religion at

Caere: Prolegomena," *University of California Publications in Classical Archaeology,* Vol. IV, No. 1. Berkeley and Los Angeles: University of California Press, 1959.

Von Mercklin, E. *Der Rennwagen in Griechenland.* Leipzig: 1908.

Michell, H. *Sparta.* Cambridge: University Press, 1952.

Moritz, B. *Grain Mills and Flour in Antiquity.* Oxford: Clarendon Press, 1958.

Muller, B. *Beiträge zür Geschichte des griechischen Söldnerwesens bis auf die Schlacht von Chaeronea.* Frankfurt-am-Main: Gottlieb and Müller, 1908.

Ollier, F. *Xénophon: La République des Lacédémoniens.* Lyons: A. Rey; Paris: F. Alcan, 1934.

Page, D. L. *Sappho and Alcaeus.* Oxford: Clarendon Press, 1959.

Parke, H. W. *Greek Mercenary Soldiers from the Earliest Times to the Battle of Ipsus.* Oxford: Clarendon Press, 1933 (= Parke, *Greek Mercenaries*).

Popp, Harald *Die Einwirkung von Vorzeichen, Opfern und Fester auf der Kriegführung der Griechen in 5 und 4 Jh. vor Chr.* Erlangen: 1957.

Pritchett, W. Kendrick "Studies in Ancient Greek Topography, Part I," *University of California Publications: Classical Studies,* Vol. I. Berkeley and Los Angeles: University of California Press, 1965 (= Pritchett, *Topography*).

Richter, G. M. A. *Attic Red-Figured Vases.* New Haven: Yale University Press, 1946.

———. *The Archaic Gravestones of Attica.* London: Phaidon Press, 1961.

———. *Catalogue of the Greek Sculptures in the Metropolitan Museum of Art.* Cambridge, Mass.: Harvard University Press, 1954.

———. *The Sculpture and Sculptors of the Greeks.* 2nd ed. New Haven: Yale University Press, 1950.

Seltman, C. *Athens: Its History and Coinage before the Persian Invasion.* Cambridge: University Press, 1924.

Smith, A. H. *Catalogue of Greek Sculptures in the British Museum.* London: British Museum, 1901.

Snodgrass, A. *Early Greek Armour and Weapons before 600* B.C. Edinburgh: University Press, 1964 (= Snodgrass, *Early Greek Armour*).

———. *Arms and Armour of the Greeks.* London: Thames and Hudson, 1967.

Tänzer, K. *Das Verpflegungswesen der Griechischen Heere.* Jena: Frommann, 1912 (= Tänzer, *Verpflegungswesen.*

Tarn, Sir W. W. *Hellenistic Military and Naval Developments.* Cambridge: University Press, 1930.

Wolter, J. "Leuctra," in Kromager, *Schlachtfeldery,* pp. 293 ff (= Wolter, "Leuctra").

PLATES

Attributions of vases to artists are all taken from Sir J. D. Beazley's ARV^2. Dates are not intended to be more than approximate indications.

NOTES ON THE PLATES

Attributions of vases to artists are all taken from Sir J. D. Beazley's *ARV*². Dates are not intended to be more than approximate indications.

PLATE 1

Victory setting up a trophy. Attic red-figured *pelike* by the Trophy Painter, middle of the fifth century B.C. (*ARV²*, p. 857, no. 2.)

The goddess is drilling a hole in the tree-trunk that forms the body of the trophy in order to hang up the shield. Sir J. D. Beazley shows that the curious double rectangle just below the helmet is the lopped end of the branch that forms one "arm."

By courtesy of the Museum of Fine Arts, Boston (Francis Bartlett Donation).

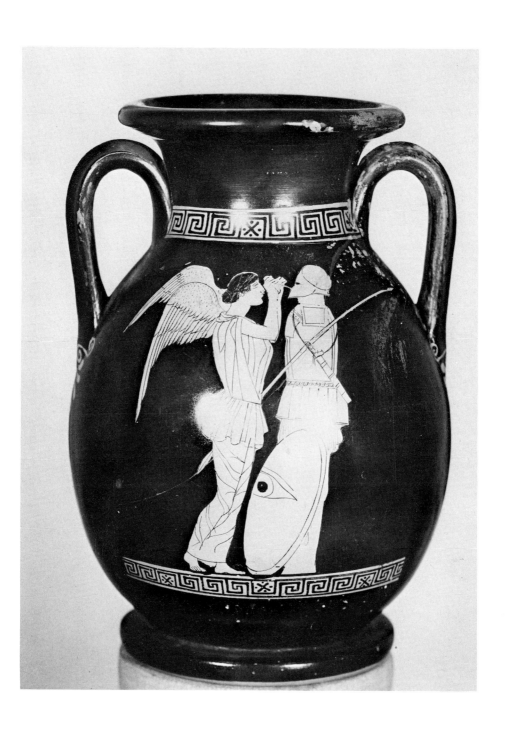

PLATE 2

a. Achilles killing the Amazon Penthesilea. Attic black-figured amphora by Exekias, about 540–530 B.C. (*ABV,* p. 144, no. 7.)
By courtesy of the Trustees of the British Museum.
b. Achilles killing Hector. Attic red-figured volute crater by the Berlin Painter, early fifth century B.C. (*ARV*², p. 206, no. 132.)
By courtesy of the Trustees of the British Museum.

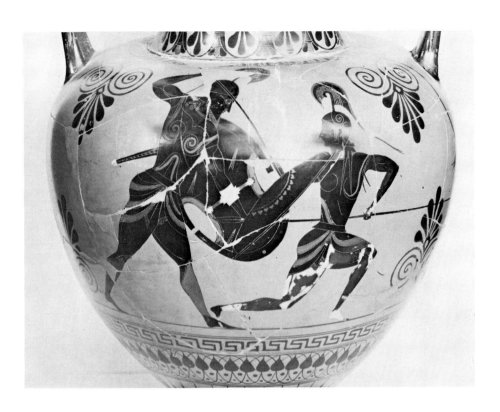

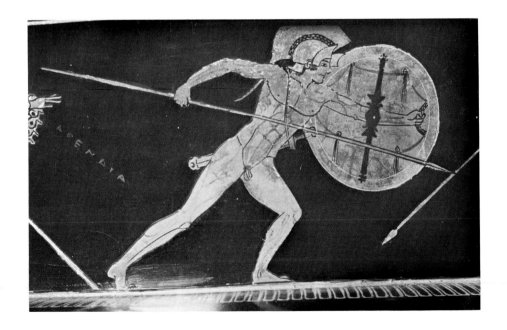

PLATE 3

Departure of young warrior (Neoptolemus). Attic red-figured amphora by the Lykaon Painter, about 440 B.C. (ARV^2, p. 1044, no. 1.)

By courtesy of the Metropolitan Museum of Art, New York (Rogers Fund, 1906).

PLATE 4

a. Amazons armed as hoplite and barbarian archer. Attic red-figured amphora; "related to the Charmides Painter," second quarter of fifth century B.C. (*ARV²*, p. 654, no. 3.)

By courtesy of the Trustees of the British Museum.

b. Hoplite with spear raised. Attic red-figured amphora by the Alkimachos Painter, second quarter of fifth century B.C. (*ARV²*, p. 530, no. 25.)

By courtesy of the Trustees of the British Museum.

PLATE 5

The arming of Hector. Attic red-figured amphora by Euthymides, end of sixth century B.C. (*ARV*^{2}, p. 26, no. 1.) By courtesy of the Antikensammlungen, Munich.

PLATE 6

Young warrior making libation before departure. Attic red-figured *hydria,* about 500 B.C. (*ARV²*, p. 1596; accession no. 98.878.)

By courtesy of the Museum of Fine Arts, Boston (Pierce Fund).

PLATE 7

Amazons arming. Attic red-figured *hydria* by Hypsis, end of sixth century B.C. (*ARV*², p. 30, no. 1.)

By courtesy of the Antikensammlungen, Munich.

PLATE 8

Young warrior arming. Attic red-figured *pelike* by the Kleophon Painter, c. 440–430 B.C. (*ARV*², p. 1145, no. 37.)

By courtesy of the Museum of Fine Arts, Boston (Francis Bartlett Collection).

PLATE 9

Warrior's departure. Attic red-figured amphora by the Kleophon Painter, c. 440–430 B.C. (ARV^2, p. 1143, no. 2.)
By courtesy of the Antikensammlungen, Munich.

PLATE 10

Athenian hoplite and fallen Spartan. Attic tombstone, late fifth century B.C. (G. M. A. Richter, *Catalogue of the Greek Sculptures in the Metropolitan Museum of Art,* No. 82.)

By courtesy of the Metropolitan Museum of Art (Fletcher Fund, 1940).

PLATE 11

a. Athenian hoplite and *b*. Victory standing beside trophy. Details of Athenian monument, late fifth century B.C. (Athens, Acropolis Museum, No. 3173.)

By courtesy of the German Archaeological Institute, Athens.

PLATE 12

Old man and two Athenian hoplites. Attic tombstone, late fifth century B.C. (Carl Blümel, *Staatliche Museen zu Berlin: die Griechischen skulpturen der V und IV Jahrhunderts v. Chr.,* III, Pl. 38.)

The object that the central figure is holding in his left hand is not the handgrip of his shield, but a spear shaft, which may have been completed in paint.

By courtesy of the Staatliche Museen zu Berlin.

PLATE 13

a. Sortie from a besieged city and *b.* file of hoplites. Details from the Nereid Monument from Xanthus, about 400 B.C. (A. H. Smith, *Catalogue of the Greek Sculptures in the British Museum,* II, Nos. 869, 931.)

By courtesy of the Trustees of the British Museum.

PLATE 14

a. Hoplites storming a fortress and *b*. Hoplites and archers. Details from the Nereid Monument from Xanthus, about 400 B.C. (A. H. Smith, *Catalogue of the Greek Sculptures in the British Museum*, II, Nos. 872, 866.)

By courtesy of the Trustees of the British Museum.

PLATE 16

Menelaus, Priam seated, Aeneas carrying shield of Paris. Attic red-figured *skyphos* by Makron, signed by Hieron as potter, early fifth century B.C. (*ARV*², p. 459, no. 1.)

The figures on either side of the handle belong to two separate scenes—the abducting of Helen on the right, on the left her meeting with Menelaus amid the flames of Troy.

By courtesy of the Museum of Fine Arts, Boston (Francis Bartlett Fund).

PLATE 17

Orpheus among the Thracians. Attic red-figured bell crater by the Painter of London E 497, middle of fifth century B.C. (*ARV²*, p. 1079, no. 2.)

By courtesy of the Metropolitan Museum of Art (Fletcher Fund, 1924).

PLATE 18

Amazons (?) armed as Thracian horseman and peltast. Attic red-figured column crater, middle of fifth century B.C. (Cecil H. Smith, *Catalogue of the Greek and Etruscan Vases in the British Museum*, III, pp. 295–296, No. E 482.)

By courtesy of the Trustees of the British Museum.

PLATE 19

"Heroically" nude hoplite, archer, and Asiatic horseman. Attic red-figures *hydria* "near Group G: delicate style," early fourth century B.C. (*ARV²*, p. 1471, no. 3.)

By courtesy of the Trustees of the British Museum.

FIGURES

NOTES TO THE FIGURES

Figure I. (Cf. pp. 98–101, and J. Kromayer, *Heerwesen*, Pl. 7, figs. 27–28).

a. Lochos of twenty-four men divided into two "twelves," each of which is divided into two "sixes." The "leader of twelve" is the thirteenth man when the *lochos* is in single file.

b. The "leader of twelve" leads his file up on the left and halts beside the *lochagos.* The *lochos* now has a depth of twelve and front of two.

c. The "leaders of six" lead their "sixes" up, each on the left of his own file, and halt beside the *lochagos* and "leader of twelve." The seventh man in the original file is now on the left of the *lochagos,* and the nineteenth on the left of the "leader of twelve." The *lochos* is formed six deep, with a front of four.

Either the "leader of twelve" must take ground to the left, and double the interval between the first and third "sixes," so that when the second "six" comes between them, the original intervals between the files will be kept (C^1), or the *lochos* will be in close order (C^2).

A   B   C¹   C²

Figure II.   Deployment of a *taxis* of four *lochoi* of twenty-four men each.

a. The *taxis* is advancing in single file with the *lochoi* one behind another. The leading *lochos* halts; the second *lochos* comes up on its left; the third on the left of the second; and the fourth on the left of the third, to make a front of four and depth of twenty-four.

b.-c. After this initial deployment, the *lochoi* may be further deployed in the manner illustrated in Fig. I, to give first a front of eight, with *lochagoi* and "leaders of twelve" forming the front rank, and finally a front of sixteen and depth of six.

This subsequent deployment would require the *taxis* to take more ground to the left, unless the intervals between the *lochoi* were originally wide enough to admit three extra files. In practice, it might sometimes be more convenient to deploy each *lochos* separately before bringing it up to its place in the line.

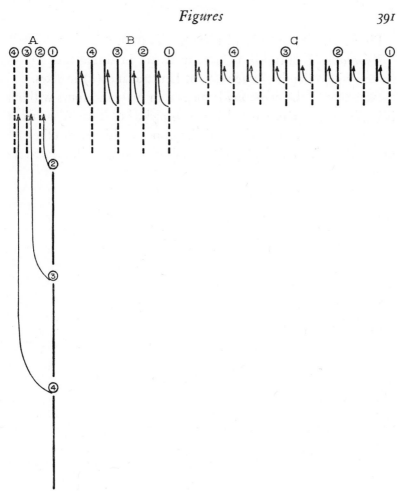

Figure III.   Spartan Drill (cf. pp. 102–104).

Enomotia of thirty-six men formed (*a*) in single file, (*b*) in threes, with a depth of twelve, as at Leuctra, and (*c*) in sixes.

Note that, if the *enomotia* is formed in twos and fours without being internally reorganized, the men picked to serve in the front and rear ranks will not be in their proper positions. In other respects the drill for deployment is similar to that illustrated in Fig. I

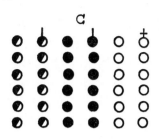

Figure IV. *Mora* Deploying into a Phalanx (cf. pp. 104–108).
Lochoi numbered I–IV.
Pentekostyes numbered i–viii.
Enomotiai numbered 1–16.

The *mora* is supposed to be advancing in column of threes with one *enomotia* following behind another. Upon the order being given to form phalanx with a depth of twelve, the first *enomotia* halts and the remainder come up on the left, one after another. Should a depth of six be desired, each *enomotia* would have to be further deployed in the manner illustrated in Fig. III.

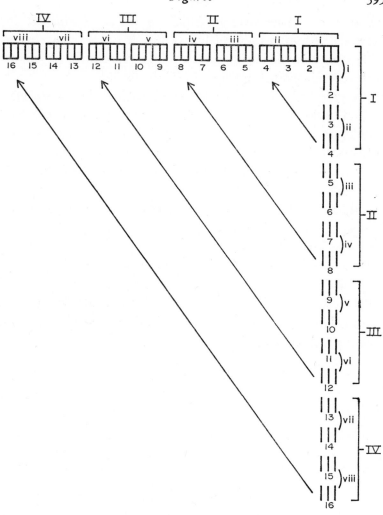

Figure V. *Mora* Meeting Attack of Enemy Formation (*a*) from left, (*b*) from right, of line of march (cf. pp. 108–110).

The *mora* is moving in column (here represented as column of threes) when an enemy appears on the flank.

The four *lochoi* simultaneously wheel to meet the enemy. Each *lochos* is still in column, and there are now four separate columns, parallel to each other, at intervals corresponding to the distances between the heads of the *lochoi* in the original column.

These columns advance "head-on" in a direction at right-angles to the axis of the original advance. When they are moving to the left, the first column is on the right (spear-hand) of the line of parallel columns; when they are moving to the right, it is on the left (shield-hand).

To deploy into *orthioi lochoi* against an enemy appearing to the front of the original line of march, the first *lochos* would halt, still in column, and the others successively would be marched up in column and halted on its left, leaving a sufficient interval between each column.

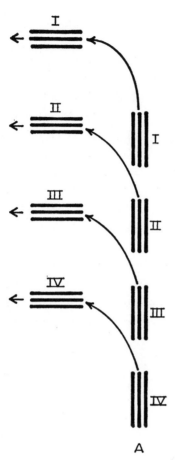

A

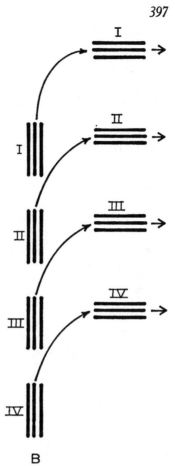

B

Figure VI. Schematic Representation of the Battle of the Nemea.

a. Position of the armies before the battle and opening movements. The Thebans advance obliquely to the right, forcing their allies to conform. The Lacedaemonians "lead off to the right," in order to "extend their wing" and outflank the enemy. The left of their division encounters the six regiments on the left of the Athenian line face to face. The Lacedaemonian right outflanks the Athenian left.

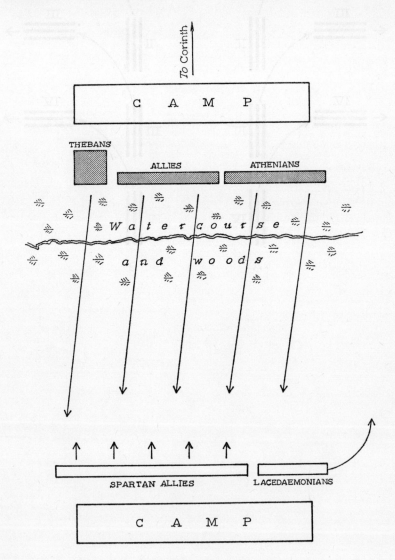

b. The Lacedaemonians, having formed a new front at right-angles to their original one, advance across the battlefield, cutting up one after another the enemy contingents returning from the pursuit of the beaten allies.

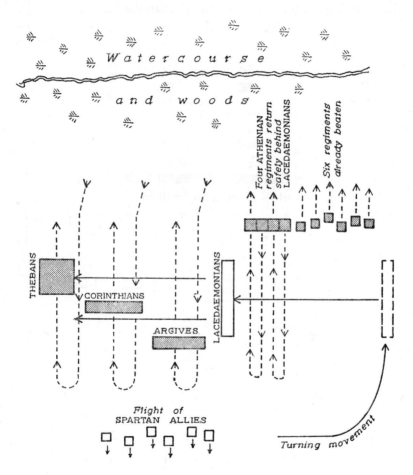

Figure VII. Schematic Representation of the "Battle of Thym-brara" (cf. Chapter IX).

a. The Egyptians halt while the two wings of their army march outwards in column, preparatory to wheeling round and then turning inwards to attack the Persian flanks.
Cyrus continues to advance into the "trap."

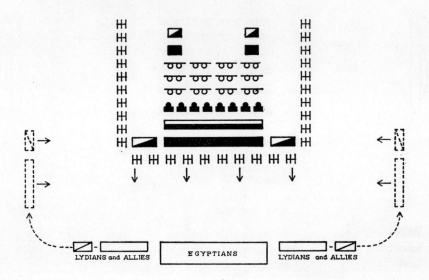

b. The outflankers outflanked.

For the sake of clarity, the Persian camels and the "Trojan and Cyrenaic" chariots of the Lydians are omitted.

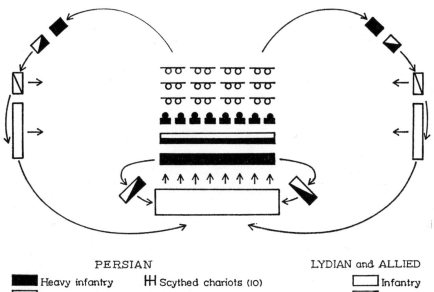

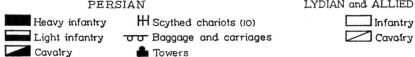

PERSIAN

Heavy infantry H Scythed chariots (10)
Light infantry σσ Baggage and carriages
Cavalry Towers

LYDIAN and ALLIED

Infantry
Cavalry

Figure VIII. Schematic Representation of the Battle of Leuctra (cf. Chapter X).

a. The four Spartan *morai* move off to the right behind their cavalry screen in order to turn the Theban flank. Epaminondas sends his cavalry to drive in the Spartan screen and follows up with the Theban infantry, advancing "obliquely" in order to break the Spartan line near its right and at a point remote from the allies.

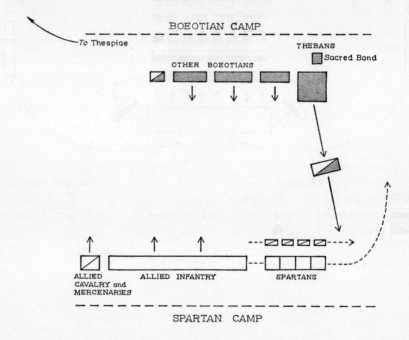

b. The main Theban mass overcomes, after a hard struggle, the Spartans directly opposed to it, including the king and his body-guard (probably stationed between the first and second *morai*). Meanwhile, the Spartans on the right attempt to carry out the outflanking movement as originally planned, but are themselves taken in flank by the Sacred Band. The Spartans on the left fall back; they have no fresh orders, and a movement against the flank of the Theban column would expose their own left flank.

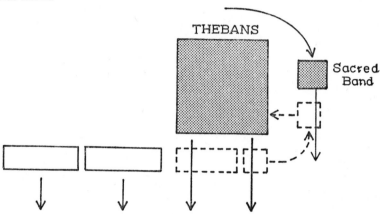

INDEX

Cyaxares, 53, 103–104

Cyprus, 34, 169

Cyrene, 159

Cyrus the Great: camp, 62; camp-followers, 46; chariots, 159, 171; equips Persians, 83–84, 132, 170–171, 187; fortified bases, 140; issues orders, 73, 75; organizes supplies, 43–45, 52; rewards soldiers, 47, 92, 102; training methods, 92, 98–99, 103–104; defeats Assyrians, 64, 76–77; defeats Croesus, 12, 146, 165–167, 172ff, 211

Cyrus the Younger, 26–27, 52, 57, 72, 87, 130, 168, 171–172, 184

Delium, 67, 142, 159, 160, 212, 216

Delphi, 4, 69, 153–154

Dema, 134–135

Demades, 38

Demaratus, 15

Demetrius of Phalerum, 94

Demosthenes (general), 65, 114, 117

Demosthenes (orator), 57, 134

Deployment, 101–102, 104–108, Figs. I–IV; of Greeks at Cunaxa, 171

Dercylidas, 53, 57, 65, 69–70, 128, 147

Dicaeogenes, 46

Dio Chrysostom, on *pilos,* 31

Diodorus Siculus: on battle of Coronea, 153; on battle of Leuctra, 197–198, 205–209; on battle of the Nemea, 143, 147; on Iphicrates, 129–131; on Sciritae, 250

Diomilus, 91

Dion, 38

Dionysius I: employs mercenaries, 27, 48, 59; helps Sparta, 57; siege warfare, 80, 112, 139

Dionysodorus, 95–96

Dionysus, 82

Doctors, 70

Dodona, 30, 33, 35, 37

Dracontius, 38

Drilae, 72–73, 138, 189

Drums, 82

Egypt, Egyptians: Agesilaus in, 64; armour, 23, 130–131, 167; Chabrias in, 167; in *Cyropaedia,* assist Lydians, 166–167, 173, 180–181, 187–189, 212, represent Thebans, 160, cities in Asia, 167–169; Iphicrates in, 129, 167

Elis, 48

DATE DUE

APR 27 '81	APR 10 '81		
GAYLORD			PRINTED IN U.S.A.